Sept 88

EARLY AUDEN

EARLY AUDEN

Edward Mendelson

Faber and Faber
London Boston

First published in 1981
by Faber and Faber Limited
3 Queen Square London WC1N 3AU
Printed and bound in Great Britain by
Redwood Burn Limited, Trowbridge, Wiltshire
All rights reserved

© 1981 *by Edward Mendelson*

British Library Cataloguing in Publication Data
Mendelson, Edward
Early Auden
1.   Auden, W.H. – Criticism and Interpretation
I. Title
821'.912   PR6001.U4Z/

ISBN 0–571–11193–9

For Barry and Valerie Bloomfield

Preface and
Acknowledgements

This book is a history and interpretation of W. H. Auden's work up to 1939, the year he left England for America. A second volume will take up his later writings.

Auden divided his 1966 *Collected Shorter Poems* into four sections, each representing what he described in his foreword as a "chapter in my life." His first two sections, dated 1927–32 and 1933–38, correspond to the two parts of this book. In the opening chapters of each I try to characterize Auden's ideas and methods during the entire period, and the remaining chapters treat separate issues in greater detail and in roughly chronological sequence.

When I refer to Auden's "first" or "earliest" poems, I mean the first poems he wanted to preserve, those he began writing in the late summer of 1927, when he was twenty years old. His juvenilia call for no more than a few paragraphs, which they receive in Chapter II.

Auden frequently revised his poems and dropped increasing numbers of them from his canon. The poems discussed in this volume were first published in book form in England in *Poems* (1930; second edition, with substitutions, 1933),* *The Orators* (1932; slightly revised second

---

* The American edition of *Poems* (1934) also includes *The Orators* and *The Dance of Death.*

edition, 1934), *Look, Stranger!* (1936, American title *On This Island*),
Letters From Iceland (1937, in collaboration with Louis MacNeice),
Journey to a War (1939, in collaboration with Christopher Isherwood),
and *Another Time* (1940). Auden's published plays during these years
were *Paid on Both Sides* (included in the 1930 and 1933 *Poems*), *The
Dance of Death* (1933), and, in collaboration with Christopher Isherwood, *The Dog Beneath the Skin* (1935), *The Ascent of F6* (1936; revised edition, 1937), and *On the Frontier* (1938). I normally quote
from the original editions, whose texts are reprinted in *The English
Auden* (1978). But where prior versions appeared in periodicals, anthologies, or pamphlets, and where these differ substantially from the versions in book form (*Spain* is a notable example), I quote the earlier
texts. Poems never collected in book form are quoted from the texts as
they appeared in periodicals or in manuscripts; with unpublished work I
have corrected spellings where necessary but have left punctuation unchanged. Some further textual details may be found in the Notes.

Many readers are familiar with the revised texts in Auden's collected
and selected editions of his poems, texts that sometimes differ considerably from the versions quoted here. Since my account of Auden's work is
largely historical, I found it essential to use the early texts even if they
were less readily accessible. In many instances, these early versions have
now been reprinted in the new edition of Auden's *Selected Poems*
(1979). Editions that contain the later, revised texts are *The Collected
Poetry*, published in America in 1945, and its British counterpart, the
1950 *Collected Shorter Poems 1930–1944* (the variation in title and
contents results from the reluctance of the British publishers to include
poems they had kept in print in other editions; the segregation of shorter
and longer poems was apparently the publishers' idea, not Auden's); a
selection published by Penguin in 1958 as *W. H. Auden* and by the
Modern Library in 1959 as *Selected Poetry*; *Collected Shorter Poems
1927–1957* (1966) and *Collected Longer Poems* (1968); a British edition of *Selected Poems* (1968); and the posthumous *Collected Poems*
(1976), consisting of the 1966 and 1968 collections together with later
work and a few early poems Auden wished to restore.

Until the middle 1930s Auden left most of his poems untitled. His
later collected editions add titles by which some of the early poems have
now become well-known (e.g. "1929" and "Lullaby"). I have used a
few of these titles for brevity's sake, but have specified that they were
appended after the first publication of the poems.

David Bromwich and Natasha Staller offered detailed comments on every paragraph of the manuscript and solved countless problems of content and style. Mr. Bromwich also provided many illuminating ideas about Auden's relation to earlier poetry—ideas I would be very proud of, had I thought of them first. Natasha Staller's expertise in the history and theory of aesthetics, and in practical matters of nuance and structure, is reflected throughout my argument. These friends, and the many others who also gave assistance, are not to be blamed for my misuse or misinterpretation of their knowledge.

Lincoln Kirstein and Michael Wood gave invaluable advice on how the book might be improved, and kept it focused on issues that mattered. Lucy McDiarmid and Elizabeth Wheeler devoted many hours to the manuscript, as did Alan Ansen, Hanna M. Bercovitch, Humphrey Carpenter, Robert Fitzgerald, John Fuller, Carolyn Heilbrun, John Hollander, Penelope Laurans, and Edward W. Tayler. Individual chapters received welcome and severe attention from Sir Isaiah Berlin, Laurence Dreyfus, and Michael J. Sidnell. Elisabeth Sifton, my watchful editor at The Viking Press, was a constant source of wisdom and instruction.

Auden's family and friends were unfailingly generous with biographical information. I am indebted above all to Dr. John B. Auden, Christopher Isherwood, and Stephen Spender; also to the late Benjamin Britten, Mrs. Janet Carleton, Gabriel Carritt, Sir William Coldstream, the late Professor E. R. Dodds, Valerie Eliot, Maurice and Alexandra Feild, Brian Finney, A. S. T. Fisher, Margaret Gardiner, Richard Hoggart, John Johnson, Wendell Stacy Johnson, the late John Layard, Robert Medley, Naomi Mitchison, Sir Peter Pears, Peter H. Salus, Iris Sinkinson, Arnold Snodgrass, James and Tania Stern, Angelyn Stevens, Mrs. Dorothy Vinter, Basil Wright, and Michael and Marny Yates.

I have relied, as always, on the intelligence and friendship of Michael Seidel. For learned and clarifying advice, I am deeply grateful to Paul Fry. Among many others who provided scholarly and critical assistance, I want especially to thank Daniel Aaron, R. Victoria Arana, Morton W. Bloomfield, Bernard Crick, Paul W. Day, Maria DiBattista, Harris Friedberg, John Hildebidle, Eric Homberger, Richard Ingber, Donald Mitchell, James Nohrnberg, David Perkins, Brigitte Peucker, Edouard Roditi, Rosamund Strode, Claire Tomalin, and the late Susanna Tomalin.

My dedication is an inadequate gesture of thanks for twelve years of friendship and encouragement. Without B. C. Bloomfield's generosity in inviting me to collaborate in his research on Auden, I would never have been in the position to begin this book.

Four books were constantly open on my desk as I wrote this one: John Fuller's *A Reader's Guide to W. H. Auden;* Samuel Hynes's *The Auden Generation;* Monroe K. Spears's *The Poetry of W. H. Auden;* and Julian Symons's *The Thirties.* Four recent essays were especially helpful: Clive James's "Farewelling Auden" in his *At the Pillars of Hercules;* Lucy McDiarmid's "W. H. Auden's 'In the Year of My Youth . . .' " in *Review of English Studies,* August 1978; Tom Paulin's "*Letters From Iceland:* Going North" in *The 1930s,* ed. John Lucas; and Peter Porter's "The Achievement of Auden" in *Sydney Studies in English,* 1978–79. John Bayley's essays and reviews provided a rich supply of useful ideas. While revising I was fortunate to have the manuscript of Humphrey Carpenter's *W. H. Auden: A Biography* and the generous help of its author, who freely shared the fruits of his research.

Auden's publishers, Random House and Faber & Faber, kindly gave permission to quote from his printed work. A fellowship from the American Council of Learned Societies afforded me the time I needed for my preliminary research.

Librarians and curators have been unfailingly patient with my numerous difficult requests. Lola Szladits at the Berg Collection of the New York Public Library and Ellen Dunlap at the Humanities Research Center of the University of Texas at Austin were especially helpful. I also want to thank the libraries of Yale, Harvard, and Columbia universities, the British Library, the Bodleian Library, the Swarthmore College Library, the library of King's College, Cambridge, the BBC Written Archives Centre, and the National Film Archive, London.

I mentioned Natasha Staller. There is scarcely room in these pages to thank her for all her kindnesses while I was writing this book, and, above all, for giving me no peace until I finished it.

Contents

XIII   Parables of Action: 2   281
XIV   History to the Defeated   304
 XV   From This Island   333

         Epilogue   365

         Reference Notes   369

         Index   393

Introduction

In childhood, before he wrote a line of poetry, Auden imagined himself an architect and engineer, the maker of a fictional landscape. Between the ages of six and twelve he devoted much of his waking thought to what he later called "the construction and elaboration of a private sacred world, the basic elements of which were a landscape, northern and limestone, and an industry, lead mining." This world was a fantasy, its fabrication a game, but the principles that gave it order were among those that governed the material world. "I decided," he recalled, "or rather, without conscious decision, I instinctively felt that I must impose two restrictions upon my freedom of fantasy." In choosing the objects that might go into his private world he must choose among objects that really exist; and "In deciding how my world was to function, I could choose between two practical possibilities—a mine can be drained either by an adit or a pump—but physical impossibilities and magic means were forbidden." He felt, "in some obscure way, that they were morally forbidden," that the rules of his game must represent both the laws of nature and the laws of ethics. Eventually, still during childhood, "there came a day when the moral issue became quite conscious." Among the equipment he needed for his imaginary mines was a device, used for washing the ore, which was available in two different designs. "One type I found more sacred or 'beautiful,' but the other type was, as I knew from my reading, the more efficient. At this point I realized that it was my moral duty to sacrifice my aesthetic preference to reality or truth."

Auden recounted these childhood decisions in later years as a way of characterizing his work as a poet. Mines were places of symbolic depths and hidden meaning, passages to a dark source of mystery and power. But even as a child he knew them also to be functioning artifacts, made for practical mundane reasons, and causing real and possibly dangerous effects. As an adult he wrote poems that found richness of meaning in the moral complexities of fact. He had no wish to achieve an imaginative triumph over common reality; he used his poetry to comprehend the world he shared with his audience, and he wrote his poems as public acts of homage to the truths he perceived. His truthtelling never led him to prefer in literature what he called "Plain cooking made still plainer by plain cooks." As in childhood he delighted in the elaborate machinery of mines, in his adult years he indulged his love of poetic artifice: "Riddles and all other ways of not calling a spade a spade," "Complicated verse forms of great technical difficulty," "Conscious theatrical exaggeration." Yet he put his dazzlingly irresponsible virtuosity to responsible use. Through it, he insisted that his poems were connected to the ordinary world by their craftsmanship, just as they were connected to it by their dedication to fact. His poems were not visionary autonomous objects, exempt from the practical and ethical standards appropriate to all other human works. They were made to be judged both for their art and for their truth.

These elements from Auden's childhood fantasy, its commitment to fact and its deliberate artifice, were present in his poetry almost from the start of his career. But in his earliest poems they were subordinate to a different element of his fantasy. "It is no doubt psychologically significant," he wrote, "that my sacred world was autistic, that is to say, I had no wish to share it with others nor could I have done so." In the same way, his first adult poetry, the work of a young man of twenty, was overwhelmingly concerned with his own emotional isolation, rather than with truths he could share with his audience. In contrast to the complex stanzaic contraptions of his later years, he wrote many of his first poems in irregular free verse. During the first twelve years of his career, the years that are the subject of this book, Auden made the difficult passage from a private poetry to a public one, from apparent formal disorder to manifest artifice, and from lonely severity to a community of meaning. When he began writing he found in his personal psychology the condition of the age. As he grew older, he sought in science and history a range and variety of knowledge that he knew no individual could hope to organize on personal or aesthetic principles alone. He began as the deliberate inventor of the new poetic language he felt his isolation required. Then he refused the imprisonment of a reflexive personal voice and chose to write in stanzaic forms that, as he said later, "forbid automatic responses, / force us to have second thoughts, free from the fetters of Self."

Two kinds of poetry, two ideas of the poet's task, two poetic traditions contend against each other in Auden's early years. Because his work, from the start, was large in its sympathies and powers, and densely linked to the traditions of poetry, the issues dividing it were those that perennially divide literature and show no signs of ever being resolved. The same tension between two kinds of art in Auden's work may also be found in the earliest poetry of Europe. Homer knew the distinction, and portrayed it in precise and vivid detail. In the *Odyssey* he tells of the poets Phemius and Demodocus who compose their songs at the command of their listeners. It never occurs to them to sing for the sake of singing. They so love their art that, when danger threatens, they protect their lyre before themselves, yet their instrument and their voice are in service to their audience, and their art responds to a specific social occasion. When Odysseus tells his story to the Phaeacians he follows their example. He chooses his words with his listeners in mind, for he needs their help to get home. Hoping to affect his audience, as he himself was affected by the songs of Demodocus, he adds some perhaps legendary embellishments—tales of one-eyed giants and man-eating whirlpools—for the urgent practical purpose of gaining sympathy and aid. All the poets in the *Odyssey* are suppliants like Odysseus or servants like Demodocus. Such a poet, surely, was Homer himself. His heirs are all poets who write as citizens, whose purpose is to entertain and instruct, and who choose subjects that would interest an audience even if a poet were not there to transform them into art.

In the *Iliad* matters are very different. Here the one person who recites poetry is Achilles when he sits in his tent singing of heroes and taking pleasure in his lyre, after withdrawing in anger from the society of his fellows. Homer specifies that Achilles has no audience for his songs; Patroclus is with him, but sits off to the side, waiting for his friend to finish. Achilles is the one Homeric hero who questions his obligations, is servant to no one and no one's fellow citizen; he sings for himself alone. His literary heirs are all poets whose first law is the law of their genius, seers who live in voluntary or psychological exile, at home only in their art. These are poets who, as T. S. Eliot wrote, "have won their own discipline in secret and without aid, in a world which offers very little assistance to that end." When they address an audience, it is no finite class or existing category of readers. It is either, on one hand, the universe or all mankind or things that don't listen, like mountains or skylarks; or, on the other, the poet himself, or someone like a sister whom he treasures as a version of himself, or the ideal reader imagined by W. B. Yeats, "A man who does not exist, / A man who is but a dream." Poets of this sort know themselves to be unacknowledged legislators, and their works reign, in Ezra Pound's words, as "lords over fact, over race-long recurrent moods, and over to-morrow."

The first critic who judged between these two kinds of poet, the civil and the vatic, was the god Dionysus. In Aristophanes' *The Frogs* Dionysus is the god of wine, but he is also a god of Athens, and he seeks a poet who can save his city from disaster. Descending into the underworld, he presides over a contest between the shades of Aeschylus and Euripides, and weighs in his scales the art of civil responsibility against the art of inner vision. Aeschylus prays to the traditional gods, invokes the ancient tradition of the poet as moral teacher, and condemns the self-centeredness encouraged by his rival. Euripides prays to a private pantheon of the sky and his own tongue and senses, claims that when he writes his extravagant modern fictions he does no harm to society, and praises the doubt and questioning his work provokes in Athens. Dionysus finds he loves both poets equally, but at last he must select one of them for his city. He chooses Aeschylus. So, in effect, did Auden.

Civil poetry and vatic poetry have separate traditions that move side by side through literary history, each giving strength to the other, and merging at times in the work of a few very great writers. During the eighteenth century the balance between them shifted. Poetry's civil purposes came to be felt as restraints on the free personal voice. The romantics inverted the ancient poetic hierarchy that saw dramatic and epic poetry as superior to lyric, poetry of action and relationship more consequential than poetic expressions of feeling. Romanticism, hearing epic resonance in the personal voice, glorified the lyric as the highest mode of poetry, and made it the vessel for philosophical and historical subjects few earlier ages would have tried to force into it. The large forms of literature and the arts left the service of specific audiences and social occasions, and became their own sufficient reason for being. Art declared its independence from local settings, and established itself instead in the neutral international context of the museums and concert halls that sprang up as its temples, bastions of its newly won autonomy.

This change in context was accompanied by changes in meaning, most strikingly in the large form of the quest. Formerly an allegory of civil obligation, the quest now became the allegory of inner discontent. In civil literature a quest hero ventured forth to seek a real goal that needed his presence, and that promised marriage and prosperity as a reward for his sufferings. But in literature that lacked external purpose, that had no audience who wanted it written, the quest, too, lost its tangible goals, and became compulsive and irresolute. The mad comic journey of Don Quixote was pursued in fatal earnest by the romantics. The price art paid for its autonomy was its desperate isolation.

Literary modernism brought the vatic tradition into the twentieth century. The lyric personal voice that predominated in the poetry of Yeats, Pound, and Eliot became the voice of prose fiction as well in the novels of Lawrence, Joyce, and Woolf. Like romantic heroes lost upon the earth, the writers of modernism felt lost in historical time: to be modern was to be disfranchised from a significant past. Vatic writing had always given credence to a lost mythical arcadia, a distant time when society was hierarchically secure and the grand manner still a natural tone of voice. Now the modernists translated this myth into a serious interpretation of history. They looked back to a recent European cataclysm that left society and art in exhausted disorder. Eliot saw the moment of change in a seventeenth-century "dissociation of sensibility ... from which we have never recovered." For Lawrence it occurred when the explorers of America brought syphilis to Europe. Yeats, convinced he lived in a debased century, dated the unbroken age in 1450, when the gyres of his historical cycles were in balance.

The poets of modernism devised their characteristic free verse as a response to the European disaster. Pound's familiar insistence on the need to "break the pentameter," and the delight with which he broke it, make it easy to forget that he and Eliot began using free verse because they were convinced the modern world was too catastrophically disordered to allow the use of older, more regular metres for any other purpose than satire. Eliot would have used formal metres if he could; "a formless age" prevented him. In British poetry of the 1920s free verse was not seen as the fluent, almost casual form it became later, and was already becoming in America. Free verse was *difficult*, and was meant to be. Eliot wrote that poets in our time are difficult by necessity, that they must "force, . . . dislocate if necessary," their language to suit their meaning. The hesitations, false starts, and broken repetitions in the free verse of Eliot and others in the 1920s—as in Auden's poetry at this time—are meant as signs of a resistance made by the poetic subject against the poet's effort to write about it. Among the historical crises faced, and in part invented, by modernism was a breakdown in what might be called the symbolic contract, the common frame of reference and expectation that joins a poet with a finite audience, and joins both with the subjects of his poems.

The modernist literary revolution hoped to clear the wreckage left by this disaster, what Mallarmé called the *"Crise de Vers."* This was a romantic revolution, intent on purifying the diction of the tribe, freeing poetry from its dependence on dead principles of form and meaning. The more naïve branches of modernism hoped that free verse might become the unencumbered vehicle of direct personal utterance, ruled only by the laws of breathing. More sophisticated writers, deriding such provincial efforts, sought to let their verse express the autonomous, even visionary order of poetic language itself. Their poetry would no longer obey the rules of allegory or the standards of mimesis, would ignore even the imaginative will of its author. The voice of poetry is not the chosen voice of the poet, said Rimbaud, because the verbal *"JE est un autre,"* is an event in language's separate disembodied world. The poet, having abandoned civil responsibility toward an audience, now sought to abandon responsibility for his poems. "The pure work," said Mallarmé, "implies the disappearance as a speaker of the poet who abandons the initiative to words"—words set in motion by the internal disorder of language, "mobilized by the shock of their inequality." But as Mallarmé added, pure poetry still finds its existence *"chez le Poëte"*: the liberation of language results not in shared truths but in a new ordering of private vision within the self. In later generations this line of modernism understood the self to be constituted *by* language, and the wordless unconscious to be organized *like* a language. No community seemed possible except the centerless, contradictory, unstable community of language itself.

As modernism worked to release the inner powers of imagination, to break the pentameter and disorder all the senses, it also, notoriously, longed for a rigid and unchanging order in the realm of politics. Modernism celebrated inner freedom as it called for outer restraint. At the same time that it pursued continuous restless innovation in literary form, it saw history ruled by unchanging historical cycles, by the eternal silence of the infinite spaces, immune from the effects of human choice. There was nothing new in this. One of Balzac's characters reports in *Illusions Perdues* that in literary Paris in the 1820s, "by a singular oddity, the Royalist romantics demand literary freedom and the repeal of the laws that give our literature conventional form; while the Liberals want to maintain the unities, the inflection of the alexandrine line, and classic themes. Thus in each faction literary opinion is at variance with political opinion." Vatic poetry praises the unique powers of heroic individuality and longs for a past when heroism was unconstrained. Its freedom from conventional form is one manifestation of its wish; romantic Royalism, like the vague fascist sympathies of modernism, is another. The heroes of civil poetry are more cunning than volcanic, more intent on finding their way back to their city than on dying gloriously and far away; and a civil poet similarly finds his artistic challenge in demands made by existing poetic forms, forms that could be completed satisfactorily rather than left in deliberate fragments. In *The Frogs* it is didactic Aeschylus who rejects vers libre for stanzaic complexity, but accepts a flawed political leader in preference to chaos and defeat. It is questioning Euripides who will cooperate only with an ideal statesman, but claims to speak the language really used by men.

Auden began writing poems in 1922, at the age of fifteen, and for the next few years he wrote mostly in the shadow of Hardy the lyricist—a poet whose early years as an architect were a distant parallel to Auden's childhood as an imaginary engineer. But in 1926, when he was at Oxford, Auden began saturating himself in the recent triumphs of modernism, which at the time was unrivalled among literary movements for its formal complexity and emotional strength. While other styles of writing seemed content to rest on the sad margins of a conventional past, modernism alone seemed to look toward a difficult and inexorable future. Its procession of landmarks stands as imposingly now as it did then: 1920 saw the publication of *Women in Love*; 1921, Yeats's *Four Plays for Dancers*; 1922, *The Waste Land* and *Ulysses*; 1923, *Birds,*

Beasts and Flowers; 1925, *A Draft of XVI Cantos* and Eliot's *Poems 1909-1925;* 1926, *Personae;* 1927, *To the Lighthouse;* 1928, *Anna Livia Plurabelle* and *The Tower.* And in 1927–28 Auden wrote the first of the intensely modernist verse he gathered in his 1930 *Poems.* For a young poet whose early ambition was to write the great poems of his generation, there seemed no turning back.

And Auden did not turn back. He was the first English writer who absorbed all the lessons of modernism, but also understood its limits, and chose to turn elsewhere. He successfully challenged the vatic dynasty after more than a century of uncontested rule. When he renounced the goals of his immediate predecessors he made no effort to revive the native lyric tradition of Hardy—now often proposed as the alternative to international modernism, but in fact another branch of the same vatic line, equally lonely and nostalgic, equally in exile from the shared life of the city. Instead he retained from Hardy the vast historical perspectives of *The Dynasts,* its conjunction of great aeons and distances with minute local detail, and put it to different use. Where Hardy stood ironically aloof from a brute mechanistic history, Auden saw an obligation to bring knowledge to the service of responsibility. He placed Hardy's perspectives in the context of a civil tradition of poetry that extended from Chaucer through Shakespeare, Dryden, and Pope. In the modernist era the chief representative of this tradition was Kipling, whose attitudes seemed to many readers to be adequate proof that his mode of writing had grown moribund or outdated. But its potential was as large as it had ever been. George Orwell did not realize when he dismissed Auden as "a sort of gutless Kipling" (a phrase he soon retracted) that he was in fact honoring him; it was precisely Kipling's "guts" that were most damaging to Kipling's genius. In 1929 Auden wrote of doomed violent heroes, "Fighters for no one's sake / Who died beyond the border." Ten years later he chose a different tone, celebrating those like Freud "who were doing us some good, / And knew it was never enough but / Hoped to improve a little by living."

In the same year, 1939, Eliot looked sadly back at the triumphs of modernism, and saw in them "rather the last efforts of an old world, than the first struggles of a new." In the midst of these triumphs, before modernism began its manifest decline, Auden was exuberantly at work, writing in ways that modernism insisted were impossible. Eliot had written of the "great labour" and "continual self-sacrifice" a writer must endure to find a tradition. Auden made tradition his ordinary experience, his daily means of perception. The poets of modernism felt they could bring tradition into the present only as battered ironic fragments, or by heroic efforts to make it new. For Auden it had never grown old.

Had Auden been alone in the course he pursued in his poetry, his career might now seem an historical dead end, offering few prospects for later writers to explore. But he was following in the same direction taken by the greatest of his near-contemporaries in Europe, Bertolt Brecht. Auden and Brecht both began as romantic anarchists, violently amoral, but matured into a chastened public orthodoxy, Christian in Auden's case, Communist in Brecht's. Renouncing the brash menacing styles of their early work, both chose didactic manners suitable for irony and celebration. Both taught through parables. Where modernism had used innovative forms to speak of historical necessity, Auden and Brecht adopted traditional forms to speak of freedom and choice. They both enlarged the genres they adopted by restoring to literary language the content and manner of historical analysis, public oratory, moral philosophy, social and literary criticism, even gossip, and they restored to poetry an encyclopedic fullness of subject matter and style; yet they never pretended that what they wrote was sufficient unto itself or that it gave order to the world. Rejecting the romantic premise that individual vision was the true source of poetry, each willingly submerged his personality in collaborations with other writers. (When their paths crossed in the 1940s they collaborated on an adaptation of *The Duchess of Malfi.*) Both kept themselves open to the full range of literature and diction, taking influences where they found them. Unlike the modernists, they used popular forms without the disclaimer of an ironic tone. Each preferred mixed styles to lyric intensity, imperfect truth to pure resonance. Neither would entrust serious issues to the inflation of the grand manner, and neither was afraid to be vulgar. Each dreamed for a time of a perfect society; each woke to the recognition that an ideal order imposed on a recalcitrant citizenry, which included themselves, would be an arid despotism.

Auden never forgot that his art could give him no privileged status. He knew he was a product of the professional bourgeoisie, that his distant ancestors "probably / were among those plentiful subjects / it cost less money to murder." The climate of his family was one of religious observance and public obligation. Both his grandfathers were Anglican clergymen. His father, George Augustus Auden, trained as a physician and was working as a general practitioner in York when his third son,

Wystan Hugh Auden, was born on 21 February 1907. The next year the family moved to Birmingham when Dr. Auden became the city's first School Medical Officer; after the first World War he was also appointed Professor of Public Health at Birmingham University. Dr. Auden had a stable and gentle character and exceptionally wide learning. Educated in natural science at Cambridge, he was also expert in archaeology and the classics. He traced his ancestry to Iceland and taught his children to share his love for the sagas. He published important contributions in public health and was one of the first officials in his field to make use of Freudian psychology. During the first World War he served with the Royal Army Medical Corps in Egypt, Gallipoli, and France, and for more than four years, from Wystan Auden's seventh through eleventh years, the family saw almost nothing of him. The eldest son, Bernard, became a farmer and spent fifteen years in Canada, and Wystan had little to do with him in childhood or after. He was closer to the middle brother, John, who had a distinguished scientific career with the Geological Survey of India, where he was also a noted mountaineer, and later with the U.N. Food and Agricultural Organization. There are signs that Wystan saw John and himself as pursuing lives that were parallel but mirror-opposites, in their careers in science and literature as well as in their emotions. Much later he saw John's two daughters almost as the children he never had.

Auden's mother had the greatest effect on his early emotional life, and her influence persisted. Constance Rosalie Bicknell had taken an honors degree in French at the University of London, one of the first women to do so, then trained to be a nurse. She planned to join a Protestant mission in Africa, but gave this up when she married Dr. Auden. Wystan recognized early on that he had more in common with his mother's emotional and imaginative character than with his father's more phlegmatic one. When Jungian terminology briefly invaded his vocabulary in later years he described himself and his mother as thinking-intuitive types, in contrast with his father, whose type was feeling-sensation. Mrs. Auden was devoutly High Anglican, and the liturgical calendar was followed in her household during the holidays. She had a firm sense of her authority within the family and tended to resent the independent lives her husband and children led outside it.

Auden's modernist poems were the work of his youthful *Wander-jahre* of exile and revolt, but by 1933, when he was twenty-six, he adopted in his political and didactic writings a socialist version of his parents' service ethic, and by 1940 he returned to their faith.

One of the last modernists, Vladimir Nabokov, wrote that art is "a game of intricate enchantment and deception." Auden wrote that "In so far as poetry, or any of the arts, can be said to have an ulterior purpose, it is, by telling the truth, to disenchant and disintoxicate." He knew that poetry, for all its formal excitement and elaboration, could never be independent, and could never adequately be understood in terms of its internal or linguistic order. The emotional power of poetry leads readers to sympathize, however subtly or unknowingly, with the attitudes it embodies. Attitudes such as nostalgia or hero-worship eventually translate into action, with results less beautiful than any poem. Knowing this, Auden found himself in the curious position of taking poetry far more seriously than his critics did who regretted his apparent lack of High Seriousness—critics who accepted the vatic principle that art was its own reason for being and who, therefore, lacked any standard of judgement that could distinguish seriousness of tone from seriousness of meaning.

When Auden wrote in opposition to the canons of modernism, he did so in the understanding that came of accepting them earlier. He explored all the fields of poetry familiar to his age, and discovered rich fields his age had neglected or abandoned. Isolated, intense, and severe in his earliest writings, he came to write poetry that, more than any other, contributed to the understanding of his time. He became the most inclusive poet of the twentieth century, its most technically skilled, and its most truthful.

Part One

~ ~ ~

THE BORDER AND THE GROUP

(August 1927–May 1933)

I

The Exiled Word

Auden begins alone. His first poems are laconic fragments, their meanings hidden. At twenty, as he finds his poetic voice, he feels little hope of communication or sympathy. A guarded border cuts across the landscape of his poetry, barring passage to refuge or escape. On one side of the frontier is a barren vacancy that permits no exit. On the other side is a vital fullness he cannot enter. Wherever he turns he finds a wall or gulf dividing the life he endures from the life he imagines. Keeping watch over "the divided face" of a would-be lover are the eyes and mouth, "Sentries against inner and outer." Knowing all ports are watched, "frontier-conscious," he sees all roads blocked by chained-up gates, secured by mythical Lords of Limit who warn that the price of crossing them is death. As he watches immobilized, desperate heroes storm the border to win a brief and futile victory—"One sold all his manors to fight, broke through, and faltered."

Auden looks down from a superior height in these early poems, and abandons the traditional past as he abandons solid ground. "Consider this and in our time," begins a 1929 poem, "As the hawk sees it or the helmeted airman." What we see is a divisive gap: "The clouds rift suddenly—look there / At cigarette-end smouldering on a border." This is a garden-border, a row of plants, but the name carries its burden of isolation even across our most familiar comforts, as a discarded cigarette intrudes its coarse modernity. Auden's tone is bravely defiant, but he knows the airman's freedom offers no escape, only a different form of isolation. He wrote an "Airman's Alphabet" in 1931, which ends on a

note of sardonic despair, and a quiet confession of the emptiness of the
airman's love:

YOUTH—   Daydream of devils
             and dear to the damned
             and always to us.

ZERO—   Love before leaving
             and touch of terror
             and time of attack.

The airman's earthbound counterpart is the spy. Divided from home,
estranged from trust, confounded by the frontier, the secret agent in
Auden's early poems enters into enemy territory, only to be forsaken by
his allies. He can communicate with no one: "They ignored his wires."
Any report of him must be drained of emotion; the proper tone is a
thin-lipped fatalism, almost at the edge of casual amusement: "The
bridges were unbuilt and trouble coming. . . . They would shoot, of
course." The agent who dares the border, whose messages go unheard,
joins all the futile heroes who "Did not believe in death," but "Whose
voices in the rock / Are now perpetual."

The nameless, faceless figures who inhabit these poems are too far off
to be recognized, too isolated for speech. They are characterized at most
by a function—airman, stranger, spy. Usually they are reduced to a pronoun or generalized as "man." Should they try to make their way back
to community and purpose, they find the roads almost vanished, the
rails blocked, and the bridges out. Barred from change and movement,
each dreams of an impossible world of energy and joy:

he dreams of folk in dancing bunches,
Of tart wine spilt on home-made benches,
Where learns, one drawn apart, a secret will
Restore the dead;

but inevitably he "comes thence to a wall." The dream stops at the
frontier.

"Outside on frozen soil lie armies killed / Who seem familiar but they
are cold." Fatal immobilizing winter haunts these early poems: "winter
for earth and us," "snow down to the tide-line," "this . . . the Age of
Ice." The "sound behind our back" we hear is more grotesquely terrify-

ing even than time's wingèd chariot: the unimaginably monstrous sound
"Of glaciers calving." In this warlike present of dead armies on frozen
soil we lie at night in our barracks and tell ourselves "the peace-time
stories" of a lost arcadia, of warmer days

> Before the islands were submerged, when the weather was calm,
> > The maned lion common,
> An open wishing-well in every garden;
> > When love came easy.

So intense is our wish for a different world that we *know* these legends
are true, "Perfectly certain, all of us, but not from the records." For the
tangible evidence left by the past tells us otherwise: "The pillar dug
from the desert recorded only / The sack of a city." There was never a
time of peace unlike the time of war we suffer now.

Auden is edgy with antagonism in these early poems. He is beset by
hostile armies, but he cannot learn precisely what he is fighting for, or
whom against. The origins of the deadly feud chronicled in his 1928
charade *Paid on Both Sides* have long been forgotten, yet the feud's hatreds continue unabated. Whatever division exists is now cause enough
for mutual destruction. The struggle Auden records in his early poems
has nothing to do with classes or nations; to the extent he characterizes it
at all, it is the battle of a dead past against an inaccessible future. The
young hope for liberation from the old; the old wish for liberation from
age. Confident in their powers, the young think themselves free from
their elders' burdens. They "sheer off from old like gull from granite."
But the past lies in wait for them, hidden like a saboteur in their psyche,
even in their genes. While sons rebel, "Fathers in sons may track / Their
voices' trick." These recurring parental voices signify a deeper persistence of hatred, its transmittal from an ancient past, binding the energies
of the newly born to the will of the forgotten dead. Each family carries
its "ancestral curse." Genetically "jumbled perhaps and put away," ignored by the new generation, the curse inevitably attacks the young.
"Escaping cannot try" to evade it; "Must wait though it destroy." But
the triumph of the curse brings little satisfaction to the old. Fathers may
succeed in putting down murmurs against what they call "Our old right
to abuse," but they are doomed by their aging flesh, left only with "Our
honour at least, / And a reasonable chance of retaining / Our faculties to
the last." In this endless war both sides are defeated. The forces of the

old diminish continually in death, while all the recruits to the army of the young must eventually defect to the other side.

Only the dead triumph. Ghosts walk through Auden's early poems, family ghosts who reach across time to hold us back from our lives. They haunt the private psyche and the public commonwealth. Their maternal jealousies impede our marriages, their fatherly patriotism sends us into battle. The daughter of one of the feuding families in *Paid on Both Sides* says hopefully of the dead, "They forget," they "shall not speak / Out of that grave stern on no capital fault." A hundred lines later the play proves her wrong. Hoping to triumph over enmity through love, she accepts an offer of marriage from the son of the opposing family. But he is killed on their wedding day in revenge for old killings, and victory is swallowed up by death.

If love could escape into the present, it might find the way to wholeness and peace, but impulsive Eros carries the dead weight of the past. Ghosts interrupt lovers, cough when they would kiss. A 1929 poem opens with this catalogue of the psychological dowry inherited by a lover:

> Before this loved one
> Was that one and that one
> A family
> And history
> And ghost's adversity.

No loving wish can compensate for archaic resentments and the adversity of ghosts. "This gratitude for gifts is less / Than the old loss." Here as so often in Auden's early poems there can be "no new year." Even the act of love itself is reduced by the ancestral curse to a border-meeting on property held in mortmain by the dead:

> Touching is shaking hands
> On mortgaged lands;
> And smiling of
> This gracious greeting
> "Good day. Good luck"
> Is no real meeting
> But instinctive look
> A backward love.

The love made now, the greeting offered, can do no more than execute inherited or instinctual patterns. "The sexual act," Auden wrote in a journal he kept in 1929, "is only a symbol for intimacy." Bound to the instincts of its evolutionary past, the body's love looks "backward" to its archaic needs. It cannot look outward to the lover standing before it now.

" 'Good day. Good luck' / Is no real meeting." Words are no better at communicating than flesh is. In another 1929 poem neither the physical nor verbal gestures of "cheek to cheek / And dear to dear" are adequate for love. As the body repeats its instinctual couplings, the mind stays absolutely alone. Auden saw the work of the mind as analytic, differentiating, abstracting, dividing. When lovers talk of love, speaking in "ambition / Of definition," love does not become recognizable and whole, but divides again—"Suffers partition." In the new atmosphere of sexual freedom in the 1920s one could hear everywhere "Voices explain / Love's pleasure and love's pain." But love itself stayed away from the conversation. "Love is not there / Love has moved to another chair." And because love is divided against itself it can do nothing to prevent the division inflicted on it. Love "would not gather / Another to another" to end their otherness. It "designs" its "own unhappiness ... and is faithless."

Auden's intractable problem in these poems is finally neither erotic nor social nor linguistic, but the irreducible fact of division itself. In 1931, when a young French poet, Edouard Roditi, sent him a draft translation of "Before this loved one," with the phrase "no real meeting" rendered as *pas une rencontre*," Auden wrote in the margin: "Can you get the sense of the *real* in. It is important. The sense is the philosophical one as in the *real* wholes in Gestalt psychology." Reviewing a new edition of John Skelton at about the same time, Auden again managed to bring in "the problem of *real* wholes." His airman's perspective, far from setting him free, left him in an extreme state of modernist isolation, capable of finding wholeness neither in himself nor in the world outside. He was psychologically too distant from his own body to be satisfied by its acts, and too distant from the rest of the world to be affected by it or to change it. The question he asked in his first poems was not What should I do now? but Of what whole can I be part?

Yet the isolation that makes him ask this question also makes it impossible for him to answer it. In the romantic psychology he accepted as true in his early twenties, Creation is Fall, and any consciousness is by

necessity an isolated consciousness. Birth initiates an absolute separation of self and world, and the unattainable goal of the fragmented life is
recovered unity of being. Auden's 1929 account of the birth trauma emphasizes the original maternal unity and its chilling loss:

> Is first baby, warm in mother,
> Before born and is still mother,
> Time passes and now is other,
> Is knowledge in him now of other,
> Cries in cold air, himself no friend . . .

The newborn infant simply "is other," defined by his separation, as in
Rousseau's grammatically parallel romantic credo *"je suis autre."* Can
this otherness end? Can love, Auden asks in a 1930 poem, "For love recover / What has been dark and rich and warm all over?" His constant
answer, in these early years, is that love cannot do this; it is baffled by
the dead. And since the dead block us from any plausible future, he
adopts the extreme romantic belief that the only escape from their
power is through our own death. The goal of our divided self is love, but
love "Needs more than the admiring excitement of union." It needs an
absolute union which, unlike the sexual act and the language of endearment, can never be broken or changed. Love, in fact,

> Needs death, death of the grain, our death,
> Death of the old gang.

If, since the romantic era, young poets have been half in love with
easeful death, that is partly because it is the one subject about which
they can be confident their elders know no more than they do. A youthful poet, especially if he feels the absence of a living tradition, may have
no useful vocation, no marriage, no citizenship to write about, may find
no coherence in the relation between an observing self and an observed
object, between language and truth. But he can look forward to a death
which may at last dissolve *all* distinctions. In Auden's earliest adult
poems, any successful transformation will occur only through death and
submergence in the undifferentiated sea. The "new conditions" of unity
he longs for may be apprehended only by dissolving the fragments of
the self. "Prolonged drowning shall develop gills," he hopes—the grim

anti-evolutionary wit casting doubt on his hope even as he expresses it. To learn unity we must endure death in "Winter for earth and us," for winter is

> A forethought of death that we may find ourselves at death
> Not helplessly strange to the new conditions

—those new conditions of wholeness and love from which we have been estranged in life. Nothing except death offers hope, and so it is the very impracticality of death as a program for achieving wholeness that becomes its strongest recommendation. *Credit quia impossibile.*

Until winter or drowning can restore unity, all Auden can admire in others is a comparable wholeness they have already achieved. He praises the "complete" beauty of a child, an adult's "Completeness of gesture or unclouded eye." But this unity proves partial after all, limited to the unconsciousness of childhood or to a physical gesture or feature. So, as the converse of his own division, Auden tries to imagine instead an undivided hero with a unity of flesh and will, a "tall unwounded leader," a "truly strong man." Like Yeats writing about the noble rich, or D. H. Lawrence about himself, Auden briefly projects a fantasy of personal wholeness and authority out of his own sense of divided isolation. Yet he knows from the start that no such leader exists. "Neither in the bed nor on the *arête* was there shown me / One with power." What he seeks is an answer to the romantic wish for self-sufficient unity—"One with power" inherent in the self, not power diffused into action, as in power to do something or power over someone. This is an instinctive erotic force, good because amoral: "on the arm" in spring, "A fresh hand with fresh power." Auden arrives at this special usage of words like *power* partly by the romantic technique that transfers to man the inherent attributes of the divine ("the Son of God with power" in Romans i.4), partly by the modernist technique that takes words whose familiar senses are transitive and uses them in an intransitive way—as Yeats uses *labour* to refer, not to anything productive, but to blossoming or dancing where the body is not bruised to pleasure soul. What Auden seeks in such words as *power* and *luck* and in some senses of *love* is a coherence that has nothing to do with purposive action, but brings an "absolute unity" of perception that will make it possible "to love my life."

Auden criticized his fantasies of wholeness even as he was writing them, but he did so mostly on the grounds that they failed. The fate of all his heroes, the Airman in *The Orators* or, later, Michael Ransom in *The Ascent of F6*, proves that they were not undivided at all, but only kept their inner disorder well hidden from their admirers. Auden at first makes no moral criticism of his disastrous heroes, because his world is too incoherent to sustain any ethical system: there action is divorced from consequence. One may try to act on one's own, but the family ghosts or impersonal evolution determines the result. And ethics will have no place either in the unified world Auden hopes to recover, a world whose wholeness will end the need for conscious action and render all standards of judgement obsolete. Even now, the disorder he experiences is, he thinks, subject to no judgement by moralists, no cure by physicians, no overthrow by revolutionaries. Efforts like theirs may alter the symptoms of a deeper and more pervasive division, the breakup of the real whole, but the universal and unspecific quality of this division makes it impossible to repair.

As the problem Auden faced in his first poems is abstract and difficult to define, so, notoriously, are the poems. Readers who try to resolve the difficulties by finding allegories of Freud and Marx, or who devise a unified narrative myth as a context for individual incidents, or who hunt out clues in the mythical landscapes of the writings of Auden's friends, largely miss the point of the early work, although they are responding to a quality that pervades it. The poems suggest that they are fragments of a larger whole but do not provide enough data to identify that whole. The reader is made to feel that some vital clue is lacking which, if one had it, could make sense of everything. But Auden hid nothing. The absence of a clue is the clue itself. The poems' central subject is their own failure to be part of any larger interpretive frame. Their metaphors refer to their own state of division and estrangement. As soon as one stops looking for the key to a set of symbols, and recognizes that the poems focus on the self-enclosing patterns that bar their way to a subject in the world outside, their notorious obscurity begins to vanish.

This argument may sound like a paraphrase of late-twentieth-century theories of poetic language as reflexive and self-referential. In fact I have been paraphrasing Auden himself. In a journal entry made in 1929 he identified his poetics and justified them by a recent change in human nature:

> Mind has been evolved from body, i.e. from the Not-self, whose thinking is community thinking, and therefore symbolic. While Yeats [in his essay "The Symbolism of Poetry"] is right that great poetry in the past has been symbolic, I think we are reaching the point in the development of the mind where symbols are becoming obsolete in poetry, as the true mind, or non-communistic* self does not think in this way. This does not invalidate its use [in] past poetry, but it does invalidate it in modern poetry, just as an attempt to write in Chaucerian English would be academic.

This is an extraordinary statement, both in its assumption that a radical and unprecedented change is occurring in the mind, and also in its extreme extension of modernist ideas. Yeats, Pound, and Eliot had all felt the loss of an earlier, nobler state of poetic language, and continually stressed how difficult was their self-imposed task of restoring it. But they never said the task was impossible, which is precisely what Auden said. He absorbed the modernist notion of a catastrophic break in literary tradition; he accepted that break as irreparable; and he set out to find a new poetic language, nonsymbolic and noncommunicative, that would give voice to the new conditions.

His earliest poems, obsessed as they are with the past, can remember nothing about it:

> Only remembering the method of remembering,
> Remembering only in another way.

The method was not enough. The poems raise the hard question of real wholes—but "To ask the hard question is simple, / The simple act of the confused will." What is "hard and hard to remember" is the answer. Separated like all the modernists from both audience and tradition, Auden could not, in his ruined world, enjoy a stable relation with any subject matter he might share with his readers. He could not be didactic,

* He is using *communistic* to refer to the way in which the realm of the senses is shared commonly by all; the word's only political undertone in this context is its bourgeois disdain for the mental life of the proletariat.

because the conditions in which questions had memorable answers were lost in the past. And he could not enjoy a sense that his own work built on a coherent tradition of which it could now become a part. A poet would now recollect older literary forms only to recognize how inappropriate they are in the present, how distant is the world where they enjoyed their proper functions. He could remember the *forms* of tradition, not its meaning—"Only . . . the method of remembering"—and could remember them only in a different, modern way. His historical evidence for such ideas would have been the Eliot of "Gerontion" or *The Waste Land,* who echoed ancient forms for only a few lines at a time, before the pressure of modern desolation twisted the forms to the breaking point.

Yet while Auden's predominant tone was one of warning and crisis, the tone suited to an apocalyptic age, he added overtones of deliberate fustian and buffoonery. There was no turning back from the disaster; best to accept it, even enjoy it as an occasion for poetry. The catastrophe seemed unsettlingly comic, whether it was pending—

> Have things gone too far already? Are we done for? Must we wait
> Hearing doom's approaching footsteps regular down miles of straight

—or certain—

> It is later than you think; nearer that day
> Far other than that distant afternoon
> Amid rustle of frocks and stamping feet
> They gave the prizes to the ruined boys.
> You cannot be away, then, no
> Not though you pack to leave within an hour,
> Escaping humming down arterial roads.

This tone manages to combine the solemn historical mourning of Eliot with D. H. Lawrence's gleeful malice, making a style that is unmistakably Auden's own, but is also remarkably unstable and elusive. Auden denies his readers a clear sense of just how they are being addressed. Is he threatening them or sharing a private joke? Are the lines in the metre of "Locksley Hall" a parody, a respectful imitation, or an unsettled mixture of both? The point is that the audience is not really being addressed at all. The unstable tone is one of the barriers Auden uses to isolate himself from his readers, or at least to keep his relation with them radically problematic. Another barrier was his impatient telegraphese, his elision of the subjects of verbs, as in:

> Can speak of trouble, pressure on men
> Born all the time, brought forward into light . . .

or

> Often the man, alone shut, shall consider
> The killings in old winters, death of friends.
> Sitting with stranger shall expect no good.

"I used to try and concentrate the poem so much that there wasn't a word that wasn't essential," he said in a letter, about ten years after writing these lines. He added that it was not the best method of reaching an audience: "This leads to becoming boring and constipated."

His first readers felt differently, and were quick to recognize the strangeness and power of his style. Like Byron, he became famous in his early twenties. Like Byron, he became famous for a style he later renounced. The elusiveness of his first poems brought consequences he never intended, effects that eventually helped persuade him to revise his modernist projects. Where the poems presented themselves as discrete parts of an unspecified whole, the poems' readers, then as to a large extent now, concluded that the poems really did imply the nature of that greater whole. The poems were taken as fragments of an activist allegory whose key, although hidden, really did exist. Auden's readers, while agreeing on this view, divided into two hostile camps: those who complained that the key was a private myth or private joke reserved for a coterie of cronies and insiders,* and those who felt *they* were the insid-

---

* But the coterie "Auden Group" so familiar to literary history was far less cohesive than its reputation suggests, and had little to do with the style and argument of Auden's poems. At Oxford, like many young writers before and since, Auden made plans to conquer the literary world with the help of chosen allies: Stephen Spender, Christopher Isherwood, Cecil Day-Lewis, Edward Upward, and others. These never met as a group. Auden "was not so much a leader," Spender recalled in *The Thirties and After*, "as a doctor and teacher among his patients, each of whom he treated as a distinct case, and separately." In the early 1930s, when reviewers and anthologists began writing of an Auden group, Auden had long since left Oxford

ers, by virtue of membership in Auden's generation, and proceeded to fill the gaps in his broken pattern with their own political and psychological enthusiasms. Stephen Spender implied in a 1932 essay that Auden saw the coming revolution as a cure for neurosis and fear—a fantasy for which Auden rebuked him. The poet Charles Madge wrote in 1933, when he was twenty-one, that Auden had saved him from the "absolute aloofness of my brain":

> But there waited for me in the summer morning,
> Auden, fiercely. I read, shuddered and knew
> And all the world's stationary things
> In silence moved to take up new positions . . .
> My states of mind were broken. It was untrue
> The easy doctrine which separated things.

Madge had it backward. Auden implied connections and relations only to announce their absence or failure. Readers hailed or denounced him as a spokesman; he never wrote as one. There were one or two moments in the 1930s when he hoped he might learn to speak on behalf of inarticulate masses, but he saw the vanity of this wish, and its half-heartedness, as soon as he tried to achieve it. When he did write with conviction of civil relations and responsibilities, in the 1940s and after, readers protested that he was distorting or betraying causes that, in fact, he had not hoped to serve. In recent years critics have often prefaced their discussion of Auden's earliest work with a faintly puzzled comment that we can no longer feel the revolutionary excitement it generated in the 1930s, but these critics have been misled by the poems' early reception. The thrill of their contemporary imagery has faded, but the poems still

---

and lost interest in the idea. He joined some of his friends' names together only once, and elegiacally, in the first Ode of *The Orators,* where a voice commands: "Wystan, Stephen, Christopher, all of you, / Read of your losses." Later he worked on separate collaborations with Isherwood and Louis MacNeice (with whom he became friendly after leaving Oxford), and he and Spender contracted to write a travel book on America which never got written because other projects got in the way of the lecture tour on which they planned to gather material. None of these books was a group manifesto or a group project. Two anthologies edited by Michael Roberts, *New Signatures* (1932) and *New Country* (1933), trumpeted the group as a new revolutionary cadre, but Auden never took Roberts' inflammatory introductions seriously. It took a BBC broadcast of a large group of modern poets to get most of Auden's literary friends into the same room at the same time, and this did not take place until 1938.

speak as urgently as they ever did of their own conditions. What we can no longer feel is the excitement produced by the first misreadings.

To say this is not to blame Auden's original audience. He scarcely made matters easy for them. His work first reached the eye of a small but influential readership when the dauntingly obscure charade *Paid on Both Sides* appeared in Eliot's quarterly *The Criterion* in January 1930. Later that year the charade and thirty short poems, none of them illuminated by a title or epigraph, appeared in a small blue-wrapped volume of *Poems* published by Faber & Faber. It is still striking to see how anonymous the poems seem, how difficult they make any speculation on the character of the poet behind them, how easy they make it to project on them meanings that might be in the air. Auden had learned the virtues of an anonymous style from Eliot, but Eliot had at least identified his special social milieus and had implicitly defined his sensibility through the personal events his consciousness chose to record. Auden refused to do even that. His poems displayed only intermittent and fragmentary correspondences with the young man visible to his friends—that improbable figure, autocrat of what he called "the dreadful literary conversations when I always talk such pompous nonsense," half genius, half poseur, who made imperial pronouncements on the cure of neurosis at one moment, at another donned a false beard and extravagant hat. In his personal life these were animated masks hiding a silent isolation. In his poems he had no need for a dramatic mask; he was invisible without one.

In an essay on "Writing" which he prepared for a children's encyclopedia early in 1932 Auden made clear not only that his sole subject at the time was dissociation from a longed-for unity, but also that he regarded *Sehnsucht* and division as the ultimate subject of all written language. Critics have ignored this remarkable essay, perhaps on the assumption that anything written for a volume entitled *An Outline for Boys and Girls and Their Parents* must be too trivial to bother with. Yet Auden used this unpromising setting to publish a manifesto of his private ideology. He wrote it in the simple sentences and homely style appropriate to its family audience, but his argument subverted every comfortable and familiar idea of language as a means of imitating or communicating. And he preceded the essay with a characteristic gesture of near-anonymity.

The editor of the book, the writer Naomi Mitchison, introduced all the other essays with long breathless accounts of the personality and accomplishments of the authors. Auden allowed her to write only this about him: "Wystan Auden (born 1907) writes poetry and teaches at a school in Scotland."

The essay itself begins by attributing the invention of language to an effort "to bridge over [a] gulf." "Life," Auden writes, "is one whole thing made up of smaller whole things. . . . So too for us, nucleus and cell, cell and organ, organ and the human individual, individual and family, nation and world, always groups linked up with larger groups. . . . The whole cannot exist without the part, nor the part without the whole; and each whole is more than just the sum of its parts." Although this is so, we are still burdened by the problem of real wholes. Failing to recognize our unity with larger wholes, we make them inaccessible to our minds.

Auden traces our false sense of isolation to the emergence of self-consciousness, an event comparable to the birth that makes the child "other": "At some time or other in human history, when and how we don't know, man became self-conscious; he began to feel, I am I, and you are not I; we are shut inside ourselves and apart from each other." There was a time in human history when this feeling did not exist, a time that man could still remember after the Fall. Auden elsewhere rejects this arcadian fantasy as the projection of a nostalgic wish. Here he portrays it in visionary detail:

> The more this feeling [of separation] grew, the more man felt the need to bridge over the gulf, to recover the sense of being as much part of life as the cells in his body are part of him. Before he had lost it, when he was still doing things together in a group, such as hunting, when feeling was strongest, as when, say, the quarry was first sighted, the group had made noises, grunts, howls, grimaces. Noise and this feeling he had now lost had gone together; then, if he made the noise, could he not recover the feeling? In some way like this language began
> . . .

Language originates in efforts to bridge a gulf, to cross a barrier, to restore wholeness. But language invariably participates in the disjunction it tries to overcome. Auden writes that language begins not in imitation or onomatopoeia, but in an attempt to recover a feeling of social unity. An animal's name imitates the noise made by a group of hunters who pursued it, not the sound of the animal itself. "In fact, most of the power of words comes from their *not* being like what they stand for." But the division of word from object runs even deeper than this. Auden's argument, by using the original group of hunters as its example, implies that language is not merely unlike the things it names, or separated by a gulf from the hearers it addresses, but violently antagonistic to both object and hearer. An animal receives its name from hunters who want to kill it:

> Before language we have the people who feel something (the hunting group), the feeling (feeling of unity in the face of hunger or danger, etc.), the object which excites the feeling (the hunted bison), and the noise which expressed the feeling. If the noise was later used to recover the feeling, it would also present to the memory the idea or the image of the animal ... Thus sounds would begin to have sense meaning, to stand for things ...

So if the hunt and the victim provided the group with its feeling of unity, and if language tries to recover the hunters' feelings, then every sentence spoken, in its recollection of the violent ritual that constituted the lost original group, makes a sacrificial victim of both its referent and its audience, and all speech is sublimated violence.

The unbridged gulf, the lost wholeness, the threat of violence: these three elements form an inseparable cluster in Auden's early poems. The distant airman and the lonely spy dwell in the same landscape of division that is scarred by the border. As the group of hunters meets the quarry with weapons ready, so, across the border dividing poem and reader, Auden hurls his ominous warnings, ranging in tone from the nursery bogey to the apocalyptic vision: "They're looking for you," "The game is up for you and for the others," "Do not imagine you can abdicate; / Before you reach the frontier you are caught," "Among the foes which we enumer / You are included," "It is time for the destruction of error." Some entire poems—"Get there if you can," "Brothers, who when the sirens roar"—amount to group exhortations and threats to outsiders, all in a rhetoric of violence and exclusion.

The band of hunters provides Auden with an origin for spoken language, but he proposes a different origin for written language. "Writing and speech are like two tributary streams, rising at different sources, flowing apart for a time until they unite to form a large river." Spoken language "begins with the feeling of separateness in space," but written language "begins from the sense of separateness in time, of 'I'm here to-day, but I shall be dead to-morrow, and you will be active in my place, and how can I speak to you?' " Where speech attempts to recover a unity among the living (and succeeds to some extent, for example at mass rallies), writing attempts an impossible union of the living and the dead. In the three years between writing his journal entry on the new noncommunicative poetry and writing this essay, Auden has turned away from praise for mental isolation to a wish to overcome it, but he remains as isolated as before. At the end of his essay he admits the defeat of writing's efforts to restore wholeness:

> Since the underlying reason for writing is to bridge the gulf between one person and another, as the sense of loneliness increases, more and more books are written by more and more people. . . . Forests are cut down, rivers of ink absorbed, but the lust to write is still unsatisfied. What is going to happen? If it were only a question of writing, it wouldn't matter; but it is an index of our health. It's not only books, but our lives, that are going to pot.

As he expressed it in a song: "It's no use raising a shout."

A few lines earlier Auden had written of literature suffering when "society breaks up into classes, sects, townspeople and peasants, rich and poor. . . . There is writing for the gentle and writing for the simple, for the highbrow and lowbrow." Auden's complaint is political only in the broadest sense of the word, not specifically partisan. Although the book in which the essay appeared was compiled from a left-wing perspective, Auden himself had no political program for resolving town and country, highbrow and lowbrow. Where the rest of the book advocates a practical communism, Auden's essay implies the fraternal visionary communism he was imagining in some of his other writings at the time. In late 1932 and early 1933, when he almost accepted the argument that communism was the one choice remaining for a wrecked society, he suggested that he came to this view more for psychological than for political reasons. In a review published in *The New Statesman* on 15 October 1932, a month after "Writing" appeared, he wrote that communism's "increasing attraction for the bourgeois"—he could not, he said, speak for the proletariat—"lies in its demand for self-surrender for

those individuals who, isolated, feel themselves emotionally at sea." In
the same way, intellectual curiosity is "neurotic, a compensation for
those isolated from a social group, sexually starved, or physically weak."
Intellectually curious, interested in communism, Auden condemns his
state of mind as a neurotic construct and disbelieves what he believes.
His one solid ground of self-knowledge is his class. "No. I am a bourgeois," he told a friend who wrote him about this review; "I shall not
join the C.P."

The Auden of later years—the avuncular, domestic, conservative,
Horatian, High Anglican poet of civilization, who sees language not as a
sublimation of violence but as a safeguard against it, and whose
"sounded note is the restored relation"—would seem to show few traces
of the anarchic stringencies of his younger self. Yet although Auden
transformed or inverted his early theories, civilized them with public
contexts, and made them responsible to a moral order, he never entirely
gave them up. The ethically sober late Auden retains the form and outline of the amorally fervid early one. A poem he wrote when he was
sixty-two, "The Garrison," brings together all the main elements of his
early work—guarded barriers and armed bands, assertions of group
unity across gulfs of space and time—for a final reunion. Its Horatian
stanzas give the form of Roman law to the old barbaric violence. I have
italicized its recollections of earlier themes:

> Martini-time: time to *draw the curtains* and
> choose a composer *we should like to hear from*,
> before coming to table for one of your
>   savory *messes*.

> Time crumbs all *ramparts*, brachypod *Nemesis*
> *catches up sooner or later* with hare-swift
> Achilles, but personal song and language
>   somehow mizzle them.

> Thanks to which it's possible for *the breathing*
> *still to break bread with the dead, whose brotherhood*
> *gives us confidence* to wend the trivial
>   *thrust of the Present,*

so self-righteous in its assumptions and so
certain that *none dare out-face it.* We, Chester,
and *the choir we sort with have been assigned to
garrison stations.*

*Whoever rules, our duty to the City
is loyal opposition, never greening
for the big money, never neighing after
a public image.*

Let us leave rebellions to the choleric
who enjoy them: to serve as *a paradigm
now of what a plausible Future might be*
is what we're here for.

"Our duty to the City / is loyal opposition"—this is a more polite, less insistently revolutionary way of saying what Auden said repeatedly in 1932: "The failure of modern education [he was a schoolmaster at the time, writing in loyal opposition] lies . . . in the fact that no one genuinely believes in our society," or, from another essay, "You cannot train children to be good citizens of a state which you despise." In Auden's later writings the young anarchist neither retreats nor recants, but he has learned the necessary cost of his independence and is willing to pay it.

The great social theme of Auden's later work is the mutual implication of violence and civil order, the penalty in human life that every peaceful well-lit city must pay to survive. As he wrote in the 1950s: "without a cement of blood (it must be human, it must be innocent) no secular wall will safely stand." This is hardly a new discovery in Western literature—it is the burden of the *Aeneid* and of Shakespeare's histories—but in English poetry since the eighteenth century it has been virtually forgotten. Both romantics and modernists focused their attention on one side or the other of this double recognition: either regarding all societies as irredeemably brutal and imagining instead a realm of universal harmony; or celebrating, with Yeats, Lawrence, and Pound, the grand isolated violence of a lofty hero. The first of these alternatives denies the real hatred in the human will, the second denies the unique humanity of its victims. Auden was able to reject both these partial visions because he reached their extreme forms early enough in his own work to sense their limits and inadequacies.

The intensely isolated and reflexive character of Auden's earliest poems has been obscured by the more public character of his later work.* It was obscured also because the critical climate was not yet receptive to it. In the atmosphere that later developed around existentialism and around structural theories of language and culture—the atmosphere propitious for the later Beckett—Auden's earliest work would have seemed comfortably at home. Late in life Auden was fascinated with the concept of prematurity in scientific and philosophical thought, the prematurity of ideas, like Vico's, that emerged before there was an audience, whether conventional or avant-garde, that was capable of absorbing them. Auden's essay on "Writing," and his manifestoes on communal theatre a few years later, are notable examples of prematurity. In them he established positions that would be occupied by an avant-garde thirty years afterward, by which time Auden himself had taken up an entirely different position. In "Writing" he offers a premature exposition of the central themes of structuralist literary theory and its successors, using a schoolroom style at the furthest possible extreme from the theoreticians' opacity. His account of language's origin in a sense of absence, and of its constant ineffectual efforts to bridge over a gap; his distinction between the sources of writing and of speech; his reflexive and interiorized concept of language's effects; his insistence on the antagonism and difference between language and its objects—all these are aspects of a late romantic theory of language, brought to a crisis by modernism, and agonized over by the young Auden a generation before Derrida and Lacan.

Like the later critical theorists who confuse the local conventions of modernism with universal truth, Auden in his early poems treats the separation of language from the world as the ultimate subject to which all writing refers. In his later poems he treats the gulf between language and world in a very different way—as a condition that must be accepted but that does not prevent language from being shared, or prevent it from illuminating and affecting a physical and ethical world whose order and events are not only verbal ones. In other words, Auden moves from a world *without* choice to a world *with* choice: from a world of limits

* It was not, however, obscured by his later revisions and rejections. When he put together his collected volumes he did his most extensive rewriting in poems that dated from around 1931–42, when he was in transition away from modernism; most of the poems he discarded were from the same period. He left the poems of 1927–30 relatively untouched.

where differences are absolute and the proper literary mode is the tragedy of helplessness and isolation, to a world of possibility where differences are overcome by mutual forgiveness and responsibility and the proper literary mode is the comedy of reconciliation. Auden's early poems are for intense love affairs that end quickly; the later poems are for marriage.

Auden's early work may be seen as the culmination of the romantic heritage in English poetry, in the same way that recent theories of poetic language are the culmination of romantic literary theory. Attempts to continue in the same course, efforts to extend the modernist revolution either in poetry or in criticism, lead to arid parodies of what came before. In each instance the next step cannot be one that moves *beyond* the last—as the idiom of progress would suggest—but one that moves in a different direction. Late romanticism, in the earliest Auden, focuses on the frontier of perception between the self and a dead inaccessible world outside—a world of discrete objects that may be put to use only by the poetic imagination. In the later Auden there is no need for a romantic imagination, because there are no objects. Instead there are *creatures*, created beings with rights of their own, and Auden is concerned more with their peculiarities and relations than with any difficulty he might have in perceiving them.

The next six chapters trace Auden's border divisions as they arise in his work and gradually change character from 1927 to 1933. One last general point should be made here. During these early years the idea of the border slowly generated its antithesis: the idea of an undifferentiated unity either beyond the border or enclosed within it. At first this was nothing more than a nostalgic dream, lost in an imaginary past. Then, in 1931, Auden reached the point where he could imagine a tangible form that unity might actually take in the present. This was the *group*. He first used the word in the "Journal of an Airman" in *The Orators*, where the group is an as yet unsolved problem, a special case of the general problem of real wholes. The Airman writes: "Much more research needed into the crucial problem—group organisation (the real parts)." Soon afterward, in a letter to Christopher Isherwood on 9 October 1931, Auden suggested that a solution had been found, a new order foretold: "I've had a most important vision about groups which is going to destroy the church." At about the same time, in an ode printed in *The Orators,* he saw the gauche and lonely finding satisfaction in "the smaller group, the right field of force."

He gave no details. But a few months later, in "Writing," he described the rise of language from the dissolution of the primal group, and then, in a letter of 28 July 1932 to the poet John Pudney, he explained why the group must now gather again:

> Re groups and sex, the two complement each other like day and night. I think there are two great desires which we are always confusing, the desire to be one of a group, building the dam or facing the tiger [illustrations that involve both a barrier and a violent confrontation, central features of Auden's imaginative world]. This is largely unconscious, impersonal and asexual though it demands physical contact. And sex, the personal conscious desire to come into a particular woman and have a child by her. If you can't get one you intensify the other. We're all sex-obsessed to-day because there isn't any decent group-life left hardly; we try to get its kick out of sex, which is one reason why we are so promiscuous. Buggery is an attempt at a magical short cut: we choose those with whom we should naturally have an unconscious group relationship and try to get that by the personal conscious contact.
>
> The problem is particularly bad in a city like London [Auden is writing from a cottage in the Lake District], which is so large, that the only group you can find, is living with your own kind, those mentally like you. This is disastrous. You end up by eating each other. The whole value of a group is that its constituents are as diverse as possible, with little consciously in common, Plurality in unity.
>
> There are some, poets are generally such, who will always be a little outside the group, critical[,] but they need the group to feel a little out of just as much as they need it to be at home in. They get more from it than they know. Without it, they have no material, must split their emotions into ever finer and finer hairs.

In its romantic assumption that the poet will be isolated even in the midst of unity, and in its sexual self-analysis, this letter has wide implications for Auden's early work. As in his poems, he is burdened by the problem of real wholes. Imagining a group, he cannot quite define one, and he offers no real example of a group that poets "can feel a little out of." What group can he be thinking of whose "constituents are as diverse as possible, with little consciously in common"? Men who build dams and face tigers probably think as much alike as do the members of those groups whom Auden deplores in cities like London. How is the group-life to be built? What is its model? Auden will find an answer to these questions later, but it will not be an answer he could have imagined when he wrote that his vision would destroy the church.

In the same month he wrote his letter to Pudney, Auden wrote a birthday poem for a friend, wishing among other things that his new year might "Create the group where for his hour / Loved and loving he may flower." This is a vague hope, little more. The closest Auden comes in his published or unpublished work to naming a benign group is a stanza (later dropped) from the 1932 poem "Now from my window-sill I watch the night." The scene is the school in Scotland where Auden was teaching:

> Permit our town here to continue small,
> What city's vast emotional cartel
> Could our few acres satisfy
> Or rival in intensity
> The field of five or six, the English cell?

But Auden was scarcely proposing this idyllic vision of schoolboy groups as a model for adult group-life—not, at least, after he moved from vision to practicalities. "Everyone knows," he wrote in a 1934 essay on his own public school, "that the only emotion that is fully developed in a boy of fourteen is the emotion of loyalty and honour. For that very reason it is so dangerous." He added: "The best reason I have for opposing Fascism is that at school I lived in a Fascist state." An adult society needs other emotions than loyalty, and needs a critical intellect as well.

The only adult groups Auden names are those organized by Nazis and Communists, and by the Oxford Group Movement. He wrote in another 1934 essay, on the Oxford Group, that all

> these movements use the same technique, the formation of a cell or small group, periodically visited by missionary officials, and the periodic gathering of cells for sudden public demonstration. . . .
>
> Its appearance and success in different and even contradictory movements suggests that the psychological importance of the small

group is beginning to be realized. Only in a group of very moderate size, probably not larger than twelve, is it possible for the individual under normal circumstances to lose himself, for his death instincts to be neutralized in the same way as those of the separate cells of the metazoa neutralize each other in the body.

He ends by noting the fascist tendencies of those groups whose members come from the middle classes and speaks of the need to find programs for the groups, larger purposes in which the smaller groups can lose themselves. Yet he also acknowledges that nothing has so far been discovered that can accomplish this—except hatred.

And so Auden arrives back at the violent antagonistic hunters in his vision of the original group. He longs for the release and self-forgetfulness a group can provide, but he must reject all existing opportunities for that release while hoping for something better in the future. He showed no inclination to join the austere sodality of the Communist Party. He felt nothing but contempt for the pious hothouse of the Oxford Group—whose members, in the last stanza of Auden's 1937 ballad, dissect Miss Gee's knee, earnestly seeking the inner life where they are unlikely to find it. In his letter to Pudney, Auden acknowledged his inevitable distance from the unity he desired: "poets . . . will always be a little outside the group, critical." He knew even then that he could not live by his promising theory. Later, in the sequence of *Horae Canonicae* he wrote in the 1950s, he would recognize that individuals lose themselves, not in a small nurturing group, but in a larger and more dangerous crowd.

The young Auden was intellectually promiscuous, embracing a new idea with brief intensity before moving restlessly to the next. He took much of what he said about the group from the visionary history proposed in the early 1930s by his friend Gerald Heard, who worked as a scientific journalist. Heard was constantly predicting an end to rationalism and a mystical revolution of the spirit. His 1931 book *Social Substance of Religion* provided Auden with a cluster of phrases and implications that he applied in his own way. Auden's paragraph on the psychological importance of the small group, for example, adapts a passage from Heard, but to a very different effect.* He seized on Heard's

---

* Heard wrote: "In the like-minded group, numbering about a dozen, the individual can experience complete release. His whole nature is not only purged: it is evolved

prophecies, as he seized on the ideas of others whom he cast as healers, in order to learn their real consequences. He never quite believed Heard's cures would work. Heard concluded his book in rapturous praise of the group as the "essential first step" toward "the salvation of civilisation": the "force of super-individual ecstasy" will bring about a reign of universal compassion and love. But Auden saw in the Oxford Groups, and in Fascist and Communist cells, the same sense of group unity being put to practical use by leaders who had little interest in universal compassion.

However strongly Auden felt his vision of groups in 1931, he was unable to translate it into a way of life. He was blocked privately, by his inability to experience the unity he supposed a group could offer, and publicly, because existing groups did not avoid hatred and exclusion. With no example before him of a group that might fulfill his wishes and his program, he could imagine the positive group only in negative terms: it would be that which could dissolve his isolation. He seems to have set the size of "the English cell," the group of five or six, in negative terms also. This was the only order of magnitude left between the larger social units to which he could as yet feel no responsibility and the smaller unit of the sexual pair in which he could as yet find no satisfaction. The group is an imaginary projection into the future of a unity lost in an imaginary past. Neither the past nor the future unity is authentic; there are no data by which either could be understood or described. Wholeness, Auden wrote, is beyond language, yet language is the inevitably futile means by which we try to recover it. In his earliest poems his language tries to cross an emptiness to a unity that cannot be found. The poems report from a condition of absence, speak to no one, and have no place to go.

---

to higher capacity and higher manifestation" (p. 307). At about the same time Heard was writing these woozy sentences, Auden was already attacking the notion of "higher" and lower modes of being; and Auden's vision of groups rejects Heard's "like-minded" idea for a different-minded one.

II

The Watershed

Auden described his transition from childhood to adulthood as the discovery of his poetic voice. "At nineteen," he recalled late in life, "I was self-critical enough to know that the poems I was writing were still merely derivative, that I had not yet found my own voice, and I felt certain that in Oxford I should never find it, that as long as I remained there, I should remain a child." He found his voice, in fact, during the summer holiday between his second and last years at Oxford, in 1927, when he was twenty, five years after he first discovered his vocation as a poet.

Until he was fifteen he had never written a line of verse. His fascination with mines and their machinery had begun to fade when he was thirteen. "Crazes had come and gone"—as he wrote in *Letter to Lord Byron*—"in short, sharp gales, / For motor-bikes, photography, and whales." Then, in March 1922, a school friend, trying to fill an awkward silence on a country walk, asked if he wrote poetry. The conviction that he should do so took hold immediately. Wordsworth provided the model for his earliest surviving verses, along with, as he recalled in an essay, "de la Mare, W. H. Davies, and even AE." All his poems in these poets' styles were trifles of adolescent nostalgia that show no signs of his adult manner, beyond their skillful metrics and their partiality to gloomy landscapes. In the summer of 1923 he discovered Thomas Hardy, and "for more than a year I read no one else." Edward Thomas shared Hardy's place after the autumn of 1924. About a year later Auden entered the university with a scholarship in natural science, but by the end of his first year he had switched to English. At around the same time, the eighteen-month reign of Hardy and Thomas—with Housman, Frost, and Emily Dickinson as their retinue—came to an end when "finally they were both defeated by Eliot at the battle of Oxford in 1926."

This battle, for a new poetry to supplant the old, was one of many skirmishes in Auden's adolescent war against his family and his class. Like most such revolts it was selective: there were parental traits he was convinced must be decisively renounced, others decisively retained. One source of friction between Auden and his parents was his loss of religious faith when he was fifteen, followed a year or two later by his parents' gradual recognition of his homosexuality. By the time he went up to Oxford in 1925 he had made plain his rejection of the family ethic of public service. Politicians, he told his friends, were lackeys who ought to be ignored. The poet's task was "the formation of private spheres out of a public chaos." A few years later, in *Letter to Lord Byron*, he recalled his undergraduate aesthetic: "through the quads dogmatic words rang clear, / 'Good poetry is classic and austere.' " Yet the severe classical tone of his pronouncements in his second and third years at Oxford, like the whole classical or T. E. Hulme phase of modernism, conceals an aestheticism not unlike that of the 1890s. A poet, Auden announced, should hold no opinions. He should use the subject of his poems merely as a peg on which to hang the verbal patterns. Oscar Wilde said much the same thing in "The Decay of Lying," which Auden had not read.* Wilde, like Auden, was the son of a doctor father and formidable mother, and his aesthetic was partly intended *pour épater les parents*. When Auden wrote about Wilde in later years he scorned his empty frivolity as if denouncing a temptation he himself had confronted and refused.

Auden first read Eliot in the spring of 1926, when he had just turned nineteen. Tom Driberg, an Oxford contemporary, showed him *The Waste Land* and, as Driberg recalled, the two read it together, "read it, at first, with incredulous hilarity (the Mrs. Porter bit, for instance); read it, again and again, with growing awe." Eliot served as a great liberator. Poetry, Auden learned, could be comic and grotesque; the extravagance of his personality was, for the first time, free to disport in his

---

* Wilde's dialogue also included a more sparkling version of Auden's evolutionary argument that mind is rapidly diverging from matter.

verse. Using Eliot's exotic vocabulary as his model, Auden brought into
his poems the science and psychology he learned in his father's library,
while discarding the traditional poetic diction and poetic subjects favored by his mother. Within two or three months, by the early summer
of 1926, the transformation of his style was complete. For about a year
he wrote almost exclusively in Eliot's driest and most satiric manner,
constantly alert to the contemporary and grotesque. Lines like these
might have strayed from Eliot's "Poems 1920"—

> In Spring we waited. Princes felt
>   Through darkness for unwoken queens;
> The itching lover weighed himself
>   At stations on august machines

—while these read like a postcard from the waste land:

> Under such pines
> I gave a penny for his thoughts. He sent
> A photograph signed, but spiders crawled across it
> Obscuring the face.

Edwin Arlington Robinson—Auden approved of his dour severity—
tempered the Eliotean extravagance somewhat. But the most fashionable
poet in the eyes of clever undergraduates in the 1920s, Edith Sitwell, left
no mark on him at all.

Most of the poems Auden wrote during his first years at Oxford describe variations on a single theme: life is a constant state of isolation and
stagnated desire—interrupted by moments of sexual satisfaction or disappointment—which the young poet unprotestingly accepts. Such is
the burden of a poem he wrote probably when he was eighteen, in 1925,
in the voice of Edward Thomas: "This peace can last no longer than the
storm / Which started it." As surely as this will pass, so "Shall I know
the meaning of lust again." Because nothing "Can change me from the
thing I was before,"* a moment of calm must suffice, a moment when
the romantic isolation from nature and those who work in nature is broken:

* Auden revised this line two or three years later to read: "Can change whatever I
might be before"—and the new syntax deftly folds past and future into a contin-
uously uncertain present.

> for this brief hour or so
> I am content, unthinking and aglow,
> Made one with horses and with workmen ...

In 1928, when Auden was twenty-one and had rejected the coherent pastoral metaphors of Hardy and Thomas for the fragmented symbolic portents of Eliot, he was still recollecting in tranquillity the same calm after the sexual storm:

> Taller to-day, we remember similar evenings,
> Walking together in the windless orchard ...
>
> Again in the room with the sofa hiding the grate,
> Look down to the river when the rain is over ...

Outside is failure and isolation: "excellent hands have turned to commonness. / One staring too long, went blind in a tower"; and we hear "our last / Of Captain Ferguson." Indoors we have peace, but the same isolation—"happy now, though no nearer each other."

The pain of sexual failure has as little effect as the transient peace of success. In a 1926 poem titled "The Letter" (it begins: "He reads and finds the meaning plain") a message in "satiric style" closes an affair. For a moment the world seems to crumble. But nature persists in her cycles, indifferent to individual pain:

> At first he looks around and hears
> Huge castles toppling to the ground
> As if the earth ceased spinning round,
> The sudden panic of the years;
> But trees and singing birds renew
> The stablished sequence of the laws;
> Creation shows no vital flaws
> For God to pay attention to.

Two years later, in a poem to which Auden eventually also gave the title "The Letter" (he discarded the earlier poem), the same pattern recurs. He can scarcely begin a new love affair before the inevitable rejection:

> Your letter comes, speaking as you,
> Speaking of much but not to come.

And once again he finds himself carried along by the repetitive cycles of nature:

> I, decent with the seasons, move
> Different or with a different love.

After any final kiss, as in a 1927 poem, "Consider if you will how lovers stand," he returns to time's dismal constancy. There is one "last look back / . . . To dazzling cities of the plain where lust / Threatened a sinister rod"—and then

>   we shall turn
> To our study of stones . . .
> Unanswerable like any other pedant,
> Like Solomon and Sheba, wrong for years.

As Auden wrote these poems of an unchanging and unchangeable world, a new element entered. In the summer of 1927 he introduced a frontier into his landscape. Unlike the moments of failure or satisfaction in his earlier poems—mere interruptions that do not alter or delimit the prevailing futility—the frontier marks a real and absolute limit, a watershed or divide isolating the mind from the cycles of unconscious nature.

Although it quickly displaced these cycles as Auden's central theme, the frontier first appeared in the background, as part of the incidental scenery of their recurring drama. In 1927, after his second year at Oxford, Auden took a holiday journey across Europe to Yugoslavia. In Zagreb, in July, he opened a sonnet in the tones of Edward Thomas:

> On the frontier at dawn getting down [from a train]
> Hot eyes were soothed with swallows . . .

Here nature still comforts. And although the poem shifts to the voice of Eliot from that of Thomas, it continues to trace the cycles of seasons and sexuality: "ploughs began," "In the dog days," "He in love . . . stiffens to a tower." No crucial change happens: "the hour deferred, / Peculiar idols nodded." Finally, the cycle begun by the dawn in the first line is completed at dusk:

A horse neighed in the half-light, and a bird
Cried loudly over and over again
Upon the natural ending of a day.

The frontier casually introduced in the poem's opening phrase seems entirely forgotten.

A month later, back in England, it was as if Auden remembered nothing else. In August he wrote a poem concerned only with borders, separations, finality, cruxes, a poem where even nature makes decisions, chooses between possibilities. Auden later entitled this poem "The Watershed," and it marks the divide between his juvenilia and the work of his maturity. His derivative early manners would persist in some of his poems for a few months more, but this was the moment when he found his own voice. In his first published volume, the 1930 *Poems*, he included two poems written before this moment, but he omitted them from the second edition published in 1933. From then on he never reprinted any poem he had written earlier than "The Watershed."*

Here is the first section of the poem:

Who stands, the crux left of the watershed,
On the wet road between the chafing grass
Below him sees dismantled washing-floors,

* Some details of publication history: In June 1927, before leaving on his European trip, and at the urging of Sacheverell Sitwell, Auden sent some poems to T. S. Eliot, who was then reading manuscripts for the firm of Faber & Gwyer (it became Faber & Faber in 1929). After some delay, on 9 September, Eliot sent a minimally encouraging rejection letter: "I do not feel that any of the enclosed is quite right, but I should be interested to follow your work." By this time Auden had written "The Watershed" and had begun to write in his own voice. A year later, in the summer of 1928, Stephen Spender produced on a hand-press, in an edition of some thirty copies, a small pamphlet volume of *Poems* chosen by Auden from his work dating back as far as 1924, but mostly from 1927–28. Possibly in 1929 Auden submitted a manuscript volume of poems to Victor Gollancz, who turned it down. In the spring of 1930 he then submitted a manuscript—possibly the same one rejected by Gollancz—to Eliot. It seems to have included only poems written after those Eliot had rejected in 1927. Faber & Faber accepted this manuscript around May 1930, and Auden then made some final substitutions. Eliot was apparently reluctant to include *Paid on Both Sides* in the book, although he had recently printed it in *The Criterion*, but it was added in proof, and *Poems* appeared in October. "On the frontier at dawn getting down" appeared only in Spender's 1928 pamphlet, but Auden reused its opening line four years later in *The Orators*.

Snatches of tramline running to the wood,
An industry already comatose,
Yet sparsely living. A ramshackle engine
At Cashwell raises water; for ten years
It lay in flooded workings until this,
Its latter office, grudgingly performed,
And further here and there, though many dead
Lie under the poor soil, some acts are chosen
Taken from recent winters; two there were
Cleaned out a damaged shaft by hand, clutching
The winch the gale would tear them from; one died
During a storm, the fells impassable,
Not at his village, but in wooden shape
Through long abandoned levels nosed his way
And in his final valley went to ground.

In these blank verse lines Auden seems to revert, in style and setting, to the poems he wrote before the "battle of Oxford." The landscape is the declining northern mine country of his schoolboy poetry,* and the verse has awkward cadences and flat descriptive patches that he would not have tolerated a few months before. But he has taken one step back in order to take two forward. He frees himself from the manner of Eliot by reclaiming from Hardy what he later called Hardy's "hawk's vision, his way of looking at life from a very great height." Added to Auden's familiar landscape, and—as the second part of "The Watershed" shows—barred from entering it, is a new figure, distant, obscure, observant. When one first reads the poem's opening line everything about this observer seems forbiddingly ambiguous. Who and where is he? Is *Who stands* interrogative or declarative? What is the missing grammatical link between that phrase and the next? Is *the crux* a crossroads or a dilemma? Does *left of* mean "remaining" or "to the left side"? And is *the watershed* a divide on high ground where waters separate, or a basin on

---

* He had in fact written a poem at school about "The Pumping Engine, Cashwell," although in a tone very different from the one he uses here. The last of its four stanzas reads:

As it groans at each stroke
Like a heart in trouble,
It seems to me something
In toil most noble.

low ground where waters gather? The word's double meaning may have
been one of Auden's reasons for choosing it. By the end of the poem all
these questions are resolved—and the crux proves to be both a crossroads and, by implication, a dilemma—but the opening refuses to give
up its meaning, and the observer of the scene is not identified at all until
the second part. Even there he is identified by negation, as a *stranger*,
alien to the scene. His estranged condition, not the landscape of mines,
is the true Auden country:

> Go home, now, stranger, proud of your young stock,
> Stranger, turn back again, frustrate and vexed:
> This land, cut off, will not communicate,
> Be no accessory content to one
> Aimless for faces rather there than here.
> Beams from your car may cross a bedroom wall,
> They wake no sleeper; you may hear the wind
> Arriving driven from the ignorant sea
> To hurt itself on pane, on bark of elm
> Where sap unbaffled rises, being Spring;
> But seldom this. Near you, taller than grass,
> Ears poise before decision, scenting danger.

Now the landscape this excluded visitor saw in the first part of the
poem was a place of barriers and separation. Because the fells—the hills
of northern England—were impassable, a miner died apart from his village and moved through abandoned geological levels, in his coffin's
wooden shape, to his final valley. In the comatose, grudging industry of
this landscape there is nothing picturesque, nothing sublime, nothing to
satisfy arcadian nostalgia. The poem attends to the place precisely because it is impenetrable, a place the miners cannot escape and the
stranger cannot enter. That stranger, "aimless," "frustrate and vexed"
by his inability to cohere with *any* surroundings, has travelled here only
to find he has got nowhere in particular. Visitor and landscape are mutually estranged. This land, cut off, will not communicate. It will be "no
accessory content" for a tourist's inventory of places seen. The stranger
has freedom and mobility but he can affect nothing: beams from his car
will wake no sleeper. He looks down from the superior height of his location and class, but he has no reason to be "rather there than here."
The natural world avoids him. The hare whose ears poise before deci-

sion knows he is dangerous. The only thing "unbaffled" in this divided world is the unconscious sap that rises inaccessibly in its abiding tree.

The spatial barrier between the land and the stranger is also a barrier in time. The land, "already comatose," is too aged, too marked by its "many dead," to join the stranger proud of his "young stock." The stranger can neither communicate with the past nor decide on a plausible future. He stands, a weak Hercules at a vague crossroads, at the crux left of the watershed; but, like the Hercules of Auden's Christmas Oratorio *For the Time Being* fifteen years later, he is "Utterly lost" and "cannot / Even locate his task."

For the Time Being was to find a solution to this Herculean uncertainty but "The Watershed" has none. It states the conditions Auden now faces; by the time he writes his next border poem, "Control of the passes" (later titled "The Secret Agent"), in January 1928, those conditions have grown even worse. This unrhymed sonnet is a masterpiece of dry foreboding. Its essential design is the same as that of the earlier poem, but the stranger has now become a spy, and the relatively mild warning to "Go home, now" has intensified into a sentence of death. The stranger had at least been mobile, and had a home, however unsatisfying, to return to; the secret agent is not only isolated but trapped. He hoped to find "easy power" by building a dam (this is one of the activities Auden assigns to the group in his letter to Pudney)—using a barrier to produce energy rather than restrict it—but he could do this only if his own people would first build the means of transport and communication. Instead they ignore him:

> At Greenhearth was a fine site for a dam
> And easy power, had they pushed the rail
> Some stations nearer. They ignored his wires.
> The bridges were unbuilt and trouble coming.

And the coming trouble is a more active and more ominous version of the listening "ears" in "The Watershed."

The secret agent, having "walked into the trap," cannot return home to the city that dissatisfied him. But now he feels nostalgia for what he left behind: "The street music seemed gracious now to one / For weeks up in the desert." The landscape leaves *him* behind: he is "Woken by water / Running away in the dark." As the poem ends he foresees the moment when his entrapment and separation will be complete: "They would shoot, of course, / Parting easily who were never joined."

This last line modernizes the last line of the Old English poem "Wulf and Eadwacer," the monologue of a captive woman separated from her lover. But Auden's poem need not be allegorized into a simple complaint about unconsummated love.* The division acknowledged at the end of the poem is present everywhere: death that parts lovers also parts mind and body, "who were never joined." It may be relevant that when Auden marked up friends' copies of his early books with dates and places of composition he often wrote in the initials of the subjects of his love poems, but with this poem he did nothing of the sort. The division it concerns is not only sexual: it is *any* separation from unity or satisfaction.

Auden made much the same point when he explained another poem, "The crowing of the cock." This dates from September 1927, a month after "The Watershed," and tells of those who see a landscape they would enter but cannot: "Blocked conduits in spate, / Delectable horizon." The last stanza describes their various futile courses:

> To breast the final hill,
> Thalassa on the tongue,
> Snap at the dragon's tail
> To find the yelp its own;
> Or sit, the doors being shut
> 'Twixt coffee and the fruit
> Touching, decline to hear
> Sounds of conclusive war.

Auden's friend Naomi Mitchison read this in *Poems* 1930 and not unreasonably complained of obscurity. "Am I really so obscure?" Auden replied. "Obscurity is a bad fault." He proceeded to explain the first two lines as "Our asymptotic movement towards emotional satisfaction," and the second two as "The result of repression. The divided self. Puritan right and wrong." If our movement towards satisfaction is asymptotic it can never reach its goal. Behind the final hill no thalassa offers a sea

* The Old English source and allegorical interpretation may be found in John Fuller's *A Reader's Guide to W. H. Auden* (1970). Like everyone else who writes about Auden I am deeply indebted to the scholarship and intelligence of this pioneering book.

change. Our movement is not a cure but a symptom of our disease, a sign of divisions too deep even for consummated love (the "touching" in the poem) to resolve. "When life fails," Auden asked in a song, "What's the good of going to Wales?"

The guarded border between Auden and any real satisfaction is too strong to be breached by sex. In Auden's earliest poems sex often serves less as a means of achieving union than as a way to evade the risks of any "real meeting" involving more than instinct. When couples go "pairing off in twos and twos," they know the proper physical act but they resolve nothing: "Each knowing what to do / But of no use." When they separate again, they are still of no use, for they will not risk a different way of life, and end their relations with a cyclical return, "Saying goodbye but coming back, for fear / Is over there." "Over there" is not a particular place, but the hidden internal source of division, "the centre of anger" that the couples make no effort to invade or change. It is safely "out of danger."

These gnomic lines are taken from "Again in conversations," a poem written early in 1929, in which sex is as empty as repetitious talk. Auden transforms this poem's declarative mood into a highly ironic imperative in a poem written a few months later, where his voice warns against the dangerous crossing from isolation to fulfillment. The poem opens on a border, "Upon this line between adventure." Best to remain here, it says, best to "Prolong the meeting out of good nature." Here good-natured sexual relations are safe; elsewhere wait the emotional dangers of commitment or abandonment:

> Forward or back are menaces.
>
> On neither side let foot slip over
> Invading Always, exploring Never,*
> For this is hate and this is fear . . .

Instead, "On narrowness stand," where there is "No anger, no traitor, but peace."

---

* Critics often maintain that Auden weakened his poetry in later years by introducing capitalized abstractions, a device he would not have used earlier. He wrote these examples when he was twenty-two.

"Peace" is less satisfactory than it may sound. Auden used the word in two related ways: when it actually occurs, peace is an evasion of real barriers and cannot endure; when it does not occur, peace is the longed-for state of real unity that can never be achieved. A real and stable peace is unattainable, for man's ordinary condition is one of anxiety and war. An unpublished 1930 poem opens with the line: "Renewal of traditional anger in peace." Real division, inherited from the traditional past, survives the diplomats' treaties. The act of love, in "Taller to-day," may interrupt anger with a moment of "peace / No bird can contradict," peace that although "passing . . . is sufficient now." But it is sufficient only "For something fulfilled this hour, loved or endured." The poem leaves open the question whether that hour was a real fulfillment or an interval when the otherwise harrowing fact of separation was peacefully tolerated. But there is an implied emphasis in Auden's choice of *endured* as the poem's final word.

The war that peace occasionally interrupts is a civil war between the broken fragments of a whole. Its forces are the mutually opposed efforts toward wholeness made by different halves of a divided city or divided self. This civil war, as Auden wrote to Isherwood in a verse letter in April 1929, is "our study and our interest."

> Although your medium is that other, Christopher,
> The most prodigious of literary forms,
> To both this is our study and our interest:
> The fortunes and manoeuvres of this civil war,
> Man's opposite strivings for entropic peace,
> Retreat to lost homes or advance to new* . . .

"Entropic peace," the peace of stasis or of dissolved distinctions, is to be found, man hopes, in "homes." Yet these homes belong either to the imaginary past or to a future yet to be achieved. The home or house (the word transcribed as "homes" is possibly "houses" in the manuscript) bears a special symbolic burden here: it is the place of an enclosed self-

* Auden reshaped this verse letter into part 1 of "It was Easter as I walked in the public gardens," first published in the 1930 *Poems.* Of the lines quoted here only the last two appeared in print, and only in the first edition of the book; they were dropped in the 1933 edition. Auden's reference to the novel as the most prodigious of literary forms is taken from Henry James's preface to *The Ambassadors,* an allusion Auden repeats in *Letter to Lord Byron* in 1936.

protective peace that is ultimately too fragile to survive. The civil war of *Paid on Both Sides* is a feud between two houses. The feud's hatred has "made a slum, / Houses at which the passer shakes his fist," while the failure of an attempted peace-making brings "the fall of an old house." The wanderer in "Doom is dark" must "leave his house," as the rider who escapes the unresolved divisions of *The Orators* rides "Out of this house." And in "Watch any day his nonchalant pauses," the repressed sophisticate who appears to be free, but is really "not that returning conqueror," stands in uneasy balance, "poised between shocking falls" which he avoids by

> Travelling by daylight on from house to house
> The longest way to the intrinsic peace.

This restates Auden's lines about "entropic peace" in his verse letter to Isherwood: the intrinsic peace is the real peace never to be attained by the divided—not through a safe daylight journey, not through any journey at all. Any deliberate movement toward satisfaction must be asymptotic and incomplete. The quest heroes of legends and fables, "The silly fool" and "The youngest son" who finally achieve their quests, are wishful fantasies, "tales in tales / Where no one fails."

Like any young man half-convinced of his superiority over the bourgeoisie from which he sprang, the young Auden tries to exempt himself from his criticism of "Man's opposite strivings." Looking down on the world around him, he sees little else than automatic processes of neurosis operating in other people. His verse letter to Isherwood details the "pity" he feels for the neurotic helplessness of his fellow man. "Our study and our interest," he tells his fellow author, is

> To trace his [man's] strategies of compensation
> "The North West Passage" to give your name to it,
> To pity his own penalties for this,
> See love transform itself to influenza
> And guilty rashes, speeding descent
> Of noble spirit, the brakes burnt out.

"The North West Passage" was Isherwood's term for the neurotic evasion of life, the elaborate compensation one makes for refusing to face one's desires and experiences directly. Auden elaborated in his 1929 journal: "*Compensation is sin.* The devil offers substitute pleasures for the divine will. Neurotic pain is the principle of Dante's Inferno. The North-West passage."

Neuroses are substitute pleasures. What are the authentic ones? Auden's answer is complex and partly self-contradictory. He wrote in another 1929 journal entry:

Pleasure

The error of Freud and most psychologists is making pleasure a negative thing, progress towards a state of rest. This is only one half of pleasure and the least important half. Creative pleasure is, like pain, an increase in tension. What does the psychologist make of contemplation and joy?

The essence of creation is doing things for no reason, it is pointless. Possessive pleasure is always rational. Freud you see really believes that pleasure is immoral, i.e. happiness is displeasing to God.

If you believe this of course the death wish becomes the most important emotion, and "reinstatement of an earlier condition" [a quotation from *Beyond the Pleasure Principle*]. Entropy is another name for despair.

Man's strivings for entropic peace amount to the despair of the death wish. "Creative pleasure" has nothing to do with personal or sexual peace; it is the making of a poem, an act that increases tension and division. To enjoy life, make a poem out of it.

Freud saw a basic opposition between Eros and Thanatos, between the two great organic impulses toward sex and death. For Auden this opposition was false. Both impulses are similar movements toward entropy, and the real opposition is between these impulses and the impulse toward creative separation:

The question is what do we mean by sex. The union or the fission of sex cells, i.e. love or hate. Freud makes sex the first and places it in opposition to the death wish. It seems to me jolly similar. . . . The real "life-wish" is the desire for separation, from family, from one's literary predecessors.

These lines attempt to realize the life-wish they describe, for the predecessor from whom Auden is separating himself in them is Freud—

whose work he discovered when his father began using the new psychology in his school medical practice around 1920, when Auden was thirteen. Auden was the first imaginative writer in English to take Freud seriously—Lawrence dismissed him, Joyce derided him, everyone else ignored him—but his earliest comments on Freud take the form of arguments over psychoanalytic doctrine. "The trouble with Freud," Auden wrote in his 1929 journal, "is that he accepts conventional morality as if it were the only one." Against Freud's quietist and conservative tendencies Auden praised the activist and progressive impulses of the psyche. Later, in 1935, he would include a compendium of Freud's teachings in an essay on "Psychology and Art To-day," and in 1939 he made him the subject of a great didactic elegy. But the detailed psychological theory in Auden's poems derived less from Freud himself than from such variously heterodox psychologists as Trigant Burrow, Georg Groddeck, Eugen Bleuler, and William McDougall. In his interpretations of artists, Auden wrote in *Letter to Lord Byron*, "Freud's not quite O.K."

His argument with Freud was in part an argument with himself. As a piece of high romantic rhetoric, Auden's statement that the real life-wish is separation from the past is unexceptionable, but it contradicts everything Auden was saying elsewhere. In his verse letter to Isherwood, written during the same month as these journal entries, he refers to man's "own penalties," the penalties he inflicts on himself for his evasions of life and for his compensations. The only penalty the poem names is psychosomatic disease: he and Isherwood see repressed "love transform itself to influenza / And guilty rashes." In his journal Auden glosses these lines in a list—headed "Body and Soul"—of "hatreds" and their consequent ills:

Hatred of the flesh. Physical Inferiority.	Boils. Skin diseases.
⎰Hatred of other people. Social Inferiorities.	⎰Infectious diseases.
⎱Hatred of physical love.	⎱Influenza.
. . .	. . .

On the one hand Auden is praising "separation" as the "real 'life-wish' " that opposes the death wish—which includes the wish for sex. On the other hand, he is condemning those who separate themselves by "hatred" and thereby generate disease. Separation is not precisely identical with hatred, but the two are closely similar, and Auden exalts the one while scorning the other.* A few months later, in the final section of "It was Easter as I walked," he will complicate matters further by writing that love *needs* death.

⌇

The edginess of Auden's early poems is partly the result of this internal contradiction. Auden at the border, Auden braving the frontier, wants to be part of a *"real* whole," to achieve a "real meeting"—but at the same time he revels in the proud creative separation that lets him look down at the world as the hawk does or the helmeted airman. Auden's indecision at the border, at the crux left of the watershed, began as indecision over how to move in space, but before long he elaborated it into the realm of time. He wanted the separation that comes with adulthood and literary maturity, "separation from family, from one's literary predecessors." But his manner was never limited to the detached laboratory stoicism that, to his first readers, offered the thrill of the absolutely up-to-date. At moments of special emotional intensity in his poems, usually moments of violent disruption or conclusive loss, a different and older note was to be heard—a faint but clear and distinct echo of Old English poems or Icelandic sagas. Auden wanted to find a language of his own, "and in our time," but he also found himself using a language of the distant past to express his experience of isolation in the present.

Just as the violence of his early poems is retained and transformed in later ones, so, correspondingly, the unbroken sense of literary tradition that informs Auden's mature work is prefigured among his modernist fragments. Auden's initial literary problem was to find independence from his literary ancestors while at the same time finding a language to write in. His reworkings of saga fragments and his echoes of Old English—both in his alliterative metres and in his direct quotations from *Beowulf*,† "The Wanderer," "The Battle of Maldon," "Wulf and

* Auden's account of the "real 'life-wish' " as separation is related to the Freudian account of the Oedipal crisis but is not derived from it. Rather, both derive from a basic and anterior romantic impulse: the urge toward self-creation, the wish to be responsible for one's being without suffering the insult of having been created by someone else. (See p. 173.)

† The title *Paid on Both Sides*, Laurence Heyworth has discovered, is a potsherd from *Beowulf*, line 1305, possibly adapted from John R. Clark Hall's 1901 prose translation: "That was no good exchange—that they should pay on both sides with the lives of friends."

Eadwacer"—are all elements of his solution. Since no poetic language can be entirely new, Auden deliberately sought his language outside the main line of transmission. When he spoke of the gangster-ethic of the sagas, he was not altogether disapproving, for it provided his language with an air of primitive illegality. In *The Orators* he added the more modern illegalities of underworld cant.*

At first, Auden's resistance to the recent literary past and his recovery of more ancient sources—both for the purpose of finding his own poetic energies—served to intensify romantic literary modes. Pound's "discovery" of Provençal and Chinese had achieved a roughly similar purpose some years before. Yet while Auden's new style severed him from the tradition favored by the immediately preceding generation, a tradition which found its ideal in the Mediterranean Renaissance, it also joined him to a very different tradition, the archaic Nordic one. Later he would recognize that his desire for a literary tradition was stronger than his wish for independence and would make his allusions and echoes more explicit. The rhymed octosyllabic couplets of *New Year Letter* in 1940, like the Horatian stanzas of many of his poems in the late 1930s, are confident of their wholeness and adequacy, as modernism's broken forms can never be, and are confident of their integration with a pre-romantic past. They learned their confidence from Auden's Old English illegalities in earlier years.

There are parallels in Auden's double sense of style—illegal yet traditional—to his double sense of history. Although he expressed vividly, in "Writing" and elsewhere, the historical nostalgia he inherited from modernism, he would constantly deny that there had ever been a past worthy of regret or that our present divisions could ever be repaired. Yet in using Old English and Icelandic literature to describe these divisions he established a literary continuity. Even when writing poetic fragments, he did not adopt the fragmentation into different national languages—bits of German, Sanskrit, Chinese—found in Eliot and Pound. His "raw provincial" taste at school for Hardy and Edward Thomas may have prepared him, when he grew more sophisticated, to make pre-Norman English the basis of his poetic language, but it did not make him insular. Its effect was to make him naturalize in his own style

---

* "Journal of an Airman" alludes to "a tan-armed *gonsil* or a *first-of-May*," meaning a homosexual boy and a young tramp. Ode IV has the line, " 'Youth's on the march' says *Jocker* to *Prushun*"—i.e. a pederastic tramp addressing his young companion.

his exotic borrowings from Rimbaud or Hölderlin or Dante; he did not call attention to their foreignness and distance, or leave them estranged as they would have been in *The Waste Land* or *The Cantos*.*

The best example of Auden's half-concealed, half-naturalized recollections of Old English is the poem beginning "Doom is dark and deeper than any sea-dingle." This seems to have been written for the lost 1930 play *The Fronny* and was first published in 1932 with the reticent title "Chorus from a Play." The poem gives no clue that its opening line derives from a Middle English prose homily, "Sawles Warde," nor that its middle section closely adapts a passage from the Old English poem "The Wanderer"—a title Auden later used for this poem, but not until 1966. The Old English lines read, in the translation facing the text in Nora Kershaw's *Anglo-Saxon and Norse Poems* (1922),

> distress and sleep together lay hold on the poor solitary, he dreams that he is greeting and kissing his liege-lord, and laying his hands and head upon his knee—just as he used to do when he enjoyed the bounty of the throne in days of old. Then the friendless man awakes again and sees before him the grey waves—sees the sea-birds bathing . . .

Auden renders this in an elliptical modern idiom and a metre based appropriately on the Old English accentual. He transforms the earlier poem's liege relationship into a sexual one, but leaves unaltered the wanderer's sense of loss:

> There head falls forward, fatigued at evening,
> And dreams of home,

* Early in his career Auden found another poet using a similar but narrower method of naturalizing the past, and for about a year he wrote some of his poems in direct imitation of that poet's voice. Laura Riding's 1928 volume *Love as Love, Death as Death* takes over the diction of Emily Dickinson and, indirectly, the metres of John Skelton and uses them in modern style, more fragmented and syncopated than the originals. Dickinson and Skelton were among Auden's adolescent enthusiasms, but he had not yet found a way of using them in his adult work. So when Laura Riding showed how, he followed her example. Riding's "All Nothing, Nothing" begins: "The standing-stillness, / The from foot-to-foot, / Is no real illness, / Is no real fever . . ." An Auden poem of 1930 begins: "This lunar beauty / Has no history / Is complete and early . . ."—and a half-dozen other poems from 1929–30 show similar ventriloquisms. The kinds of poetry he wanted to write after 1930 required a less thin-lipped style, and so he worked Emily Dickinson out of his system and began taking his Skelton, like his Old English, straight from the source.

Waving from window, spread of welcome,
Kissing of wife under single sheet;
But waking sees
Bird-flocks nameless to him* . . .

Nothing could be more different than Auden's manner with "The Wanderer" and Ezra Pound's with its companion poem "The Seafarer." This is Pound's rendition of Old English:

May I for my own self song's truth reckon,
Journey's jargon, how I in harsh days
Hardship endured oft. . . .

   Nathless there knocketh now
The heart's thought that I on high streams
The salt-wavy tumult traverse alone.
Moaneth alway my mind's lust
That I fare forth, that I afar hence
Seek out a foreign fastness. . . .

Pound's metrical echoes of Old English are technically less accomplished than Auden's, and he translates the poem into something that resembles not contemporary diction, but a farrago of misremembered and imaginary Englishes—including something of the diction of Browning's Caliban.

Although Pound wrote "The Seafarer" before he had completely modernized himself to his own standards, the comparison with Auden is not unfair. Even in the later *Cantos* Pound was still using archaic diction whenever matters turned nostalgically serious. Pound emphasizes the historical distance of his poem's subject. He stresses the absence from the debased modern world of the proud heroism celebrated in the older poem—although he has to do some retouching to bring out the lonely romantic virtues that are inconveniently obscure in the original. The Seafarer's world, for Pound, may be gone for ever, but its powers are recoverable in the poet's heroic transforming imagination, and only there.

---

* The poem diverges here from the Old English and continues: ". . . ; through doorway voices / Of new men making another love." But the poem does not recommend this new (homosexual?) love; it hopes for the "joy" and "day of his returning" to the home he left, and for a "lucky" and "leaning dawn."

For Auden, in contrast, "The Wanderer" is thoroughly available to the present. He makes no fuss about translating the social isolation of the Old English poem into the psychological isolation of his twentieth-century one. He does not much care if his readers recognize that his lines derive from an ancient source.* The point in Auden is not that a distant past has been laboriously recovered for the present, but that a statement about present loneliness and anxiety can be made in terms that the past freely provides. The ancient poem has always been contemporary; there is no need to "make it new." But while the archaic words of "The Wanderer" give Auden a living poetic language, they offer him no further comfort. He knows that what makes them contemporary is the persistence of the sorrow they proclaim, a sorrow that will never pass away.

---

* Similarly, in an example from a few years later, those who do not recognize the words "Airs, waters, places" in Sonnet IX of *In Time of War* as a title from Hippocrates miss an interesting detail but are neither excluded from understanding the poem nor made to *feel* excluded by a show of linguistic strangeness. In contrast, Auden violated his own practice when he obscured his meaning with obsolete syntax in the phrase "will his negative inversion" in the 1929 poem "Sir, no man's enemy." He wrote in a friend's copy in the 1940s: "I bitterly regret the day I was snobbish enough to use an archaic genitive (=will's). I've been asked what this line means ever since."

III

Family Ghosts

For two years Auden lived without obligations or responsibilities, free to do as he wanted. From the time he left Oxford in the spring of 1928 until he took his first job as a schoolmaster in the spring of 1930, he could devote all his energy to the pursuit of his "real 'life-wish' " for separation from his family and from his literary predecessors. First in the slums of Berlin, then in the rich houses of London, he preached to himself and his friends the liberation of impulse and the wisdom of desire. But as he shed his outer constraints he found he was burdened by an inner necessity that until now had been hidden. Before this time his poems spoke of entrapment in space, of borders blocking passage to a country with easy power; now they spoke of entrapment in time, of psychological restraints transmitted as if genetically from the past. The "ancestral curse" (the phrase is from the 1929 poem "Under boughs between our tentative endearments") took hold, as proliferating "ghosts" impeded the impulse to freedom with their archaic hatreds. Auden wrote in his 1929 journal: "The Tyranny of the Dead. One cannot react against them." *Paid on Both Sides* is a study in that tyranny.

It is an autobiographical study also. Annotating a friend's copy of the play in the 1940s, he called it "A parable of English Middle Class (professional) family life 1907–1929." The dates are the year of Auden's birth and the year he put the finishing touches on his play, which opens with the birth of the hero and ends with the defeat by the ancestral curse of his first adult efforts to love. Nothing in the play's manner suggests that its allegory is personal. With its double perspective of ancient legend and modern psychology, its rapid and drastic shifts of tone—from farce to dream play to lyric, from the stridencies of battle to the metaphysics of sex-in-the-head—it seems to exclude any reference to the private life of its author. Such exclusion was precisely what Auden told his friends he wanted for his poetry, but the impersonal elements he chose as his material from the world outside himself corresponded exactly to his private concerns. His literary anonymity was a thoroughly romantic anti-romanticism, as obsessed with the self it excluded as an earlier romanticism was with the self it expressed. The central personal meaning may be invisible in Auden's early work, but its outline can be traced along the edges of the impersonal meanings that surround it. *Paid on Both Sides* is subtitled "A Charade," and a charade implies a solution.

However opaque the manner of the play, its story is simple. It is a tragedy of revenge. Two mill-owning families have been feuding for generations. The son of one family, John Nower, and the daughter of the other, Anne Shaw, fall in love. A truce is declared on the occasion of their engagement. But on their wedding day one of the Shaws, urged on by his mother, murders Nower, avenging the Shaw brother whom Nower had earlier killed. The feud reopens as the play ends. The setting is modern northern England, but the prevailing legal system, or lack of one, recollects the sagas and their gangster-ethic from an ancient past. The play's language similarly fluctuates from schoolboy slang to alliterative Old English pastiche; all the murders are reported in the rhythms of Old English verse.

Hatred, here as throughout Auden's early poems, survives matrilineally: "His mother and her mother won." In the opening scene John Nower is born on the same day his father is killed by Red Shaw. (Red is Shaw's coloring, not his politics.) Nower's mother resolves to see her son pursue "Unforgetting" vengeance, wills that his "new ghost" must learn "from old termers what death is, where." The morning of Nower's birth is to be an "unforgiving morning," one that will bind the future to old hatreds. As for Nower's adulthood, his mother warns, using the sagas' laconic portentousness, "There'll be some crying out when he's come there."

In the second scene, after an interval of twenty years (this is obscure in the printed text because, Auden explained to a friend, he forgot to specify it in the stage directions), Nower reappears as a young man. He ambushes his father's killer and reports the success of his revenge in archaic metre:

Day was gone Night covered sky
Black over earth When we came there
To Brandon Walls Where Red Shaw lay
Hateful and sleeping Unfriendly visit. . . .

There he died Nor any came
Fighters home Nor wives shall go
Smiling to bed They boast no more.

Immediately afterward Nower's men discover a spy, the elder brother
of the Shaw who will kill Nower at the end. Nower orders him shot.
This task accomplished, one of Nower's men asks, "Will you be wanting
anything more to-night, Sir?" Nower answers, "No, that will be all
thank you," and then, sitting alone, finds himself for the first time in a
state of moral isolation, left to make his own decisions and utterly incapable of doing so. For the first time, ancestral habits fail to give sense or
order to his life. He soliloquizes:

Always the following wind of history
Of others' wisdom makes a buoyant air
Till we come suddenly on pockets where
Is nothing loud but us . . .
Our fathers . . . taught us war,
To scamper after darlings, to climb hills,
To emigrate from weakness . . .
But never told us this, left each to learn,
Hear something of that soon-arriving day
When to gaze longer and delighted on
A face or idea be impossible.

He longs for an evolutionary past, "Younger than worms," when there
was no need for choice at all. Finally, as a deleted stage direction in
Auden's typescript makes clear, "He sleeps," and dreams a play-within-
a-play. From this inner drama of his own psyche he will awake determined to end the feud through love. Putting aside ancient hatred,
Nower chooses to live *now*.

His dream is the mechanism of his change; its cause lies in the waking
action that precedes it. The feud's origins are lost to memory, and
therefore impervious to psychoanalytic cure. But at last Nower is *satiated* by the killings: "Will you be wanting anything more?—No, that

will be all." Auden's 1929 journal distinguishes "The two forces" in human psychology:

> Security.   Habit.   Deeper in the mine, or higher in the air.
> Satiety.   Mutation.   Persisting in folly brings wisdom.

The journal goes on to define habit as "the inheritance of thoughts and emotions. Parental authority." This is the motive force that sustains the murderous feud. "Death," the journal explains, is "failure to get rid of metabolic products, i.e. interest in the past." To cure the feud, to arrest habit, to lose interest in the past—all this requires the other force, satiation. Elsewhere in the journal Auden suggests that a psychoanalytic quest into the past for the origins of division cannot possibly help to resolve it:

> Freud says it is better to recollect infantile experience than to repeat this [i.e. infantile experience]. This is wrong. Recollection does nothing. If [as Blake wrote] the fool would persist in his folly he would become wise.

Satiation does, apparently, permit Nower to be cured. In the words of the play's Chorus, it "makes us well / Without confession of the ill," without, that is, any Freudian revelations of hidden causes.*

Nower's dream takes the form of a trial, in the course of which he kills his own past and then with the help of a comic healer—the first of many in Auden's poetry—emerges reconciled and renewed. Father Christmas presides at the trial, which, like the charade in which it is set, takes the form of a Christmas pantomime, with elements of the traditional mummers' play. The inner play, as always, points to the interpretation of the outer one. For both trial and charade, the goal is to bring in a New Year and new conditions. The spy whom Nower had just ordered killed is the accused, Nower the accuser. At first, when Father Christmas calls for evidence, Nower can only rattle off a jingoistic speech echoing the public rhetoric of 1914–18: "We cannot betray the dead. As we pass their graves can we be deaf to the simple eloquence of their inscriptions. . . ."

---

* Auden was to see this point very differently in America in 1939, when he elegized Freud who "told / The unhappy Present to recite the Past / Like a poetry lesson till sooner / Or later it faltered at the line where / Long ago the accusations had begun . . . / And was life-forgiven and more humble . . ."

This speech emerges from Nower's mouth, but the words are those of his ancestral voices. Here the psychological problem of the tyranny of the dead enlarges into an urgently public one. Auden's generation, reminded constantly of its escape from the slaughter of their fathers and brothers in the Great War, might easily become guilt-ridden enough to welcome another war as a means of compensation. John Nower's dream will cure him of the fevers of patriotic rhetoric as well as the rigidities of family hatreds.

In the midst of the trial the back curtains open, and "The Man-Woman appears as a prisoner of war behind barbed wire, in the snow." The Man-Woman's speech is notoriously the most obscure moment in the play, but its obscurity is appropriate to a language that arises from the deepest unconscious sources—heard only in dream, from behind a barrier, at the furthest recess of Nower's psyche. The Man-Woman is less a person who combines the two sexes than a personification of the repressed erotic impulse toward union and love which the feud has kept prisoned behind barbed wire, frozen out in the snow.* The Man-Woman sadly accuses Nower of evading and demeaning Eros. "Love was not love for you but episodes, / Traffic in memoirs": you kissed in order to tell. When sexuality persisted in its attentions, "you made that an excuse / For playing with yourself, but homesick because / Your mother told you that's what flowers did."† The Man-Woman goes on to

---

* Auden combined two sources here. R. J. E. Tiddy's *The Mummers' Play* (1923)—the comic doctor in *Paid on Both Sides* also speaks lines taken from this book—refers to the traditional man-woman character as possibly the "survival of an endeavour to promote fertility by the mere fact of wearing a woman's clothes." And Proust, on the first page of *Sodome et Gomorrhe*, uses "*hommes-femmes*" as a term for homosexuals. Auden dismissed Proust in his journal—"all his talk about the 'man-woman' seems astoundingly superficial and quite meaningless"—but it is clear that the Man-Woman in the charade embodies a hidden reference to Auden's sexuality. In a mood of Madame-Bovary-c'est-moi, soon after writing *Paid on Both Sides*, he told Stephen Spender, "I am the Man-Woman." Presumably he was alluding not only to his homosexuality but also to the role he imagined for himself as an agent of healing impulse and as an isolated noncommunicative poetic voice which must warn, as the Man-Woman does in the charade, that "where I am / All talking is forbidden."

† Compare this entry in Auden's 1929 journal:

> Among the educated classes the child very soon connects [?by] suggestion the idea of physical contact and sexual acts. When he does gratify the first, he thinks he wants the second, i.e. when he sleeps with his friend he gets an erection. "Mother told us that's what flowers did" [the child explains to the friend].

list Nower's other evasions—coldness, fear, his sense of sex as recreation—and concludes, satiated, "Now I shall go." At this point Nower interrupts, crying "I can't bear it," and shoots the spy. The lights go out. When they come up again the jury is gone. A doctor enters, cures the spy by extracting an enormous tooth from his body and exorcising the ancestral curse: "This tooth was growing ninety-nine years before his great grandmother was born. If it hadn't been taken out to-day he would have died yesterday." The spy gets up, and he and Nower, reconciled, plant a tree. "Sharers of the same house," divided aspects of the same self, they are free from their ancestral past, "know not the builder nor the name of his son" and "Now cannot mean to them." They have come through.

When Nower wakes from this dream he calls for his horse and rides to the house of his enemies to propose marriage to Anne Shaw. Yet even now the feud continues around him, as another Nower and another Shaw are killed for vengeance. Nower's cure is not enough. As Auden wrote in his 1929 journal, "Freud's error is the limitation of neurosis to the individual. The neurosis involves all society." And although the play has the drama of Nower's divided psyche at its center, it does not therefore reduce all its other issues to allegories of personal psychological disorder. The play's social disorder is an entirely separate problem, one which Auden, in 1928, does not even attempt to solve.

Nower hopes to live up to the promise of his name. He breaks his ties to old complexities: "All pasts / Are single old past now." When he talks of love with Anne Shaw he contrasts his memories with his new emotions: "These I remember," he says of childhood events, "but not love till now. We cannot tell where we shall find it . . . and what others tell us is no use to us." But Anne knows the present is still surrounded by the feud's enduring hatred. She urges Nower to leave with her, to go where the feud cannot follow. He insists that they remain. His heroic ambition—so his earlier speeches suggest—is to rebuild, not escape, the world around him, and to defeat, not flee, the dead. When Anne argues that there is no need to oppose the dead, that they do not speak from the grave, Nower replies by enumerating their legacy: "slinkers, whisperers, . . . what dreams or goes masked, embraces that fail, . . . touches of the old wound." All must be cured; such is the pride of his heroism.

In the private realm of his psyche, Nower's murder of the Shaw spy induced the mutation of his cure. But in the public realm of the feud, this same murder is remembered with undiminished intensity by those who have not been cured at all. There are two kinds of time in *Paid on Both Sides:* a personal time in which mutation is possible and the dead past can be barred from the living present, and a social time that never changes, is never renewed, where habit rules unchallenged. At Nower's wedding to Anne, when the ceremony brings their private love into the public realm, social time triumphs. The language of the play returns at the end to the language of its opening. In a speech that complements Nower's mother's earlier threats of vengeance, the spy's mother now shames her younger son into killing Nower—breaking the truce and resuming the feud. Then Anne's final speech over Nower's dead body echoes his mother's opening lines about his infant self and dead father. This speech takes the place of the final scene of a Shakespearean tragedy: comparative nonentities, ordinary men, survive the lost hero, and Anne foresees—laconically, eloquently—"An empty bed, hope from less noble men." She

> had seen joy
> Received and given, upon both sides, for years.
> Now not.

The real whole is still guarded by dead sentries.

I have been describing the published text of *Paid on Both Sides,* with its emphasis on personal cure and personal defeat. But when Auden began work on the play he was thinking only about social and family disasters. Two separate typescripts exist of the play, one finished in July or possibly early August 1928, which Auden never published,* and another, corresponding in all important details to the printed versions, which Auden prepared in Berlin in December the same year. He wrote the first version at the end of his final term at Oxford, intending it for a semi-public performance as a country house charade at a friend's home in August. The friend's family looked at the script, and, as Auden told Isherwood, "They refuse to do the play, as they say the village won't stand it." This first version, half the length of the final one, almost ignores the issue of personal psychology, entirely omits Nower's dream

---

* It has now been printed as an appendix to *The English Auden.*

and cure, and gives no clue to his motivations. Nower himself is not even mentioned until the announcement of his engagement to Anne Shaw. No mutation, no inner psychological change, prompts him to discover love. It simply happens, and Auden may have regarded the play's structural echoes of *Romeo and Juliet* as a sufficient substitute for personal motives. The July text emphasizes only the matter of the inherited past and what might be called the social genetics of "habit." There is nothing at all about Christmas or New Year, and not even a distant hope of personal renewal. Auden even denied personal names to his minor characters, using instead the biological symbols for filial generations—F′ and F″, FF′ and FF″—as if to say that all that mattered about them was the distribution of their genes.

The December version is of course very different from this, and its changes resulted from changes in Auden's life. In August 1928, not long after leaving Oxford, he spent three weeks at Spa in Belgium—"staying with a psychologist," he said in a letter. Exactly what happened there is unknown. Almost certainly he took some sort of treatment, and there are indications that he did this in the hope of altering his sexual preferences. Little could have been accomplished in so short a period, and little was. Auden seems to have regarded the whole episode, then and afterward, with amused disdain. The poems he wrote on his return to England showed no change in his conviction that his isolation was congenital and incurable.

Yet in the one poem he wrote during his weeks at Spa he found the terms in which, a few months later, he would welcome the prospect of a cure. The poem itself denies that prospect, but it states it as at least a possibility. This is the poem, later incorporated into the December text of *Paid*, that begins "To throw away the key and walk away"; technically, it marks Auden's first use of the slant-rhymes with initial consonance (*right/rate, wall/well*) that he found in Wilfred Owen's "Strange Meeting" and used frequently in the next two years. In content, the poem is a chronicle of defeat: yet another of Auden's voyagers goes across the border to a dead end. But the opening lines propose—what the following lines will deny—that by consciously and deliberately rejecting the past one can make a real and immediate change. One needs no guide or teacher to initiate change, no Freudian retrospection (and the poem says nothing about mutation and satiety, which would not enter Auden's vocabulary until a few months later):

To throw away the key and walk away
Not abrupt exile, the neighbours asking why,
But following a line with left and right
An altered gradient at another rate
Learns more than maps upon the whitewashed wall
The hand put up to ask; and makes us well
Without confession of the ill. . . .

Yet such a departure, for all its decisiveness and ease, cannot make us well at all. The source of illness is too deep:

It may examine but cannot unwind
Bandage of flesh nor diagnose the bane
Which has for some time now attacked the bone . . .

And in the poem's second verse-paragraph the journey "Crossing the pass" leads to an exhausted isolation, "Too tired to hear except the pulse's strum," and finally to "Rock shutting out the sky, the old life done." The final phrase carries a faint suggestion of a new life to follow, but the rest of the poem, and the rock shutting out the sky over the tomb, make clear the irony in this. Auden dropped the lines about the bone's bane within a few weeks of writing them, but it is evident that he did this not to alter the poem's vision of defeat but to clarify its structure. Now the whole first half states the efficacy of departure, while the second half replies with a catalogue of dire consequences.

There matters stood at the end of the summer. Psychoanalysis had raised the question of change but had not resolved it; in his poem Auden had tried another solution and rejected it also. But now he was receptive to a better and more plausible solution, if there were one to be found.

In this mood, in the autumn of 1928, he went to Berlin. His parents had offered him a year on the Continent, and because everyone else with artistic ambitions went to Paris he chose Berlin instead. He arrived there probably in September and stayed about nine months. He seems to have regarded the city largely as an amusement park for the flesh. Berlin was an extension of the Cosy Corner, the proletarian *Lokal* where he relaxed and made friendly pickups. The change in his life that occurred in Berlin had nothing to do with Berliners. Its catalyst was an Englishman named John Layard who was living in Berlin at the time; a mutual friend at Oxford had suggested that he and Auden get in touch. As Auden recalled in *Letter to Lord Byron:* "I met a chap called Layard and he fed / New doctrines into my receptive head." The immediate cure—which Auden had looked for in a vague way in Spa—Layard's doctrines now promised in extensive and plausible detail.

Layard was an anthropologist in his late thirties who, some years before, had suffered a complete nervous breakdown and had been treated by Homer Lane, an American psychologist working in England. By the time Lane died in 1925—having been hounded first out of the governorship of a reformatory and then out of England by charges of sexual misconduct with his women patients—Layard had become his disciple. He preserved transcripts of Lane's teachings as sacred texts. Although Layard's name turns up in the December text of *Paid*—Nower's father is killed while riding to "speak with Layard," presumably in hope of a cure—his importance to Auden in 1928 was the entrée he provided to Lane's ideas.

Lane built his theory on the romantic doctrine that man's impulses are good, a doctrine whose history in modern times extends from Rousseau through Nietzsche to D. H. Lawrence. To act on one's deepest impulse is to be happy and virtuous, immune to neurosis, "pure in heart," a living beacon to the tormented and the ill. To deny one's impulse is to rebel against the inner law of one's own nature, and the self-imposed punishment for this rebellion is physical and mental disease. Every illness is in fact psychosomatic and points the way to recovery, since the disease manifests in twisted form a feared or repressed desire. Syphilis results from sexual guilt, cancer from foiled creativity. Indulge the desire and the disease will be cured.*

---

* Layard, without quite intending to do so, served as a living example of the efficacy of Lane's ideas. On Lane's death Layard had only partly recovered from his nervous breakdown, and during the months after he met Auden he sank again into a severe depression. (In the poem "It was Easter as I walked" Auden alludes to "A friend's analysis of his own failure / Listened to at intervals throughout the winter.") In the spring of 1929 Layard announced his intention to kill himself. Auden, giving Layard back his own teachings, made no effort to stop him: if this were Layard's impulse he should be free to act on it. Finally Layard did act. He put a revolver in his mouth and fired—but he had aimed up his nose and managed to miss his brain. Remembering Auden's attitude, he made his way to Auden's flat, handed him the revolver and asked him to finish him off. Auden instead took him to a hospital. Layard's obedience to his inner impulse almost left him dead, but it also succeeded in curing him. Within a few weeks he had recovered from his bullet wound and his mental de-

The contrast between Lane's teachings and the Freudian teachings which Auden already knew could not have been greater. Where Lane developed the romantic doctrine of man's original virtue, Freud pessimistically distrusted the violent and anarchic id. Where Freud attributed civilizing virtue to sexual sublimation, Lane celebrated the release of impulse. Where Freud hoped to do little more than reduce the sufferings of his patients to the ordinary misery of mankind, Lane promised happiness and freedom. (In fact John Layard seems to have exaggerated the romantic optimism of Lane's thought, but was true to its basic premises.) Lane's teachings were less like Freud's than like D. H. Lawrence's in his anti-Freudian book *Fantasia of the Unconscious* (1922). Auden probably encountered this book sometime before he met Layard; certainly he was quoting it a year or so later. But he would have hesitated to borrow ideas directly from one of the literary predecessors from whom he said he must separate himself. Because Lane had nothing to do with literature, Auden could take over his doctrines as if they had never been used by a writer before. Once he had appropriated the basic theory from Lane, he was free to borrow details from Lawrence.

Auden copied out in his notebooks various charts and tables in which Lane summarized his ideas. But when it came to using the ideas in his poems, Auden found their specific form less important than the general promise they offered of renewal and cure. Auden first gave voice to this promise in a poem he wrote in November 1928, within a few days or weeks of his first meeting with Layard:

> There is the city,
> Lighted and clean once, pleasure for builders
> And I
> Letting to cheaper tenants, have made a slum
> Houses at which the passer shakes his fist
> Remembering evil. . . .
>
> But love, sent east for peace
> From tunnels under those
> Bursts now to pass
> On trestles over meaner quarters
> A noise and flashing glass.

---

pression. Soon he was back in England where he published important contributions to psychology and anthropology, one of which was to provide Auden with the basic idea for *The Orators*.

Feels morning streaming down . . .
Nowise withdrawn by doubting flinch
Nor joined to any by belief's firm flange
Refreshed sees all
The tugged-at teat
The hopper's steady feed, the frothing leat.

Auden had never written in a tone anything like this before. He allows no irony, no threats, no ambiguous silence to intrude on his vision of triumph.*

In Auden's notebook this poem appears as an independent work, and there is no way of knowing whether, at the time he wrote it, he planned to use it as one of John Nower's speeches in a revised *Paid on Both Sides*—a context in which the poem's promise is qualified by Nower's defeat. (Verses undoubtedly written for the revised version of the charade appear in Auden's notebook in the following month.) Whatever Auden's plans for it, the poem marks his discovery of a rhetoric for hope and metaphors for freedom. Now he could write about a future that had hitherto been closed to his poetry.

Visiting England at Christmas 1928, Auden proclaimed Lane's doctrine to his friends in extravagant and unqualified terms. But by this time he had almost certainly finished rewriting *Paid on Both Sides*—by New Year's Eve he had the typescript ready to send to Eliot for *The Criterion*—and the new version shows that he was not so thoroughly converted by Lane's teachings as he allowed his friends to believe. To the July text he added Nower's mutation, dream-psychomachia, and cure, but he also added the monitory speech of the Man-Woman (written within a few weeks after Nower's vision of love's triumph) and left virtually unchanged the final scenes in which the feud starts up again and Nower is killed. Lane offered hope for an inner cure, but Auden knew already it was little more than a hope as long as the world outside remained contagiously diseased.

Among his friends, Auden blazoned the ideal of the Pure-in-Heart,

---

* Eighteen months earlier, silence interrupted a poem that reads like an unfinished fragment of this one. "Some say that handsome raider still at large," it begins, "in truth is love." When love returns from his journeys he calls order, "greets, repeats what he has heard / And seen, feature for feature, word for word." But here the poem ends, silent on the contents of love's report, silent on the effect it has on those who hear it. (The poem was later incorporated into *Paid on Both Sides*.)

the man free from sexual guilt and repression, and he amused himself by
posing as an example. In private he knew himself to be the opposite. On
page after page of his 1929 journal he analyzed his homosexuality as an
inner disorder whose cure he could never hope to find. His sexuality had
nothing to do with the real impulses whose release, in Lane's view, produced happiness and virtue. "It is not always realised by half that the
attraction of buggery is partly its difficulty and torments," he wrote in
one entry. In another he observed that "All buggers hate each other's
bodies as they hate their own, since they all suffer under the reproach,
real or imaginary[,] of 'Call yourself a man.' " He evidently went to
Berlin, as he went to Spa, in the hope that his year there might change
the character of his sexuality. If Berlin could not end his homosexuality
entirely, at least it might help him to overcome his arrested development. "I am having the sort of friendships I ought to have had at 16 and
didn't," he wrote to a friend. "The sort of Homosexuality which should
remain when I have done has the same cause as cancer, the [displaced]
wish to have a child." Before he left England for Berlin in 1928 he became engaged to marry a nurse from his home city of Birmingham.
When he returned, in July 1929, he knew he could not go through with
it, and broke off the engagement. He told a friend in a letter, "This is a
criticism of me not of marriage."

   He traced his sexuality to the past he had inherited. It was, he wrote
in his journal, "a criticism of the mother," comparable to a heterosexual's pursuit of whores. "Buggery seems a more unconscious criticism of
the mother as a love-object. Whores a more conscious rejection against
her sexual teaching. The bugger presumably though finds his mother
more satisfying . . . i.e. the bugger got too much mother love, so sheers
off women altogether, the whorer too little, so must always have another." Homosexuality was transmitted matrilineally, like hatred. Many
years later, in his poem "The Cave of Nakedness," Auden alluded to his
homosexuality as "certain occult / antipathies" of which he knew "perhaps too much."

In his first published book review, in *The Criterion*, April 1930, Auden
wrote that "The only duality is that between the whole self at different
stages of development." This duality he tried to realize in Berlin, but
nothing (in the words of a 1929 poem) could "cancel the inertia of the

buried." *Paid on Both Sides* served as a large general statement of the problem of cure and change, of the weight of habit that stalled mutation. In the poems he wrote after he finished the charade he took up more specialized aspects of the problem and examined them in detail.

In an August 1929 poem, "On Sunday walks," his subject is the specific etiology of the divided condition. This is the longest and most elaborate of the poems he wrote in the irregular two-stress line and abstract fragmented diction he purloined from Laura Riding during 1929–30. The opening lines set a scene of apparent calm, a scene whose hidden tensions the rest of the poem will expose:

> On Sunday walks
> Past the shut gates of works
> The conquerors come
> And are handsome.

These conquerors, like John Nower, try to live up to the glories of their family heritage, but by their own efforts they defeat themselves. Their heritage, although they do not know this, is a nostalgic legend, transmitted matrilineally, so in trying to maintain it they trap themselves in a delusion. The mothers, "Not meaning to deceive," nonetheless want their sons to remain dependent on them. So their "Wish to give suck / Enforces make-believe." The acts that earlier generations had done because of plausible fears "Of fever and bad-luck" are now romanticized into the make-believe ordeals of a legendary quest, with "A need for charms / For certain words / At certain fords." This is the quest the young soon persuade themselves is the authentic standard by which to measure their adult lives. The deeds their ancestors performed simply for "livelihood" have been transformed into a heroic but fictive display of "tallness, strongness / Words and longness, / All glory and all story." What makes these legends so believable is the presence of visible traces of the ancestors, traces misinterpreted by the living. The ancestors built houses—"Though over date / And motto on the gate / The lichen grows"—and, through the erotic rights of the seigneur, left genetic traces of their illicit unions—"That Roman nose / Is noticed in the villages." The effect of all this on the legitimate sons is a neurotic split between their self-imposed waking calm and their uncontrollable nightmare of entrapment. They dream of a guarded divisive border where

> Pursued by eaters
> They clutch at gaiters
> That straddle and deny
> Escape that way . . .

The stifling effect of this inner disorder is the subject of "The strings' excitement," written in April 1929—the poem to which Auden later gave the title "Family Ghosts." This poem has an impenetrable density appropriate to its subject and to Auden's difficulty in writing about it. He tried to compose it in terza rima, a form that structurally imitates ancestral influence by making each stanza take its outer rhymes from the middle line of the preceding stanza, but the pattern is defective twice in the poem's eight stanzas. Auden first adopted in this poem a rhetorical stance he would use repeatedly during the 1930s: he addresses a lover, but does so to express his inability to love. The only link between poet and lover is the simple fact of visual perception: "It is your face I see." Even his emotions are not his own but those provided him by his family ghosts. As in *Paid on Both Sides,** where our fathers taught us to "scamper after darlings," so, here,

> morning's praise
> Of you is ghost's approval of the choice,
> Filtered through roots of the effacing grass.

Our erotic impulses diverge from erotic expression, and can only project onto the empty sky a stern repressive deity forbidding love: the strings and drums that sound out in the opening line "Are but the initiating ceremony / That out of cloud the ancestral face may come." And so our erotic acts are reduced to empty signs, "subaltern mockery," as infertile as they are frequent—"Loquacious when the watercourse is dry."

"It is your face I see." But you threaten my peace, are "the visible enemy." To find safety, my fear warns me, "It is enough to turn away the eyes." Yet it is too late to escape the disorder that now threatens from both within and without. "There's no peace in this assaulted city." At last "all emotions to expression come," but they do so by "recovering

---

* The poem is in fact a direct offshoot from the charade. The fifth stanza is extracted and revised from the opening chorus of the July 1928 text of *Paid*, a poem that had been cut and rewritten for the December text where it is spoken by the character named Walter.

the archaic imagery," by reverting to the ancestral past that gives them form. What another poem calls "backward love" here regresses to its evolutionary origins. "This longing for assurance takes the form / Of a hawk's vertical stooping from the sky." And "These tears" move even further back, to the inanimate condition of lunar tides, "The lunatic agitation of the sea."* Love corresponds to the death wish in Freud, seeking "the reinstatement of an earlier condition" and the inanimate state of entropy which Auden called in his journal "another name for despair." So, in the poem's final stanza, the close of the cycle initiated by the sexual excitement of the opening line, is a cry for the end of all action and energy, a glacial age with no possibility of change:

> this despair with hardened eyeballs cries
> "A Golden Age, a Silver . . . rather ["better" in a manuscript] this,
> Massive and taciturn years, the Age of Ice."

"My family ghosts I fought and routed": so Auden reported forty years afterward. In 1929 they seemed immovable. He recognized their sleights and springes, he foresaw their vengeance, but knowledge gave him no power to resist. Auden differed from other victims of the ancestral curse only in enduring the irony of his knowledge in addition to the pain of his defeat.

He gave that irony dramatic form in *Paid on Both Sides*. Standing outside the action of the play, unseen by all its characters, a Chorus observes the doom it cannot change. While the characters move ignorantly to destruction, the Chorus knows exactly what will happen. Its speeches, which divide the play into a Shakespearean five-act structure, all begin with images of birth or springtime or the ambition of the young, and end in the inevitable defeat. Only a few lines separate their bracing openings—"To throw away the key and walk away," "The Spring unsettles sleeping partnerships," "The Spring will come"—from

---

* The line introducing the tears reads: "These tears, salt for a disobedient dream"—a brilliantly elaborate play on three senses of the word *salt*. These *saline* tears are, in the Shakespearean sense of the word, *lustful* in pursuit of a false dream, a dream disobedient to the inner law of one's own nature—a disobedience for which tears are, in another obsolete sense of the word, the *sharp, bitter* punishment.

their dire conclusions—"The last transgression of the sea," "The out-of-sight, buried too deep for shafts," "Rock shutting out the sky, the old life done." In the last lines of its final speech the Chorus foresees a fertile world, altogether elsewhere, with "Big fruit, eagles above the stream," but that world has no human population. "Better where no one feels." The Chorus alone knows the mechanism of the curse, that "His mother and her mother won." But it takes no comfort in its ineffectual knowledge, and knows that it too is observed by an unseen and pitiless eye:

> O watcher in the dark, you wake
> Our dream of waking . . .
> Your sudden hand
> Shall humble great
> Pride, break it . . .

Auden's Chorus differs from its historical predecessors—the classical *prologus*, the Chorus in *Henry V*, the musicians in Yeats's Irish Noh plays—in the enormous gulf that divides its knowledge from that of the characters. In devising a Chorus that knows what the characters do not know (and *why* they do not) Auden made an important innovation in modern drama. He achieved on stage the distant ironic perspective that the modern novel had already achieved, a perspective from which characters are seen as doomed victims of a world whose order they can never understand. Conrad in *The Secret Agent* had shown his readers the links that join the various characters, but in the eyes of the characters themselves there remained a final and impenetrable mystery. Joyce in *Ulysses* never let Leopold Bloom in on the secret that his actions repeat those of Odysseus thousands of years earlier. In plays and narratives written before the twentieth century this ironic distancing seldom occurs; by the final scene in virtually all epics, dramas, and novels, all that the narrator and audience knew about the characters and their world has also been learned by the characters themselves. When the *lacrimae rerum* note predominated, as in the *Aeneid*, the hero might be left ignorant of his place in the larger scheme of things, but at least he knew there was a scheme of things, not only tears.

In the aftermath of romanticism the community of knowledge between characters and their authors broke down. The intensity of understanding that gave the romantic artist his heroic stature isolated him as well. Perceiving more than other men, he lost hope of communicating with them. Finally he became imprisoned in his own perception. There are signs of the increasing distance of the artist from his subject in the novels of Meredith, George Eliot, and Thomas Hardy; a final separation occurs in Hardy's 1903 epic-drama *The Dynasts*, where the action is observed from the far reaches of space by Phantom Intelligences who alone perceive in human events the workings of the Immanent Will. But Hardy was writing "simply for mental performance"; it was Auden who first made this ironic distance visible on the stage.*

Between the knowing Chorus and the doomed actors in *Paid on Both Sides* opens a gulf—the gulf dividing thought from action, consciousness from habit, mind from nature, hope from fate. Homer Lane had promised that to cross this gulf required only the free impulse of love. But, as the secret agent knew in Auden's poem a year before, the bridges were unbuilt, and trouble coming.

---

* The charade was frequently performed at university theatres beginning in 1931. A few years later some French dramatists, André Obey, Jean Cocteau, and Jean Anouilh, wrote modern versions of Greek tragedy using choral voices much like the one in Auden's play, and from France the device spread to the rest of Europe and America (as in Thornton Wilder's *Our Town*). T. S. Eliot partly anticipated Auden's Chorus in the implicitly dramatic figure of Tiresias in *The Waste Land*, although Tiresias's role as universal witness is more apparent in the notes to the poem than in the poem itself.

IV

The Evolutionary
Defile

At twenty Auden was young enough to hope that the passage of time
would suffice to end his isolation. Two years later, as his loneliness persisted, he sought a more drastic and deliberate means of change. He
faced his difficulties as a healer would—tracing causes and experimenting with cures. He saw man's inner pain as a consequence of evolution:
mind had been evolved from body, and their divergence had now
reached the point of crisis. Yet the mind, Auden argued, had also
evolved to the point where, unlike its evolutionary predecessors, it could
choose to end its pain by choosing the next stage in its development.

What was to be done? In 1929 Auden considered two very different
answers to this question. At first, in Berlin during the spring, he rea-
soned that man's suffering would end when the parting of mind from
body was at last complete. Mind, he wrote, must divorce itself from its
origins in nature. It must learn to overcome its nostalgia for the palpable
delights of the flesh and learn to be satisfied with the incommunicable
privacy of abstract thought. The body, then, could be left alone to indulge its simple habitual pleasures, coupling thoughtlessly with other
bodies in a communism of the flesh. As long as Auden was living among
German working-class adolescents whom he regarded solely as (in a
phrase from his journal) "good drinking and sleeping companions,"
whose language he spoke imperfectly and to whom in any event he had
little to say that he could not communicate by gestures, this fantasy of a
self-delighting mind and habitual body seemed almost plausible. And as
a poet's theory of life it at least had the merit of following logically from

the theories with which more than a century of romanticism had hoped to solve its persistent dilemma, the relation of the perceiving consciousness to the perceived world of objects.

This first theory collapsed quickly enough, both from its own inadequacies—the mind was wrong to think it wanted only to be left alone—and from changes in Auden's circumstances. When he returned to England during the summer and lived among his own family and class, he could still consider himself a mental isolate but he could no longer treat everyone else as merely unconscious bodies. He now tried replacing his first theory with its exact opposite. Instead of finding happiness through greater separation, the mind, he argued, must choose its own dissolution into unconscious unity, must deliberately renounce the privacy it had been granted by evolution. Consciousness must return to its source in nature, a source that nature itself wished it to find. Only there could the mind recover the lost love it had always desired.

Auden's metaphor for the first of these theories was *weaning;* for the second, *drowning.* In the end, neither of these liquid metaphors could stand as a foundation for change.

Auden tested his first theory in his 1929 journal. In a long entry, probably written in April or May, he explained its historical basis:

> The progress of man seems to be in a direction away from nature. The development of consciousness may be compared with the breaking away of the child from the Oedipus relation. Just as one must be weaned from one's mother, one must be weaned from the Earth Mother (Unconscious?). Along with the growing self-consciousness of man during the last 150 years as illustrated for example by Dostoevsky, has developed Wordsworthian nature-worship, the nostalgia for the womb of Nature which cannot be re-entered by a consciousness increasingly independent but afraid. Rousseau is a nice example of the two tendencies. The motor-car and other improvements in quick transport are altering this and I am glad. The first sign of change is an impoverishment in feeling, noticed and criticised by many. This is a necessary accompaniment of weaning; every adolescent feels it. May it be a prelude to a full individual life of the mind, and Admiration of Nature become, like an adult's admiration for his

mother, a free interest in and liking of a world, good in itself but distinct from us . . .

The swelling rhetoric of this last sentence is significantly hollow, and its maternal simile too sanguine to be true. Auden is concerned far less with such agreeable matters as "free interest" and "liking" than he is with the process of disjunction and the impoverishment of feeling. In another entry he writes that "As far as we can see the development of the body is finished. In which case it should be encouraged to form habits, to become generalised, communistic; the direction of the body is to love all men." And again: "Only body can be communicated." The mind gladly keeps to itself, its relation to the flesh limited to a nobleman's formal hauteur as he addresses the stupid peasants huddled around his gateway. "I want something suggesting the seigneur here," Auden told Edouard Roditi, advising him how to translate the "gracious greeting" offered to a sexual partner in the poem "Before this loved one." As the body goes off to play among its habits, the mind must preserve its imperial self-sufficiency. What Auden wants is both absolute isolation and absolute community, one for the mind, the other for the flesh. For the moment his double wish is a personal one. But in his essay on "Writing" he will also attribute it, although with a greater sense of its futility, to language itself—language that stands in violent opposition to its objects while at the same time it tries to recover the unity that body enjoyed before language occurred.

The spirit of D. H. Lawrence walks heavily among these journal entries. Auden condemns the "heresy" of "Unitarianism," which denies that any distinction between mind and body really exists. This heresy can take two forms, either the effort of "Pagans . . . to convert mind into body," resulting in madness or apathy, or the effort of Christendom to "turn body into mind" by subjecting it to ideal standards, an effort that results only in disease. Our real development is toward dualism, but our "second error," after Unitarianism, is that "we have tried to develop . . . in the wrong direction":

We have tried to make the body more and more individualistic (Hygiene) and the mind more and more communistic (Newspapers). The result being that on the one hand we lose the capacity to love and on the other we lose the capacity to think. The love of one's neighbour is a bodily, a blood relationship, the development of the mind is one

more and more of differentiation, individualistic, away from nature. . . .

"It is the body's job to make," he concludes, "the mind's to destroy."
And the importance of the sexual act is that it performs both these tasks
at once. In sex there is "a mixture of mind destroying itself and body
making itself. To body, the child is more body like itself, the assurance
of body's immortality; to mind, the child is new mind, hostile to itself,
the assurance of the destruction of its ideas."

These evolutionary doctrines provided Auden with the basis—or the
excuse—for a literary theory he had been developing since his first year
at Oxford. He set out the theory in detail in his 1929 journal, especially
in the entry in which he predicts that "we are reaching the point in the
development of the mind where symbols are becoming obsolete in poetry, as the true mind, or non-communistic self does not think in this
way."* Before he had published a line outside school and university
magazines, Auden was advancing a literary project that, if followed exactly, would make it new with a vengeance. After sufficing for three
thousand years, the symbolic method must go; the mind was satiated
with symbols and was now undergoing a mutation that would lead it to
the free play of abstractions. Poetry would no longer imitate or instruct.
"The essence of creation," he wrote in another entry, "is doing things
for no reason; it is pointless."

In practical matters of poetic craft, this program required Auden to
favor abstract ideas over concrete metaphors and to concentrate on syntactic ingenuity rather than imagistic epiphanies. In his 1929 journal he
contrasted "Three types of verbal dexterity:"

A. α) The picked word.	*Antres vast and deserts idle.*
β) Rhyme discoveries.	*Your head would have achèd*
	To see her naked.
B. The manipulation of common	*Where you would not, lie you*
abstract words.	*must.*
	Lie you must, but not with me.

B is the rarest and means the most to me I think. There is always something exhibitionistic, and Society for Pure English about Aα. But what a
temptation, and how satisfied one is with oneself when one does it.

---

* This entry is quoted in full in Chapter I, p. 11.

But his rhetoric and examples demolish his intended argument. Stating his preference for abstraction, he appends a hesitant "I think"; and he does not hesitate to report the satisfactions of the style he hopes to reject. His choice of examples may have shown him how little he wanted to reject it. His "picked words" are from Shakespeare (the rhyme discoveries are from Skelton), but for abstract manipulations he descends to A. E. Housman when he could easily have found examples in Shakespeare's sonnets. His schema makes a large implicit claim for historical progress from the sixteenth to the twentieth century, but it undercuts the claim with examples that demonstrate historical decline. Auden did ascend into the realm of abstractions to write some spare stringent poems during the spring of 1929—"Love by ambition," "Before this loved one"—but he found the atmosphere too rarefied to sustain his ambitions for long.

↩

> Coming out of me living is always thinking,
> Thinking changing and changing living . . .

Thus Auden characterized himself in a poem written in the spring of 1929. His "living" was a life of thought, constantly changing into new thought, which for him was new life. This was not, he argued, a retreat from real life into illusion. In his journal, at the same time, he dismissed the whole question of art *versus* life: "To me writing is the enjoyment of the living."* The glut of gerunds and participles in both poem and journal results from Auden's early enthusiasm for Gertrude Stein, but his theory of perception is virtually the same as Wordsworth's. His memories of past sensations give rise to his feelings in the present: "*Am* feeling as it *was* seeing," he continues in the poem. And the theme of the poem, as of the speculative entries in his journal, is the romantic theme of the relation between nature and mind.

This poem is the second of four, all in a loose blank-verse line, which Auden wrote as separate poems during 1929 but reworked, probably

---

* The journal itself illustrated his theory. Although the entries for the first few weeks appear in the form of a diary, they were demonstrably written out at the end of the period they cover, as a literary reconstruction of past events. Auden did not know at the time that Boswell had used the same technique in writing out his journals two centuries before.

late in the year, as four parts of a single poem. The full text is familiar under its later title "1929" and begins: "It was Easter as I walked in the public gardens." Auden thought enough of it to make it the centerpiece of the 1930 and 1933 editions of *Poems*, the sixteenth poem in each sequence of thirty. Critics have assumed it to be unified and consistent, but this assumption has led to interpretive difficulties. The poem is grandiose and expansive in a manner new to Auden's work, but it is torn between two contradictory arguments, one based on the theory of weaning which Auden held early in 1929, the other based on the theory of drowning he adopted later in the year. The first two parts of the poem conform to the first theory; the fourth part to the second theory; while the transitional third part exists in two versions, the manuscript supporting the first theory, the published text the second.

The first two parts, written in April and May, illustrate the journal entries Auden was writing at the same time. Here again, the mind's weaning from nature is still incomplete, and consciousness feels nostalgia for the world it is leaving behind. The poet of the second poem is a "homesick foreigner" in both national and evolutionary senses. He watches from his customary superior position, this time on a harbor parapet, as a colony of ducks floats on the water beneath him. Unlike the poet, these simpler products of evolution

> find sun's luxury enough,
> Shadow know not of homesick foreigner
> Nor restlessness of intercepted growth.

In context this last line refers to the mind's disturbingly incomplete separation into its solitary independent life, but Auden derived the line from a very different context in a book by Trigant Burrow, *The Social Basis of Consciousness* (1927). Burrow, like Lane, insists that impulse must not be intercepted by repression, but he extends this argument to include the whole social organism: "Seen clearly, man's restlessness today is, after all, the restlessness of intercepted growth. The tremors we are experiencing at this moment throughout the political and economic world undoubtedly owe their impulse to the awakening of a new order of consciousness."

Burrow goes on to predict an "overwhelming disruption of the social personality," through, he implies, a second world war far more destructive than the first. Auden takes this up in the next lines of his poem:

All this time was anxiety at night,
Shooting and barricade in street.
Walking home late I listened to a friend
Talking excitedly of final war
Of proletariat against police . . .

The poem makes no move to embrace this socially apocalyptic future. The lines refer to the battles between communists and police that began on May Day 1929 in Berlin and continued for almost a week, not far from where Auden was staying. Yet he did not think the matter important enough to mention in his journal (which he was keeping only intermittently by this time), where the sole reference to the working classes during the following weeks is his approval of them as drinking and sleeping companions. As for the revolution, in his poem he will not even discuss it.* He listens to his friend talk of the brutality of the police, "Till I was angry [with the friend], said I was pleased [to squelch him]." This line is normally read differently, as a statement of Auden's anger at the police and his pleasure at the prospect of revolution; but the poem does not report that he *was* pleased, it reports that he *said* he was pleased--and a constant burden of Auden's early work is the gulf between manifest speech and hidden thought. For the moment, his interest is not in the common world of social change but in a strictly private development of the life of the mind, and he quotes from Trigant Burrow while diverging from Burrow's argument. A few months later he will return to it.

Now, however, he dismisses his friend's vision of final war to turn to his own account of the growth of consciousness. He begins with the differentiation of birth, when the baby, having been "still mother" in the womb "now is other . . . himself no friend." Man's mind is alone in his flesh, he is estranged from himself, and "unforgiving is in his living." Sex cannot break his loneliness: "Body reminds in him to loving, / Reminds but takes no further part"—as a journal entry calls the sex act merely "a symbol for intimacy." The only unity Auden can imagine in

---

* Two months before he had alluded in another poem ("Under boughs between our tentative endearments") to his generation's ignorance of, among other things, "What industries decline, what chances are of revolution." He did not suggest these matters were therefore important: the poem's subject was the ancestral curse whose power is independent of economic and political change.

the poem or in most of his journal entries is a romantic unity in the perceiving mind:

> Yet sometimes man look and say good*
> At strict beauty of locomotive,
> Completeness of gesture or unclouded eye;
> In me so absolute unity of evening
> And field and distance was in me for peace . . .

For a moment this unity of perception offers peace and forgiveness, and
Auden is undisturbed that his forgiveness is self-forgiveness only. He
can live in peace with his memories of failure and his knowledge of nature's distance because his Wordsworthian moments are intimations of a
free new life of the mind. The unity of evening

> Was over me in feeling without forgetting
> Those ducks' indifference, that friend [Layard]'s hysteria,
> Without wishing and with forgiving,
> To love my life, not as other,
> Not as bird's life, not as child's,
> "Cannot," I said, "being no child now nor a bird."

The life of the mind, where living is always thinking, must forgive the
body for its indifference and be glad of its own mature isolation. The
mind may look through its windows to the world outside, but it must
leave those windows shut.

One of the barriers Auden accepts for the mind is the barrier of diction. The very odd grammar Auden uses in some passages of this poem
may seem arbitrary, but it illustrates his historical argument. The absolutely uninflected verbs in a phrase like "man look and say good," verbs
whose forms are unaffected by tense, number, or person, signify a new
mutation in the evolution of language. Verb forms tend to simplify as
older languages develop into newer ones; Modern English has reached a
highly advanced stage, and few inflections in its verbs and nouns still
remain.† The poem proposes the next logical step. Where Joyce had sat-
irized a chaotic future English in the last paragraphs of the "Oxen of the

---

* Good is not an illiterate substitute for the adverb well; it is what the man says. In
one manuscript the phrase reads: "man look and say 'good.' "
† Auden referred to this evolution in his essay on "Writing."

Sun" chapter in *Ulysses*, Auden uses the new forms "without wishing and with forgiving." As with other aspects of evolutionary change, he is disturbed less by the change itself than by its present incompleteness. Thus his diction in the poem varies, depending on whether he is writing from a communicating self that narrates his recollections in verbs close to those of Modern English, or whether the poem is quoting the thoughts of a "non-communistic self" that is more advanced in development and so uses almost no inflections at all. The grammatical inconsistencies are a result of the insufficient weaning that is the subject of the poem itself.

Auden's evolutionary theories have poetic as well as linguistic consequences, which he raises explicitly in the unpublished manuscript version of the first of the "1929" poems. The manuscript—the verse letter to Isherwood discussed briefly in Chapter II—dedicates to Isherwood the play Auden was then beginning to write.* In his journal Auden wrote that he did not want "any characters, any ideas in my play, but stage-life, something which is no imitation but a new thing."† So, in lines that only partially survived in the published version, Auden describes the origins of the play's stage-life, origins that are obscured by the mutated form of the play:

> Out of the common incidents of life
> And individual strength or weakness
> With general commentary upon their nature
> A work of art must have its genesis.
> So this play has its living origins:
> The death from cancer of a once hated master,
> A friend's analysis of his own failure . . .
> Always with success of others for comparison,
> The happiness, for instance, of my friend Kurt Groote
> Absence of fear in Gerhart Meyer
> Young, from the sea, the truly strong man.

The play's new life is an analogue of spring's awakening, "Season when lovers and writers find / An altering speech for altering things." And al-

* The play's first title was *The Reformatory;* it was completed in collaboration with Isherwood as *The Enemies of a Bishop*. See Chapter XII.
† This, like the entry quoted on p. 11, inverts Yeats's essay "The Symbolism of Poetry." All artists, Yeats wrote, have "sought for no new thing . . . but only to understand and to copy the pure inspiration of early times . . ."

though Auden's green thoughts inevitably turn, "forced by the feeling of identification" (in the manuscript text), to memories of death and failure, these only remind him of what he, his play, and the spring must leave behind: "all of those whose death / Is necessary condition of the season's setting forth." Like his sailor friend who emerges "Young, from the sea," he and his play must be weaned from the past.

There is in all this a faintly unpleasant whiff of Strength Through Joy, mitigated by one's sense that Auden is trying to make himself believe something he cannot. He had spent the preceding year detailing the persistence of the ancestral curse in the young who think they can "sheer off from old like gull from granite." Now he hoped to attain the same newness through self-forgiveness and unity of perception, although he knew he had little chance of success. By the time he wrote the third of the "1929" poems, in August, after his return to England from Berlin, he was still hoping to be weaned, but his tone had changed, and he added an ominous suggestion that death, not independence, was the only possible step that remained in his development.

This third poem moves both toward home and away from it. As the poet makes his physical return to his family's summer cottage and "the frightened soul" returns to the natural "life of sheep and hay / No longer his," his psychological movement is in the opposite direction, away from nature and family:

> he every hour
> Moves further from this and must so move,
> As child is weaned from his mother and leaves home . . .

"But taking the first steps," he "falters, is vexed." His departure is a painful one, burdened by "the difficult work of mourning" his lost unity. Yet there is hope for a new life:

> as foreign settlers to strange country come,
> By mispronunciation of native words
> And by intermarriage create a new race
> And a new language, so may the soul
> Be weaned at last to independent delight.

At this point, however, the poem steps back to contemplate mysteries it has not yet taken into account. There may be more to the future life than the soul's independent delight. In the manuscript text the final

verse paragraph moves from the excitement of solitary consciousness—
the "tireless excitement of verbal manipulation" that brought the poem
itself into being—toward a very different mental life, the unconscious
and unchosen life of dreams. And dreams may point to something that
solitary consciousness can never comprehend:

> Startled by the violent cry of a jay
> I turned.indoors to compose these verses
> For tireless excitement of verbal manipulation . . .
> Composed them, scattered the embers of the fire
> And climbed the stairs to a dreaming sleep,
> That curious criticism of the day's actions,
> Or, as it may be, a desire of Nature's,
> Her kindly forethought that we find ourselves at death
> Not helplessly strange to the new conditions.

Auden lifted this final line from J. W. Dunne's *An Experiment with
Time* (1927), a book concerned with dream prescience as, among other
things, a preparation for death. Dunne continues almost buoyantly:
"And we must die before we can hope to advance to a broader understanding." The thought of death led Auden to borrow the elegiac tones
(later muted for the published text) of Yeats's "In Memory of Major
Robert Gregory," but, more important, these lines contain the first suggestion in Auden's work that there is something to be learned from unconscious nature that a free mental life cannot provide on its own: dream
prescience may be Nature's kindly forethought. Auden's conviction that
he must divorce his mind absolutely from nature has evidently been
shaken. Soon it will collapse entirely.

Up to now I have been emphasizing Auden's project of division from
nature. But a contradictory project, a movement toward dissolution *in*
nature, was quietly taking shape in his work at the same time. In the
midst of his celebrations of division he also began to denounce it. He
was able to hold these diametrically opposed positions because he used a
different set of metaphors in writing about each. Whenever he promoted
division, as in the argument described in the past few pages, he used
evolutionary and biological metaphors. When he attacked division he
turned to religious metaphors instead. Thus, among his meditations on

weaning in his 1929 journal, this Blakean intrusion occurs: "*Humanism:*
Will never do since it believes that the duality of the Higher and Lower
will is inevitable and desirable. This dualism is the result of the Fall, i.e.
the dissociated consciousness of man. We can only live properly when
this fissure is repaired." In another notebook later the same year, he gave
a revised account of the division between body and mind, using a new
set of metaphors: "Body and mind are distinct but neither can exist
alone, nor is there rightly a rivalry between them. Attempts to turn
body into mind (Manichaeism) or mind into body (Arianism) lead to
disease, madness, and death." When he exalted division he had used
Newspapers and Hygiene as parenthetical illustrations rather than
Christian heresies.

The same notebook makes an elaborate equation of the language of
religion and the language of psychology (both Freudian and Lawrentian) in the form of a travellers' phrase book:

Glossary of Christian and Psychological terms

Heaven		The Unconscious	
Earth		The Conscious Mind	
Hell		The repressed unconscious	
Purgatory		The consulting-room	
The Father	{Body?	The Ego-instincts	The self ideal
The Son	{Mind?	The Death-instincts	The Not-self ideal
The Holy Ghost		The Libido	The relation between these two opposites
The Madonna		Nature	
The Four Archangels		The four great ganglia of the body	
Satan		The Censor	
The Devils		The repressed instincts	
Hell-Fire		Unhappiness, disease, and mania	
The Fall of Man		The advent of self-consciousness	
. . .		. . .	

And in his review for *The Criterion*, April 1930, based in part on this
notebook, he again uses Christian metaphors to flail duality:

> The reason is an instrument, and cannot of itself control or inhibit
> anything; what it can do is cause one desire to modify another. . . .

Dual conceptions, of a higher and lower self, of instinct and reason, are only too apt to lead to the inhibition rather than the development of desires, to their underground survival in immature forms. . . . That which desires life to itself, be it individual, habit, or reason, casts itself, like Lucifer, out of heaven.

The dual conception of "instinct and reason" that he condemns in print (in sentences that show him very much in search of a prose style) is not readily distinguishable from the dual conception of habit and thought he had been promoting in his notebooks. Concealed behind the variant metaphors is a major contradiction. He is arguing two opposed positions, and he does so even in this review, where the sentences that set out to deny the dual conception of *higher* and *lower* include metaphors like *underground* and *cast out of heaven*, which covertly reaffirm it.

At the close of the first of the "1929" poems, written in April, the individual act of choice seemed "a necessary error"—etymologically, a wandering away from unconscious nature, after which there could be no turning back. By the time Auden wrote the fourth poem, in October, he had resolved his mixed feelings by abandoning all hope for an independent mental life. It was "time for the destruction of error." Now he saw the sad end of differentiated existence: "The account of growing, the history of knowing" ends with

> Living together in wretched weather
> In a doorless room in a leaking house,
> Wrong friends at the wrong time

—Gerontion's house, not much improved by the rainy season.

Now Auden's goal is a new unity and a new love. This needs more than growth and knowledge, more than the meeting of two bodies and the satisfied withdrawal of the mind afterward—

> Needs more than the admiring excitement of union,
> More than the abrupt self-confident farewell.

What love requires is the thorough loss of the self in death, the "death of the grain," which Auden was more likely to have taken from Gide than from Paul. Love needs the death not only of Auden's seigneurial self but of all who share his pride. Love

> would leave them
> In sullen valley [i.e. the grave] where is made no friend,
> The old gang to be forgotten in the spring,
> The hard bitch and the riding-master,
> Stiff underground; deep in clear lake
> The lolling bridegroom, beautiful, there.

In these lines Auden follows Trigant Burrow to the point where he had refused to follow earlier. In May he quoted Burrow on intercepted growth, but ignored Burrow's call a page or two later in the book for "the recognition of our collective unconsciousness." But now, in October, he senses a global warning in the autumn air. The apocalypse Burrow predicted is about to occur in all its transforming fury:

> In sanitoriums they laugh less and less,
> Less certain of cure . . .
> The falling leaves know it, the children,
> At play on the fuming alkali-tip
> Or by the flooded football ground, know it—
> This is the dragon's day, the devourer's:
> Orders are given to the enemy for a time . . .
> To haunt the poisoned in his shunned house,
> To destroy the efflorescence of the flesh,
> The intricate play of the mind, to enforce
> Conformity with the orthodox bone . . .

This is no final war of proletariat against police but a psychological apocalypse in which the dragon, the devourer, and the enemy are figures only slightly updated from the Book of Revelation.

Not long after writing this fourth poem Auden went back and revised the last verse paragraph of the third. He threw out all references to conscious thought and unconscious dream. Now the forethought of death's new conditions was no gift of nature to a solitary dreamer, but a warning of global transformation:

> Startled by the violent laugh of a jay
> I went from wood, from crunch underfoot . . .
> As I shall leave the summer, see autumn come . . .
> See frozen buzzard flipped down the weir

And carried out to sea, leave autumn,
See winter, winter for earth and us,
A forethought of death that we may find ourselves at death
Not helplessly strange to the new conditions.

Through this rewriting and some lesser changes elsewhere Auden combined the four poems into a seasonal cycle. He increased their scope and grandeur, but he also raised new problems. The separate poems were each internally consistent, but the sequence as a whole begins with unequivocal hopes for the mind's weaning from nature and ends by calling for the opposite, the mind's dissolution in death. The revised version of the third poem holds both positions in the course of a few lines. And while the full sequence looks forward to the coming spring when the old gang will be forgotten, it says nothing of how the new year might be different. The novelty predicted at the end is contradicted by the recurring seasonal cycle affirmed by the rest of the poem. The urgent rush of images is compelling enough, for most purposes, to rescue the poem from the effects of its internal disorder. But the same irresolution, set in a political context, will have more damaging consequences eight years later in the hortatory stanzas of *Spain*.

The danger signs were already visible in an improbably uplifting poem Auden wrote immediately after finishing the last part of "1929." The poem, which begins, "Which of you waking early and watching daybreak," promises the new spring that was left pending in the earlier poem. It is filled with optimistic equations of beauty and truth, and finds in each new dawn "truth's assurance of life—that darkness shall die . . . Shall bless the new life and die." No death seems to be required of us, and little discomfort. The mental life is no longer isolated; dreams have nothing to do with death. Instead, kindly nature sees to it that through the

immediate day-dream
Or nightly in direct vision the man is nourished,
Fed through the essential artery of memory
Out of the earth the mother of all life.

Now man suffers no evolutionary disjunction, but carries in his veins "all that were living flesh at any time." Of this massive population, all "plead to be born" in man's own fulfillment. Auden is versifying the teachings of Homer Lane as transcribed by his followers and published in *Talks to Parents and Teachers* (1928): "All organic life may be represented as a wish. Man, the highest form of life, is in himself the product of the cumulative wishes of all organic life in past ages. Man is the embodiment of the master-wish for perfecton of the universe, and is therefore essentially good. The motive-power of goodness is love, and love is compulsory." Man's goodness is a product of nature, of whom the poem affirms: "Yes, she is always with him and will sustain him." She offers proof of her presence in pastoral communions "with horses behind a dripping wall" or more directly in orgasm, when man "is one with all flesh." No matter what failures man may witness—as Auden did in the early parts of "1929"—"the dawn of each day is still as a promise . . . Of peace and life, that he despair not." He may look to "security upon earth and life in heaven." It all sounds easy.

Whatever Auden's reasons for writing this wretched poem, he scarcely took it seriously for long. He tried, too late, to have it removed from the proofs of the 1930 *Poems*, and as soon as it was published he called it "pompous trash." Within a month of writing it he had gone on to write two sardonic poems in which nature does not nourish but abandons. Each new stage of evolution approaches neither goodness nor perfection, but is merely an experiment which nature will soon discard in favor of another. The two poems amount to an incomplete dialogue between man and nature: a cry of pain from the one, a dry rebuff from the other.

"It's no use raising a shout," the first of these poems, is the song of a man whom evolution has left behind. Where the badness of Auden's previous poem exposes the failure of its argument, here the gawky doggerel verse is entirely functional. Based probably on a song in the repertory of Sophie Tucker, for whom Auden felt a half-ironic fondness, the poem is affecting and bathetic at once. To express Auden's most painful sense of isolation it borrows the shopworn styles of the popular lyric. The singer is doubly trapped, both in his separation from nature and in his futile escape from his mother. His weaning failed:

> A long time ago I told my mother
> I was leaving home to find another:
> I never answered her letter
> But I never found a better.

The evolution of mind, as D. H. Lawrence warned, has sundered it from
the lower nerve centers:

> In my spine there was a base;
> And I knew the general's face:
> But they've severed all the wires,
> And I can't tell what the general desires.

General puns on the impersonal generalized instincts of the flesh and
the commanding power of instinct which the mind has forgot. "In my
veins there is a wish, / And a memory of fish." So Lane had said; but the
body's wish and memory are no help at all. "I've come a very long way
to prove / No land, no water, and no love." Each stanza ends with the
helpless cry:

> Here am I, here are you:
> But what does it mean? What are we going to do?

In the second poem, "Since you are going to begin to-day," the evolutionary life force itself speaks to man. (Auden later added the flippant
title "Venus Will Now Say a Few Words.") It begins by identifying the
present rulers of the earth, the confident bourgeois who

> climb with bare knees the volcanic hill,
> Acquire that flick of wrist [for tennis] and after strain
> Relax in your darling's arms like a stone . . .

But their satisfactions are illusory:

> joy is mine not yours—to have come so far
> Whose cleverest invention was lately fur;
> Lizards my best once . . .

Omnipotent evolution, and no one else, enjoys freedom to choose and
change. All human action follows evolution's absolute control. The
world is her political prison, we her prisoners:

> For you amusements, feelings at a ball
> Are, could you realise it, as horrible

> As printed statements signed with shaking pen
> Under conditions of extreme pain.

"Nor even is despair your own": it is a sign that evolution is abandoning you, "that I wish to leave and to pass on, / Select another form, perhaps your son." Yet he will come no closer than you to freedom or perfection. For the young as for the old, Venus will be *Venus abscondita*.

> My treatment will not differ—he will be tipped,
> Found weeping, signed for, made to answer, topped.*

To try to escape evolution's powers is merely to confirm the barriers by which it blocks all freedom: "Before you reach the frontier you are caught." And the fate of those who try to escape through space is to be stopped dead in time, "Holders of one position, wrong for years." Auden borrowed this last phrase from an earlier poem he wrote about the futilities of love ("Consider if you will how lovers stand"); in its new setting it indicates the absolute futility of all personal attempts to change.

↩

By the end of 1929 Auden's evolutionary speculations had outgrown the confidence in which they began a few months before. He now saw the mind's treasured autonomy as a painful delusion, the product of an evolutionary power whose influence no consciousness could escape. And he saw the body trapped in the disordered isolation it had stupidly copied from the mind. Where he had looked forward to freedom he now saw abandonment.

One emotional if illogical corollary of this grave vision is a compensating fantasy of a golden age where there was no unhappiness and therefore no wish for freedom or change. The romantic image of the lost age is the innocent child. In one of Auden's poems the intense romanticism at the heart of his earliest work breaks through his clinical and monitory styles to produce this very image of perfection. The poem is "This lunar beauty," at one time titled "*Pur*," written during Auden's first month as a schoolmaster, April 1930. The subject is the unchosen

---

* *Topped* is prison slang meaning *hanged.*

beauty of a schoolchild, a beauty still "complete and early," as yet un-contaminated by family ghosts. This beauty is "lunar," as untouched and virginal as Diana. As yet it "Has no history," and "like a dream / Keeps other time" from ours. Our adult time, in contrast, is that of "the heart's changes / Where ghost has haunted / Lost and wanted," isolated in consciousness. But this childhood beauty "was never / A ghost's en-deavour," not the work of the ghost in the machine, the mind that in adults gives character to the features. Here, until childhood passes, nei-ther love nor sorrow can intrude:

> Love shall not near
> The sweetness here
> Nor sorrow take
> His endless look.

Early and late, Auden denounced Wordsworthian nature-worship as an illusory nostalgia, but here he adopts a thoroughly Wordsworthian worship of a child. It is a Wordsworthian technique, also, to compare the beautiful to a dream, and a romantic assumption that the realm where beauty is truth cannot be altered by those who look in on it. If, in reading this poem, we put aside the pedantic question of how the family ghosts are supposed to restrain themselves until after the child reaches puberty, a question that insists on being asked in an era that sees child-hood through Freudian lenses, the poem succeeds as a masterpiece of crystalline beauty. But it is also one of Auden's first efforts to "refuse the tasks of time" (as he later put it in *The Age of Anxiety*) either by dying out of time or by finding some arcadian locus not yet affected by it. His retraction or palinode of this poem came seven years later, in "Schoolchildren," where, making no attempt at verbal music, he admit-ted bluntly that in every schoolchild "the sex is there, the broken boot-lace is broken"; while the reality beneath his abstract hope for a new life in the young child is that "The professor's dream is not true."

V

Trickster and Tribe

At Oxford Auden maintained that poets should take no interest in politics. Then, in Berlin, when he wrote about society, he did so in biological terms, as if the division of the lower classes from the bourgeoisie were sexual not economic, a result of the evolutionary separation of body from mind. Now, in London in the autumn of 1929, Auden added the social revolutionary to his dramatis personae of healers and apolitical agents, and he began his slow transformation into a public poet.

Auden recognized all along that the social world was stratified, but until he came to London he interpreted the different strata as different degrees of self-consciousness and mental isolation. At the highest level of all was the "tall unwounded leader," who presides over the poem "From scars where kestrels hover," written in Berlin early in 1929. The leader has no politics other than his exile and elevation. He stands alone atop a rocky cliff, "looking over / Into the happy valley" he will never enter. Beneath him on the social scale are his doomed companions—plural not singular—"Fighters for no one's sake, / Who died beyond the border." Unwounded, the leader survives them because he lives in his singular mind and never fights. The evolution of mind has reached the point where isolation is all:

> bravery is now
> Not in the dying breath

> But resisting the temptations
> To skyline operations.

Beneath leader and companions move the sea-level masses of "summer visitors," tourists in the woods of exile, tamely seeking heroes to follow. But when visitors gather, "leaders must migrate: / 'Leave for Cape Wrath to-night.'" This summons sounds dramatic, but the journey is empty, a recollection of a drunken purposeless drive Isherwood once made. Behind the high drama of the leader's journey is an ironic futility. The relations of leader, companions, and masses are summed up in Auden's later title for the poem: "Missing."

Remove the leader from the lonely crags of adolescent fantasy, set him in the civil adult world of money and work, and the drama disappears from his story. Only the ironic futility remains. When Auden came to London in September 1929, after a month or two with his family in Birmingham and the Lake District, he found himself more isolated than he had ever been when standing on a distant fell. He had a twenty-two-year-old's intellectual pride, but no published work to show for it. He lived on his allowance from his parents and had little to do in London beyond some intermittent tutoring. The friendships he made there seem to have been more distant than those he made elsewhere.

The first poem he wrote in London suggests that he arrived with a half-serious fantasy of himself as a secret agent behind enemy lines. This fantasy the poem proceeds to demolish. The poem is addressed to the poet, giving him his agent's orders; but the orders are all in the form of questions and warnings. The first stanza turns away from a border, away from even a futile hope of change, and refuses to hear the words of those who escaped to sea:

> Will you turn a deaf ear
> To what they said on the shore,
> Interrogate their poises
> In their rich houses . . . ?

Will you, the poem asks, live as a spy, but have no purpose for your spying? For the first time, Auden's secret agent feels revolutionary sympathies, which he keeps secret from the wealthy he lives among. But he *does* nothing. Will you examine their acts and gestures, the poem asks, but do this passively—carry no "bombs of conspiracy / In arm-pit secrecy"? Will you serve as companion to the personified "death" who rules here, wheel him "anywhere / In his invalid chair"?* You will take no action of your own, will only serve death and, chameleon-like, take on the coloring of your surroundings—"Salute with soldiers' wives / When the flag waves," hard as this may be. As an agent you will have no power of agency, no occasion for pride. "Hard to be superior," when one's exile is rewarded with

> No recognised gift for this;
> No income, no bounty,
> No promised country

—nothing to give comfort but the sight of others' defeat, the death of those who struggle, and the chilling triumph of entropy in "cold's victorious wrestle / With molten metal."

Will you question their poises? the poem asked at the start. Auden later added a title from Blake: "The Questioner Who Sits So Sly"—and who, as Blake continued, shall be silent by and by.

What is especially unsettling about this poem is that its subject, the figure it addresses, is absolutely faceless and anonymous. As he does nothing, he communicates nothing. His doom is "Never to make signs." The poem itself is equally uncommunicative. It does not in fact predict that "you" will be subservient to those around you, will act only in imitation of their actions; it affirms nothing at all, restricting itself to the interrogative and conditional moods. Will you do *x*? it asks. Hard to do *y*, it warns. All Auden can communicate in this ironic self-portrait is his own invisibility, his own poetic refusal to communicate. In his essay on "Writing" two years later, he will describe written language as an attempt to bridge a gap in time, an attempt made because people "feel alone, cut off from each other in an indifferent world where they do not live for very long." In writing this poem he does not even make the attempt. Instead of communicating with a reader, the poem leaves a record of isolation and failure for the reader to discover as one might discover

---

* Auden's tactless allusion to the husband of one of his London hostesses: an army colonel, paralyzed from the waist down. I don't know why death's "anecdotes betray / His favorite colour as blue" in this poem; perhaps because it is the color of recent corpses.

an archaeological relic. The only success the poem predicts—in its one
straightforward indicative statement—is the success felt by its reader:

> A neutralising peace
> And an average disgrace
> Are honour to discover
> For later other.

When Auden compiled *Poems* in 1930 for publication he placed this
poem at the start of the book,* as a rebuke to his literary and personal
isolation. Nothing that followed it could answer this rebuke. Instead, at
the close of the volume, in the poem that he wrote immediately after
"Will you turn a deaf ear," he appealed to some external agency to impose from without the change he could not make from within. "Sir, no
man's enemy," it begins, addressing a distant ambiguous deity, like the
watcher in the dark in *Paid on Both Sides*—here addressed as Sir for
strictly literary reasons, in imitation of the religious language of Gerard
Manley Hopkins. This deity is a convenient fiction, defined by his ability to clear up all the problems that Auden found insoluble. The poem
calls on him to cure the "exhaustion of weaning" into independent life,
to make those "in retreat" to a backward love turn forward again. He is
to "Harrow the house of the dead," in imitation of Christ, with the purpose of defeating the family ghosts. Like an electric generator he is to
send "power and light"—with a private pun on Auden's erotic use of the
word *power*. And he will accomplish what Homer Lane had promised
one's own impulse could achieve: a cure for the intolerable neural itch,
the liar's quinsy, the distortions of ingrown virginity, an end to the habitual "rehearsed response." For an embodiment of unrepressed impulse
and healing love, he seems a curiously authoritarian figure—prohib-
iting, correcting, covering with beams as if from a watchtower. The
poem in which Auden addresses him is less a prayer than a logical and
ironic exercise. The imitation of Hopkins is a matter of rhetoric not belief, and the deity invoked is unlikely to offer much comfort in the real
world. The psychological apocalypse Auden evoked a few weeks later at
the end of the "1929" sequence was unlikely to do any better.

But during this autumn, when most of his poems were reporting the

---

* *Paid on Both Sides*, which precedes it in published copies, was added at the last
minute, after bound proof copies had already been prepared.

ironic indifference of evolution, Auden made one brief oblique approach to more political matters. The poem "To have found a place for nowhere" opens with a summary account of colonialism: "the creation / Of nation from nation" by settlers who

> come
> With girls and guns
> And letters home,
> Turn vantage spots
> To neighbour plots
> While wards and banks
> Give many thanks.

The poem is quick to diverge from this into more familiar psychological territory: the border journey to "Cross any Alp"; the ancestral curse that leaves each heir "With loathing remembrance / And a growing resemblance"; and the repression of change by habit, "putting the unoccurred / Upon its word." This perfunctory little poem, which perhaps was prompted by a colonial among Auden's London circle, survived only into the 1930 *Poems* before he discarded it. But for the first time in his work he had bracketed neurosis and capitalism, "wards and banks," as he would continue to do throughout the 1930s. It was only a matter of time before he would bracket the two great healers, Freud and Marx.

After this one brief allusion, he wrote nothing more about such matters while he stayed in London. He took his first large step toward the fields of political economy in poems he wrote after returning to his family home in Birmingham early in 1930. In an abrupt change in his poetic language, he enlarged his vocabulary to accommodate a wide range of contemporary objects, the bric-à-brac of the twentieth century. Where all his earlier poems together had stocked only a few items of recent manufacture—motorcars, searchlights, drinks called "sidecar" and "C.P.S."—he added in the space of two poems written in March and April 1930 a helmeted airman, arterial roads, typists, power stations, pylons, high tension wires, motor-bicycles, chain-smoking, electric signs, sunbathing, holiday and prisoner-of-war camps, "monster stores," and, by name, Freud, D. H. Lawrence, and Homer Lane. Before this Auden had observed his historical moment with a surgeon's ironic distance. Now he settled in.

The world had changed in the past six months. After the Wall Street crash in October 1929, European industry lost a large portion of its market and credit. Unemployment in Britain, already severe, grew rapidly worse. Each of Auden's up-to-date poems, "Consider this and in our time" and "Get there if you can and see the land you once were proud to own," threatens global disaster. It is later than you think, warns the first; are we done for? asks the second. Each poem acknowledges the political aspects of the approaching crisis, and each acknowledges economics by alluding to the distance between places where money is made and where it is spent. But in writing these poems Auden lays claims to the crisis as a proper subject for psychological analysis and cure, as if he intended to rescue political problems from the political mind. The climate in both poems is tense with social disorder and economic alienation, but the inevitable cataclysm predicted by the first, and the potential cure demanded by the second, are psychological in nature.

"Consider this" opens in flight over the rich in mountain hotels and farmers on stormy fens. Their social classes are isolated from each other, and each is isolated from the inner life, "Supplied with feelings by an efficient band" heard on the wireless. This divisive time is ripe for a great upheaval, a psychological night of the long knives. Now is the time for the triumph of the *inner* enemy, the "supreme Antagonist" who personifies the fears and repressions that oppose love. The Antagonist had always found victims, but in this stalled landscape of late capitalism, with its silted harbors and derelict works, there is no defence against his epidemic,

> Which, spreading magnified, shall come to be
> A polar peril, a prodigious alarm,
> Scattering the people, as torn-up paper
> Rags and utensils in a sudden gust,
> Seized with immeasurable neurotic dread.

As the people are doomed, so is the ruling class. "Financier, leaving your little room," dons, clergy, hedonists, "The game is up for you and for the others." There is no escape beyond the border, "Not though you pack to leave within an hour," for your fate is

> To disintegrate on an instant in the explosion of mania
> Or lapse for ever into a classic fatigue.

After finishing this poem Auden compiled what he called "a text book of Psychology in doggerel verses," a group of some twenty squibs on personal neurosis he had written during the previous year. (Examples: "The friends of the born nurse / Are always getting worse." "Nothing-to-do / Works all day through.")* He seems to have been clearing his desk of personal matters in order to make room for public ones.

In the next poem he wrote, in April 1930, the crisis of the moment manifests itself as economic ruin and social alienation:

Get there if you can and see the land you once were proud to own
Though the roads have almost vanished and the expresses never run . . .

Far from there we spent the money, thinking we could well afford,
While they quietly undersold us with their cheaper trade abroad . . .

"Have things gone too far already?" Must we wait and

listen for the crash
Meaning that the mob has realised something's up, and start to smash;

Engine-drivers with their oil-cans, factory girls in overalls
Blowing sky-high monster stores, destroying intellectuals?

But the poetic form in which Auden heralds these political urgencies casts doubt on the prospects for a political solution. The "Locksley Hall" stanza serves to remind us that almost a century after Tennyson's prediction the Parliament of Man has not yet convened. Something outside politics will be needed to cure the world's disorder. Although at twenty-three Auden did not say what might accomplish this, he made it clear that the cure for the political symptoms would be personal and psychological. Those who might have helped cure us are lost:

Lawrence was brought down by smut-hounds, Blake went dotty as
he sang,
Homer Lane was killed in action by the Twickenham Baptist gang.

---

* He compiled, under the title "Case-Histories," the ones that were not too obscene to be published, and submitted them to *The Adelphi*. The magazine printed two small samplings in July and December 1931, after Auden had apparently lost interest in them. As he wrote to Isherwood: "I agree about the Adelphi but it was not altogether my fault. I sent the swine about 20 of those things a year ago, and heard nothing from them; and forgot about them till they suddenly sent me the magazine."

Now we need more than the healer's hand. To keep the mob from gathering, to keep the drivers at their engines and the girls in their factories, we must—the prescription is breathtakingly implausible—cure ourselves:

> Drop those priggish ways for ever, stop behaving like a stone:
> Throw the bath-chairs right away, and learn to leave ourselves alone.
>
> If we really want to live, we'd better start at once to try;
> If we don't it doesn't matter, but we'd better start to die.

This tautological cadence, after the superficial tones of the rest of the poem, suggests Auden's unease with his subject. He had now acknowledged that there were problems more serious than solitary neurosis, and having admitted public issues into his poetry he could not get them out again. If he had no cure for himself, what could he offer others? In an unpublished song (probably for the lost play *The Fronny*), a few months later, he surveyed the ordinary life of the English in seven dry repetitive stanzas, with disturbing off-rhymes—

> I saw them stoop in workshops
> I saw them drink in clubs
> I saw them wash for meetings
> I saw them pay for cabs

—until, in a final couplet, he picked up his hat to walk away from a diseased nation whose healer was yet to appear:

> I saw them and said as I took my hat
> "No doctor in England can cure all that."

In three years Auden had exhausted most of his precocious hopes for satisfaction in the lonely mind or the unconscious body or some vague evolutionary future. Now, gradually, he began thinking in very different terms. Where once he wavered between isolation or dissolution, weaning or drowning, he now sought unity in a world where other selves were as real as his own. Where once he had rejected the past as a malevolent prison, now he sought to remember the truths of history.

With personal humility came poetic strength. An ethical dimension gradually deepened and transformed a world he had once understood in terms of free impulse and dead constraint. At first he could only frame these matters in rhetorical questions or invocations of hope; he would secure them in the indicative mood later.

The change began with a change in vocabulary. Two poems Auden wrote during the summer of 1930 use, without irony, words like *restore, remember, recover, return*. The magnificent prayer for the wanderer in the last lines of "Doom is dark" would have been unthinkable in earlier poems:

> Bring joy, bring day of his returning,
> Lucky with day approaching, with leaning dawn.

The wanderer has been dreaming of home and the spread of welcome. For the first time, Auden dreams of these things also.

Knowing the sterile limits of the mind's free creative play, he hopes to revive memory instead. Trapped in a continuous present, he looks back for help. Another poem written this summer opens: "To ask the hard question is simple." The mind's proud challenge to the world outside is in fact an evasion. In the failed sexual relations to which the poem alludes, "The ears listening / To words at meeting" and "The eyes looking / At the hands helping" are dissociated from what they perceive. To the isolated mind the physical world of sound and sense has become a world of mere objects—words and hands without purpose or meaning—and so the senses "Are never sure / Of what they learn." It is this mental isolation that "Makes forgetting easy," as the mind absorbs no significant detail and knows only the fact of its own consciousness: "Only remembering the method of remembering." As two lines from a manuscript version of the poem put it: asking the hard question "Is beginning history easily / Without history to recall." The mind, self-enclosed, can recognize nothing but its inadequate fictions, and remembers "Only the strangely exciting lie."

In this poem Auden identifies the ethical and emotional consequences of the privacy he has not overcome. The mind is "Afraid" to remember the real knowledge it has lost through evolution, that physical knowledge that is still directly accessible to sheep, bird, and fish in the three realms of earth, air, and water. Lacking a real subject, the mind is not, as it had thought, free at all. It is forced to repeat the divisive past it has unwittingly inherited, and "ghosts must do again / What gives them pain." The results are "Cowardice," "Coldness," and a lost drifting "Obedience" that cries for a master. Here in summary is Auden's account of what he would soon call "the failure of the romantic conception of personality": a personality obsessed with its own fictions, alienated from nature, proclaiming freedom while crying for a master.

Where the romantic personality was—this poem hopes—there love shall be. In rhetorical questions, forceful in tone, tentative in assertion, the poem asks if memory of the real past can make possible a real meeting in the present. "Shall memory restore ... The face and the meeting place"? "Can love remember / The question and the answer"? And can memory, for the sake of love, "recover / What has been dark and rich and warm all over?"

Like Forster's Margaret, he would connect; like Woolf's Clarissa, he must assemble. But the political issues Auden had raised prevented him from closing his circle, as Bloomsbury had done, around his own social and intellectual class. He wanted a wider unity-in-diversity, and during the next two years he would hope to find it in what he called the group.

Given the problems he had set himself and his characteristic patterns of thought, as well as the climate of the times, it was almost inevitable that Auden should turn to the group as an answer to his isolation. He always preferred to think in terms both archaic and contemporary. Freud had recently identified the primal horde, the band of brothers, as the earliest form of human society; and the group had emerged as the unit of the newest political moments, in the form of Communist or Fascist cells and in the Oxford Groups of the 1920s. Auden had already made a glancing allusion to the companions of a tall unwounded leader. Now he returned to them for a closer look.

A group requires a language common and also special to those within it, a language that gathers the group within its own borders and excludes those outside. Auden had earlier tried to find the abstract language that would be appropriate to the private acts of the mind. He now sought the different language that might constitute a group. But the companions of the tall unwounded leader were doomed companions, and the language Auden found was the language by which groups fail.

The Orators, the long poem that included most of Auden's work from the autumn of 1930 to the autumn of 1931, is an account of everything a group ought not to be. It is also a study of language, a transcript of the rhetorics that make a group coalesce and decay. Auden began it as a deliberately negative vision of groups, but as he worked on it, and after he published it, he came to recognize that he had favored his negative vision more than he thought, and not simply because he could find no alternative. The failed group focused on a leader, and Auden was reluctant to give up the privileges of the seigneurial mind. He set out to write a satiric attack, but *The Orators* chose to be written differently. Its bafflingly elusive tone emerged in part from the divisions Auden recognized in himself only while he was writing it. He would write greater books when he learned to live with these divisions, but *The Orators*, which he later called "a case of the fair notion fatally injured," has a pungency and extravagance that he never equalled.

The title *The Orators* indicates how far Auden's attention had shifted from the noncommunicative poetry of his 1929 journal to the effects of language on its audience. The book is subtitled "An English Study," and while the adjective refers to both the language and the nation, it applies best to the English language; most of the book's imaginative landscape is Scottish. What is consistent between Auden the self-enclosed literary artist of 1929 and his orators in 1931 is that they are all isolated: the orators are isolated even as they communicate. Their language persuades and compels—even, like family ghosts, retaining its authority after an orator's death—but it does not unite an orator with his audience, and the community it establishes is false.

The form of the work is Auden's invention. It has a Prologue followed by three Books and an Epilogue. The first and third Books are each spoken by a number of different voices in sequence, the second Book by a single voice.* At first Auden seems to have intended to write only the first Book, "The Initiates," which traces the development of a group around a hero and its degeneration after his death. But while writing "The Initiates" Auden got the idea of complementing it with the "Journal of an Airman," the story of the hero told from his own perspective. After writing these two prose Books he then added "Six Odes," which attempt something of a synthesis of them. The whole volume is organized, between its Prologue and Epilogue, as a dialectical triad: a thesis of variously purposeful rhetorics in "The Initiates," an antithesis of pri-

---

* Some ten years after writing *The Orators*, and having dismantled it into separate poems for inclusion in his 1945 *Collected Poetry*, Auden used the same structure for a very different study of oratory and rhetoric, *The Sea and the Mirror*. His only structural change was the inversion of the central sequence, so that the first and third parts are spoken by single voices, the second by a series of voices.

vate noncommunicative notebook entries in the "Journal," and a synthesis in formal odes that are both personal statements and public acts.

To say this is to attribute a precise formal order to a volume whose
surface disorder is its most obvious characteristic. *The Orators* reads
like an expressionist autobiography, and its personal background has
much to do with its curious tone. When his leisure-class season in London, and his allowance from his parents, ended in the early months of
1930, Auden took a job teaching in a rather different setting, Larchfield
Academy at Helensburgh, near Glasgow, a small down-at-heels prepar-
atory school. Auden never felt useful or at home there—as he did at his
second school, the Downs, a few years later. He grew friendly with his
Larchfield colleagues (some have bit parts in *The Orators*), but the atmosphere set by the headmaster, whom Auden and his friends despised,
was not encouraging. The book is the work of a subversive writing from
within: the grand-guignol quality of some of its details, its wild violence
against the established order, may reflect Auden's sense that he could
accomplish nothing more practical than this in reality. His literary
dogma had shifted from the classic austerity of his Oxford years. Now,
as he wrote John Pudney while working on the book, "On the whole I
believe that in our time it is only possible to write comic poetry; not the
Punch variety, but real slapstick."

"The Initiates" takes place in a parody of school, with some details
taken from suburban life; a summer holiday follows in "Journal of an
Airman," with recollections of two weeks Auden spent in a scout camp
in the summer of 1930; finally there is a return to school in the "Six
Odes." Auden uses these three settings to satirize the class that rules a
diseased England, a class whose adult life is trapped in the habits of
childhood. He writes as a domestic anthropologist, portraying his society as the product not of deliberate social choices but of unexamined
mythical beliefs. If an implicit purpose of the book is to bring the nature
of these myths to consciousness that they might be changed, Auden
complicates this by using the book also as a vehicle for self-analysis.
Each of his many fictional orators is in part a portrait of the artist; and
when Auden reread the book after publication he was disconcerted to
find that what he had intended as criticism sounded like an endorse-
ment. His uncertainty of tone and perspective resulted largely from his
indecision about his public role: was he a satiric prophet innocent of the
flaws he exposed, or could he speak only of his personal disorders? After
four years in which he had been diligently widening the gap between

himself and his audience, he could not immediately discover a public rhetoric that might close it up again.

Finally *The Orators* baffled everyone, even its author. Auden's preface to a new edition in 1966 begins:

> As a rule, when I re-read something I wrote when I was younger, I can think myself back into the frame of mind in which I wrote it. *The Orators*, though, defeats me. My name on the title-page seems a pseudonym for someone else, someone talented but near the border of sanity, who might well, in a year or two, become a Nazi.
>
> The literary influences I do remember more or less [Perse, Baudelaire, Ludendorff's *The Coming War*, Lawrence on the unconscious]....
>
> The central theme of *The Orators* seems to be Hero-worship....

It was not only the passage of time that made the book so obscure. Even when he was writing it he seems to have felt it needed more explanation than any of his other work. There is more exposition of *The Orators* in his surviving letters than of anything else he wrote in his English years, possibly in his life. When the book was at the publishers in 1932 he got cold feet over the prospect of launching it without public warnings, and suggested adding this prefatory note:

> I feel this book is more obscure than it ought to be. I'm sorry, for obscurity, as a friend once said to me, is mostly swank. The central theme is a revolutionary hero. The first book describes the effect of him and of his failure on those whom he meets; the second book is his own account; and the last some personal reflections on the question of leadership in our time.

From his editorial desk at Faber & Faber, Eliot, who had experience in such matters, advised Auden not to apologize for obscurity; the preface was dropped. And in the months after the book was published Auden's explanations kept changing in emphasis as his attitude to the public role of poetry altered. More than anything he had written earlier, *The Orators* raised problems he did not know how to resolve, and prompted him to find solutions he would have refused to consider when he began.

The Orators is Auden's only published work that is virtually impenetrable without certain keys. He freely gave those keys to readers who bothered to ask—the book's meaning was never, as some unhappy critics imagine, reserved for Auden's friends, who were as puzzled as anyone—but the keys cannot possibly be deduced from the text alone. This is entirely in keeping with the book's subject. As Auden wrote, both early and late, *The Orators* is about hero-worship. To his followers, the hero seems to offer the missing keystone in the structure of their world; but just as that hero is absent, lost, or defeated, so the key to the book's interpretation is also lost from the book itself, and the text like the group is left fragmented and obscure. The difference between this and Auden's earliest work is that now the key really exists but is absent; then, the key did not exist at all.

The "Prologue" establishes Auden's familiar tension between mother and son, which pervades the work until a prayer to a father just before the end. The story told by "The Initiates" is an anthropological account of a tribal band, more English than aboriginal, located among such contemporary props as aircraft hangars and newspapers, much as the ancient feud in *Paid on Both Sides* is set among mills and bicycle pumps. The point of placing the exotic practices among familiar settings is in both instances the same. In *Paid* the archaic enmities that civilization thinks it has long since abandoned survive with full virulence in the distortions of the modern family, and in *The Orators* the outlandish customs supposedly found only in savage races—the "dance of males" and the cleansing with a "vegetable offering"—recur every day among the English bourgeoisie as field sports and sponge bath. As a savage tribe assures its victory by a war dance in a clearing, so the wars of England are won on the playing fields of Eton. Auden felt no need to search among distant archaic places, as Lawrence did in Mexico, for the primitive mind. It was now and in England.

Auden gave his clearest account of "The Initiates" in a letter to Naomi Mitchison in August 1931:

> In a sense the work is my memorial to Lawrence; i.e. the theme is the failure of the romantic conception of personality; that what it inevitably leads to is part 4 ["Letter to a Wound"].
>
> Formally I am trying to write abstract drama—all the action implied. The four parts, corresponding if you like to the four seasons and the four ages of man (Boyhood, Sturm und Drang, Middleage, Oldage), are stages in the development of the influence of the Hero (who never appears at all).

Thus Part 1. Introduction to influence.
      Part 2. Personally involved with hero. Crisis.
      Part 3. Intellectual reconstruction of Hero's teach-
           ing. The cerebral life.
      Part 4. The effect of Hero's failure on the emotional
           life.
The litany is the chorus to the play.

The tribal band in "The Initiates" clusters round a hero who, as in Auden's earlier poems, proves to be the missing leader of doomed companions. The different rhetorics in the four parts are suited to the different stages in the group's development. Part 1 is an "Address for a Prize-Day." The speaker, an old boy down for the day, with no special responsibility to the initiates gathered before him, analyzes three varieties of privacy that stand in the way of forming a group.* As a warning to the schoolboys in their *rite de passage* he elaborates on Dante's three categories of sinners in Purgatory: those guilty of excessive love toward self or neighbor, of defective love of God, and of perverted love. The first two can be cured and made ready for initiation into the group. The third is irredeemable, "those who never have and never could be loved." These must be cast out, "have got to die without issue"—which is hardly Dante's view of the matter, as all souls in Purgatory are eventually received into Paradise. Also unlike Dante, the prize-day speaker does not think in terms of absolutely free moral choice, but in terms of organic health and disease, the terms Auden preferred at the time. The large subject of the "Address" is the health of "England, this country of ours where nobody is well." Those guilty of defective or excessive love can be cured by their initiation. But the perverted lovers, the lost, are either incurable or, worse, were "never ill," so well-armored against emotion that not even their repressed or deflected impulses have any effect on their surface life. At the end of the "Address" they are put through a fatal parody of initiation, one that will dispose of them entirely. They are the scapegoats whose exclusion, in itself, constitutes the group:

* The opening is Auden's parody of a sermon from his schooldays: "Commemoration. Commemoration. What does it mean? What does it mean? Not what does it mean to them, there, then. What does it mean to us, here now?" In his autobiographical *Lions and Shadows* Isherwood transcribed Auden's spoken rendition of the original sermon: "Sn Edmund's Day.... Sn Edmund's Day.... Whur ders it *mean*? Nert—whur did it mean to *them, then, theah*? Bert—whur ders it mean to *ers, heah, nerw*?"

All these have got to die without issue. Unless my memory fails me
there's a stoke hole under the floor of this hall, the Black Hole we
called it in my day. New boys [earlier initiates] were always put in
it. . . . Well look to it. Quick, guard that door. Stop that man. Good.
Now boys hustle them, ready, steady—go.

What makes this black comedy so unnerving is that the "Address"
also includes, among its grotesqueries and absurdities, some of the same
imaginative analysis of contemporary malaise that Auden was making in
his own voice in his other writings. Auden believed part of what he was
parodying; throughout the 1930s he was both attracted and repelled by
natural metaphors for human disorder, metaphors that implicitly deny
free choice.* But even as he endorsed some aspects of the "Address" he
was also using it to warn against the tendency of oratory, like any devil,
to quote scripture for its purpose. The ultimate appeal of all the orators
in the book is for self-surrender and the abandonment of choice, an appeal that can only succeed if their audience suspends its critical faculty;
and there is no better way to accomplish this than by offering enough
scraps of plausible argument to satisfy the intelligence and put it off
guard.

   And, in fact, by the start of the second part of "The Initiates" the
group has taken in its new self-surrendering members, who have inter-
nalized the initiating arguments they heard in the "Address." This second part, "Argument," is divided into three sections, the first and third
spoken by a single initiate, the second a choral litany spoken by the entire group. The initiate speaks of all the group's acts in reference to the
central hero. Around the leader's name they organize their secret codes
and their linguistic systems of totemic exclusion. They "Speak the name
only with meaning only for us, meaning Him, a call to our clearing."
They gather in a band of brothers, isolated from women, but offer tribute to the maternal powers on which their energy draws.† There is a
"tale of sexual prowess told at a brazier followed by a maternal song."
When they leave on a mission for the hero they leave the women behind:

---

* In a diagram dating from 1929–30 (and reprinted in John Fuller's *A Reader's
Guide to W. H. Auden*, p. 56) Auden gave an unironic version of the prize-day
speaker's three categories of defective love and the corresponding diseases.
† Auden surely observed at school a group's self-identification with its leader and
the libidinous feelings in the group itself, but he found his observations confirmed
by Freud in *Group Psychology and the Analysis of the Ego* and *Totem and Taboo*.

> Girls, it is His will just now that we get up early. . . . When we shuffle
> at night round up-country stoves, although in waders, a dance of
> males, it is your hour. . . . Parting by hangars we are sorry but reborn.

Their tribal life is half a fantasy of exotic adventure ("Interrogation of
villagers before a folding table, a verbal trap"), half a fantastic vision of a
bourgeois family, with the "goggles, a present from aunts" and the crucial departure "down the laurelled drive."

The choral litany in the middle of "Argument" prays for grace to
personifications of the two aspects of the Audenesque group: the solitary hero and the communal gathering. It begins with schoolboy prayers
to the heroes of adventure fantasy ("O Bulldog Drummond, deliver
us"), continues with adult appeals to pubs as meeting places ("O Jack
Straw from your Castle, hear us"), and concludes with all England
praying to a sadly inadequate focus of unity for a diseased nation, the
king: "that it may please thee to calm this people, George, we beseech
thee to hear us." Such are the saviors chosen by the English, the initiates
whom Auden saw in the politically uneasy year 1931 waiting for their
redeeming hero.

All hero-worship ends in what Auden's letter to Naomi Mitchison
calls "Crisis." No secular savior can equal the hopes of his youthful followers. In the final speech of "Argument" this crisis takes the dramatic
form of a betrayal of the leader and the "sudden disaster" of his death.
Now a "witless generation" plays on the steps of his monument, ignoring the inscription. A priest opens his mouth to speak in commemoration, "but the wind is against it." All power gone, the hero subsides into
a dead past.

But not for long. The effect of his initial influence on the group is to
make its members long for the security he offered. Part 3, "Statement,"
opens in a chaos of nostalgia. In the midst of a potentially endless list of
the various "talents" of the group's members, now without any central
order or focus ("One is obeyed by dogs . . . One jumps out of windows
for profit . . . One makes bedsteads"—all the lists in this section are
parodied from the Old English *Exeter Book*), a few sentences intrude of
a fragmentary narrative of the lost hero. His initial "Summon" is recalled, then fragments of his most elementary rules ("Do not listen at
doors," "Always think of the others"), and finally his death, reported by
the telegraph boy who brought death notices of fathers and elder broth-

ers during the Great War: "Have seen the red bicycle leaning on porches and the cancelling out was complete."

The speaker's response to the emotional vacancy left by the hero's absence is to construct a visionary orthodoxy from his teachings. Like all orthodoxies it is largely an adaptation of various traditions of wisdom, many of them used in ways unimaginable to their originators. So "Statement" begins its orthodoxy with a Genesis in the participial style of Gertrude Stein ("An old one is beginning to be two new ones"). It includes a naming of the animals ("Fish is most selfish; snake is most envious") and proverbs out of Blake and the Old English maxims. It continues through a quasi-Levitical code based on Lawrentian primitivism ("The man shall love the work; the woman shall receive him as the divine representative"), organizing society around the aegis of the remembered hero ("The leader shall be a fear"), and setting out the rituals of sacrifice ("The murderer shall be wreathed with flowers; he shall die for the people"). It concludes with a Revelation according to Lawrence, derived from the intimations of apocalyptic immortality in the "Cosmological" chapter of *Fantasia of the Unconscious*. In Lawrence the sun and moon are brought forth from our own deaths; in "Statement" something more obscure happens, with the sun on the right, the moon on the left, and the "action of light on dark" that simply "brings forth."

Yet the hero who gave these counsels is dead. Without his charismatic presence the group must disintegrate. The initiates who were once joined by a common love are now isolated in their loss. The leader's absence replaces the leader himself as the focus of their emotional life. "Letter to a Wound," part 4 of "The Initiates," is addressed by one of their number to the emptiness left in his psyche by the leader's departure. The name of the surgeon who pronounced the wound incurable was Mr. Gangle; the wound, that is, is a break in the ganglia of the nervous system. At first, the letter recalls, the self-regard demanded by the wound was a humiliation; then the source of an adolescent pride in one's own loneliness; finally the object of comfortable but issueless affection. "The surgeon was dead right. Nothing will ever part us." No other love is possible. Without the leader at the center, the rest of the group no longer holds any interest—"only yesterday, I took down all those photographs from my mantelpiece"—and the aging initiate settles into permanent privacy and calm. Behind this sinisterly comic pastiche may be heard a sentence from Freud's essay on "Mourning and Melancholia": "The complex of melancholia behaves like an open wound, drawing to itself cathectic energy from all sides . . . and draining the ego until it is utterly depleted."

Auden told Naomi Mitchison that the theme of the work was the failure of the romantic conception of personality. What he did not say was that the work was retrospective self-criticism also. Both the Initiates of the first Book and the Airman of the second dramatize aspects of Auden's emotional life and his literary ambitions. The Initiates stand for that tendency in the romantic personality that asks for a prior hero to serve as a model for its growth—a Lawrence or a Lane. The Airman stands for the wish to stand alone. Each ends in isolation, the first passively, the second actively, and the failures of each confirm the restraining power of the past. The Initiates find no satisfaction in following an absent leader, while the Airman, pursuing his lonely pride, finds his independence illusory. The Airman, like Auden two years earlier, tries to separate himself from parents and predecessors, but like Auden adopting Old English models, can do this only by finding an alternate set of ancestors instead. He ends as dependent as he began. The romantic personality, Auden suggests, having lost a unified community, tries to compensate through its isolated will to power; but as a result it forfeits unity and power together. The romantic hero, for all his claims to autonomy, begins by assuming his own unfreedom: he knows that the isolation he enjoys was caused by historical or psychological fate, not by his own choice. Denying freedom at the start, he cannot discover it afterward. He tries to be self-creating and self-sufficient, but he invariably finds he must take some heroic predecessor as a model. Seeking to become himself, he becomes a version of someone else instead. From Don Quixote onward, the imaginative hero has proved to be a literalist: he gets it all out of books, from Milton's Satan or Homer's Ulysses. In "Statement" the initiate answers the hero's summons by "cursing his father, and the curse was given him." Leaving his father, he takes the hero's curse of isolation on himself, exchanges one predecessor for another, and never frees himself from the curse he pronounces on the past.

The internal tension that Auden describes in both the Initiates and the Airman, the tension of the self-contradictory desire to achieve independence through imitation, finally breaks into a "wound." And this wound, the personal analogue of the "gulf" that Auden's language explicitly hopes to cross, becomes the sole interest of the divided self. What may lie on the other side of the gulf no longer matters. The really fascinating subject is one's personal abyss. And thereby come coldness, cowardice, and obedience that cries for a master.

The ironic progress of the Airman takes a direction opposite to that of the Initiates. They began gathered in a hall, tried to find a focus for their small society, mourned a lost leader, and ended in discrete self-regarding fragments. The Airman begins alone, worries over "the crucial problem—group organisation," slowly acknowledges his reliance on an ancestor, and finally accepts the undifferentiated unity of surrender and death. Like Auden writing in his 1929 journal that "The essence of creation is doing things for no reason, it is pointless," the Airman opens his journal with an aimless regimen of "self-care." "Self-care is carefree," a matter of "minding one's own business." The Airman distinguishes self-care, which is absolutely isolated and self-absorbed, as he says it ought to be, from self-regard, which attends to the outside world but interprets public "news as a private poem." "One must draw the line somewhere," he writes, in praise of borders; there must be "awareness of interdependence." With this program in mind the Airman then seeks to find some means of delimiting and unifying a group.

Yet when he tries to suit the action to the word, he finds nothing he can do. His resolution is sicklied o'er by guilt. Secretly worshipping his "real ancestor," his uncle, he still does nothing to "avenge" his foul and most unnatural death—though examples gross as earth exhort him. Maternal opposition puzzles the will; he is too much in the sun. Unpregnant of his cause, uncertain of his purpose, he puts an antic disposition on, marking time with practical jokes. At the end he realizes he can end his isolation only if he will lose the name of action, and accept total "absorption" into the undiscovered country of the enemy he opposed. Leaving his journal to report him and his cause aright, he chooses "self-destruction, the sacrifice of all resistance." The rest is silence.

Who is the Airman, and what does he have to do with the problem of groups? While Auden was writing the book he seems to have thought the answer was reasonably clear. He explained to Naomi Mitchison:

> I am now writing the second half, which is the situation seen from within the Hero. It is in the form of a *Journal of an Airman*. The flying symbolism is I imagine fairly obvious. The chief strands are his

Uncle (Heredity-Matrilineal descent and initiations), belief in a universal consipiracy (the secret society mind), kleptomania (the worm in the root). I am finding it very difficult but am getting along slowly.

Evidently the difficulties were enough to frustrate his conscious intentions. In August 1932, three months after publication, he gave this answer to a reader's request for help:

Orators
   I am very dissatisfied with this book. The conception was alright but I didn't take enough trouble over it, and the result is far too obscure and equivocal. It is meant to be a critique of the fascist outlook, but from its reception among some of my contemporaries, and on rereading it myself, I see that it can, most of it, be interpreted as a favourable exposition. The whole Journal ought to be completely rewritten.

He goes on to identify "Goering in Germany [as] a good example of the kind of figure I had in mind," an intention almost unrecognizable in the finished work. But although he said he ought to rewrite the Journal, when he had a chance to do so for a reset second edition in 1934 he made only some minor omissions and resexed the Airman's lover from female to male. The equivocal obscurity of the Journal—and its autobiographical elements—proved indispensable after all.

In this same letter Auden makes clear the anthropological origins of *The Orators:* "The genesis of the book was a paper written by an anthropologist friend of mine about ritual epilepsy among the Trob[r]iand Islanders, linking it up with the flying powers of witches, sexual abnormalities etc." The friend was John Layard, and his paper, in the *Journal of the Royal Anthropological Institute,* July–December 1930, is the hidden key to *The Orators.*

Layard's paper is in two parts with separate titles. The first is "Malekula: Flying Tricksters, Ghosts, Gods, and Epileptics"; the second, more theoretical part is "Shamanism: an Analysis Based on Comparison with the Flying Tricksters of Malekula."* The opening section is an account of sorcerers on Malekula who, the islanders believe, can fly. These

* Malekula is in fact in the New Hebrides, not the Trobriands; in his letter Auden was conflating Layard's work with Malinowski's.

flying tricksters sometimes kill their enemies, at other times merely play practical jokes on their friends. Unlike all other initiation rites in Malekula culture, which are transmitted patrilineally, the rite by which a trickster is initiated is transmitted from a maternal uncle to his nephew. The tricksters share many peculiarities with epileptics, and Layard speculates that their reported power of flight may derive from the "well-known epileptic aura [which] is the feeling of a cold wind blowing across the face." Layard believes that the tricksters are not in fact epileptics, but that they derive their rites from close observation of epileptic fits. In the Malekula culture, he speculates, those responsible for the rites of re-animating the dead (we call them priests) noted the resemblance between their own rituals of death and rebirth and the apparent death and rebirth of an epileptic who falls into unconsciousness and then rises again. The priests found it expedient, on both practical and spiritual grounds, to use epileptics in their rites, but when there came to be too many rites to be served by the limited supply of epileptics, the priests began to induce a deliberate hysterical epilepsy instead. As they learned to work themselves into fits of real unconsciousness, they also took over the incidental peculiarities of epileptics such as the sensation of flight and, so Layard argues, irresponsibility and homosexuality.

The special character of the Airman should now be clear. He too traces his ancestry to a maternal uncle; he is a practical joker; he can fly; in his kleptomania his hands, like an epileptic's, act against his will; he initiates others into his order ("The new batch of recruits arrived this morning . . . very excited about to-morrow"); and his order itself is a recent historical introduction whose props and symbols of flight take the place of an earlier reality, as in the case of the imitated fits on Malekula:

> The aeroplane has only recently become necessary, owing to the progress of enemy propaganda, and even now not for flying itself, but as a guarantee of good faith to the people, frightened by ghost stories, the enemy's distorted vision of the airman's activities.

That is, the essential quality of the Airman is not his ability to fly, but his understanding of "ancestor worship," which his enemy falsifies as "ghost stories," tales of literal communion with the dead. (The Malekula tricksters likewise gain their power from the spirits of the dead.) Ancestor worship is essential because it involves a recognition of dis-

tance—which, claims the Airman, makes love possible. He has no sympathy with his father or mother, with whom he shares "likeness," but he
worships his uncle, with whom he shares an "awareness of difference—
[that is,] love." "The airman is the agent of this central awareness."

But who is the "enemy" who opposes the Airman, who warned him
in his youth against his own impulsive nature and against the role he
would eventually accept as his own? Who were "they" who warned:

> whatever you do don't go to the wood.
> There's a flying trickster in that wood

—advice that the Airman, in a poem in his Journal, sees himself rejecting, "following his love" to find "consummation in the wood." Because
Auden could not criticize the Airman while writing in the Airman's
own terms, readers of *The Orators* have taken the enemy at the Airman's word, as a personification of repression, bourgeois stuffiness,
timid restraint, and so forth. The enemy is indeed all these things, but
only from the perspective of the Airman. The distinction between the
Airman's *we* and the enemy's *they* implies a contrast, not so much between instinct and repression, although the Airman claims it to be that,
as between two different kinds of organization, each of which sees the
other in distorted terms. It is possible to recognize this only with
Layard's paper at hand, because although Auden set out to use the relatively neutral distinctions Layard makes in his paper between different
kinds of order, the result sounds like an attack on that perennial target,
the bourgeoisie. Layard's paper makes it possible to reconstruct the original conception that was blurred in the finished work.

In the first part of his paper Layard observes that although the flying
tricksters of Malekula have rites of initiation, they have no social organization of any kind: "Though there appears to be a form of initiation,
they cannot be said to constitute a society, since so far as I know there is
no common lodge, and so little mutual assistance that they are as liable
to direct their attentions against one another as against the rest of mankind." In itself this observation is of little interest, and Auden borrows it
only to introduce some mutual distrust into the Airman's camp (as he
does also in "Address" and "Argument" earlier in the work). But in the
second part of his paper Layard compares the ecstasy of shamans with
the initiation rites of flying tricksters in order to develop something of a
general theory of social organization. Both shamans and tricksters experience spiritual possession, epileptoid symptoms, apparent death and re-

birth, and flight; both have a widespread and fairly uniform religion but lack any organization "such as is found elsewhere between the different practitioners of a homogeneous cult." Both shamans and tricksters have religious systems based on moments of real personal unconsciousness, whether epileptic or hysterically induced; while other religious systems, which have developed into unified organized forms, are based not on actual unconsciousness but on *ritual* death and resurrection, mimetic rites which "become highly organized and collective." The trickster's vision comes to him singly, through private unconsciousness; his system, Layard writes, therefore cannot become organized. Rituals of death and rebirth, on the other hand, are conscious and collective, and do permit systems to be organized. (Layard closes with a footnote pointing out the "disintegrating effect of 'individual inspiration'" in Christendom, "where Catholicism, firmly based on ritual, remains united, while the Protestant sects, the foundation or revival of which is frequently accompanied by manifestations of a hysterical order based on direct communication with the deity, tend ever to divide and multiply.")

Now the Airman understands none of this. He believes a social organization can come into being by itself, provided no one interferes by setting up codes of law or habit. His Journal opens: "A system organises itself, if interaction is undisturbed." And the entries that follow try to refute the enemy dogma that "first causes and purposive ends" are required for any "orderly arrangement." The true means to organization, he writes, is simply "self-care or minding one's own business," which is his definition of the second law of thermodynamics—the law that states that when heat is freely exchanged between two objects, the hotter always loses energy to the colder. What the Airman neglects (although Auden, with his scientific literacy, may have assumed readers would have no trouble spotting) is that the real consequence of this law is not an orderly arrangement at all, but the random disorder of entropy, a condition without form, pattern, or potential. The Airman simply doesn't know physics. Undaunted by ignorance, he denounces his enemy's brand of order as repressive.* As the Airman sees it, the

---

* He offers a geometrical pattern that serves as "A Sure Test" for recognizing the enemy. Ask the person you suspect to pick out a form from the pattern; a "friend" will choose one of the regular forms that are immediately evident, while the enemy will impose his own order and choose an irregular arbitrary form instead. Auden lifted the diagrams from Wolfgang Köhler's *Gestalt Psychology* (1930), where the oddly shaped form is one that does not constitute a "real whole."

enemy's organization is the result of bourgeois caution whose "catchwords" are "insure now—keep smiling—safety first." What the enemy
seems to possess is not the true vital order that arises from self-care, but
a dead structure of false limits and restrictions, maintained by a secret
conspiracy: "The effect of the enemy is to introduce inert velocities into
the system (called by him laws or habits) interfering with organisation." And these, the Airman continues approvingly, "can only be
removed by friction (war)"—which is why the enemy takes such an
"interest in peace societies." The Airman believes that all existing order
is an enemy plot and is convinced, in a vaguely Rousseauistic way, that
if the existing order were removed, a true order would emerge inevitably
as a "natural result."

He is wrong. What he cannot understand is that his loony physics is a
projection of his contradictory desire for order and no order at once.
There is clearly an element of parodic autobiography here, as the Airman, like Auden himself, tries to find an order that will bear no indebt-
edness to systems received from the past. And like Auden, the Airman
knows he is far from solving his modernist dilemma: "Much more research needed into the crucial problem—group organisation." This is, to
put it mildly, an understatement. As long as the Airman retains his
trickster-shaman belief in the adequacy of his private vision, it does not
matter at all how much research he devotes to the problem of groups;
having asked the question in self-contradictory terms, he will never find
an answer. The real consequence of his vision, at the end of the Journal
as at the end of "The Initiates," is chaos and isolation.

Furthermore, the Airman, in spite of all precautions, has been infected by the enemy—which is another way of saying that the internal
tension and division he attributes to others are aspects of himself as well.
He is divided against himself, and his inner divisions cause the neurosis
that keeps him isolated from the world outside. Between the Airman
and "E," whom he loves, stands the Airman's secret guilt of kleptomania. In an early review Auden had written of "theft, that attempt to
recover the lost or stolen treasure, love." Here, the Airman's desire for
love has been displaced into his attempt to steal for himself alone. The
tension of this self-perpetuating division increases throughout his Journal until, as the final battle approaches between his camp and the
enemy, he suddenly recognizes that his own division gives the enemy its
strength. "My whole life has been mistaken. . . . The power of the
enemy is a function of our resistance, therefore . . . The only efficient

way to destroy it—self-destruction, the sacrifice of all resistance." This elaborates what he had already written in his opening pages, a mad inversion of an initial madness. By dividing himself from the enemy, he now believes, he blocked his own way to unity; in effect, he brought his enemy into existence. Entirely on his own, he has drawn a border and established a system of barriers and limits; this is precisely what the enemy thrives on.

His recognition comes when he is able to interpret a dream he has already transcribed in his Journal, a dream about the uncle he worships as his real ancestor. He used to believe that the verdict of suicide on the uncle's death was a lie, that his death must be avenged. But the dream says something different. In it, the Airman sees a newspaper, bordered in black, with his uncle's photograph and the words "I have crossed it." When the Airman resolves to cease his resistance, he understands that his uncle willingly crossed over the border that stood in the way of unity. The Airman will now do the same, and follow his uncle to surrender and death. As in Nower's cure in *Paid on Both Sides*, a revelatory dream overturns the fatal logic of revenge, but the ironic consequence is the dreamer's death.

So, in one sense only, the Journal's opening statement, that systems organize themselves spontaneously, proves true. The Airman's sudden conversion, his change from resistance to surrender, reflects the psychoanalytic doctrine that such events result from hidden imbalances in the mind, imbalances that create strains so severe they can be relieved only by an abrupt and ultimately futile conversion. But this is not at all what the Airman had in mind.

At the end, the Airman is ready to cross the border. By giving up resistance he will dissolve the barriers between his enemy and himself. But to cross the border in Auden's earliest poems is to die. As his last day dawns, the Airman is serene, his kleptomania cured, his "Hands in perfect order" (an echo of Wilfred Owen's report, in two letters shortly before his death, that his "nerves are in perfect order") like the epileptics mentioned by Layard who stand motionless immediately prior to their fit. But instead of the apparent death of an epileptic, the Airman faces a real death. He writes a farewell letter to "E," in pious obedience to what he imagines to be enemy orders: "O understand, darling. God just loves us all, but means to be obeyed." The final entry in his Journal records the moments before he takes off to crash or surrender on the enemy side:

3.40 A.M. Pulses and reflexes, normal.
           Barometric reading, 30.6. . . .
           Fair. Some cumulus cloud at 10,000 feet. Wind easterly and
               moderate.
           Hands in perfect order.

His calm is more terrible than any of his fantasies of violence.*

One last point about the Airman. Layard notes the childish irresponsibility of the Malekula tricksters, and claims that epileptics are equally childish—which is one reason for the schoolyard atmosphere of *The Orators.* He then notes certain similarities between Malekulan tricksters and Malekulan ghosts, observing that the initiation rites of the latter include an act of anal intercourse. He suggests that the childishness found among epileptics, ghosts, and tricksters takes the form of homosexuality and supports his argument with examples of ritual homosexuality among shamans. Layard sums up these matters as "the suppression of the adult side of the conflict."

The Airman and his uncle are both homosexuals, and the exclusion of women is a recurring issue in "The Initiates." In the same way Auden uses the Airman and Initiates to criticize his own youthful theories of personality, he uses the Airman's Journal to score another complaint against his own homosexuality. In his long letter to John Pudney a few months later† he wrote of homosexuality as "an attempt at a magical short cut: we choose those with whom we should naturally have an unconscious group relationship and try to get that by the personal conscious contact." The magical short cut, carried into the life of a community, is precisely a childish evasion of conflict and difficulty. The Airman's homosexuality blocks him from the organized relation of marriage—the province of his mother, who disapproved of the uncle—and leaves him in disordered isolation. In a review written a year later Auden was to claim that "nearly all homosexual relations" are of the kind where "the object is really non-existent." The metaphoric wound

* In yet another of his explanatory letters to readers, in December 1932, Auden wrote: "The airman's fate can be suicide or Rimbaud's declination"—*declination* in the original sense of turning aside, as in Rimbaud's decision to stop writing and renounce his youthful ambitions; there are allusions to Rimbaud's "*Adieu*" in the final paragraphs of the Journal. Auden added: "*The Orators* is too bloody obscure I know." (Letter to Henry Bamford Parkes, now in Colby College Library.)
† Quoted in Chapter I, p. 23.

to which one of the Initiates writes his love letter is in part the Initiate's isolating homosexuality, fostered by the rituals of school. A year before writing *The Orators* Auden had suffered a real wound, an anal fissure, which was not in fact the result of sexual relations but which he explained psychosomatically to friends as "the Stigmata of Sodom." This is the wound he suffers *in propria persona* in the first Ode, where he wakes to "a bed, hard, surgical / And a wound hurting." In "Letter to a Wound" he recalls its onset "only last February," in 1930. Throughout "The Initiates" and "Journal of an Airman" Auden unsettlingly draws his own features on the figures he satirizes and attacks. He suggested in his 1966 preface that his unconscious motive "was therapeutic, to exorcise certain tendencies in myself by allowing them to run riot in phantasy."

In different ways, this same radical uncertainty of tone pervades the "Six Odes" at the end. These take up the problems of national and group purposes raised earlier, but where "The Initiates" was clearly satirical, the Odes are not sure whether they celebrate or parody the positions they take. Auden's abandoned 1932 preface called them personal reflections on the question of leadership in our time. That question remained open.

The first Ode is a dream vision, its stanza an elaborately overgrown variety of the Pindaric. The themes are loss, isolation, and the possible means of rescue. A "voice" that the poet hears on waking in his hospital bed tells him and his friends to "Read of your losses." It pictures for them a Europe reduced to the futility of "self-regarders." Then the voice asks—as Auden will hear other voices ask in the 1930s—to be saved. But with no means of salvation at hand, Auden can only "pause hesitant" while a troop of "all the healers" rush forward. They are an odd lot: "granny in mittens, the Mop, the white surgeon [of Auden's wound], / And loony Layard." Waking from his dream, he hears a beggar outside the window suggest that what may be approaching, instead of a cure, is a more painful political convulsion from "East Europe." The beggar's tone promises no harmonious socialism, but an avenging fury:

> Have you heard of someone swifter than Syrian horses?
> Has he thrown the bully of Corinth in the sanded circle?
> Has he crossed the Isthmus already? Is he seeking brilliant
>   Athens and us?

Auden is not the beggar, and he does not welcome a revolution imposed
from above, but he doubts that leaders and healers may be able to prevent it.

The remaining Odes trace an implicit narrative, looser than that in
"The Initiates" but roughly parallel to it. The impulsive group unity
celebrated in the second Ode stales in the third; we then welcome the
renewing powers of a leader in the fourth; and we serve under him,
somewhat anxiously, in the fifth.

The narrative begins in Ode II with a cheerful parody of Pindar by
way of Hopkins. A school rugby team is celebrated with erotic praise,
its triumphs blazoned:

> Success my dears—Ah!
> Rounding the curve of the drive
> Standing up, waving, cheering from car,
> 　　The time of their life . . .

Life-inducing Eros is summoned to flow in their veins as it flowed into
nature in the seven days of creation:

> Heart of the heartless world
> Whose pulse we count upon . . .
>
> From darkness your roses came
> In one little week of action
> By fortunate prejudice to delighting form
> 　　And profuse production;
> Now about these boys as keen as mustard to grow
> Give you leave for that, sir, well in them, flow,
> Deep in their wheel-pits may they know you foaming and feel
> 　　　　　　　　you warm.

The "sir" is from Hopkins, rhetorically lowered from a personal god to
a generalized erotic power; and the "Heart of the heartless world" is
from Marx ("Religion is the sigh of the oppressed creature, the heart of
a heartless world and the soul of soulless conditions. It is the opium of
the people"), rhetorically heightened from rigorous scepticism to theatrical exuberance. This is a poem that delights in the performance of
athletes in order to delight in its own.

But its comfortable vision of childhood "Joy docked in every duct" is shadowed by adult consequences. By Ode III a decline from group promise to lonely aftermath has already begun. Now we are among schoolboys (or exiles? or mental patients?—the poem leaves all three possibilities open) who arrive full of hope, crossing a border into their new life as a group: "All meet on this shore." Our initial pleasures fade quickly as the unchanging self-regard of group life makes itself felt:

> We shall never need another new outfit;
> These grounds are for good, we shall grow no more,
>> But lose our colour . . .
>> Peering through glasses
>> At our own glosses.

Until at last our "nerves grow numb"—"Accepting dearth / The shadow of death."

After two Odes in the first-person plural, Ode IV returns to the singular. It proclaims a leader who deserves unequivocal obedience and praise, but this hero proves to be the infant son of the writer Rex Warner—a tyrant like all infant children, but only a domestic tyrant. In his 1966 preface, arguing that in the work as a whole "it is precisely the schoolboy atmosphere and diction which act as a moral criticism of the rather ugly emotions and ideas they are employed to express," Auden says that in this Ode, "I express all the sentiments with which his followers hailed the advent of Hitler, but these are rendered, I hope, innocuous by the fact that the Führer so hailed is a new-born baby and the son of a friend." But Auden's difficulty throughout *The Orators* (as his qualifying *I hope* implies) is that he has no alternative to the ugly feelings he is trying to criticize. His effort to replace them with benign variants is no more effective in literature than it is in life; the malignant originals always return. So while the Ode spiritedly recites the deficiencies of the proletariat, the upper class, youth, and all politicians, hailing in their stead the infant John Warner who will "save John Bull," it also commends the leader-theory that is still the only practical politics Auden knows.

Auden finds this Lawrentian leadership nowhere in Europe. He was writing in October 1931, when it was still almost possible to describe Mussolini, the Polish dictator Pilsudski, and Hitler as "the ninny, the mawmet and the false alarm." The proletariat, "All of them dunces," can scarcely take charge of society; nor can "our upper class . . .—they won't pass—" nor our youth, "most of them dummies who want their mummies." Our only hope is an infant Führer whose imaginary new order will display the primitive fascistic virtues Lawrence demanded in his *Fantasia*:

> The few shall be taught who want to understand,
> Most of the rest shall live upon the land;
> Living in one place with a satisfied face,
> All of the women and most of the men
> Shall work with their hands and not think again.

Fortunately for the poem, Auden's new order includes changes impossible ever to achieve: "The official re-marriage of the whole and part," and "The two worlds in each other's arms" in a restoration of the real whole. Auden's political alternative to an intolerable society is an impossible vision. About ten years later he commented in a friend's copy of this poem: "Can't bear this."

Even at the time he wrote it he knew that the real consequences of its joyful *Führerprinzip* was the divided psyche of the fifth Ode, which he dedicated—perhaps pityingly—to his pupils. We are in a setting that is both a school and a barracks. The group to which we belong (this Ode returns to the first-person plural) displays all the forms of organization the Airman despised: we parade in front of the Cathedral, are blessed by the bishop, file in after the choir boys. In short, we are the Airman's enemy. We read newspapers (which to the Airman, as to Auden in his 1929 journal, are one of the "Enemy Gambits . . . against the awareness of difference" and therefore against love); we are "aware of our rank"; we are "alert to obey orders."

Yet we also resemble the Airman in that our own division causes the war we endure. Our fear of the other side is what gives the enemy their strength. We "have made from Fear" their laconic captain, and their avenging forces are our own repressed impulses transformed into seven deadly sins: "Wrath who has learnt every trick of guerilla warfare," Lust who would hug Love to death. Our internal barrier is too hidden and too dangerous for us to understand: "They speak of things done on the frontier we were never told." In a sense the Airman and the Initiates were right. We shall never be parted from our wound, we exist because of our own conflicts. The Ode looks back into history to seek out a golden age, but finds only the record of the sack of a city. We and the

Airman are two sides of the same eternally divided psyche. As Auden would soon recognize, to think in terms like these only perpetuates division and, by reducing real social issues to fantasy-projections of psychological conflicts, makes external standards for choice and action impossible to find. When he reprinted this Ode in the 1940s he gave it the title "Which Side Am I Supposed to Be On?"*

Finding no resolution possible in the book's own terms, *The Orators* ends by looking elsewhere for help or escape. Its conclusion echoes that of *Poems* 1930 in its prospect of unspecified change and its appeal to a fictional deity. As the "Sir" of "Sir, no man's enemy" was in part a construction made from the syntax of Hopkins, so the "Father" addressed in the sixth Ode is the one auditor who can unravel the syntax of the Scottish Metrical Psalms, a syntax Auden renders like this:

> These nissen huts if hiding could
> Your eye inseeing from
> Firm fenders were, but look! to us
> Your loosened angers come.

The Ode begins with the appeal: "Not, Father, further do prolong / Our necessary defeat." This is the defeat of both sides in our inner conflict, a defeat that will be followed by their reconciliation. The fiction that this is "necessary," not merely in the sense that it is a precondition of our cure, but also in the sense that it is inevitable—and can be postponed but not prevented—will become more serious in Auden's political poems a few years later. For the moment Auden is only miming an act of prayer, with little hope that his imitation will result in change, or that the necessary defeat can ever occur.

And since he does not expect his prayer to be answered, he follows the last Ode with an "Epilogue" where there is still no resolution but, rather, a sudden exit for an unspecified Elsewhere. Now Auden is no longer subverting from within, but his departure is no more effective in any practical sense than were his fantasies of destruction. To the timid question, "Where are you going?" asked by "reader," "fearer," and "horror," the answer flung back by the departing "rider" is: "Out of this house." This is a memorable ending, but an empty one. It leaves behind

---

* Possibly an allusion to a union organizing song, popular among Communists, which Auden would have heard in America. It demanded to know "*Which* side are you on? Which side *are* you on?"

a host of unresolved contradictions, with an air of having done something decisive about them. The conclusions of both *The Orators* and *Poems* are entirely different from the formal resolution either of comedy in marriage or of tragedy in death, both of which refer to events that actually occur in the world of the audience. Auden's endings in these early books refer instead to fantasies of change. They are formal means of bringing a book to an end when the disordered world of the book itself permits no resolution that would be plausible in reality.

Yet the overwhelming futility of Auden's negative vision of groups seems spontaneously to have generated a positive one. At about the same time he wrote the Epilogue to *The Orators*, in October 1931, he told Isherwood he had just had his "most important vision about groups." If, as seems likely, this was substantially what he described in his letter to Pudney, it gave Auden his first hope of a practical alternative to absolute isolation on one hand and absolute submergence and submission on the other. He began to see how he might participate on both sides of a division at once. Poets, he told Pudney, "will always be a little outside the group," yet "without it, they have no material" and are doomed to endless division—"must split their emotions into ever finer and finer hairs." Poets "need the group to feel a little out of just as much as they need it to be at home in." So there is no need to ride across a border out of this house: the poet can stand at the doorway, mediating between the undifferentiated group inside and his differentiating language "a little outside." This is still only a primitive sketch of Auden's later dialectical understanding of self and society. He knows he needs a group, but he does not know why a group might need a poet, and his vision has nothing to do with the responsibilities of a citizen. He has not yet found what he would call, in a much later poem, "a place / I may go both in and out of." Yet although his vision has not brought him to the door of any real community, he is at least ready to stop riding away.

VI

Private Places

Around the time he was finishing *The Orators* Auden began to demand of literature that it perform a public service. Three years after he welcomed a new noncommunicative poetry, he explicitly attacked modern writing for its failure to communicate. Reviewing a novel by David Garnett in the French magazine *Échanges* in December 1931—his second published review, and his first on a literary subject—he criticized the book in terms that would not have been out of place in a review of his own 1930 *Poems:*

> I think that Mr. Garnett is not very interested in individuals or even their relations . . . but that he is very interested in the human soul. I feel certain that the situations and incidents of this tale are profoundly significant to him, a revelation—call it an allegory if you will—of the nature of life. The reader is aware of this excitement but is not allowed to share it.
>
> The reason for this failure in communication seems to me very important; it is characteristic of much of the best modern work . . . Writers have been so afraid of saying what they don't mean, that what they do say, when not backed up* by private associations, their own foreknowledge of their meaning, means very little. It is inadequate to say that this is merely a reaction against Victorian overstatement; they both have the same cause—fear. . . . The non-committal manner

---

* The French printers set "lached up," but "backed up" seems likely to have been what Auden had in mind. His hand was barely legible at the best of times.

is not a change of heart but only an advance in sophistication, a double bluff. The trouble is, not that these artists have no vision, but that they remain self-regarding; they are afraid of making fools of themselves over it.

In short, what keeps literature private is the same isolating cowardice Auden had explored in his poems.

But how to overcome fear and speak one's meaning? As he acknowledged in his essay on "Writing" at about this same time, the problem could not be solved within the confines of language itself. Individual loneliness, in writers as in everyone else, resulted in part from an isolating society. In a review of a new edition of John Skelton, for the January 1932 *Criterion*, Auden defended Skelton not only for his language but, emphatically, for his social function. "In criticizing a satirical poem, I do not see how one can avoid reference to the abuses attacked. A satire, like an advertisement, should be a public service." This was easier in Skelton's day:

> I should be very sorry to see Skelton used as a convert's stick to beat the poor old Reformation with; but it is evident that there was less gap [the word is characteristic], both in language and interests, between the man-in-the-street and the intellectual in his time than in the age, say, of Pope; and that is the kind of society most favourable to good satire.

In Pope's day as in ours, satirists could talk only about other writers, not about public issues; yet "Which is the major subject: that of *Why come ye not to court* or of the *Dunciad*, Wolsey or Grub Street?" Which subject is suited to a wider audience? Furthermore,

> responsibility is now so diffused that the personal figure which satire demands is hard to find. A modern satirist in search of a subject would be far more likely to select a *Criterion* dinner [i.e. the contributors to Eliot's quarterly] than a newspaper peer. Mr. Wyndham Lewis, for example, even when he is attacking fundamental abuses attacks them *through* certain writers which the majority of people have never read.

So it is refreshing "to turn to the pages even of *John Bull* where, if one disagrees, one at least is clear what it is all about." Better still to turn to poets like Skelton "who, using a language as direct as that of Burns, takes as his subjects matters of which the accidents may be peculiar to his times but the substance is common to all, and not least to our own." (The reference to Burns is proleptic: Auden began using variations on the Burns stanza a few months later.)

To follow Skelton's example a poet would need a society as unified as his. Only in such a society is a universal and direct poetic language possible; only in such a society can an artist serve without damaging his art. The poet's task, Auden was now ready to believe, is to promote a new unified society, for its own sake and for the sake of his poetry.

To do this meant breaking free of his poetic privacy, leaving his solitary landscapes for common ground, replacing personal allusions with public faces. He needed a community of interest, a place to belong in. Through the use of mysterious personal names, unknown to his readers, he had enforced the privacy of his earliest poems. This had led to charges that he indulged in coterie writing, but the names were even more private than his accusers suspected: no one but Auden knew the significance of them all. Captain Ferguson, of whom we hear our last in "Taller to-day," was a sadistic master at a friend's school; Gerhart Meyer and Kurt Groote in "1929" were proletarian friends in Berlin; "the Mop," listed among the healers in the first Ode of *The Orators*, was Auden's name for the mother of one of his Larchfield Academy colleagues, unknown to his friends elsewhere (although he may also have used the name for a London friend); and so on through Gabriel, Derek, Olive, Allen and Page and all the rest. He made his preferences clear in the dedicatory poem to *The Orators*:

> Private faces in public places
> Are wiser and nicer
> Than public faces in private places.

Until the spring of 1930 all the names in his work honored private faces. Then the political themes of "Get there if you can" demanded public ones instead, for the poem lists betrayers and seducers who block us from our lives, who "with their compelling logic . . . whispered 'Better join us, life is worse.' " In an early manuscript the list is exclusively public:

Bishops and headmasters, Plato, Pascal, Bowdler, Baudelaire,
Led their massed and storming squadrons, managed deadly engines
there.

But when Auden revised these lines for publication in the 1930 *Poems*, he scrambled in some names of a different kind:

> Newman, Ciddy, Plato, Fronny, Pascal, Bowdler, Baudelaire,
> Doctor Frommer, Mrs. Allom, Freud, the Baron, and Flaubert.

The slapdash quality is entirely deliberate, Auden's way of stepping back from public themes as he first approaches them. The historical figures on the list share a reactionary pessimism; the poet among them is not pardoned for writing well. The private references are a very mixed bag. Ciddy was a nickname for Auden's prep-school headmaster, Fronny a dissolute contemporary of whom we shall hear more in a later chapter, Doctor Frommer a Berliner who frequented the same louche bars Auden favored, and Mrs. Allom the loquaciously pious mother of an Oxford friend. The Baron is presumably that arch-deceiver Charlus.

Eighteen months later, when Auden wrote Ode IV of *The Orators*, all the names he used enjoyed public currency—names of politicians, aristocrats, writers, censors—but with these outlandish exceptions:

> Bob and Miss Belmairs spooning in Spain,
> Where is the trained eye? Under the sofa.
> Where is Moxon? Dreaming of nuns.

A few years later Isherwood revealed in *Lions and Shadows* that these names came from the fantasy world of Mortmere which he and his friend Edward Upward invented in their university days and peopled with various grotesques, among them the sinisterly elegant Moxon and the formidable woman painter whose name they spelled Miss Belmare. But the coterie air this revelation gave to Auden's lines was misleading. The Mortmere names served as apt disguises for the real targets of Auden's satire, who could not be identified in print:

> Middleton Murry's looking in pain,
> Robert and Laura spooning in Spain,
> Where is Lewis? Under the sofa.
> Where is Eliot? Dreaming of nuns.

(Robert Graves and Laura Riding were together on Mallorca; Lewis was Wyndham Lewis.) Auden kept the joke hidden even from Isherwood, sending him a manuscript with the Mortmere substitutions while preserving the originals only in his notebook.

Public references now almost entirely crowded out private ones. In the same month he wrote Ode IV, October 1931, Auden wrote his first public-service satire, the flyting of "Beethameer, Beethameer, bully of Britain" (Beethameer = the press lords Beaverbrook and Rothermere). This poem springs less from partisan convictions than from Auden's psychological objection to the false community established by newspapers—an objection he shared with the Airman in whose Journal he published the poem—but its tone is emphatically public. Over the next few months he made a few last desultory private references, but after the early months of 1932 all the personal names in his poems were well-known already to his audience. The rule-proving exceptions were names in elegies and epithalamia where the private names played roles made familiar by poetic convention, and names in the verse-letters and "Last Will and Testament" that he and Louis MacNeice wrote for *Letters From Iceland* in 1936, which explicitly celebrate friendship and implicitly invite readers to draw private parallels of their own.

Place names also came out of hiding. In his earliest work Auden had named places he loved, but as he looked down on them from his hawk's eminence, he did not imagine they had any need for him; nor did he share his love for them with anyone else. The settings of *Paid on Both Sides* are two houses, Lintzgarth at Rookhope and Nattrass at Garrigill. They sound like the imaginary haunts of a modern gothic sensibility, but houses with these names exist in the north of England, about twelve miles apart from each other, divided by the border between Cumberland and County Durham. Auden wandered in that countryside in early adolescence. Like the other place names in the play, they can be found on large-scale maps, yet few readers could have known where to look. The "possible bases" in *The Orators* include "Vadill of Uirafirth, Stubba, Smirnadale, Hammar and Sullom." All readers must have assumed, as F. R. Leavis did in a review (*The Listener*, 22 June 1932), that "Those names come from a boy's romantic map." In fact they are in the Shetland Islands, but Auden could not have expected anyone to know it other than Shetlanders, a rather small segment of his readership. None of the names appeared in standard atlases.*

* Sullom Voe became notorious thirty years later as an ecologically questionable tanker port. Auden had a good eye for possible bases.

Other names in these early poems sound too generalized even for a romantic map, and were apparently drawn from a map of poetic symbols—The Tower, for example, in the envoi to Ode IV of *The Orators*:

> The couples are coming now out of The Tower
> Love has its licence, the darkmans its power,
> Linking their arms they pass up the hill
> Motions their own though not what they will.

A slang dictionary will identify *the darkmans* as thieves' cant for *night*, but The Tower, surely, is a symbolic fiction, a place of erotic ceremony sacred to some imagined ritual, a focus for a dream-community where Eros is reconciled to the Will. It is that, in a way. In Helensburgh, where Auden was teaching at Larchfield Academy, The Tower was the name of a cinema. Behind the vague poetic evocation is an almost comically domestic setting, but one virtually inaccessible to almost everyone who was likely to read the poem. Auden's maps were real, but he kept them tightly folded.

Auden was training himself in a topography of the actual, but for the moment his landscape forbade him to participate in it. From the time the exhausted land rejected a visiting stranger in "The Watershed" until *The Orators* was complete late in 1931, the Auden country remained secret and hostile, opposed to free passage, denying security. In "Between attention and attention," a poem written in May 1930, we can neither get away nor learn where we want to get away from:

> These wishes get
> No further than
> The edges of the town,
> And leaning asking from the car
> Cannot tell us where we are.

We carry our isolation with us, and can register only "Acreage, mileage," the superficial "easy knowledge / Of the virtuous thing" that is the undivided earth. The romantic assumption behind these lines is that the world of nature, the earth itself, is the locus of both virtue and *virtù*, right action and erotic power, but that our divided consciousness, "The divided face," bars our access to it.

These inner divisions gradually took on outer forms. They became visible as armed implacable guardians, wrathful against all who would transgress them. The first of these guardians, and the model for the rest, rose from the earth in the summer of 1930, in a poem which begins by asking rhetorically "Who will endure" the perils of a "Journey from one place to another." In this poem's landscape "nothing passes / But envelopes between these places." An angry sentry blocks the way:

> There is no change of place . . .
> For no one goes . . .
> Further through foothills than the rotting stack
> Where gaitered gamekeeper with dog and gun
> Will shout "Turn back."

The figure of the border sentinel, after this first brief appearance in Auden's work, now dropped from sight for almost two years. When it returned it had changed, as the frontier it personified had changed. The border hindered; now it could protect. Where Auden had seen himself banished without, he now felt safely within. Where he dreamed of a loving community, he now imagined he had found one.

This thorough reversal of attitude and emotion took place in a series of partial stages. While writing *The Orators* in 1931 Auden realized that the group he sought to establish would need a place to feel at home in. His first image of a landscape of refuge appeared in the September 1931 sestina "We have brought you, they said, a map of the country," a poem he incorporated in "Journal of an Airman." Auden made no pretence of treating this country as tangible rather than symbolic. In effect, it was a landscape generated from the recurring end-words of the sestina form— *country, vats, wood, bay, clock, love*—and had no referent in the world outside. The traveller in this poem finds consummation when he ignores the restraining advice of his elders and "sees for the first time the country." In the last line the clock strikes its welcome: "This is your country and the hour of love."* Yet any hope that such a place and time might be found in the actual world is denied by a later poem in the Airman's Journal, the poem beginning "There are some birds in these valleys" (and later titled "The Decoys"). This poem exposes an innocent-

---

* Until shortly before Auden's death all editions printed "the *home* of love," a typist's misreading of the manuscript. The rest of the poem refers to both maps and clocks in each stanza, so this final line requires a resolution in time as well as space.

seeming landscape as a fatal trap. The Airman's promised country is not a datum of his experience but a projection of his wish.

Yet shortly after finishing *The Orators* Auden was surprised to find himself in something very like the landscape of consummation. In November 1931, in the lyric "That night when joy began," he wrote for the first time of a love that persisted "day by day." On the first night, he recalls, he waited "for the flash / Of morning's levelled gun." It never appeared, but even now the poet cannot quite believe he is safe. He speaks of love's persistence in negative terms, as the absence of an enmity he can still remember. As love "Grows credulous [the word has an ominous undertone] of peace," it still keeps watch over its landscape for intruders from without:

> As mile by mile is seen
> No trespasser's reproach
> And love's best glasses reach
> No fields but are his own.

Auden lavished technical bravura on this report of his happiness. He had already been using slant-rhymes with rich consonance (hill/hall) in long-lined couplets. Now, in shorter lines giving much less room for maneuvers between the end-words, he elaborates this device into a stanzaic pattern where lines in the pairs 1–3 and 2–4 use vowel-rhyme (s*een*/r*ea*ch, repr*oa*ch/his *ow*n), while the same end-words are also linked in the pairs 1–4 and 2–3 by rich consonance (s*een*/hi*s ow*n, repr*oach*/r*each*). The poem takes on even greater complexities when it is read as a sequel to a lyric written a month earlier, in October 1931, the exquisite miniature beginning "For what as easy." Here love's failures in previous years seem to be redeemed. The "ghost" is not "houseless," but is satisfied in the flesh; nor has the mind's isolation left "the word forgotten"—the word "Said at the start / About heart / By heart, for heart." Lovers can feel reticent but unambiguous delight, even as they "Go kissed away / The data given / The senses even." Thus love begins, but the second lyric shows Auden's double sense of hope and fear over its prospects. Even in its more welcome aspect, the border still threatened.*

---

* In his erotic poems Auden retained the laconic abstract style of Laura Riding (see p. 44n) more than a year after he renounced it in his psychological and political poems for the more expansive and explicit styles of the *Orators* Odes. The last lines

Yet this was the time of Auden's vision of groups, and he now began to seek a real community that might fulfill his vision, an enclosed, protected place that was more than a poetic metaphor. Near the end of a long poem he wrote in February 1932 he discovered he had always been there.

The poem, first published under the title "A Happy New Year," is in two parts, the first satirically rejecting the old year, the second turning expectantly to the new. Auden's model for the first part is the Prologue to *Piers Plowman* (although the verse form is the rhyme-royal Chaucer wrote at the same time Langland was writing his alliterative verses). He sees a dream vision of "The English in all sorts and sizes," but unlike Langland, who had his vision in the Malvern Hills, Auden is displaced from his vision's content. He experiences it in Scotland, on a hill over Helensburgh, Loch Lomond below him. Also unlike Langland, he has no absolute standard by which to judge what he sees, no allegorical Lady to provide interpretations. He is on his own when the vision fades,

> Leaving the mind to moralise
> Upon these blurring images
> Of the dingy difficult life of our generation.

His moralizing in the second part has little to do with the vision in the first—so little that he dropped the first part soon after publication. The second part, later republished as a separate poem, begins: "Now from my window-sill I watch the night." It is New Year's Eve. In an early manuscript the night is a *gulf* (a word Auden used for the first time in his essay on "Writing" a few weeks before), and over that gulf he meditates an end to his isolation:

> Now from my room I look out at the night
> The church clock's lighted face, the green pier light
> Burn clearly on the borders [*changed to* Burn at the edges] of a gulf

---

of "For what as easy," celebrating contentment through a series of negatives, are almost pure Riding: "Fate is not late / Nor the ghost houseless / Nor the speech rewritten / Nor the tongue listless / Nor the word forgotten / Said at the start / About heart / By heart, for heart." This inverts the content, while preserving much of the tone, of Riding's lines about emotional emptiness in her poem "All Nothing, Nothing": "The stamping does not steam, / Nor impatience burn / Nor the tossing heart scream / Nor bones fall apart / By tossing of heart . . ."

> On which I lean and ask myself
> What difference the year can bring about.

By the fourth stanza (to return to the published text) the year has already reached spring, "this season when the ice is loosened," when desire "for the long lost good"—somewhat ominously—"like a police-dog is unfastened."

At dangerous moments Auden habitually resorted to the rhetoric of prayer. So, abruptly, the poem addresses the genii of borders who had disappeared from his poetry for the past two years:

> O Lords of Limit, training dark and light
> And setting a tabu 'twixt left and right:
> The influential quiet twins
> From whom all property begins,
> Look leniently upon us all to-night.

What we learn of these Lords of Limit is that they consolidate the self Auden had earlier hoped to divide. They are the principles by which a person or thing is constituted, the enclosing limits that differentiate and distinguish. From them "all property begins"—not in the economic sense but in the deeper Latinate sense that derives from *proprietas*, that which is proper to a thing and makes it itself, not something else instead. It is a Lord of Limit who, in *The Phoenix and the Turtle*, pales at the sight of lovers losing their individuality in each other: "Property was thus appalled / That the self was not the same." But in the ordinary world that lacks these fabulous unions, *proprietas* generously establishes personal selves, and so makes possible communication and love between one self and another.

Auden's image for the Lords of Limit is redoubled from the gaitered gamekeeper with dog and gun in his 1930 poem:

> in my thought to-night you seem
> Forms which I saw once in a dream,
> The stocky keepers of a wild estate.
>
> With guns beneath your arms, in sun and wet
> At doorways posted or on ridges set,
> By copse or bridge we know you there . . .

The Lords are as angry as the gamekeeper, still "Quick to be offended, slow to forgive," but Auden's relation with them is a new covenant. He has now identified them with the witnesses in the Book of Revelation, as interpreted by D. H. Lawrence in *Apocalypse*, published in 1931. To Lawrence the two witnesses "put a limit on man. They say to him, in every earthly or physical activity: Thus far and no farther.... They make life possible; but they make life limited ... They are the enemies of intoxication, of ecstasy, and of licence, of licentious freedom."

In earlier years Auden feared the powers that kept him back from the border; now he senses that their opposition rises from love, not hate. He realizes that the border might exist to protect him from what lies beyond. The angry warnings of the Lords of Limit make him value the inner coherence they enforce. Their "sleepless presences endear / Our peace to us with a perpetual threat." After years of absolute isolation, he knows it is to the Lords'

> discipline the heart
> Submits when we have fallen apart
> Into the isolated personal life.

The frontier has been transfigured.

What has not altered is our disease within. "We have no invitation, but we are sick" and strain to cross the guarded limit of community, seeking isolation and danger. The nature of the Lords is such that "we shall only pass you by a trick"—that is, by acting as a solitary trickster, like the Airman whose goal is the disorder of others' lives and whose fate is the disorder of his own. Auden, who had finished *The Orators* only a few months before, is already praying to his household gods to hold him to the world of shared distinctions that the Airman had seen as enemy territory. The poem prays to the Lords of Limit to guard this small community—the school, the English cell—from the Airman's fantasies of chaos and violence:

> what if the starving visionary have seen
> The carnival within our gates,
> Your bodies kicked about the streets,*
> We need your power still: use it, that none

---

* This is adapted from Lawrence on the witnesses: "Hence the men in the cities of licence rejoice when the beast from the abyss, which is the hellish dragon or demon of the earth's destruction, or man's bodily destruction, at last kills these two 'guard-

O from this table break uncontrollably away
Lunging, insensible to injury,
Dangerous in a room, or out wild-
-ly spinning like a top in the field,
Mopping and mowing through the sleepless day.

To a schoolmaster it seemed relatively easy to exorcise that saturnalian visionary the Airman, and easy to celebrate the enclosed comforts of the group. But what was easy to achieve in the school's small field of rule, custom, and limit would prove more difficult in the larger world.

In Auden's poetry until 1932 the schoolboy was the measure of all things. The adult world seemed a public school writ large. Schools educated no one to move beyond them; the adult world retained the tribal rites and immature relations of the dormitories—although the fun turned ugly. Growth or change was possible only through biological evolution or a personal change of heart, never through the workings of society. Then, for a brief transitional moment early in 1932, commemorated in "A Happy New Year," Auden valued the school as a pattern for a loving community. He dismissed England but embraced "the English cell." Yet he soon realized that this could flourish only in an England that had found a coherence of her own. By May 1932, in the poem "O Love, the interest itself in thoughtless Heaven," he was praying to feel toward all of England the same tie he felt to the small group, although he had in mind a different England of the future, an England so transformed that she deserved his love. From this prayer sprang his revolutionary preachments of 1932–33 (the subject of the next chapter) and another change in his attitude toward schools.

Auden had decided soon after he left Oxford in 1928 that he would eventually become a schoolmaster—although his allowance from his parents would suffice for more than a year before he needed a paying job. When he finally began teaching at Helensburgh, two months after he turned twenty-three, he had little love for the work. His letters to Spender show that he resented having to earn a living while Spender

---

ians' . . ." In a manuscript version of the poem Auden included a version of Lawrence's account of the witnesses' triumphant return from death on the third day.

and Isherwood enjoyed the *rentier* life in Berlin. But for all his language of revolt in *The Orators*, Auden remained the "Son of a nurse and doctor," and had absorbed their work ethic and commitment to public service. He could not retreat into bohemianism or into an ironic contempt for his responsibilities. His prose writings, which until September 1932 had concerned only literature and psychology, now began wrestling with "Problems of Education"—the title of one of his reviews—and for about nine months he wrote about little else. He argued that "an unsatisfactory educational system is one of many results, not a cause," of "the fundamental abuses of a society." An excessive interest in child welfare is "often a propitiation of the feelings of guilt" over one's failure to attack society's corruption at the root. Working as a schoolmaster, Auden saw himself in a hopeless position. "Education, whatever it pretend, can do nothing for the individual; it is always social." And the "failure of modern education lies . . . in the fact that nobody genuinely believes in our society, for which the children are being trained." He and his colleagues might labor to bring about change in their pupils, yet their efforts would be wasted until a fundamental change in society made training in citizenship a goal worthy of their efforts. "In the meantime some of us will go on teaching what we can for a sum which even in its modesty we do not really deserve. Teaching will continue to be, not a public duty, but a private indulgence."

When Auden began writing on education in September 1932 he had not yet found a rhetoric in which to raise social questions, much less answer them. In *The Orators* all available public rhetorics had been commandeered by the forces of instinctive group-unity and unquestioning hero-worship. For his first review he used a Lawrentian life-affirming prose that was certain to delight the editors of *Scrutiny* who commissioned it,* but was otherwise ill-adapted to the matter at hand. The review begins by glancing quickly at three books written from within the educational establishment, then, after only one paragraph, forgets the books entirely. In the rest of the piece Auden takes up general questions about education, using the rhetoric most opposed to the official solemnities of the headmaster, the rhetoric of Lawrence demanding in *Fantasia of the Unconscious* that all schools immediately be shut:

---

* Their annual denunciations of Auden's immaturity did not begin until two or three years later, after he got Lawrence out of his system.

It is going on. It is going to be like this to-morrow. Attendance-officer will flit from slum to slum, educational agencies will be besieged by promising young men who have no inclination to business, examiners chuckle over a novel setting of the problem of Achilles and the Tortoise, fathers sell grand pianos or give up tobacco, that little Adrian or Derek may go to Marlborough or Stowe.

Like everything else in our civilization, the system we have made has become too much for us; we can't stop the boat and we can't get out into the cold sea. The snail is obeying its shell.

The content of this matters far less than the linguistic solidarity the style proclaims between Auden the schoolmaster and Lawrence the prophet of impulse.

The assumptions behind our schooling are hollow: "Education, all smoothly say, is the production of useful citizens. But, good God, what on earth is a useful citizen just now?" Liberal reformers fail to see what really matters: "Before a man wants to understand, he wants to command or obey instinctively, to live with others in a relation of power; but all power is anathema to the liberal. He hasn't any. He can only bully the spirit." What can a teacher do? "Dearie, you can't do anything for the children till you've done something for the grown-ups. You've really got nothing to teach and you know it."

A few weeks later, in *The New Statesman*, 15 October 1932, Auden attributed the bourgeois's interest in communism, not to social or political concerns, but to communism's demand for self-surrender from those who, "isolated, feel themselves emotionally at sea." Auden's language in this review and others is overwhelmingly psychological, although he insists that the educational issues he addresses are social ones. Here he takes up the Lawrentian blunderbuss for a quick blast announcing that "man's nature is dual, and . . . each part of him has its own conception of justice and morality. In his passionate nature man wants lordship . . . mystery and glory. In his cerebral nature he cares for none of these things." Two and a half years before, Auden blamed "dual conceptions" like this one as "the cause of disease, crime and permanent fatigue." Then, he wanted to maintain distinctions between an internally unified self and the world outside; now he wants to make connections. Yet he still lacks a language in which to do so. Education, he writes, is always social; but in the next sentence he is back to the "growth of an individ-

ual," which "cannot be planned; it is the outcome of passionate relationships."

Although Lawrence's language proved useless for practical social argument, abandoning that language did not make the problem easier.
Auden's next review, in *The Criterion* for January 1933, specifically acknowledges his lack of a social rhetoric. The two books at hand are
about social aspects of sex, but he soon turns his attention to education
and the state. He sees his own difficulty in finding a language for social
criticism as a weakness which society inevitably exploits—a point made
earlier not by Lawrence but by I. A. Richards. Everywhere, one hears
voices speaking only about personal issues, and so criticism of society
has become impossible. "Whoever possesses the instruments of knowledge, the press, the wireless, and the Ministry of Education, is the dictator of the country; and, my friends, it becomes increasingly difficult to
overthrow a bad one because imitating our voice, he makes us believe
that he does not exist." Our language bars us from understanding and
choice. "You cannot train children to be good citizens of a state which
you despise," and you cannot alter that state until you have a language
in which to understand it.

Auden's complaint against the limits of the language available to him
should be read as a poet's complaint as well as a citizen's. Politics and
sociology offered adequate rhetoric for the arguments he wanted to
make; what he needed was a way of incorporating this rhetoric into a
memorable language for poetry. He began to recognize that the literary
manner he inherited from his modernist predecessors had rendered
practical social issues invisible by assimilating all experience into a private introspective order. The rhetoric of modernism was based on two
great organizing principles, each of which excluded the characteristic
patterns of the social order. These principles may be called, in critical
shorthand, the Image and the Gyre. The Image is the poetic focus of
private vision in all its individual variety: the moment in Pater, perception of inscape in Hopkins, the epiphany in Joyce, the vortex in Pound
and Lewis, Yeats's "masterful images because complete," Pound's ideo-
grams, Eliot's still point. The Gyre, which is less often recognized as a
crucial element in modernism, is the outer complement to inner percep-

tion, the great cyclical order that controls the fate of nations. The Gyre has its basis in cyclical theories of time derived from esoteric traditions, but in modernism is used to give order to otherwise discrete Images. In effect, it is the Image of the universe itself, or of eternity where, Yeats wrote, "all the gyres converge in one." The most elaborate example is the complex set of cycles Yeats traces in *A Vision*. Another is the recurring circular pattern on which Joyce arranges events in *Ulysses* and *Finnegans Wake*. Between Gyre and Image there is no independent third realm. Whenever a modernist writer takes up matters that fall between these two extremes of scale, he does so either by projecting the Image outward, as Yeats does when he makes a terrible beauty the goal of a political poem, or by reducing the Gyre inward, as Joyce does in organizing Bloom's wanderings according to a cyclic pattern he discerns in the *Odyssey*.

Both Image and Gyre are visual metaphors, elements in the modernist alliance between poetry and painting. Such metaphors, and the symbolist aesthetic on which they rely, made possible the triumphs of vividness and elaboration that characterize modernism's greatest works. But those triumphs were won at a cost. In their imaged world, human motive was fruitless or unknowable, and all causality mysterious and obscure. Only art could make order: the uncontrollable mystery on the bestial floor mattered less than the marbles of the dancing floor, breaking bitter furies of complexity. Instead of motivation and consequence, cause and effect, modernism saw the brief intensity of the Image and the unwilled determinism of the Gyre. Such a world was the product of necessity not choice, and no one could choose to alter it.

As Auden sought a poetic language of choice and community, an alternative to the Image and Gyre, Bertolt Brecht was tackling the same problem. He had already recognized what Auden now began to understand: that to turn away from the closed intensity of modernism required more than an enlargement in vocabulary and style such as Auden had begun in 1930. It required a thorough change in the artist's relation to his audience. Instead of composing his unique experience into idiosyncratic structures, or transmitting the forms of his vision to an audience of the aesthetically initiated, an artist must convey knowledge that is not exclusively his own, and that he and others can put to use. He must become a teacher both of theory and of practice.

While Brecht was getting on with the job, Auden, in his reviews on education during the school year 1932–33, kept insisting he had nothing to teach. In the last of these reviews, he was almost ready to jettison language. Writing in May 1933 for *The Twentieth Century*, he charges that his literary language is so corrupted by its limited reference that teaching it to the young cannot serve to make them critical. Better for an English class to study advertising, "part of the environment [to] which literature is a reaction," than literature itself. Better still to get as far away from language as possible:

> Our education is far too bookish. . . . A boy in school remains divorced from the means of production, from livelihood; it is impossible to do much, but I believe that for the time being the most satisfactory method of teaching English to children is through their environment and their actions in it; e.g., if they are going to read or write about sawing wood, they should saw some themselves first: they should have plenty of acting, if possible, and under their English teacher movement classes as well, and very, very little talk.

⌐

In Auden's verse, meanwhile, the Lords of Limit, the mythical patrons of schools, reappeared under a new and darker aspect. They were no longer benevolent guardians of the coherent personality, shepherding pupils "Who to their serious season must shortly come." Now they emerged as the secret dictators of all society, generous only to those who stayed fixed within narrow bounds. Late in 1932 Auden wrote a dialogue poem for them, in which they call themselves simply "the Two." A few months later he published it under the title "The Witnesses," after Lawrence's *Apocalypse*. But just as Auden had discarded Lawrence's prose style in writing about education, now he discarded Lawrence's favorable opinion of the Two. The Lords of Limit who protected the pupil in space became the Witnesses who bar his progress in time.

In manuscript, the poem spoken by the Witnesses is not the separate work that Auden published, but a song inserted in a much longer poem, a dream vision in cantos which Auden left unfinished around the end of 1932. In this longer poem, as in "A Happy New Year," the Two preside over education, and the poem itself is again based partly on *Piers Plow-*

man. The poem (of which the next chapter gives a more detailed account) presents the Witnesses as the authors of all textbooks used in schools, the powers who decide what knowledge will be granted to the young. Auden borrowed his dream-vision's structure from Dante: as in the *Commedia,* the first part is a journey through an urban Hell which is metaphorically a human body. The Witnesses occupy the brain and stand for what Auden called in his 1929 journal the non-communistic isolated mind whose task it is to separate and destroy. They live behind a "steel door sealed as a safe's," propped up in a double bed like the cranial hemispheres, "Little, old, as like as two peas." Their power over schooling is absolute, but they themselves are products of society. "We're simply the servants of a system, you know," they answer when asked to aid in a case of injustice. Both their power and their isolation are the consequence of repression. Named (alas) Titt and Tool, they have no relation other than their names to these organs of satisfaction and desire, but are repressed transformations of desire—sex in the head. Lawrence had written that the "mind is the dead end of life," and in a 1930 song Auden echoed him:

> What's in your mind, my dove, my coney;
> Do thoughts grow like feathers, the dead end of life . . . ?

From these dead ends, education builds the ramparts of the social order.

In their song the Witnesses retain few traces of their gamekeeper origins, but they still "guard the wells" and are "handy with a gun," and to transgress their limits is to die. They tell the story of a would-be hero, an exploring conqueror, who defied all boundaries and restraints until, at last, "He came to a desert and down he sat / and cried." Sitting alone, he asks:

> for what
> Was I born, was it only to see
> I'm as tired of life as life of me?
> let me be forgot.
>
> Children have heard of my every action
> It gives me no sort of satisfaction
> and why?

> Let me get this as clear as I possibly can
> No, I am not the truly strong man,
>   O let me die.*

The Truly Strong Man, and his opposite, the Truly Weak who defies the Lords of Limit, is an idea that brings into focus Auden's divided wish for private satisfaction and public responsibility. He and Isherwood had shared the idea at least as early as 1929. Isherwood claimed in *Lions and Shadows* that he found it among Eugen Bleuler's case studies; Auden claimed in a 1934 book review that he found it in William McDougall's *Outline of Abnormal Psychology* (where, as it happens, McDougall was in fact quoting Bleuler). Whoever found it first, they agreed on its meaning. The Truly Weak, Auden wrote, takes to "blind action without consideration of meaning or ends"; he pursues what Isherwood called the futile compensatory North-West Passage. In 1929 Auden began writing his relevant case-histories of Truly Weak neurosis, e.g.,

> Pick a quarrel, go to war
> Leave the hero in the bar
> Hunt the lion, climb the peak
> No one guesses you are weak.

He wrote many of these, and used some in his 1930 "text book of Psychology in doggerel verses," but at the time he could name only one counter-example, one instance of personal calm: "Gerhart Meyer / From the sea, the truly strong man." The trouble with using this as a model is that Gerhart Meyer was a sailor Auden met in Berlin, and it was much too late for bourgeois intellectuals to follow his example. Until Auden found a plausible model for what he called "the transformation of the Truly Weak Man into the Truly Strong Man" (in 1934 he thought T. E. Lawrence might serve), he was able to identify the Truly Strong only by his absence. His review in 1934 cites, in very loose paraphrase, Bleuler's account of the man who said after cutting the throats of his wife and family: "No, I am not the truly strong man.

* This is among Auden's earliest uses of a modified Burns stanza; the first was "A Communist to Others," written about three months before. (See p. 143.)

The truly strong man lounges about in bars and does nothing at all."*
And that is all Auden knows about him. While the Truly Weak dies
searching for the North-West Passage, the Truly Strong, utterly un-
afraid, does nothing.

   This priggish ideal served Auden reasonably well as a model of inner
coherence in 1929. But by the end of 1932 he saw the inaction of the
Truly Strong in a somewhat different light—as the only way of life
the repressive Witnesses would tolerate. "Don't make the mistake,"
they warn, "of thinking us dead." Two years later, when he had made
peace with the Witnesses (and had dropped the parts of their song that
told the story of the Truly Weak), he reused their monitory closing
stanzas in the play *The Dog Beneath the Skin* as authentic guidance for
those embarking on a quest. In the context of the 1932 dream vision, in
the mouths of the textbook masters, the same warning had a more sinister tone:

> For I'm afraid in that case you'll have a fall;
> We've been watching you over the garden wall
>   for hours,
> The sky is darkening like a stain,
> Something is going to fall like rain
>   and it won't be flowers.
>
> When the green field comes off like a lid
> Revealing what were much better hid

—and so forth, as the Witnesses accumulate images of dread from the
nursery and the apocalypse. When they end by offering positive advice
on how one might avert their fury, they have only this to say:

> Be clean, be tidy, oil the lock,
> Trim the garden, wind the clock:
>   Remember the Two.

Like Auden's planned school curriculum of wood-sawing and movement classes, it is a limited program.

* The lounging in bars—and in the 1929 quatrain "Leave the hero in the bar"—is
Auden's embellishment, misremembered from a phrase in Bleuler's original about
"barroom gossip" driving the man to murder.

VII
Looking for Land

Auden's politics, when he first formulated them, were those of a very intelligent young man in the early 1930s—young enough to believe revolution inevitable, intelligent enough to be sceptical of its benefits. The worsening Depression, more severe than any in the industrial era, threatened to fulfill Marx's prediction of a final crisis of capitalism. During the summer of 1932 Auden began to see the Communist critique of bourgeois society as a redoubled form of his psychological critique, and one that might bring about real change. Late in the year he thought he was in the midst of a "conversion" to Communist belief; but he also knew he was too much of a bourgeois ever to join the Communist Party or ally himself directly with the working class. His politics remained a matter more of attitude than action, and although for a few months late in 1932 he tried on various articles of Communist faith, he found none that seemed to fit.

The communism he imagined for himself was idiosyncratic, with large admixtures of D. H. Lawrence and Gerald Heard. The mix varied according to the audience for whom Auden happened to be writing. He offered the mass readership of the *Daily Herald* a simple prescription based on economic self-interest: if you want to gain the high standard of living made possible by the machine, he told them, "you must first establish a Socialist State in which everyone can feel secure, and, secondly, have enough self-knowledge and common sense to ensure that machines are employed by your needs, and not your needs by the machinery." Addressing the educated progressive audience of *The Twen-*

tieth Century, the journal of the short-lived Promethean Society, he was less hopeful: "some kind of revolution is inevitable, and will as inevitably be imposed from above by a minority; in consequence, if the result is not to depend on the loudest voice, if the majority is to have the slightest say in the future, it must be more critical than it is necessary for it to be in an epoch of straightforward development." In the rarefied atmosphere of Eliot's *Criterion,* the important issues were more psychological than political, and there could be no illusions about the virtues of either the new order or the old: "If we want a decent sex life, happy human relations, if we want to be people at all, and not behaviorist automatons, we must see to it that our dictators can have no personal or class axe to grind and we must hurry or it will be too late."

Auden readily followed Marx in insisting that the majority should be made more critical—better aware of the structure of society, better prepared to change it—but he was uncertain how they would become so. The schools could not accomplish this didactic task. "Education succeeds social revolution, not precedes." The educational ideals of liberalism, with its hatred of power and stress on personal relations, made matters even worse: "unconsciously the liberal becomes the secret service of the ruling class, its most powerful weapon against social revolution." Yet revolution, when it comes, will inevitably be imposed by a minority who will have no wish to make the majority more critical. Auden repeatedly traced this circular dilemma in his essays and reviews, never claiming to have found an adequate solution. And he knew enough to keep his distance from any party that proposed an inadequate one.

He was at least certain he must overcome the isolation he had welcomed a few years before. He must learn to think of himself not as a solitary consciousness, not even as part of a small group, but as one man among millions, one whose fate would coincide with the fate of the majority. It was not enough to emulate the psychological health of the Truly Strong whose calm inaction left society unchanged.

As Auden gradually approached this new sense of things, during the first half of 1932, his poems also came to see the world in different ways. He began "A Happy New Year" from the superior distant heights of the first part but shifted to a more humane horizontal for the second, where he looked out on his school and town. By April, two months later, in the love poem "The chimneys are smoking, the crocus is out in the border," he had so thoroughly rejected his hawk's perspective that he had become something a hawk sees from above:

> A hawk looks down on us all; he is not in this;
> Our kindness is hid from the eye of the vivid creature.

Love and our common nature—the two meanings of *our kindness*—require a common level, a shared landscape unknown to airmen. Yet even here, lovers stand in a divided world. A garden-border cuts across the poem's first line, and, everywhere, opposed to love, are the "white death" and his spies, "hostile, apart / From the belovèd group"—from the sexual couple which is a special case of Auden's general theory of groups. Auden's goal in this poem is a stratagem that will allow the small group to survive death's hostile interest, a stratagem by which the small group may dissolve at last into a larger unity.

The poem opens with a lover's lament over separation.* He is alone in the midst of an otherwise renewing world, where spring has begun and a "communist orator"—changed to a "political orator" in the 1936 revision—lands like a sea-god at the pier. This is the first Communist in Auden's work, and he appears as one of the many aspects of spring renewal from which the poet is excluded. What matters most to the poet is his own divided love, which reminds him how fragile was the harmony he shared when "Last week we embraced on the dunes and thought they were pleased." Then, we thought ourselves one with nature when alone together; but it was through the feeling of that "hour of unity" itself that we have become aware of the gulf between our private unified "world" and the disordered "world" outside. The ominous "double-shadow" we cast in our single embrace warned of that threatening outer division.†

---

* The affair reported in "For what as easy" and "That night when joy began" ended when Auden's partner moved to another town.
† I am trying, without much confidence, to make sense of one of Auden's most tangled stanzas. Its convolutions are the sort which suggest that Auden didn't quite believe what he was not quite able to say. The stanza reads as follows (the word in brackets appears in both surviving manuscripts but in no printed text):

> For our hour of unity makes us aware of two worlds:
> That [one] was revealed to us then in our double-shadow,
> Which for the masters of harbours, the colliers, and us,

Death outside threatens inner love, but now Auden has a stratagem against death. All the evidence in his poetry indicates that love cannot survive, but the visionary politics he has begun to embrace offers new promise. The trick is to accept the division that separates two lovers, in order to find instead a general unity in which they can dissolve their separate personalities and so, ultimately, join not only with each other but with everyone else. The death two lovers cannot defeat on their own may be defeated by millions. So the poet explains that his lover *should* "leave me and slip away . . . allaying suspicion" on the part of the white death. "What we do for each other now must be done alone," assert the early texts (altered, presumably, when Auden noticed the sexual double entendre). But our departure from each other is only a pretence, for we remain joined by our "trust." "If we can trust we are free" from death's divisions. Since physical love had almost invariably failed in Auden's early poems, now he tries to imagine that separated love, in a larger unity of trust, may survive in its place.

This is very odd. The trust Auden has in mind in this poem depends not on vows or responsibilities but on joining ("implicating") one's private wish to a larger wish for unity. It has little to do with personal love or even physical satisfaction. Since the world's divisiveness blocks our way to erotic unity (desire's "straightest" route), we must deflect toward something greater. This general unity is not the unity of social revolution, not the promise of the communist orator, since it is desired equally by the workers and the rich:

> For our calculating star,
> Where the divided feel
> Tears in their eyes
> And time and doctors heal,
> Eternally sighs.

Since the previous stanza speaks of metaphoric "spies on the human heart," hostile to our unity, and since the following stanza describes the desire of the "friendless" "white death" for us, this stanza may perhaps be unfolded to mean something like this: In the divided shadow we cast in our hour of unity, it was revealed to us that we are *shadowed* by that world of death which always sighs for us—sighs for the divided, sighs for the loving—and longs to reduce us to the passivity of the "white death." If this reading is awkward and unconvincing, at least these are qualities it shares with the poem.

And since our desire cannot take that route which is straightest,
Let us choose the crooked, so implicating these acres,
These millions in whom already the wish to be one
    Like a burglar is stealthily moving,
    That these, on the new façade of a bank
    Employed, or conferring at health resort,
    May, by circumstance linked,
    More clearly act our thought.

The poem leaves unexplained this great change in the collective mind, this wish to be one that moves among millions, *now*. But Auden's next poem will identify this change as an evolutionary mutation, fated from the beginning of time. The dire sense of evolution's indifference that Auden felt earlier has yielded, for a month or two, to a meliorative faith out of the woozier pages of Gerald Heard. Mankind, Heard predicted, was about to ascend from individualism to a new "super-consciousness of a purely psychologically satisfying state." Auden's love poem ends by summoning "boatmen, virgins, camera-men, and us" to a universal dance of this super-consciousness, a dance in which "our joy abounding is, though it hide underground." But this apolitical vision of dancing fraternity has a confidence that in the youthful Auden is thoroughly off-key. The whole poem is marked by the characteristic badness of his moments of poetic inauthenticity and deliberate self-deception, and I doubt he believed a word of it.*

A month later, in May 1932, he again foresaw visionary unity in his mind's eye, but now he saw it approaching in one country only. A transformed England was to be the vanguard of evolution. "O Love, the interest itself in thoughtless Heaven," he began, praying for the human heart to be simplified and made whole. By the third stanza he turned from the individual heart to the nation at large, "our little reef . . . This fortress perched on the edge of the Atlantic scarp." Here Love's power is urgently needed. In the great economic depression, dreams of progress and empire die; industry declines; but the crisis is ultimately one of understanding. All through "these impoverished constricting acres" the English lapse into single vision and Newton's sleep:

* Its tone is reminiscent of Auden's 1929 poem "Which of you waking early," with its concluding vision of "truth's assurance of life . . . Of security upon earth and life in heaven"—the poem on which Auden's second (and final) thoughts were that it was "pompous trash."

> The ladies and gentlemen apart, too much alone,
>
> Consider the years of the measured world begun,
> The barren spiritual marriage of stone and water.

Yet "at this very moment of our hopeless sigh" a new unity begins to approach us. The next stage of our evolution, another "dream" somehow coded in the biological past, "long coiled in the ammonite's slumber," is about to come true. A few years before Auden had seen the ancestral curse emerge in a family's heir by a similar mechanism; now he indulges himself with an evolutionary fantasy to the effect that our isolation and division have grown so severe that the next mutation must bring a recovered unity. In his love poem the previous month he saw that unity as a dance of joy. Now he has a more ominous image. There will be no dancing. A great change will cut through all our familiar pleasures. It is

> prepared to lay on our talk and kindness
> Its military silence, its surgeon's idea of pain.

And the poem ends with the change making its inexorable approach, bringing apocalyptic marriage out of the distant past into our immediate present. The change, "called out of tideless peace by a living sun"—or, in the 1936 revision, "out of the Future into actual History"—has as its metaphor the mythical origins of England itself:

> As when Merlin, tamer of horses, and his lords to whom
> Stonehenge was still a thought, the Pillars passed
>
> And into the undared ocean swung north their prow,
> Drives through the night and star-concealing dawn
> For the virgin roadsteads of our hearts an unwavering keel.

Splendid as this rhetoric is—and the retention of the subject of the verb *drives* until the end is splendid indeed—it leaves some doubts. The source of the image is Canto XXVI of the *Inferno*—which Auden will quote at length in his play *The Ascent of F6*—where Ulysses repeats the false counsel that drove his men past the Pillars of Hercules to swing south into the uncharted ocean, only to be destroyed by a storm of divine wrath. (Auden's phrase "tamer of horses," a common epithet in the

Iliad, is part of the same cluster of Homeric references.) The Ulyssean disaster suggests that Auden lacks full confidence in his new visionary Merlin. Evolution is not quite so sudden as he wants to believe, nor its timing quite so convenient.

It is a short step—at least in literature—from visionary to practical politics. If the new order seems unlikely to happen by itself, perhaps it can be made to happen. Auden knew that Communists were arguing in these terms in Germany and England, but he only listened seriously when a writer he admired began to follow their example. Edward Upward, Isherwood's collaborator on the Mortmere fantasies, had turned to politics and a stringent literary realism around 1930. Auden and Isherwood at first thought Upward's new attitudes alien and extreme, but they could not ignore them. Isherwood looked to Upward as his literary mentor, and since Auden to some extent saw Isherwood in the same light, Upward's influence reached Auden both directly and indirectly. Before 1932 Auden had read some essays and stories Upward had written about his first contacts with the Communist Party, which he did not formally join until 1934; and in the late spring of 1932 Auden read the journal in which Upward chronicled his growing sympathy with communism.

One of Upward's prose pieces maintained that writers need the working classes and could choose to help them. When Auden wrote his long letter to John Pudney late in July he adapted this argument to his own nonpartisan purposes. Poets, he said "need the group . . . They get more from it than they know." But he resisted the political content of Upward's argument for only a few more days. In August he wrote a poem in the voice of a Communist who addresses an "unhappy poet," telling him, almost in Upward's words, "You need us more than you suppose / And you could help us if you chose." The earliest manuscript of the poem opens, "All you who when the sirens roar"; when Auden sent a copy to Isherwood shortly afterward, this became, "Comrades, who when the sirens roar"; and when it was published in September he added the title, "A Communist to Others."

The voice of this poem is not Auden's but that of a Communist telling Auden what he needs to learn. The ventriloquism is not entirely convincing. The Communist is supposedly a member of the working class, "a nasty sight" and proud of it, but he is well-informed in the intellectual fashions of the bourgeoisie—mysticism, psychoanalysis, Cambridge liberalism, and so on. D. H. Lawrence seems to figure far more prominently than Marx in his pantheon. He has more to say about the psychology of groups and the failings of poets than about communism as such. He concludes his poem, in stanzas Auden dropped after first publication, with a mystically erotic vision, a group ecstasy of "Brothers for whom our bowels yearn / When words are over," all held "in unseen connection" by "Love outside our own election." The Party would not be pleased to learn that its stalwart orator found this vision in the final pages of Gerald Heard's *Social Substance of Religion*, where Heard explicitly rejects a Marxist economic communism, "driven not by love, but by hate," for a communism of emotion and eros. Heard argues that if the ordinary man can feel love for his fellows, not a sexual love as much as a manifestation of "the general energy of life," "then there is no need for a proletarian dictatorship to transform him." Auden's poem bends to the pressure of Marxism but does not yield to it.

A month later he wrote a companion poem, the song "I have a handsome profile." This tone-deaf doggerel alternates between the lonely voice of a bourgeois—"I own a world that has had its day"—and choral voices threatening change. The approaching revolution has little to do with economics or politics, though it is fueled by the discontent of the workers. It proves, in the final stanza, to be a revolt of the young:

> Your son may be a hero
> Carry a great big gun
> Your son may be a hero
> But you will not be one
> Go down with your world that has had its day.*

One thing that is now certain about revolution, whoever makes it, is that it will be violent: great big guns, not virgins and boatmen dancing. After Auden exorcized the fantasies of the Airman he never again romanticized violence. His political poems in the summer of 1932 use a heady rhetoric of apocalyptic upheavals, but he turns his attention

---

* This pairing of a long poem and a shorter song in reply repeats the pairing three years earlier of the poem spoken by evolution, "Since you are going to begin today," and the song of the man abandoned by it, "It's no use raising a shout."

almost immediately to the real acts of personal betrayal that will inevitably attend any violent change. A month after "I have a handsome profile," he wrote the monitory ballad "O what is that sound which so thrills the ear." This is a quietly terrifying dialogue between two lovers, a ritual exchange of anxious questions in long lines of verse and calm cold answers in shorter ones. At the end, the betraying lover escapes the pursuit of the scarlet soldiers, leaving the betrayed to the mercies of the state:

> O where are you going? stay with me here!
>   Were the vows you swore me deceiving, deceiving?
> No, I promised to love you, dear,
>   But I must be leaving.
>
> O it's broken the lock and splintered the door,
>   O it's the gate where they're turning, turning;
> Their feet are heavy on the floor
>   And their eyes are burning.

However mixed his feelings about social revolution—it was a few weeks after writing this poem that he wrote his warning about dictators with a personal or class axe to grind—Auden had largely recast his early psychological theories into emphatically political terms. He returned to the "Glossary of Christian and Psychological terms" he compiled about three years earlier (see p. 76) and added a third column. Now the chart looked like this:

Social terms	*Glossary of Christian and Psychological terms*		
Society, the happy	Heaven	The Unconscious	
Matter	Earth	The Conscious Mind	
Society the unhappy	Hell	The repressed unconscious	
The revolution	Purgatory	The consulting-room	
The collective	The Father	{Body?} The Ego-instincts	The self ideal
The individual	The Son	{Mind?} The Death-instincts	The Not-self ideal
History	The Holy Ghost	The Libido	The relation between these two opposites
Nature	The Madonna	Nature	
The C. Party	The Four Archangels	The four great ganglia of the body	

The capitalist system	Satan	The Censor
The ruling classes	The Devils	The repressed instincts
Starvation, war, unemployment	Hell-Fire	Unhappiness, disease, and mania
The appearance of class distinction	The Fall of Man	The advent of self-consciousness
. . .	. . .	. . .

Although the Christian terms remain firmly rooted at the center of this chart, Auden's interest has shifted leftward across the page. By the end of 1932 he was ready to discard or postpone all his old projects for psychological healing until after a thorough social upheaval. "What is the use of trying to remove complexes from individuals when the society into which they will go demands that they should have them?" Properly understood, neurotic and lonely sexual relationships are a political issue: "Big business encourages them because human relations are bad for trade." The healers' art has been usurped by industrial capitalism for its own ends. The modern levelling of sex differences, for example, proves to be a means of social repression:

> To big business and for its trivial but exhausting tasks of mass pro-
> duction, an intermediate pert adolescent type is the most suitable; it is
> advertised for and obtained. The effect of mother on son, son on wife,
> so dear to the healers, is the process by which the valuable product is
> manufactured.

After the isolating darkness of his psychological questioning, Auden, at twenty-five, writes as one who has emerged into daylight, even if he is still somewhat blinded by it.

Auden's movement out of private places into the public arena corre-
sponds to a parallel development in his literary method. His first poems had called attention to their fragmentary quality—they started and stopped in the middle of things, and refused to give any hint of the contexts in which they might be read. Whenever Auden put together a poem longer than about a hundred lines, he would combine existing fragments into a sequence rather than devise a large form at the outset.

The first poem in the 1928 pamphlet *Poems* (the edition hand-printed by Spender, not the 1930 Faber volume) consists of eight poems written separately over a period of two and a half years, and now strung together on a fragile thematic thread; an earlier version in manuscript used some different fragments. He employed a similar method with greater success in gathering and rewriting the four "1929" poems. *Paid on Both Sides* was put together by writing a prose context around some existing poems, with new verses added where needed. *The Orators* has a large and fairly coherent form, but the Odes seem to have been tacked on as an afterthought, and parts of the "Journal of an Airman" were apparently sketched in around poems already written.*

All this improvisation from isolated fragments could be considered suitable to a poetry whose aim was to express fragmentation itself. But as early as 1929 Auden was objecting to his own style, and doing so from the standpoint of bourgeois values. In his journal he wrote:

> *Work*
> Damn this laziness. I envy the ease of so many writers. I sit down for an hour or so and think of about two lines. Is this genuine difficulty or just lack of concentration. My work is scrappy. I want to do something on a larger scale. Or must I wait till I am fifty. My flabbiness of mind, inability to think, obscure sensibility disgusts me. I know what I write is obscure. Too often this is just being too lazy to think things out properly.... Laziness is impatience.

At last, during 1932, he set out to write larger and more coherently patterned poems. He knew it would not be easy. A unified long poem requires an extended commitment to the poem's subject, a commitment very different from that needed for a lyric. At one extreme of critical theory, in the territory exemplified by the Arnoldian touchstone and other affective ideas of what poetry ought to be, a long poem is regarded

---

* Auden often reused lines or stanzas of discarded poems when writing later ones, but Isherwood was writing more as a novelist than a historian when, in 1937, he explained Auden's early obscurity thus: "If I didn't like a poem, he threw it away and wrote another. If I liked one line, he would keep it and work it into a new poem. In this way, whole poems were constructed which were simply anthologies of my favourite lines, entirely regardless of grammar or sense. This is the simple explanation of much of Auden's celebrated obscurity." In fact there are no such poems, and the earlier rejected poems are no less obscure than the poems to which they donated, at most, one or two stanzas or lines.

as a contradiction in terms. Similarly, all modernist long poems—*The Waste Land, The Bridge, The Cantos, Paterson* and so on—shift abruptly from one short fragment to another, from one style to another, in an imagistic procession. Auden's earliest long poems had been like this, but now he was ready to try for something different: works that recommend a large social unity by embodying a large poetic unity.

At first his distance from *any* material kept him from developing the complex response a long poem required. The opening part of "A Happy New Year," early in 1932, was his first attempt at a consistent long poem: about three hundred lines, mostly in rhyme-royal. But the stanzaic form gives no coherence to the poem's satiric dream vision, nor does Auden's personal voice give much order: he passively observes a vision that begins for no good reason, changes focus at random, and ends for no better reason. All he preserved of "A Happy New Year" after its first publication was its shorter second part, with its celebration of the small group.

Undaunted, Auden soon began an even more ambitious project, a poem he described to friends as "my epic." This was the dream vision in cantos which includes "The Witnesses." He worked on it from September 1932 until abandoning it, about two-fifths complete, late in that year or early in 1933. Had he finished it he would have written some three thousand alliterative lines. Once again he adapted medieval forms. As "A Happy New Year" had taken its basic outline from Langland—a vision of a fair field full of folk—and its verse form from Chaucer, the new poem took its outline from Dante—a guided spiritual journey through darkness into light—and its verse from Langland. Both these 1932 poems are anatomies of modern England, but the second has wider range and greater detail and, unlike the earlier poem, searches for the cause and cure of the disorder it records.

The first canto traces a night voyage downward through an urban Hell; the second, of which only the opening passages were written, moves in daylight to a house on a hill, presumably the site of a Purgatorial struggle. The first canto indicates that the second was to include a confrontation between the rich at a hunt and a group of Communist rebels hiding in the countryside. Auden wrote nothing about the Paradise in which, presumably, the poem was meant to conclude. Despite the consistent alliterative form, the poem is exceptionally unstable in tone, shifting from portentous visions of urban horror to an elaborately joking riddle on an electric razor, without much success at either extreme. The methods that worked well in *Paid on Both Sides* were difficult to renounce when they were no longer needed. As in "A Happy New Year" Auden does little more than observe the landscape through which he moves, even though he now has an active companion and guide, a Virgil under the name of Sampson, loosely modelled on Gerald Heard. Auden has come down from his superior height, but he has brought his distance with him. His Florentine original was a political exile who could still respond personally to the souls he met on his journey; as an English poet following in Dante's path, Auden is a psychological exile who swears loyalty to his guide but otherwise shows no emotions at all. It is hard to imagine what he could say to any Beatrice who might be waiting at the height of his Purgatory.

Near the opening of the second canto Auden makes his most elaborate and explicit statement of the problem of borders. Here, for the first time, the border is a problem he does not face alone. He can discuss it with others and, perhaps, thereby resolve it. Sampson-Heard calls the border a "limen" and speaks of the "colossal shadow" that it casts over life. Auden (the poet, not the poetic pilgrim) found this word in *Social Substance of Religion*, where Heard writes of a "limen" which "rises between" the two sides of the mind. Heard commits a minor solecism here. In the original Latin sense, and the modern psychological one, *limen* does not mean a barrier but a threshold. (Heard may have confused the word with *limes*, frontier.) Probably Auden knew this, and wanted the proper sense to be detected as an undertone in Sampson's answer when Auden-as-Dante asks, "What did you mean when you mentioned limen?" The answer summarizes all Auden's concerns with barriers, divisions, watersheds, and the disjunction between matter and mind:

> "The barrier," he answered, "which divides
> That which must will from that which can perceive,
> Desire from data; the watershed between
> The lonely unstable mad executives
> We recognize in banks and restaurants as our friends,
> And that lost country across which
> Dreams have made furtive flights at night
> To reconnoitre but have never landed,*

* I have inserted this comma because the next phrase is parallel with the one beginning "across which," and follows logically from the words "that lost country."

Where dwells the unprogressive blind society,
Possessing no argument but the absolute veto. . . ."

The limen is every barrier in the divided self: between active will and passive senses, between the wish and the reality. On one side of this watershed is the aspect of man which executes action in the physical world, the aspect of ourselves we can also recognize in others through their visible acts. (Auden's "unstable mad executives" are a whimsical personification of Heard's "outer, executive, unstable side of man's nature.") On the other side is the private subjective realm, absolutely isolated from the objective world, whose essential feature is its "blind" self-enclosure, its "veto" over any intrusion from outside. Much later, and far more economically, Auden will refer to these two aspects of man as the Self and the I.

The limen, Sampson-Heard continues, is the ultimate subject of the romantic poetry of loss—"Hills that the famous sang sighs over like a Shelley"—and the cause of all religious longing for the One. Our task now is not to sigh over the impasse, but to tunnel through, "and pierce we must." Should we fail, the stress within us will be so great that, however calm we appear to others and ourselves, we shall soon "in a scandalous explosion of the stolid perish."

All this psychological analysis is from the unfinished second canto; the first is reserved mostly for public matters—social division and economic crisis. But in calling the barrier between the public and private worlds a *limen* Auden potentially redefines it as a threshold, a wall that might open as a door. The poem points toward a double reconciliation in its unwritten third canto—a psychological reconciliation between the divided aspects of the mind, and a political one in which the victors of the coming revolution will have no class axe to grind. Gerald Heard, who dismissed economic matters from his projected communism of love, seems an inadequate guide to Auden's final Paradise and, like Dante's Virgil, must presumably be left behind at the height of Purgatory. If Sampson-Heard has Virgil's merits, he also has his limitations. Like Virgil before the gatekeepers of the city of Dis, Sampson can do nothing to persuade the Witnesses to help an unemployed friend. The presumably reconciled forces of communism and psychology would change all this at the end of the poem, but what form could their reconcilation take?

Auden was not yet ready to accept the Christian terms at the center of his three-part glossary, but while he was working toward his vision of Paradise, he thought of himself as moving toward belief. At about the time he was finishing his first canto, in December 1932, he explained to a reader who had asked about *The Orators* that the book had been, "as I didn't realise when I was writing it, a stage in my conversion to Communism." In fact he would soon arrive at a very different religious experience, not a conversion at all, certainly not to communism, but he knew he was approaching an impasse and communism seemed the only way through it.

In this same letter Auden foresaw a dark night of the national soul, which he described in terms corresponding to his own crisis of belief: "England will get worse and worse till there is an utter defeat and then it's possible I think that as we have often done before we shall stand the winner." But in his cantos Auden could portray only the faintest outline of the Communists who might bring England's salvation. What he says of them has nothing to do with the Party or the Soviet Union or any political praxis. All he can report is that they have withdrawn from the poem's world. As Sampson explains:

> "From factory, warehouse, foundry, shop,
> Garage and depot, men have gone from this town,
> Slipping away without warning or reason;
> In twos and threes they have taken to the hills.
> Our companions in the morning [i.e. the rich] would
>
> >   compel them back.
> The measure of their success we shall see together."

A few lines earlier one of these men made his escape by smashing a window and jumping through. Auden portrays the departure, but his second canto breaks off before the reappearance. Like the Truly Strong Man, these Communists do nothing. In "A Communist to Others" Auden had evaded the problem of portraying a revolutionary hero by letting him speak about his class enemies rather than himself. Later, in *The Dog Beneath the Skin* in 1935, the hero leaves his village to join "the army of the other side," an army not otherwise defined. Spender's comment on this play applies equally to the poem in cantos: both imagine "a society defeated by an enemy whom the writers have not put into the picture because they do not know what he looks like, although they thoroughly support him."

Auden's contradictory and unattainable purposes finally brought him to a halt. For about four months after he abandoned his cantos he seems to have written no verse at all. Then, in April 1933, in a new tone of voice, he began again.

First he dismissed his grandiose ambitions in favor of comic self-knowledge. Instead of an epic dream vision of England he wrote a mocking dream vision about himself. This poem, unpublished in Auden's lifetime,* opens with crisp pedantic exactitude:

> The month was April, the year
>   Nineteen hundred and thirty-three,
> The place a philosopher's garden
>   In Oxford, the person me.
> The weather was mild and sunny
>   As prophesied by Old Moore;
> I fell asleep in a deck-chair
>   And this is what I saw.

Auden assigns a date to his vision, just as in the first line of his cantos he had specified the date as 1932, "In the year of my youth when yoyos came in." In this new vision he has no guide. He dreams he is a sea gull, looking down alone on a ship in the ocean:

> I didn't have to be told
>   That she was looking for land,
> But her steering was so peculiar
>   I couldn't quite understand.

The sea gull cannot see as the hawk or the helmeted airman sees; he flies down to get a closer look. What he finds is the good ship *Wystan Auden Esquire*, a private place, drifting aimlessly in open water, searching not very efficiently for solid ground.

Her captain and crew represent Auden's faculties in a crudely allegorical way. The captain, who proves to be a woman with the formida-

---

* It is now in *The English Auden*.

ble traits of Auden's mother, stands for his will. The mate, who looks
and sounds like Auden's father, acts on the will's commands. There is a
wireless operator representing speech and the senses, an engineer, a
cook, a stoker, and so on. Two passengers are along strictly for the ride.
One is the Duke, who amuses himself with the cabin boy, in a parody of
Auden's sexual attitude to the working class. The other is the Professor,
who represents the poetic faculty. Never was a poet so isolated in his art
as the Professor is. Ignoring everyone around him, he does nothing but
make cat's cradles—the allegorical equivalent of autonomous poetic
structures. The interest he takes in this harmless amusement is entirely
technical:

> The Professor went on muttering,
>   "I was right: at Position A
> Navaho index strings—
>   Yes, this must be the way."

This apparent nonsense is compiled from terms used by anthropologists
to describe the making of string-figures, technical terms equivalent to
the prosodic and rhetorical terms used by poets.* So much for the fire-
breathing politics of Auden's verse during the previous year.

The destination of this personal *Narrenschiff* is not to be found on
the ship's chart, which like the map used for hunting the Snark is a perfect and absolute blank. The ship's goal is nothing less than the impossibly reconciled Utopia that Auden never got around to describing in
his cantos. As the captain explains:

> "I would remind you we are sailing
>   To the Islands of Milk and Honey
> Where there's neither death nor old age
>   And the poor have all the money.
> The wells are full of wine,
>   New bread grows on the trees,
> And roasted pigs run about
>   Crying 'Eat me, if you please!' "

* The verb *to Navaho*—to perform a certain complex operation characteristic of
Navaho Indian string-figures—is not in the *OED*; it was first used and defined by
Kathleen Haddon in *Cat's Cradles from Many Lands* (1911).

On those Islands, desire and its object meet. Society's disorder is re-solved and public wrongs made right. The ancestral curse and the fam-ily ghosts can have no effect there, since no one grows old and dies. Auden is doing his best to make it impossible for him to take his youth-ful fantasies seriously.

A storm, the captain announces, is approaching the ship; the crew must go without rations until it passes. The wireless operator reports that he has received messages telling of "calmer water / If we steer our course to the east," but the captain will have none of it. As the storm comes up, everyone goes below decks except the Professor and captain. The Professor is still making cat's cradles though "the water was up to his neck." The captain is acting very oddly indeed, but she manages none the less to put an end to Auden's earlier projects:

> Alone on her bridge the captain,
>   While the gale whirled shriller and colder,
> Was eating the chart, and now
>   Took the musket from her shoulder,
> Loaded it and began to fire
>   Wildly at sky and sea,
> Then suddenly she turned round
>   And levelled it straight at me.

When the captain of the *Auden* fires at the sea gull Auden, the dreamer Auden wakes in his Oxford garden—where "The table was laid for tea."

The stormy waters that in Auden's dream engulfed his craft had ap-peared in different forms in earlier poems. At first the waters of impulse were frozen solid. The scene of transient love in "Taller to-day" was "far from the glacier," but not far enough to omit it from the poem. A year or so later the waters settled "deep in clear lake" where drowning might perhaps lead to new life in the spring. Both glacier and lake are passive. Here the storm rushes forward, too quickly and inexorably for escape.

The waters take a different but equally active form in a poem Auden wrote the following month, May 1933—the sestina beginning "Hearing of harvests rotting in the valleys" (later titled "Paysage Moralisé"). Now, instead of dreaming of a chaotic storm or a passive lake, he asks if flowing waters might make fertile his barren landscape. For the first time he hopes neither to be somewhere else, nor changed to some transfigured condition, nor held to the safety of a small group, nor joined with the masses. Instead, epitomizing in the simple emotional term "sorrow" all the unhappiness that gives rise to vain hopes of escape, he asks if that glacial unhappiness could "melt." If this could happen, he would no longer be caught in his wish for an impossible change, but would be free to work responsibly, would be free to rebuild the broken fragments of his world.

Within the exigencies of the sestina form Auden achieves a masterful symbolic play of psychology and history. The poem offers a summary account of civilization in terms of action and desire. We live in sorrowful cities, trapped by an inhospitable landscape. Looking back to a time we imagine to have been less sorrowful than ours, "We honour founders of these starving cities." But our nostalgia for the past has no basis in historical fact; it is the projection of our present unhappiness. Our image of the heroic past is false: the will and energy we admire in the city's founders is only the inverted "image of our sorrow." They lacked as we do the decisive happiness we project onto them, and it was their own futile hope of a cure "That brought them desperate to the brink of valleys." As we dream now of a past without sorrow, they dreamt then of a happy future, "of evening walks through learned cities." That their dream was futile is proved by our unhappiness now. Their new cities brought no peace, only a different dream of some distant place never infected by sorrow:

> Each in his little bed conceived of islands
> Where every day was dancing in the valleys . . .
> Where love was innocent, being far from cities.

These are the Islands of Milk and Honey, an Enlightenment dream shattered daily when "dawn came back and they were still in cities." No fantasy could distract them for long, since "hunger was a more immediate sorrow."

Now romantic visionaries came, promising unity and peace on utopian islands. Yet of those who went forth in quest, "So many, fearful, took with them their sorrow," and got no farther than other "unhappy cities." Other travellers, "doubtful," "careless," "wretched," came no closer to Utopia. And so the centuries of search and dream leave us with the same sorrow in which these cities began.

The sestina's envoi states our circumstance bluntly: "It is the sorrow." No more need be said. The nurturing sea lies frozen—

> shall it melt? Ah, water
> Would gush, flush, green these mountains and these valleys
> And we rebuild our cities, not dream of islands.

Only in the last line do "these cities" become "our cities." The melting
flood, if it comes, will release our private dream into public responsibility. What the watershed divided, now will gather in the valleys.

Auden in this poem is fully conscious of the difficulties he has set for
himself. The ancient founders and explorers, the thinkers of the Enlightenment and the dreamers of the Romantic age, all hoped to escape
or to diminish human sorrow, but Auden's hope is different. Knowing
that sorrow is everywhere and can never lessen, he hopes instead that it
may *melt*—change its form, become available for use, make a vineyard
of the curse. No reason or logic offers any promise that this might happen. But in imagining the results of this miraculous event Auden infuses
his poem with the accentual energies of Gerard Manley Hopkins' religious poetry: "water / Would gush, flush, green these mountains and
these valleys." Hopkins used such language as a sign of faith's conquest
of rational limits. Auden, less confident, can use it, for the moment, only
in the conditional mood, to express a possibility. Yet after years of entrapment in a language of irony and contradiction, sorrow and self-
defeat, he speaks in a language of hope.

Part Two

≠≠≠

THE
TWO
WORLDS

(June 1933–January 1939)

VIII
Lucky This Point

On a warm June evening in 1933 the sorrow melted. That night Auden experienced what he later called a mystical vision, probably the only such event in his life. He characterized it as a *vision of agape*, one in which, for the first time, he knew what it meant to love his neighbor as himself. His vision revealed neither sexual intensity nor undifferentiated groups nor social revolution, nor any of the extreme personal and public ordeals he had imagined as the only possible escapes from privacy. But while it lasted his isolation dissolved.

He wrote about the vision twice. Within a few days or weeks he celebrated its mood in the poem he later entitled "A Summer Night." In 1964 he returned to it and wrote a detailed factual account in a prose essay on the varieties of mystical experience. Then, in 1965, he suggested the vision's importance to him by arranging his *Collected Shorter Poems 1927–1957* in sections corresponding to "a new chapter in my life," and opening the second of these sections with "A Summer Night." The book's other chapter-divisions mark visible concrete events: Auden's arrival in America in 1939, his first summer in Italy in 1948, his purchase of a house in Austria in 1957. His placement of "A Summer Night" marks an equally decisive passage and arrival, one that occurred invisibly and intangibly as he sat in an English garden one evening in 1933.

His prose account, prepared thirty years after the event, appears in the introduction he wrote for Anne Fremantle's 1964 anthology *The*

Protestant Mystics. This essay divides mystical experiences into four different types: visions of "Dame Kind" (nature), Eros, Agape, and God. Under the heading "The Vision of Agape" he writes: "Since I cannot find a specific description among these selections, I shall quote from an unpublished account for the authenticity of which I can vouch." For rhetorical purposes—he needs an *exemplum*—he presents the account as independent evidence, but his mask of anonymity is thin enough to be transparent; no one has access to anyone else's visions. Although he speaks of quoting from an account, his quotation seems to be all there ever was of it: the typescript of the essay shows minor stylistic revisions being made in the account while it was typed. It is important enough to reprint in full:

> One fine summer night in June 1933 I was sitting on a lawn after din- ner with three colleagues, two women and one man. We liked each other well enough but we were certainly not intimate friends, nor had any one of us a sexual interest in another. Incidentally, we had not drunk any alcohol. We were talking casually about everyday matters when, quite suddenly and unexpectedly, something happened. I felt myself invaded by a power which, though I consented to it, was irre- sistible and certainly not mine. For the first time in my life I knew exactly—because, thanks to the power, I was doing it—what it means to love one's neighbor as oneself. I was also certain, though the con- versation continued to be perfectly ordinary, that my three colleagues were having the same experience. (In the case of one of them, I was able later to confirm this.) My personal feelings towards them were unchanged—they were still colleagues, not intimate friends—but I felt their existence as themselves to be of infinite value and rejoiced in it.
>
> I recalled with shame the many occasions on which I had been spiteful, snobbish, selfish, but the immediate joy was greater than the shame, for I knew that, so long as I was possessed by this spirit, it would be literally impossible for me deliberately to injure another human being. I also knew that the power would, of course, be with- drawn sooner or later and that, when it did, my greeds and self-regard would return. The experience lasted at its full intensity for about two hours when we said good-night to each other and went to bed. When I awoke the next morning, it was still present, though weaker, and it did not vanish completely for two days or so. The memory of the experi-

ence has not prevented me from making use of others, grossly and often, but it has made it much more difficult for me to deceive myself about what I am up to when I do. And among the various factors which several years later brought me back to the Christian faith in which I had been brought up, the memory of this experience and asking myself what it could mean was one of the most crucial, though, at the time it occurred, I thought I had done with Christianity for good.

Some biographical details may be added. Auden was twenty-six at the time and had been teaching at the Downs School, near Malvern, for the past academic year. His three colleagues were a master and two matrons at the school. "A Summer Night" adds the detail that he lies in bed at night out on the lawn—as did much of the school during that unusually warm season. (When it rained he put up an umbrella over his head and went back to sleep.) The astronomical and meteorological details in the poem are consistent with those recorded for 7 June 1933 and a day or two before and after.

The prose account is the work of Auden the middle-aged churchgoer writing about Auden the young atheist, but there is no reason to doubt any of it. Even without "A Summer Night" as contemporary evidence, it would be clear that, in Auden's words, "something happened" around June 1933 that brought an exalted note to his prose and verse. The most striking evidence is a book review he wrote for *The Criterion*, probably in July, in which he celebrated as the solution of all problems that had baffled him earlier "intensity of attention or, less pompously, love." He was writing about *The Book of Talbot*, a worshipful biography of the explorer Talbot Clifton by his widow, Violet. On the face of it nothing could have seemed less sympathetic to the young Auden. His earlier *Criterion* reviews concerned such matters as crime, sex in the Soviet Union, problems in education, instinct and intuition, and medieval poetry. *The Book of Talbot* recorded, often in purple prose, a married love that was more persistent than passionate and that was shared by two believing Roman Catholics from the upper classes. Auden waved away all his own objections in a concluding crescendo of praise: "One may be repelled by Roman Catholicism; one may regard the system of society which made Talbot's life and character possible as grossly unjust, but I cannot imagine that anyone who is fortunate enough to read this book, will not experience that sense of glory which it is the privilege of great

art to give." The sense of glory and that final emphatic *give* are signs of
the charity he discovered in his vision of agape.

A dispassionate reader of *The Book of Talbot* may suppose that, for
all its emotional power, Auden gave rather more glory to the book than
he received from it. Carried aloft by his vision, he found loftiness everywhere. What mattered most, he said, was not Talbot's life and adventures, but his widow's absolute love for the subject of her book:

> *The Book of Talbot* is a great book, not because he went to Ver-
> khoyansk, the coldest place in the world, but because Lady Clifton
> would have been just as interested in his adventures if he had gone to
> Wigan.
>
> It shows more clearly than anything I have read for a long time that
> the first criterion of success in any human activity, the necessary pre-
> liminary, whether to scientific discovery or to artistic vision, is inten-
> sity of attention or, less pompously, love.

At a stroke, love solves his old "problem of *real* wholes" by making
those wholes both real and communicable: "Love has allowed Lady
Clifton to constellate round Talbot the whole of her experience and
make it significant. One cannot conceive of her needing to write another
line; one feels she has put down everything." This means *The Book of
Talbot* was everything Auden's early poems were not. He had presented
fragments of his experience, never the whole; his poems were ambiguously "significant"; no reader could feel he had put down everything.
Auden's early language kept its secrets; Lady Clifton's language communicates. As a language of love it expresses intense personal need, yet
makes no complaints of inadequacy or incompleteness. This is a paradox
of love that Auden had imagined solving only in death. For personal and
ideological reasons it had never occurred to him that married love—of
all things—could solve the paradox equally well, and leave one free to
write about it.

Six years before, at Oxford, Auden declared that the subject of a
poem was merely the peg on which to hang the poetry. A poem was a
verbal pattern that referred largely to itself. Now he reverses himself.
Literary technique is incomplete without the cohering power of love. It
is Lady Clifton's "single-minded devotion" to her subject that "gives her
her remarkable technical skill at combining the words of Talbot's diary

and her own comments into a consistent texture of narrative." That is to say, love makes possible a union of isolated individual perspectives in a coherent work of art, one broader and larger than any single point of view could allow.* Love transforms isolated fragments into an harmonious whole by making it "possible for her to say things which in isolation look silly." All this argues that technical skill *results* from love of subject: a radically anti-modernist position that Auden would continue to hold, in a less exalted way, throughout the 1930s. No attitude could be more thoroughly opposed to critical claims, as common then as now, for the formal autonomy of art. No attitude could lead more directly to an effort to restore poetry to a didactic relationship with its audience.

To explain why *The Book of Talbot* is important more for Violet's love than Talbot's adventures, Auden borrows a lesson of the master: "Henry James once said, reviewing a batch of novels: 'Yes, the circumstances of the interest are there, but where is the interest itself?'† How easily might that have been true of a book like this." Auden had alluded to James's question before, in writing about his own literary privacy. In the Airman's Journal in 1931, he inserted a baffling little dialogue poem, full of private references, which opens with the question:

> To return to the interest we were discussing,
> You were saying . . .

The poem then proceeds disjointedly through various unfinished anecdotes of Auden's life among his friends—the *circumstances* of the interest—and closes with the opening voice asking again: "Yes, but the interest." The question mark at the end is implied, not printed, because there is no hope of an answer, no trace of "the interest itself." In the 1932 song, "I have a handsome profile," when the doomed bourgeois says he will write a book about his dying world, choral voices ask, "But where is the interest." In the same year the first line of "O Love, the interest itself in thoughtless Heaven" identified the interest as love, but placed it outside the realm of human thought and action. Finally, in

---

* Auden would turn this idea into practice in the long series of collaborative writings which he began the following year.
† This is slightly misquoted from a passage on Arnold Bennett in James's essay "The New Novel."

1933, *The Book of Talbot* showed that love, the interest itself, could be brought down from heaven to earth and inscribed in a book.

"A Summer Night" brings love very much down to earth, down to "this point in time and space," and so far from thoughtless heaven that for the first time in Auden's career he associates love with conscious choice rather than simple instinct. The worlds of Eros and responsibility coincide as never before: "this point" is both a place of love and "chosen as my working place." For the first time, Auden is neither astonished nor wary at a love that lasts longer than an hour or a night, and knows he will wake to "speak with one / Who has not gone away." This poem, in fact, marks the first time in his work that he manages to speak with a lover at all. Earlier there had been either touching or talking, but never both.

This is the full text, with stanzas numbered for the benefit of the discussion that follows. Half-concealed in the third stanza may be found the ring that symbolizes the married love Auden praised in *The Book of Talbot:*

1   Out on the lawn I lie in bed,
Vega conspicuous overhead
   In the windless nights of June;
Forests of green have done complete
The day's activity; my feet
   Point to the rising moon.

2   Lucky, this point in time and space
Is chosen as my working place;
   Where the sexy airs of summer,
The bathing hours and the bare arms,
The leisured drives through a land of farms,
   Are good to the newcomer.

3   Equal with colleagues in a ring
I sit on each calm evening,
   Enchanted as the flowers
The opening light draws out of hiding
From leaves with all its dove-like pleading
   Its logic and its powers.

4 That later we, though parted then
 May still recall these evenings when
  Fear gave his watch no look;
 The lion griefs loped from the shade
 And on our knees their muzzles laid,
  And Death put down his book.

5 Moreover, eyes in which I learn
 That I am glad to look, return
  My glances every day;
 And when the birds and rising sun
 Waken me, I shall speak with one
  Who has not gone away.

6 Now North and South and East and West
 Those I love lie down to rest;
  The moon looks on them all:
 The healers and the brilliant talkers,
 The eccentrics and the silent walkers,
  The dumpy and the tall.

7 She climbs the European sky;
 Churches and power stations lie
  Alike among earth's fixtures:
 Into the galleries she peers,
 And blankly as an orphan stares
  Upon the marvellous pictures.

8 To gravity attentive, she
 Can notice nothing here; though we
  Whom hunger cannot move,
 From gardens where we feel secure
 Look up, and with a sigh endure
  The tyrannies of love:

9 And, gentle, do not care to know,
 Where Poland draws her Eastern bow,
  What violence is done;
 Nor ask what doubtful act allows
 Our freedom in this English house,
  Our picnics in the sun.

10 The creepered wall stands up to hide
 The gathering multitudes outside
  Whose glances hunger worsens;
 Concealing from their wretchedness
 Our metaphysical distress,
  Our kindness to ten persons.

11 And now no path on which we move
 But shows already traces of
  Intentions not our own,
 Thoroughly able to achieve
 What our excitement could conceive,
  But our hands left alone.

12 For what by nature and by training
 We loved, has little strength remaining:
  Though we would gladly give
 The Oxford colleges, Big Ben,
 And all the birds in Wicken Fen,
  It has no wish to live.

13 Soon through the dykes of our content
 The crumpling flood will force a rent,
  And, taller than a tree,
 Hold sudden death before our eyes
 Whose river-dreams long hid the size
  And vigours of the sea.

14 But when the waters make retreat
 And through the black mud first the wheat
  In shy green stalks appears;
 When stranded monsters gasping lie,
 And sounds of riveting terrify
  Their whorled unsubtle ears:

15 May this for which we dread to lose
 Our privacy, need no excuse
  But to that strength belong;
 As through a child's rash happy cries
 The drowned voices of his parents rise
  In unlamenting song.

16   After discharges of alarm,
All unpredicted may it calm
    The pulse of nervous nations;
Forgive the murderer in his glass,
Tough in its patience to surpass
    The tigress her swift motions.*

The goal of this poem, from its large structure down to its details of metre and rhyme, is reconciliation. It hopes to join the private and public realms; the present, past, and future; and the opposing powers of instinct and choice. For all its improvisatory air its structure is directed single-mindedly toward its reconciling cadence. The poem begins with a present moment of unity, moves through a time when that unity is broken, and ends with its recovery in another form. This pattern occurs in the poem as a whole and also in both its halves. In the first eight stanzas the pattern informs the private realm of friendship and love; in the second eight, the public realm of society and revolution. In the final stanzas the two patterns and the two realms join.

Even in the opening lines opposites are reconciled. The very first line places the poet both "out" and "in" at once; the second stanza sets the scene as one that is both "chosen" and unwilled ("lucky"), a place of work and sexy leisure. He discovers it and is discovered by it: in Stanza 5 he learns he is glad to look in eyes that return his glances, while in Stanza 3 he is metaphorically discovered, drawn out of hiding, by an opening dove-like light. (These latter metaphors, with their distant echoes of the Annunciation, suggest religious resonances Auden was not yet prepared to acknowledge more directly.) The poem, like its opening line, moves both out and in. In Stanza 6 the first line rushes outward to the four cardinal points of the compass, "North and South and East and West"; the next line arrests this outward motion by stating a relation with "Those I love"; and now the arrested motion turns to evening repose as all "lie down to rest." The moon that sees them all cannot comprehend the love that joins them—its perspective is too distant to tell a church from a power-station or sense the love that informs our gardens.

---

* All the early versions of the poem—a typescript, the text in *The Listener*, 7 March 1934, and that in *Look, Stranger!*—are verbally identical, except that the book version misprints "voice" for "voices" in Stanza 15. I have followed the punctuation of the book version, with minor emendations in end-line pointing. The *Listener* text is titled "Summer Night"; other 1930s texts are untitled.

This love is the unity of the poem's present. Although it must break, it will survive in memory. This pattern of breaking and recovery, the poem's central mode of reconciliation, would be quite conventional were it not for one extraordinary detail. We shall recall our lost moment of unity not simply out of nostalgia, but because our recollection of it will fulfill the real purpose it has in occurring now. We experience it in order that we may recall it later. Our unity is not at all like a modernist image or epiphany, valuable for its immediate intensity, but an event whose full meaning exists only in time's extension. This idea is present in Stanzas 3 and 4, although partly obscured by Auden's practice of ending stanzas with a period where grammar would demand a lighter stop. In Stanza 3 he sits "Equal with colleagues in a ring." This sentence, despite the period at the end of the stanza, continues in the subordinate clause that opens Stanza 4. He and his colleagues sit in their ring *"That"* later, though parted, they may recall its enchantments. Auden's prose account mentions four persons, a number whose visual counterpart is normally a square or cross (as in the cardinal points of Stanza 6). But the poem makes an imaginative transformation, and sets the four colleagues in a ring, because the ring is an emblem of the poem's sense of ultimately unbroken time. Miranda's love song in *The Sea and the Mirror* will make the same statement of cause and effect:

> So, to remember our changing garden, we
> Are linked as children in a circle dancing.

The ring is our seal of faithfulness even in change. The 1940 poem "In Sickness and In Health," its title borrowed from the marriage service, identifies it as a wedding ring: "this round O of faithfulness we swear." And in fact Auden was faithful to his image of the faithful ring, recalling it in these poems years after he wrote "A Summer Night."*

When Prospero ends *The Tempest* by gathering the wise and the royal together—"Please you, draw near"—Antonio is still silent, having neither asked nor accepted forgiveness. When Auden forms his charmed and loving circle he too acknowledges an unloved and unloving world

---

* He alludes to this aspect of his vision of agape in a passage near the start of Part III of *New Year Letter* (1940) in which he describes a vision of pure Being: "O but it happens every day / To someone. . . . / But perfect Being has ordained / It must be lost to be regained."

outside. We need not look to the future to face separation. It exists now, dividing those protected within our ring from those we never invited.

From the moment Auden found his poetic voice he was alert to the outsider who was barred from community, but at first he scarcely regarded the exclusion as unjust. When he himself was the outsider, he tried to claim that he had chosen or accepted his position. As he grew older all this changed: he learned that the pain of exclusion was real, and that some of its victims were innocent and unwilling. "A Summer Night" includes an allegory of this change. In the poem's first half, with its mood of calm celebration, the excluded Other is one who can feel no pain at all: the orphaned moon staring blankly at love's marvels. But by the second half, it is not only the moon who is left out of our sunny picnics. There are "multitudes" gathering, whose hungers cannot be satisfied by our love feast.

To do justice to these wretched multitudes—even to become aware of them—the poem must shift from the private affective realm to the public economic one. At its midpoint, in the final line of Stanza 8, the poem subjects its vision of love, for the first time, to the irony of a different perspective. In our enclosed gardens we endure with a sigh love's "tyrannies"—a word that acknowledges the existence of more painful tyrannies elsewhere. The first line of the poem's second half admits we "do not care to know" about those tyrannies, or about political violence, or about the "doubtful act" of inequality that allows us our prosperity and peace. In these transitional lines Auden poses the moral paradox that would become familiar in the writings of George Orwell: the paradox of one's love for the English calm and recognition of its manifest virtues, while at the same time one knows it to be sustained by hidden injustice in colonies and mines.

At the moment the poem reaches this divided sense, a border rises abruptly into view. The garden no longer rests at the center of a compass rose from which love extends without limit. Now the "creepered wall *stands up* to hide" the few "Whom hunger cannot move" from the many "Whose glances hunger worsens." Where the poem's first half managed to be *out* and *in* at once, the second divides our "freedom *in* this English house" from the "gathering multitudes *outside.*" A vision of love, like Nower's curative dream in *Paid on Both Sides*, can dissolve personal division, but social division remains.

Yet those divisions too will be broken—by revolution within and without. While the wretched threaten its walls, our world inside has lost its "wish to live." Their external revolution will fulfill our fantasies of destruction, those apocalyptic projections which "our excitement could conceive, / But our hands left alone." Since we cannot resolve thought and action, the crumpling flood will resolve it for us. It will realize our dream of dissolution, and sweep away all that we valued. Auden had hoped for that flood a few weeks earlier in "Paysage Moralisé"; now he foresees its imminent arrival, and his hope is balanced by regret.

Where "Paysage Moralisé" hoped to rebuild its cities after the flood, "A Summer Night" hears the actual "sounds of riveting." These contemporary sound effects, with their faint Socialist Realist overtones, accompany a more ancient image of the waters receding from Ararat. Auden's politics in this poem are more visionary than practical. He imagines a garden of Eden in the first half (Stanza 4) and a New Jerusalem in the second. In Stanza 14 the new city and the new wheat spring up while Leviathan lies gasping on the strand. The new order is ruled not by workers' committees but by love. The public revival of the city in Stanza 14 corresponds to the private recollection of love in Stanza 4, and the poem concludes by praying that these two recoveries might become one. The love we feel now may "belong" to the rebuilding strength of the future. The drowned parental voices of the private life will rise through the happy childish cries of the new order as death is overcome by charity. Personal love, transfigured into public concord, will have power to calm nations and grant even the murderer forgiveness and peace. With the tough patience of a persistent love whose emblem is the equals' ring, the new Love will surpass the "swift motions" of violent enmity.* Yet at the depths of the poem's harmonies, in the slightly awkward and tentative character of its hymns to the future, is a sad presentiment that its political hopes are unlikely to prove true.

"A Summer Night" is curiously reticent about the source of its exaltation. Auden's earlier poems did not scruple to invoke the name of Love or provide intimate reports of Love's actions and desires. This poem uses the word *love* only once, in the relatively weak sense of wide friendship (Stanza 6), a sense in which Auden had not used the word before. Where the word *love* is virtually demanded by the poem's argument, in the two concluding stanzas, Auden refuses to use it. Stanza 15 speaks of "this" which should need no excuse in the revolutionary fu-

---

* "The tigress her swift motions" adapts Wilfred Owen's vision of warriors in "Strange Meeting": "They will be swift with swiftness of the tigress."

ture and for which we dread to lose our privacy; but the poem nowhere says what "this" is. Nor, in Stanza 16, does the pronoun "it"—that which calms and forgives and is tough in "its" patience—refer to any antecedent more specific than the word "this" in the stanza preceding. There is no mystery about the unnamed antecedent of these two words: it is Love. And as the syntax makes clear, it is not "Our privacy" we dread to lose, but the Love the privacy made possible.*

Auden evidently had reasons of his own for suppressing Love's name in his one poem that seemed most to require it. He had effectively profaned that name by using it to refer to various loves that were less than fully human—either the simple impulsive Eros which the "it" of this poem has patience to surpass, or the interest itself in an impossibly distant heaven. To use the same name for the power he would later call agape would amount to a desecration. In his prose writings, however, this state of affairs was exactly reversed. There he used the word *love* only once, in referring to the absence of love as the motivation for theft. In this light his review of *The Book of Talbot* may perhaps be forgiven its quality of gush.

Love's transformation brought with it a transformation of other forms of desire, and for a moment even dispelled the nostalgic wish that burdened Auden's earlier poems. Before this, Auden kept trying vainly to convince himself of the error of nostalgia. When he wrote nostalgically he made use of a characteristic pattern of three elements in sequence: a lost undivided Eden, a barrier, and an inescapably divided Present. In "A Summer Night" he makes no effort to dismantle this durable pattern of thought, but instead pushes it forward in time, so that the coherent moment of unity is no longer in the past but in the present. Now the divisive barrier does not block us from a desired imaginary past, but instead will rise up in the future, as the later moment of the parting of friends. Unable to exorcise his nostalgic wish, Auden accepted its structure, and learned to render it harmless.

In Auden's work during the next five or six years this historical pat-

---

* Revising the poem for the 1945 *Collected Poetry* Auden apparently recognized how elusive he had been, and altered "this for which we dread to lose / Our privacy" to "these delights we dread to lose, / This privacy"; and in the final stanza changed "it" to "them" (i.e. the delights). Although the new "delights" allude to the "opening light" in Stanza 3, the change drastically alters the force of the poem. Around 1942–43, when he made these revisions, Auden's protestantism was too calvinistically severe to grant much authority to mystical visions of love.

tern developed into two different and contradictory versions, which in some instances occupied the same poem. On the one hand, he retained the modernist nostalgia for a coherent arcadian past, but added to this a corresponding revolutionary projection of a utopian future. On the other, he made explicit the historical idea implied in his Old English recollections, the idea that history is essentially continuous and that Eden and Utopia are fantasies that evade the tasks of the present. This newly explicit sense of continuity would also find expression in the form and texture of his poems, whose eager acceptance of received metres paid homage to the unbroken patterns that persist in human time, while his increasingly accessible vocabulary and diction reversed the evolutionary movement toward isolation in his earliest work. His new sense of time brought with it a new sense of the feasibility of education. The past could teach the present. Education was no longer to be postponed in hopes of a revolutionary future; it was urgent now.

Important as these new attitudes were, they manifested a deeper and more crucial change. Until this time Auden had understood repetition—in nature, history, and poetry—as the romantics and modernists understood it, as a mortifying compulsion, a doom to which everyone was condemned and which heroes struggled to escape. Throughout Auden's earliest poems "ghosts must do again / What gives them pain." All this changed in "A Summer Night." Repetition now became the ground of memory, the medium of love, and for the first time Auden praised events that occurred a second time.

This was a prodigious step, made in opposition to the reigning assumptions of almost two centuries of philosophy, psychology, and art. In romantic thought, repetition is the enemy of freedom, the greatest force of repression both in the mind and in the state. Outside romanticism, repetition has a very different import: it is the sustaining and renewing power of nature, the basis for all art and understanding. The detailed history of repetition deserves a book to itself; here it will suffice to note that repetition lost its moral value only with the spread of the industrial machine and the swelling of the romantic chorus of praise for personal originality. Until two hundred years ago virtually no one associated repetition with boredom or constraint. Ennui is ancient; its link to repetition is not. The damned in Dante's Hell never complain that their suffering is repetitive, only that it is eternal, which is not the same thing. In *Le Neveu de Rameau* Diderot portrays a novel and still quizzical rejection of repetition, one that does not quite lead to action in the way it

soon would elsewhere. Among the earliest literary figures who decisively and actively rejects repetition is Goethe's Faust. When Faust asks
Mephistopheles if there is a way to regain youth without resorting to
witchcraft, he is advised to take up the repetitive life of a rural farmer,
cultivating his garden. This is precisely what Voltaire's Candide learned
to accept only a few decades before, but Faust will have none of it. He
wants no reliable satisfactions of any kind, only continual change and a
perpetual unease that will call into being ever new interests and desires.
He accepts a wager with the devil which he can lose only when he asks
the passing moment to linger, to repeat itself in the next moment. For
Faust, accepting repetition means accepting death.

In his passion for novelty Faust is a man of his time and ours. The
romantic urge toward originality established a new link between repetition and anxiety—specifically the Oedipal anxiety that one might prove
not to be an original being in oneself, but only a repetition of one's pro-
genitors. What Freud interpreted as the Oedipus complex had less to do
with sexual desire—Freud's explanation—than with a romantic tradition of which Freud himself was a representative. Oedipal desire was
the intense and final form of Cartesian and bourgeois individualism, a
desire to become one's own creator, entirely sufficient unto oneself, by
supplanting one's father and conceiving oneself on one's mother. Outside the psychological realm, at the same time, industrialism altered and
augmented the forms of repetition found in nature, to the point where
the absolutely unchanging repetition of the machine became a part of ordinary existence. Repetition was thus given over from nature to satanic
mills, and it *became* compulsive repetition.

Since the end of the eighteenth century this set of attitudes took hold
wherever progress was the dominant idea. In the arts it took the form
of the modernist doctrine of continuous formal innovation; in education,
the abandonment of rote learning; in politics, Marx's explicit faith that
the nineteenth-century revolution would be the first that did not repeat
earlier ones; and so on. In religious thought, however, in the tradition
extending from Kierkegaard to Eliade, repetition came to be celebrated
as the attribute of eternity; since it could not be denied altogether, it
was granted honorary status in a realm absolutely distinct from human
history.

The cost of originality is a solitary and incommunicable sense of time.
In eighteenth-century empiricism (and in different terms in St. Augus-
tine), time withdrew from the universe at large to the inner

events of the mind. But time's privacy did not become ironically disquieting until the romantic era, when a figure like Rip Van Winkle emerged from folklore into sophisticated fiction as an avatar of personal alienation from large historical change. The privacy that still seemed fabulous to Washington Irving became domestically real for Dickens and George Eliot: their characters are isolated by events in a past hidden even from the characters themselves. The same was true of Freud's patients only a few years later. In the twentieth century this philosophical and literary convention became a popular commonplace, as men and women learned to think of themselves as congeries of neurosis trapped in distant childhoods, and aging badly.

Auden consistently associated nature with the idea of repetition, and the conscious mind with uniqueness and novelty; what changed after 1933 was the relative value he placed on each. In the texture of his verse, he used the repetitive elements of metre to represent the experience of events in nature, and the unique rhetorical stress of an individual line, its variation on a metrical ground, to represent the experience of unique events in history. His 1929 journal entries calling for the innovatory mind to break free from the repetitive body (which should now be "encouraged to form habits") were consistent with his free-verse poetics at the time. Modernist free verse, like the irregular ode of earlier centuries, requires each stanza and each poem to find a unique architecture. "For it is not meters," Emerson wrote, "but a meter-making argument that makes a poem . . . and adorns nature with a new thing." Poetry based on this romantic principle subordinates the repetitive elements of verse to an ever-changing originality, and is almost invariably written from a private and self-conscious perspective. In contrast, verse in which repetitive elements are dominant—whether the aristocratic couplet or the homely ballad stanza—tends to be written from the common point of view of a social or intellectual class, and has little to do with inner vision or original genius. Tennyson dramatized these contrasts in *Maud*, indicating through broken form and irregular metre the isolation of madness, through symmetrical form and consistent metre the shared world of sanity and love.

Orthodox modernism, in adopting a free-verse poetic, did not entirely renounce regular metres, but restricted them to satiric or elegiac use. Formal speech served to rebuke the formless disorder of the present, what Yeats called "this filthy modern tide." *Hugh Selwyn Mauberley*, the Sweeney poems, "The Fire Sermon" in *The Waste Land*, all depend for their effect on contrasts between ancient form and modern chaos. Before 1933 Auden used regular metres in similar ways, as in the accusations of "Get there if you can," the flyting in *The Orators*, the apocalyptic darkening of popular lyric in "It's no use raising a shout," or in poems like "We made all possible preparations," where truncated versions of regular metre suggest a formal order just beyond the speaker's grasp. In "A Communist to Others" and "The Witnesses" Auden commandeered the peaceable stanza of Robert Burns and reshaped it as a vehicle for satiric onslaughts. He was obeying the modernist canon, spelled out by Eliot in his 1917 "Reflections on *Vers Libre*," that regular metres like these would be allowed to survive only if the historical record proved they could be put to aggressive use. In the new order, Eliot said, "formal rhymed verse will certainly not lose its place. We only need the coming of a Satirist—no man of genius is rarer—to prove that the heroic couplet has lost none of its edge since Dryden and Pope laid it down. As for the sonnet I am not so sure." In the same 1933 summer when Auden first used a variant of the Burns stanza in "A Summer Night" for celebration and praise, he also wrote a sonnet sequence.

The gently comic rhythms of "A Summer Night," its calm glow of domesticity and romance in the opening stanzas, accommodated, in a way new to modern poetry, the poet's body. Auden's cheerful reference to his selenotropic feet at the far end of the bed is the first sign of a crucial divergence from the modernist tradition: he celebrates the ordinariness of the flesh. Instead of Eliot's fastidious distaste, or Lawrence's supercharged glorification, Auden wrote with an amused and grateful tolerance of the flesh he had never chosen. Yeats found the body interesting only when ideally beautiful or grotesquely decayed; Auden found it a fit subject for great poetry even at its most banal. He learned to take the body on its own terms—solidly there and with rights of its own, incapable of love but necessary for love's works. The body was the human locus of the repetition he was learning to accept, a creature comically but gratifyingly bound to cycles of sex, nutrition, breathing, and sleep. In choosing a metaphor that might convey the proper tone of the flesh, Auden repeatedly made his feet stand for the body that stood on them. A "martyr to corns," he became expert in the body's comic resistance to the mind's ambition to sublimity. In the most solemn poem of his career, his meditation on the crucifixion in "Nones," it is the body that restores the order which the will tries to destroy, and even here the body demands a low pun in which to make its serious point: in the calm after the murder, "We are left alone with our feat."

For Auden to write a poem like "A Summer Night" at the crest of the modernist wave was a manifest gesture of independence. Yet it was also an early gesture of allegiance to the augustan literary tradition that would unmistakably— in the rhymed octosyllabic couplets of *New Year Letter*—become his real home. Even beneath the loud dissonances of his earliest poems some softer harmonies can already be heard. His Old English and Icelandic recollections had conformed to the modernist mode by asserting the privacy and discontinuity of the present; but they also asserted a continuity between the present and the equally disordered past evoked by epic and saga. In recalling the past of Skelton not Sidney, in travelling to Berlin not Paris, Auden declared his independence from the previous literary generation while extending and endorsing their sense of isolation. What he did not expect at the time was that his movement toward independence would lead him eventually into a larger tradition of community and obligation.

His vision of agape pointed the direction he would later follow. But the vision faded, and "A Summer Night" accurately foresaw a time of loneliness and separation. For the next few years Auden would explore various routes, some very circuitous, that he hoped might lead back to the vision's wholeness, and he would learn how "large the hate, / Far larger than Man can ever estimate," that love must overcome. He had rested for a moment at a "lucky" point. Now he would "stand where luck may vary, out or in." Only in the early 1940s would he again find it absolute and unvarying, and by then the word *luck* had become for him what it had always been implicitly, a synonym for grace.

IX

The Great Divide

When the vision faded Auden again found himself on the frontier. Now
he was immobilized at the dividing line itself, on the edge separating
two realms, "Unable to choose either for a home." On one side was the
visible, urgent, public world of nature and social responsibility that
promised a future of unity and peace. On the other was the hidden,
guilty, private world of thought, desire, and loneliness whose future
offered only transience and death. Now, more than at any other time,
Auden was divided: between the public summons and the private wish;
between "The liberal appetite and power" with its confident look toward the future, and "The intricate ways of guilt" with their twisted
ties to the past; between social or family obligations and erotic impulsive
love; between communism and psychology; between the tangible work
of the hands and the abstract work of the mind; between the beauty of
Alcibiades and the intellect of Socrates; between, in his own summary
statement of 1938,

> Heaven and Hell. Reason and Instinct. Conscious Mind and Uncon-
> scious. Is their hostility a temporary and curable neurosis, due to our
> particular pattern of culture, or intrinsic in the nature of these facul-
> ties? . . . Does Life only offer two alternatives: "You shall be happy,
> healthy, attractive, a good mixer, a good lover and parent, but on con-
> dition that you are not overcurious about life. On the other hand you
> shall be attentive and sensitive, conscious of what is happening round
> you, but in that case you must not expect to be happy, or successful in

love, or at home in any company. There are two worlds and you cannot belong to them both. If you belong to the second of these worlds
you will be unhappy because you will always be in love with the first,
while at the same time you will despise it. The first world on the other
hand will not return your love because it is in its nature to love only
itself. . . .*

While in his earliest work Auden had no hope of altering the divisive
loneliness that was his main subject, in his work after June 1933 he both
explored his division and sought to resolve it. The present chapter offers
a sketch-map of the central rift in Auden's landscape, the frontier between the private and public worlds, with descriptive notes on its more
intransigent obstacles. The chapters that follow describe his various
projects for overcoming the frontier—some visionary, some practical—
in the approximate sequence in which he focused his attention on them.
A concise list of these projects might read something like this:

Erotic—joining the two worlds through sexual love and personal growth,
Redemptive—saving mankind from its divisions by personal example and direct
    cure,
Didactic—teaching an audience, through parables, to unlearn hatred and learn
    love,
World-historical—allowing the problem to be solved by determined forces
    working on an international scale, and
Escapist—abandoning the problem altogether and finding comfort on an island
    of refuge.

Even at the time he knew none of these efforts would suffice. As early as
1934 he intimated a different course when he praised those who, whatever their immediate ends, "for our greater need, forgiveness, also
work." In 1938 he concluded his summary statement of division with
this tentative expression of hope: "Yes, the two worlds. Perhaps the Socialist State will marry them; perhaps it won't. . . . Perhaps again the
only thing which can bring them together is the exercise of what Christians call Charity . . ."

* The occasion of this outburst was the biography of A. E. Housman by his brother
Laurence, which Auden was reviewing in New Verse, January 1938.

Auden's poems in the 1930s imply the personality that wrote them: seriously comic, with a growing moral sensibility and a set of experiences subject to biography. In his earliest poems he chose anonymity; in 1936, in *Letter to Lord Byron*, he provided a full-length physical portrait and a shilling-life that gives you all the facts. He adopted dramatic masks, but they corresponded to the face beneath. He devised a style to accommodate the private and public worlds, "From natural scenery to men and women, / Myself, the arts, the European news." The more ambitious an Auden poem in the 1930s, the more likely it was to make a bravura turn from Eros to Ares and back. He needed only a few stanzas to move between the slow luxuriant loll of

> Easily, my dear, you move, easily your head
> And easily as through the leaves of a photograph album I'm led

and the quick forced march of

> Ten thousand of the desperate marching by
> Five feet, six feet, seven feet high.

What made this fluent inclusive style possible was another palace revolt in Auden's pantheon. As Eliot supplanted Hardy in 1926, now Yeats supplanted Eliot in 1933. The conventional portrait of Yeats at the time highlighted his communion with spirits and his erotic regret. Auden evidently recognized, long before this became a commonplace, that Yeats also had something different to offer. It was Yeats alone, among contemporary poets, who could address specific political issues from a personal perspective. It was true that Yeats's repertory of effects depended on some very creaky machinery: cyclical notions of history antithetical to Auden's concern for freedom and choice, political nostalgia for an imaginary hierarchy of cultured nobles and eloquent peasants, and a revived Irish mythography—Cuchulain stalking through the Post Office, in Yeats's later phrase. Auden joked about bequeathing "the phases of the moon / To Mr. Yeats to rock his bardic sleep," but he also felt he could take over the sensible aspects of Yeats's style and leave the silliness behind. Yeats had endorsed the goal Lady Gregory found for herself in Aristotle, and considered it accomplished: "To think like a wise man, but to express oneself like the common people." Alluding to this in 1936, a few months after Yeats published it, Auden was hopeful but realistic: "Personally the kind of poetry I should like to write but can't is 'the thoughts of a wise man in the speech of the common people.' "

Whenever Auden followed Yeats's example he took up positions that contradicted his beliefs. Yeats had established connections between the public and private realms by two distinct methods. On the one hand, he wrote about public figures who were also his personal friends, and whom he treated as personal symbols. It was possible to do this on the small scale of Irish politics, impossible on the larger scale of England and Europe. On the other hand, he joined the local and universal by treating them both as aspects of the lunar cycle, manifestations of imaginary beings like the Gyres. When Auden tried to adapt Yeats's voice to a poetry that included both personal psychology and political history, but not as secondary expressions of a lunar cycle, he found himself inventing imaginary beings of his own. Auden's bestiary sounded far more plausible but it was no less unreal. "History" was the most notorious of his chimeras. In the poems he wrote in the 1930s, but later rejected with the greatest vehemence, History moved independently of human choice and knew where it was going; and it was History that nations and individuals either defied at their peril or followed in triumph. There were some related beings, like "Time the destroyer," but History made the loudest noise and moved with the greatest force.

At the time Auden was using these mythical beasts to give order and urgency to his poems, he knew he was violating his gifts. It did not take him long to start writing poems of self-rebuke that gave examples of earlier poets who struggled against their gifts: "Matthew Arnold," "Rimbaud," "In Memory of W. B. Yeats," part of "Caliban to the Audience." He contrasted these with examples of artists who accepted and obeyed their gifts, even at the cost of their own vanity and comfort: "Pascal," "Edward Lear," "At the Grave of Henry James." Using Yeats's methods in contempt of his own gifts, Auden was forced repeatedly to learn the same warning lesson. Yet he also kept hoping to avoid this lesson, because he wished to find words that might cure the world's divided condition and his own. Yeats's voice, for all its hidden dangers, seemed the only instrument available.*

* Around 1942, when the Yeatsian fever had abated, he made emphatic allusions (in *For the Time Being*) to the Eliot of *Burnt Norton*, as if in a cleansing gesture of apology. After this, the voices of Yeats and Eliot disappeared from his work almost entirely.

He could not doubt the urgency of the times. As his private moment of visionary unity receded, the public agonies of European war grew ever more threatening. "These moods give no permission to be idle," he wrote; "Language of moderation cannot hide." Yet the familiar journalistic account, so reassuringly symmetrical and naïve, of the young Auden setting out to conquer the twin nemeses of fascism and neurosis is much simpler than the truth. Like many young men of radical sympathies in not quite revolutionary times, he was not so much *engagé* as anxious to become *engagé*, and he was searching as much for the will to act as for actions to perform. Communism and psychoanalysis, he wrote, used the same basic method of "unmasking hidden conflicts." For a year or two after 1933 he hoped that something—he was not sure what—that combined aspects of both might succeed in joining divided purposes in a single direction and "Make action urgent and its nature clear." But his hopes focused less on the practice than on the theory of each, theories he knew had not yet been realized and feared never could be realized. Even his hopes in the theories could not sustain him for long. The tone of his English writings for public places in the 1930s seldom had the assured complexity of his writings for private ones. "Let us honour if we can / The vertical man": Auden was never quite able to do so. Much later he would recognize that the gulf between private passion and public responsibility ought, in fact, to be a central subject of political writings, and he would explore the issue in his 1950s sequence *Horae Canonicae*. In the 1930s the issue was at times an embarrassment he tried to shout or laugh away.

Around 1934 he imagined that T. E. Lawrence was one of those who "exemplify most completely what is best and significant in our lives, our nearest approach to a synthesis of feeling and reason, act and thought." Lawrence's life was "an allegory of the transformation of the Truly Weak Man into the Truly Strong Man." Yet when Auden based a poem on Lawrence, the 1934 sonnet "A shilling life will give you all the facts"—all the facts about one who conquered empires yet loved someone living quietly at home—he was no better able than "astonished critics" to understand the Lawrentian synthesis. Two years later he found the truth behind his astonishment: the synthesis had never happened at all. The climber-hero of the 1936 play *The Ascent of F6* is a partial portrait of Lawrence as the Truly Weak Man to the end, his spectacular heroic acts prompted by childhood neurosis, indentured to the private realm and exploited by the public one. Lawrence gave only the illusion of reconciling the divided worlds. The border between them remained sealed all along.

Indeed, the border proved to be a wide and complex territory in itself. Simple heroism was baffled by it. As Auden was to write later, in "Mountains," "what looked like a wall turns out to be a world." One could spend time there, and be unable to leave again. To cross the border had once meant death in a far country; now one died slowly at the border itself. One might attain at last a transforming knowledge of one's divisions, but the transformation killed. The hero of *The Ascent of F6* climbs toward a goal that is both the mountain border between two colonial empires and the reconciliation of his own divided self. To attain this goal he must die. The isolated lovers in the 1938 play *On the Frontier*, who meet in dreams at the border between their warring countries, imagine in death a "lucky" future when

> Others like us shall meet, the frontier gone,
> And find the real world happy.

They too die in their moment of understanding and forgiveness. The real world remains divided, its border endures.

Auden sensed it might endure forever. Even the passions he dramatized of its doomed heroes might be nothing more than a fantasy of escape from our divided lives. The air of crisis and revelation that seemed appropriate to the frontier landscape could easily become the seedy atmosphere of customary indecisiveness, the unsettled condition turn stale. In his poem about Dover—the border-station between England "within" and "without . . . the immense improbable atlas"—a whole city "has built its routine upon these unusual moments" of exile and return. Here the frontier crisis has become a dull sterile ritual. "All this show" of dramatic approaches to the port by land and sea

> Has, somewhere inland, a vague and dirty root:
> Nothing is made in this town.

Frontiers make nothing happen.

Auden's hope that the small undifferentiated group might be able to dissolve the frontier came to an abrupt end in June 1933. The enlightening powers of agape taught each individual self the unique value of other selves in all their incorrigible variety—"The healers and the brilliant talkers, / The eccentrics and the silent walkers, / The dumpy and the tall." Auden began to see his interest in the group as an evasion of the personal responsibility that comes with personal uniqueness. Writing on "The Group Movement and the Middle Classes" in 1934 he criticized the interest taken by others in the Christian revivalism of Moral Rearmament, but he was implicitly condemning his earlier attitudes as well. A young bourgeois seeks the security of the group, he wrote, because the beliefs and economic security of his class had been severely shaken. Modern science has called into question the bourgeois faith in "character," in the ideal of the disinterested scholar-athlete, a faith which presupposes the superiority of the conscious will—the will of the ego—over all other mental faculties. Since Auden himself has never held this faith he can write as a disinterested observer. But then he turns autobiographical. Economic change, he continues, has called into question the dominant position of his class:

> There must be many families like my own, whose members, two generations ago, had substantial incomes from investments, who are now entirely dependent on the salaries they earn.
>   . . . The unemployed young university graduate is unlikely to starve, but he will have to live at home, ask for his pocket-money, and endure the mutely resentful anxiety of his parents. Thus insecurity threatens him from within and without: within, his belief in himself and his world, and without, his material situation.

So, desiring security, the young bourgeois has two courses open to him, "Liberalism or Irrationalism . . . Liberalism involves faith in reason and he has never had that. His Liberalism has always been Utopian, emotional, feeling indulgent and full. . . . No, he can only exchange one dictatorship for another, that of the conscious [will, not reason] for the unconscious." So he turns to the emotional satisfactions of the group.

Groups enable a small number of people to lose their self-consciousness and anxiety, but this leads to serious political dangers. Since the group is irrational, "it lays itself open to having its thinking done for it by more intelligent and less scrupulous people"; and whatever beneficial effect it may have cannot be extended to larger social units.

> The problem of all modern communities ... is of finding for the masses as a whole a suitable object on which to focus the life-hostile, destructive death instincts, or rather of placing these at the disposal of the life instincts, as they are for the individual, for instance, in the sexual act.
>
> So far mankind has discovered only one method, war. Given a suitable hate-object—the Kaiser, Marxists, Bourgeois, we can feel really loving towards the neighbours who share it.

The frontier between the isolated private world and the collective public one could indeed be crossed, but only by the combined force of "Ten thousand of the desperate marching by," saluting a Leader as they pass. The solution was more dangerous than the problem.

The alternative Auden offers to the irrational group is rational liberalism. He writes in a footnote that "Modern Liberalism recognizes the power and importance of the Unconscious, but while admitting the weakness of reason, believes in its necessity and value. . . . Ethically, it manifests itself as a reverence for life. Politically as socialism, scientific, not Utopian. As typical Liberals of this kind, I would mention Freud . . . and Schweitzer in the world of thought, Nansen in the world of action."

Freud, Schweitzer, and Nansen are among the liberal heroes Auden named in his poetry from 1934 to 1936, but at the same time he recognized how weak their powers were against the gathering Fascist armies. Auden came tentatively, half-heartedly, to believe that the only opposition to fascism that had a chance of success must be as united and collective as fascism itself. Was such a worthy opposition possible? Communism made claims for itself that sounded quite plausible. Its origins in Marx's rationalism, and its professed assent to his summons to conscious analysis, were polar opposites of fascism's appeal to violent irrational fantasies of blood and race. Yet, in practice, communism had its own violent irrationalities, and demanded of its followers a suspension of disbelief that Auden was unwilling to provide.

Throughout the 1930s Auden readily accepted Marxist interpretations of the past, but he did not commit himself to any specifically Marxist program for the future. In *Letter to Lord Byron* in 1936 he wrote a brief history of art in materialist terms—tracing romanticism directly to the Industrial Revolution, finding the source of the artist's heroic isolation in the rise of the *rentier* class—and thoroughly enjoyed his chance to deflate pomposity and idealism. (This materialist attitude persisted with only slight changes into his religious commitment, in later years, to the visible created world.) But when he looked to the future he wrote vaguely about "international democracy" and "planned socialism," and quietly evaded the question of how these visions were to be made real. At the time of the Spanish Civil War, when Stephen Spender and Cecil Day-Lewis and other friends were mounting the rostrum to endorse Party orthodoxy, Auden kept his distance. The Communist Party, whatever its claims for itself as the Future's agent in the Present, proved to be united, like any fascist cell, by common hatreds and the willing surrender of choice to a Leader's will. Auden did not speak in support of the Soviet Union, and when, in the mid-1930s, he praised Lenin it was either in the same breath with T. E. Lawrence, as a personal not a political example, or in a list of healers and truthtellers that also included such unlikely revolutionaries as Kafka and Proust. Of Lenin's successors he said nothing at all.* He allowed himself to hope that what followed the Russian Revolution would not recur after an English one, but he knew better than to rely on it. His only published reference to the Party was in the context of a brief pseudonymous note on surrealist art. Challenging the claims of some surrealists that their release of the repressed unconscious had revolutionary merit, he wrote that conscious analysis is what revolution demands, and that "There is a rough and ready parallelism between the Conscious and the Unconscious, and the Masses and the Communist Party." But the context makes it clear that the last two terms should be inverted, and the error may be telling.

In America, late in 1939, Auden looked back over his political history and sought to name his motives and mixed feelings. He was nominally writing a review of Alvah Bessie's memoir of the Spanish Civil War, but he devoted most of the review to his own experience. At school, trapped in an intense group life, he realized that he was one of those

---

* Early in 1934, while casting about for a new job, he was curious enough about the Soviet Union to draft a letter asking if it might be possible for him to teach English there. Nothing came of this; it is possible he never sent the letter.

for whom it is awful, who, because their talents require a solitude
which is denied them, are unhappy and in consequence unpleasant . . .
The effect on myself of being forced to lead this social life was to create precisely that justificatory "looking-down" that Mr. Bessie can
rightly call perverse, a reaction which, since my fellow man was always a member of my own class, was a not unimportant factor in my
adoption of left political views.

That is, his disdain for his fellow bourgeois, in compensation for the solitude they denied him, eventually helped him to sympathize with those
who rebelled against their political power.

I left school a confirmed anarchist individualist, but after a few years
became dissatisfied with this attitude and adopted, though more in
theory than in practice a view of Mr. Bessie's[:]

It was necessary . . . to work in a large body of men, to sub-
merge myself in that mass, seeking neither distinction nor pre-
ferment, and in this way to achieve self-discipline, patience and
unselfishness.

I say more in theory than in practice, not because I never tried it,
but because when I did, my former experience at school was repeated;
my character did not become better; it became worse. I lost what little
discipline, patience and unselfishness I possessed.

So when a few weeks before writing this he had dismissed "the clever
hopes . . . Of a low dishonest decade," he had in mind not only the collective political hopes shattered by the Spanish War, the Hitler-Stalin
Pact, and the German invasion of Poland, but his own clever hopes to
lose himself in a political cause or a utopian future.

Some of these hopes rang false from the start. In 1935, using a strat-
egy he would soon criticize the surrealists for using, he attributed social
purposes to his work that could not plausibly be found there. He was
sent an essay on contemporary drama, especially on his and Isherwood's
The Dog Beneath the Skin, in which the author, John Johnson, argued
that the new theatre hoped to change society through psychological revelation rather than by direct social action. Auden told Johnson he meant
nothing of the kind: "You must of course say what *you* think, but I do
think 'an external effort like the Russian Five Year Plan' [Johnson's dis-
missive phrase] is quite as essential if not more so than the inner change.

The kind of drama I'm trying to write has a good deal to do with my social views." A reader of the play may doubt this. When, near the end of *The Dog Beneath the Skin*, a chorus insists the inner change is not enough, what it means is that the inner change ought not to be limited to the middle class. In the cadences of the biblical prophets, inflated just enough to remain on this side solemnity, the chorus warns the nation while it mocks the scribes and pharisees of Bloomsbury:

> Do not speak of a change of heart, meaning five hundred a year and a
>   room of one's own,
> As if that were all that is necessary. In these islands alone there are
>   some forty-seven million hearts, each of four chambers.

The doom of these millions is psychological not economic: "Man divided always and restless always: afraid and unable to forgive." The chorus ends with an injunction to "Repent ... Unite ... Act," with a line or two of comment between each imperative. This owes more to Eliot's "Datta ... Dayadhvam ... Damyata" than to politics, and does not offer much help to anyone working out the details of an external effort like a Five Year Plan.

At about the same time he was writing this chorus, late in 1934, Auden wrote in a book review that "People and civilizations are saved by a change of heart." If personal change is not enough in itself, Auden tries to make it suffice by adding civilization to his metaphor; but civilizations have no hearts to change. The phrases that follow in the same sentence (after a semicolon) emphasize the confusion of categories: "whether physical violence, loathsome as it is, is necessary to secure it, or whether if we are concerned enough, it can be brought about by 'mental fight' alone, we cannot answer ..." Auden at least ended the sentence by insisting that those capable of mental fight—in the private realm—must "not lose patience" and attempt violence instead.

Personal change in the present might lead to public change in the future, but there could be no assurance that matters would thereby improve. In his second essay on Skelton, published early in 1935, Auden referred to "the period of criticism by the Intelligentsia ... which always precedes a mass political movement." The intelligentsia of Skelton's time hoped that by a change of heart corrupt institutions could be cured without changes in the "dogmatic system." In this, the intelligentsia were opposed to the revolutionary who "attributes the corruption directly to the dogmas, for which he proposes to substitute another set which he imagines to be fool-proof and devil-proof." Neither faction was able to cure Reformation society. Their heirs are no more likely to cure society today.

Despite all these difficulties Auden saw at least one small way in which his poems could help reverse the inwardness of the modern age: "It seems to be a rough-and-ready generalisation that the more poetry concerns itself with subjective states, with the inner world of feeling, the slower it becomes ... Thus the average pace of mediaeval verse compared with that of later more self-conscious ages is greater, and no poetry is more 'outer' than Skelton's." By writing his rapid public poetry in the years after 1933 Auden made a technical contribution of his own to the new "outer" age he hoped was just beginning to emerge.

He predicted the characteristics of the new age in another 1935 essay, "Psychology and Art To-Day," written for a collection titled *The Arts To-day*. Instead of the new age of disconnected body and mind he described in his 1929 journal, he foresaw an age of unity and integration. He divided European history since the fall of Rome into three distinct periods: the Middle Ages, an interregnum of capitalism and subjectivity extending from the Renaissance to the present, and a third period "just beginning" of planned socialism and international democracy. A chart, divided into three columns, provides details. It shows the first and third periods as integrated, each enjoying a unified political system and world view. The medieval world joins two realms in a symbolic relation, "The visible world as a symbol of the eternal." Comparably, the socialist third period joins two realms through perception, "The interdependence of observed and observer." Both these periods overcome division, as the middle period grievously does not. It is split between two incompatible world views, one "official," the other in "opposition," each of which contrives to subdivide matters even further. The official view is one of "The material world as a mechanism," while the opposition sees "The spiritual world as a private concern." Neither, obviously, can unite the visible world of matter to the invisible world of spirit. A similar pattern may be seen in "Personal Driving Forces." In the medieval period the driving force is a cooperative union between the human and divine, "Submission of the private will to the will of God"; while the new socialist period is moved by a union of two psychological worlds, "The unconscious directed by reason." But in the divided middle period the two antagonistic world views each grant dominion to one half of reality, the official view seeing "Conscious will" as the personal driving force where the opposition sees "Emotion."

This schema reveals more about Auden's pattern of thought at the time than it does about European history. In diagrammatic form it sets out the structural basis for his concept of the frontier: a realm that, besides dividing two other realms from each other, is further divided within and against itself. Spatially, this is a map of a redoubled border, treacherously resistant to anyone who would cross it. Temporally, it is a special instance of a commonly accepted historical myth that may be called *cataclysmic*. This myth, which is essential to the romantic tradition in literature and philosophy, sets a cohesive Eden and, potentially, a cohesive Utopia within the realm of actual history, rather than as ideal images outside human time. The myth looks back to an abrupt catastrophic loss of happiness, and forward to a sudden revolutionary renewal. The trouble with all this, and the stumbling block for Utopians, is the myth's failure to suggest a plausible means of transition from a divided present to a unified future. Individualism is not easily unlearned: the children of divided generations carry into adulthood the isolation they learned from their parents, and their children will learn it in turn. (The transition from an undivided Eden to a divided present, although no less a fantasy, is easier to imagine: the idea of Fall is so universal that it seems to demand no special justification when illicitly applied to events in history.) Auden admits the difficulty in an introductory note to the chart, where he writes that it "ignores the perpetual overlap of one historical period with another, and highly important transition periods, like the Renaissance." This gives away the show. To include such transitions would be to acknowledge that the supposed periods of unity must already have contained the germ of the divisions that put an end to them.

Auden chose to present his vision of a socialist future in the course of an essay about psychology. He follows his chart with the comment that "Freud belongs to the third of these phases, which in the sphere of psychology may be said to have begun with Nietzsche . . . Such psychology is historically derived from the Romantic reaction, in particular from Rousseau . . ." That is, despite the chart's prediction of socialism and democracy, the only details Auden provides about the transition to the future are developments in psychological theory. About the political world he says nothing, beyond observing that both Marx and Freud are rationalists who "start from the failures of civilization, one from the poor, one from the ill." Of the mutual accusations of the psychologist and the revolutionary, each one claiming the other ignores the most important issues, Auden concludes evenhandedly that "Both are right." It follows that "as soon as socialism attains power, it must learn to direct its own interior energy and will need the psychologist."

In 1935, two months after the publication of *The Arts To-Day*, another volume of essays appeared, *Christianity and the Social Revolution*, a product of the traditional effort to reconcile socialism and religion. This book included an essay by Auden, titled "The Good Life," which reads as if it had been written by a polite antagonist of the author of "Psychology and Art To-day." In this second essay Auden contrasts communism with psychology, religion, and social democracy. While he is reticent about his preferences, he gives communism most of the best lines, shows little sympathy for social democracy, and goes so far as to accuse psychology of reducing itself to "a quack religion for the idle rich" by failing to tell the neurotic that his grievance against society is legitimate and that society must be changed. The essay's final sentences throw down a challenge to Christians, who "will have to see if what occurred in the first century can occur again in the twentieth. A truth is not tested until, oppressed and illegal, it still shows irresistible signs of growth." (Auden soon abandoned the ordeal-by-illegality as a test of truth, if he ever believed in it at all; its tendency to give equal support to fascism and to communism would have proved an embarrassment.) The essay says nothing of what a communist society might actually be like or what practical means should be taken to secure it.

There matters stood in the summer of 1935, with Auden vaguely predicting an integrated future while slighting the problem of how to bring it about. Then, in September, he set out to make a practical contribution as an artist. He joined a Film Unit that operated with some degree of autonomy under the unlikely aegis of the Post Office and made documentaries for a national audience from a socialist point of view. Although Auden had written political stage plays like *The Dog Beneath the Skin*, these had not yet been produced for anything larger than a coterie audience, and he had done little work on the practical details of production. In the Film Unit he worked full time and had direct responsibility for the results. What happened during his documentary season is a story for a later chapter; what matters here is the conclusion he reached—that his class background and artist's perspective gave him nothing useful to say on political issues, and that his efforts to make socialist propaganda amounted to a self-indulgent luxury. He gave up his job in the Film Unit after less than five months.

By this time the meaning of his tripartite pattern of historical thought had thoroughly changed. In a poem he wrote in February 1936, the same month he left the Film Unit, he transposed his schema from the field of history almost into the field of religion, and replaced its political optimism with a more tentative statement of faith. This poem was "The Creatures," written for a song cycle by Benjamin Britten on the relations of animals and men. The poem is based on the same structure Auden used for his chart of European history, but the content is radically different. Now he represents *all* human time as the irresolute divided middle realm between two unified realms that lie beyond history, occupied by the unthinking and unknowing creatures. This *homeostatic* vision of time, the opposite of the cataclysmic, sees all human history as fallen and divided, with Eden and Utopia as imaginary ideals outside of time, and that can be neither remembered by nostalgia nor realized by revolution.

In Auden's poem it is the animals, not any political systems, that "are our past and our future: the poles between which our desire unceasingly is discharged." The image is of a spark gap, with the creatures as the solid poles and mankind as the electrically charged emptiness between, a place of unceasing discontent and desire. As always in Auden's characteristic pattern, the middle realm is so divided against itself that resolution on its own terms is impossible:

A desire in which love and hatred so perfectly oppose themselves that
we cannot voluntarily move . . .

Auden's image for the wholeness of the animal world is not the conventional image of a single peaceable kingdom opposed to the human one, but two realms both unified in the same way: "our past and our future." This double image allows the creatures to take their place in Auden's pattern, where they embody both our wish for a lost arcadian innocence—

Their appearances amid our dreams of machinery have brought a
vision of nude and fabulous epochs

—and our wish for a new utopian order—

> Their affections and indifferences have been a guide to all reformers
> and tyrants.

To use a word Auden applied to the creatures in another poem, they are
"finished": their development is complete. We, in contrast, are so
thoroughly divided in our wish that we cannot even attempt to satisfy
either of our desires, and "cannot voluntarily move." So we wait passively for some involuntary force that might impose change, "the extraordinary compulsion of the deluge and the earthquake." This is the
same hope Auden had expressed at an earlier moment of uncertainty,
just before his vision of agape, when he waited for sorrow to melt and
his landscape to be flooded. This time the flood will not come, and the
animals stay separate in their "Pride so hostile to our Charity." Yet in
the poem's last line, Charity, which is neither desire nor compulsion,
may resolve our bafflement and division, and bring us the wholeness the
creatures never lost:

> But what their pride has retained, we may by charity more gen-
> erously recover.*

Throughout this poem, and especially in this final line, Auden is
adapting a literary source that attributes reconciling power not to Charity but to "reason and freedom." Schiller's essay *Über naive und senti-*
mentalische Dichtung says of natural objects such as flowers, streams,
and birds: "*They are what we were;* they are what *we should once again*
become. We were nature just as they, and our culture, by means of reason and freedom, should lead us back to nature." Schiller's is one of the

---

* Images of irresolution between two worlds occur frequently in Auden around this
time. The most memorable are in a poem written within a month of "The Creatures," "Now the leaves are falling fast":

> Whispering neighbours, left and right,
> Pluck us from the real delight;
> And the active hands must freeze
> Lonely on the separate knees.

Here, as in "The Creatures," no extraordinary compulsion will change the divided
present: "And the nightingale is dumb, / And the angel will not come." As we are
separated "left and right," so we are blocked forward and back. On one side march
"Dead in hundreds at the back," in fascist regression, "Arms raised stiffly to reprove
/ In false attitudes of love." On the other side, "Cold, impossible, ahead," is the inaccessible future whose "white waterfall could"—if we had any hope of reaching
it—"bless / Travellers in their last distress."

earliest and most elaborate statements of the romantic tendency to look toward the natural or infant past to learn what ought to be regained in a higher form in the future. This past was variously embodied in nature or children or the art of Greece—and the last is an example taken up by Marx, in words almost identical to Schiller's, as a model for the revolutionary future. A century and a half after Schiller, Auden is less confident that the liberal virtues of reason and freedom will restore the wholeness of nature, and his hope that charity might accomplish it instead is still only tentative. He does not yet identify charity, as he will two years later when writing on Housman, as "what Christians call Charity," and the word's resonances are still only potentially religious.*

In writing "The Creatures" Auden abruptly shifted from his didactic and documentary styles to one he borrowed from the least politically didactic of poets—the Rimbaud of *Les Illuminations*, who abandoned everything when he grew disillusioned with his *alchimie du verbe*. In Auden's *New Year Letter* in 1940, the imaginary tribunal sitting in constant session on his poems still included "The young *Rimbaud* [whom] guilt demands," his silent presence requiring Auden to justify his own writings as worthier than silence.

In the weeks after writing "The Creatures" Auden became uncharacteristically reticent about politics, and wrote more love poems than in any comparable period in his career—"Let the florid music praise," "Underneath the abject willow," "Dear, though the night is gone," "Night covers up the rigid land," "Fish in the unruffled lakes," and some lighter songs as well. After making these offerings to Eros, he then further rebuked his political ambition by killing off the hero of *The Ascent of F6*, whose fantasies of public power were based partly on his own. He also revised the poems he had written since *The Orators* for publication in a book—titled *Look, Stranger!* in Britain, *On This Island* in America—and systematically blunted the partisan thrust of the poems that dated from his revolutionary days in 1932. "The sun shines down on the ships at sea" lost seven of its eleven satiric quatrains. "A

---

* He had conjoined the words *charity* and *recover* on an earlier occasion, but in a relation that was the syntactic opposite of that in the last line of "The Creatures." A chorus written in 1934 for the unpublished play *The Chase*, and reused in *The Dog Beneath the Skin*, tells the audience to "Choose . . . that you may recover both your charity and your place." Here, in a vaguely Marxist homily, charity is the object to be recovered, and we have only to choose in order to regain it. In "The Creatures" and afterward it is the *means* of recovery, and far more difficult to find.

Communist to Others" lost its title and six of its twenty-two stanzas, and the opening word *Comrades* became *Brothers*. "I have a handsome profile" disappeared altogether. In "The chimneys are smoking" it was no longer a *communist orator* who lands like a sea-god at the pier, but a mere *political orator* instead. Dedicating the book to Erika Mann—he had married her the year before so that she could become a British national when Goebbels took away her German citizenship—he declared allegiance to the realm of personal responsibility:

> Since the external disorder, and extravagant lies,
> The baroque frontiers, the surrealist police;
> What can truth treasure, or heart bless,
> But a narrow strictness?

And as for uniting thoughtless Heaven and the Hell of consciousness, Auden sighed soon afterward in *Letter to Lord Byron* that it was impossible after all. But he did not sigh very deeply:

> The match of Heaven and Hell was a nice
>   Idea of Blake's, but won't take place, alas.
> You can choose either, but you can't choose twice.

Yet almost as he was writing these lines Auden was preparing to choose again, and to return to the field of direct political action.

This was not at all what he anticipated a few months before when, in June 1936, he left England for a holiday summer in Iceland, and deliberately left politics behind. He persuaded Louis MacNeice, the least politically minded of his poet friends, to join him for much of the trip, whose official purpose was to gather material for a travel book. Auden also had personal reasons for going North. His family traced its origins to Iceland, and his childhood had been nourished on the sagas. He wanted an interval in which to "reflect on one's past and one's culture from the outside." Iceland's sharp, cold sanity promised an escape from the madness of Europe. (And from more personal dilemmas: "One goes North," he remarked to MacNeice, "in order to escape from sex.")

Auden found sanity in Iceland, and a peaceful society without class divisions. He also found Goering's brother making a more serious visit, and parties of Nazis seeking the Aryan ideal. Within a few weeks of his

arrival he heard the first news of the Spanish Civil War. There could be
no refuge in Iceland, or anywhere else. The war in Spain threatened to
become the war in Europe. Soon the public realm would engage everyone—"Obsessing our private lives," as he wrote when the thing happened, in September 1939. After returning to England in the autumn of
1936, he and MacNeice put together a volume of *Letters From Iceland*.
The book repeatedly emphasized that the holiday had ended, perhaps
had never really begun. In the book's letter to Isherwood, Auden put it
this way:

> If you have no particular intellectual interests or ambitions and are
> content with the company of your family and friends [what he would
> call Heaven in the Housman review], then life on Iceland must be
> very pleasant, because the inhabitants are friendly, tolerant and
> sane. . . . But I had the feeling, also, that for myself it was already too
> late. We are all too deeply involved with Europe to be able, or even to
> wish to escape. Though I am sure you would enjoy a visit as much as
> I did, I think that, in the long run, the Scandinavian sanity would be
> too much for you, as it is for me. The truth is, we are both only really
> happy living among lunatics.

In December 1936, with *Letters From Iceland* finished, he decided to
join the International Brigade and fight in Spain. To Professor E. R.
Dodds, a family friend and the personal confidant he most respected, he
explained: "I so dislike everyday political activities that I won't do them,
but here is something I can do as a citizen and not as a writer, and as I
have no dependents, I feel I ought to go." A few days later he added:

> I am not one of those who believe that poetry need or even should be
> directly political, but in a critical period such as ours, I do believe that
> the poet must have direct knowledge of the major political events.
>   It is possible that in some periods, the poet can absorb and feel all in
> his ordinary everyday life, perhaps the supreme masters always can,
> but for the second order and particularly to-day, what the poet knows,
> what he can write about is what he has experienced in his own person.
> Academic knowledge is not enough.
>   I feel I can speak with authority about la Condition Humaine of
> only a small class of English intellectuals and professional people and
> that the time has come to gamble on something bigger.

I shall probably be a bloody bad soldier but how can I speak to/for them without becoming one?

These letters give two opposed reasons for going out to Spain. The first justifies his decision to fight as something he "can do as a citizen and not as a writer," while the second explains that he made his decision for the sake of his writing. One letter concerns the public realm, the other the private: he does not speak of both at the same time.

When he finally left for Spain he had decided not to fight after all, but to drive an ambulance instead. He arrived in Barcelona in the middle of January 1937 and soon went on to Valencia, where he was forced to bide his time. A wall of bureaucracy stood between him and an ambulance, and the local officials preferred to put him to work writing propaganda for broadcast. The transmitter he was given to use seems to have had so small a range that the only English audience it could reach was among the international volunteers, who had already made up their minds to fight and probably knew more about the war than Auden did. He stopped broadcasting after a while and wandered toward the Aragon front, intending to stay a month. But after a few days he returned to England, where he said little or nothing about his visit.

Many years would pass before he discussed the mixed feelings he brought back from Spain. Like many others, he was disillusioned by what he found there. Nothing weakened his conviction that fascism was an absolute evil, but he could no longer imagine that those who directed the struggle against it were, by necessity, good. The civil war that began as a battle between Fascist invaders and a democratically elected Republic soon changed to a struggle between the agents of Hitler and the agents of Stalin; and Stalin had reasons for wanting his agents to lose. As the command of the Republican armies fell into the hands of the ruthless and unjust, as the lies told on their behalf grew louder and more corrupting, those who opposed Franco on moral grounds faced an impossible dilemma. As Auden told an interviewer later: "Any disillusionment of mine could only be of advantage to Franco. And however I felt, I certainly didn't want Franco to win. It is always a moral problem when to speak. To speak at the wrong time may do great harm. Franco won. What was the use [of speaking out]? If the Republic had been victorious, then there would have been reason to speak out about what was wrong with it."

For Auden himself this dilemma had two immediate consequences, one manifest, one hidden. The first was an elaborate pattern of self-contradiction in his political writings—especially in the poem *Spain* which he wrote soon after his return. The second was a new seriousness about his hitherto vague religious feelings. This, too, he discussed only long after the event. In a 1955 essay about his return to Christianity, he wrote of his arrival in Barcelona, where he found the churches closed and no priests to be seen:

> To my astonishment, this discovery left me profoundly shocked and disturbed. The feeling was far too intense to be the result of a mere liberal dislike of intolerance, the notion that it is wrong to stop people from doing what they like, even if it is something silly like going to church. I could not escape acknowledging that, however I had consciously ignored and rejected the Church for sixteen years, the existence of churches and what went on in them had all the time been very important to me. If that was the case, what then?

Before this he had treated religion mostly as a source of metaphors and structural cadences, to be used when he reached an intellectual or emotional impasse. Religious language had provided him with rhetorical solutions to problems that, outside rhetoric, remained unsolved. Now, unexpectedly, religion was demanding to be taken seriously, insisting that it might have personal importance beyond its use in writing poetry. And its imperatives further complicated Auden's already divided politics.

For the moment, Auden dealt with the problem by saying nothing about religion and by talking much more scrupulously about politics. In his first days in Valencia he had sent a propagandistic vignette, a scene from a socialist travelogue, to *The New Statesman:* "everywhere there are the people . . . a revolution is really taking place . . . once a man has tasted freedom he will not lightly give it up," etc. Two or three months after his return, when he was asked for a statement on the war, he responded with a small masterpiece of tact and circumspection:

> I support the Valencia Government in Spain because its defeat by the forces of International Fascism would be a major disaster for Europe. It would make a European war more probable; and the spread of Fascist Ideology and practice to countries as yet comparatively free of them, which would inevitably follow upon a Fascist victory in Spain,

would create an atmosphere in which the creative artist and all who care for justice, liberty and culture would find it impossible to work or even exist.

These resonant words say nothing about the merits of the Valencia Government.*

Whatever might happen in Spain, Auden felt that liberty and justice were doomed there. Franco's defeat might delay a broader European disaster, but could not prevent it from happening. It seemed only a matter of time before the rest of Europe joined Spain in facing two intolerable alternatives, conquest by fascism or division into two armed camps. The Moscow trials gave little cause for encouragement. Spain gave less.

Auden still allowed himself to hope that some place of resolution and refuge might be found, but his pattern of thought, his sense that life might "only offer two alternatives," made it impossible for him to find its image. On his return from Spain he wrote of "Our hours of friendship"—a personal reconciliation—blossoming into "a people's army"—a public instrument of enmity and killing. His metaphor contradicted itself, as if his own poem would not accommodate the union he was trying to propose. The same thing happened the following year, in 1938, after his return from a journey to China to report on the Sino-Japanese War. Once again, in the "verse commentary" to the sonnet sequence *In Time of War* (but significantly not in the sonnets themselves), he tried to reconcile private intentions and public acts; and once again the poem did not cooperate:

> Here danger works a civil reconciliation,
> Interior hatreds are resolved upon this foreign foe,
> And will-power to resist is growing like a prosperous city.

---

* Auden wrote his statement around June 1937, for inclusion in the pamphlet *Authors Take Sides on the Spanish War*. Another statement on Spain, frequently cited as Auden's contribution to this pamphlet, reads: "The struggle in Spain has X-rayed the lies on which our civilisation is built." But this sentence comes from a statement by Jenny Ballou, which appeared on the same page. The misattribution may be traced to Hugh Thomas's book *The Spanish Civil War;* from there it has proliferated widely. Professor Thomas also misidentified the pamphlet's publisher, but while in later editions of his book he corrected this latter error, he added still another quotation misattributed to Auden, this one from a *New English Weekly* article written in fact by George Orwell. The only work Professor Thomas correctly attributes to Auden is *Spain*, which he misquotes.

There is nothing "prosperous" about armed resistance, and the lines un-
easily recall Auden's less encouraging argument, in his essay on the
Group Movement, that only hatred can unify individuals into purposive
groups. Should the foreign foe be defeated, the resolved hatreds would
once again unravel in civil strife; which is precisely what happened.
Even in the same poem, a few stanzas later, Auden severely qualifies his
vision of prosperous unity by observing that thousands are prepared to
give up freedom as the price of unity, ready to heed the dictators who
urge them to "Leave Truth to the police and us." Millions more, he
adds, are almost ready to follow.

At this point in the poem Auden tries to rescue his vision of unity
from the dictators by placing it in the hands of the just. He hears this
better unity recommended by the multitudes of the humble who
"through the ages have accomplished everything essential," and
who now speak from "the dust of the dead." They urge us all to find a
common justice, for "among the just, / And only there, is Unity com-
patible with Freedom." Auden displays a propagandist's tact in putting
this noble sentiment in the mouths of the dead. Unlike the embarrassingly warlike living, the dead have nothing to argue about, and can
recommend unity without being expected to do anything about it themselves. "O happy the free cities of the dead," Auden wrote in a lyric.
There "no one need take trouble any more."

As the "Commentary" concludes, Auden hears no less than "the voice
of Man" praying for a unifying justice. This prayer is addressed to no
one in particular and ends by contradicting itself. As in *Spain*, where
"the nations combine each cry," and beg the life-force for order and
purpose, so in the "Commentary" the voice of Man asks for both public
unity and a private warmth that will melt the glacier of the "frozen
heart." The voice asks for the release of the "forces of the will" so that
they may "rally"—the poem does not say how—and make "a human
justice." The hidden paradox of a human justice made by men isolated
by guilt, in a poem where the only unifying power is hatred, erupts in
the vividly self-contradictory metaphors of the final stanza. Here the
poem asks that the lost and trembling powers of the will combine,

> Till they construct at last a human justice,
> The contribution of our star, within the shadow
> Of which uplifting, loving, and constraining power
> All other reasons may rejoice and operate.

In a single line, justice is a gift of light, the contribution of a star, and a barrier to light, as it casts a shadow in which all reasons may rejoice. Human justice is as contradictory an idea, in this poem, as the metaphors that describe it, and the pattern of rhetoric resists the force of the argument.

Auden's poetic language was so firmly committed to indicating the truth it cannot embody that it was unable to express without self-contradiction a belief that Auden did not hold. In fact, when his voice found his own propagandistic intentions too intolerable, it simply refused to speak them and gave way to the voice of some other poet instead. In this instance the other voice is that of Shelley, the poet Auden attacked most vehemently and consistently throughout his career. The conjunction of *shadow* and *power* comes directly from the opening line of Shelley's "Hymn to Intellectual Beauty"—"The awful shadow of some unseen Power . . ." When Auden writes in the voice of a poet he despises, he is certain to be saying what he knows is untrue. His stanza's hope that human justice can be established by will ignores the conviction he stated explicitly in the sonnets to which the "Commentary" was appended. "We are articled to error," he wrote; we "never will be perfect like the fountains."* Eventually he would learn, by hearing the catch in his own voice and the intrusive accents of Shelley and Yeats, that he was temperamentally bound by canons of truthfulness that seemed to him at the time to have been suspended by political necessity. But, as he said privately after his return from Spain, political exigence was no excuse for lies.†

---

* Yet the hope for change persists faintly in the word *articled:* one is articled to apprenticeship, but for a fixed and finite term.
† The stanza discussed here was a revised version made in 1938 of a stanza written in 1934 for the unpublished poem beginning " 'Sweet is it,' say the doomed" (see Chapter XI, p. 243). The stanza first appeared in print in 1936 in the first edition of *The Ascent of F6* where, in a slightly different form, it concluded one of the hero's overheated prayers. Neither of these early versions includes the contradiction of star and shadow, and neither refers to political matters like human justice—only "the human vision . . . of one great meaning / Linking the living and the dead, within the shadow," etc. The contradictory cluster occurs in the 1938 text only. Sometime after 1940 Auden removed it, by making the "contribution of our star," instead of justice itself, our willingness to "follow / The clear instructions" of a divine Justice whose source is elsewhere. Later still he found this patching insufficient and dropped the "Commentary" entirely. He told friends it was "too New Deal."

The cold fury that marked Auden's attacks on Shelley emerged almost certainly from his recognition of the dangerous degree of sympathy which in fact he held for Shelley's purposes and style. Eliot also dismissed Shelley, but then Eliot could not have sounded like Shelley if he tried. Auden felt tempted to sound very much like him indeed. This was scarcely Shelley's fault, but when Auden published his strongest attacks, in the early months of 1936, he was rebuking the vanity and ignorance of his own political writings and Shelley generously took the blame. Reviewing Herbert Read's *In Defence of Shelley* in *New Verse*, April–May 1936, Auden found "the bulk of [Shelley's] work, with the exception of a few short pieces, empty and unsympathetic." Auden's specific objections derive largely from Eliot's. Shelley "never looked at or listened to anything, except ideas"; his abstractions, not being the products "of a richly experienced and mature mind," are "empty and their expression devoid of poetic value." What Auden wants from poetry instead of immature abstraction is "plenty of news." "I cannot believe—and this incidentally is why I cannot sympathise with Mr. Read in his admiration for abstract art (symbolic art is another matter)—that any artist can be good who is not more than a bit of a reporting journalist." While "the journalistic side of an artist can easily and frequently does kill his sensibility," there must always be a tension between sensibility and a concern for the facts, or else the artist will be tempted to yield to the vanity of his poetic imagination—a vanity that Auden felt had marred his own political writings before 1936. This tension was as important in everyday life as it was in art. Broadcasting more than half-seriously "In Defence of Gossip" in 1937, he concluded: "never hesitate to invent, but invent *in detail*"—unlike Shelley.

Auden's review was one of many warnings to himself in these years, warnings he ignored in writing *Spain* in 1937, the "Commentary" in 1938, and "September 1, 1939." Of the latter poem he wrote, some years later, that it was "infected with an incurable dishonesty." Its infection, like that of his other large public poems, was its implicit claim to have joined the realm of the private will to that of the public good, when in fact the union had been made through the force of rhetoric alone. There had been "no real meeting," only what he would later call "vain fornications of fancy." By his own standards, if not those of his readers, these public poems failed, and, for a time, their failure convinced him he should not write public poetry at all.

Yet *Spain* and the "Commentary" are best understood not as public poems but as utopian poems. Just as nostalgia sighs for a world lost in the imaginary past, so utopianism—nostalgia for the future—dreams of a world only imagination can build. A nostalgic wish arose repeatedly in his earliest poems, but it was always explicitly and deliberately rejected as fantasy a few lines later. When a utopian wish arose in his poems of the 1930s, the denial took the more devious and involuntary form of self-contradiction.

Auden tried briefly, late in the 1930s, to force the two worlds together with the adhesive of simile. For a year or two, especially in the otherwise magnificent sonnets of *In Time of War*, he scattered the word *like* over dozens of pages, using it to connect aspects of the world of the emotions with heterogeneous aspects of the world of cities and armies. He learned this technique from Rilke, who used it with subtlety and control. Auden used it to make one unlikely conjunction after another. Anxiety found itself linked by simile to a grand hotel; a phrase went packed with meaning like a van; talent was yoked to a uniform, an attack of shyness to the divisions of class, tears (the lachrymal kind) to dirty postcards. This habit took hold in English and, especially, American poetry and persisted there for about twenty years, long after Auden had abandoned it.

Auden's reckless similes, his shifts into self-deceiving ventriloquism, his "preacher's loose immodest tone," were all symptoms of an inner conflict on whose outcome depended the course of his career. In the late 1930s, on the battlefields of Auden's poems, two literary traditions, two ideologies of art, struggle for supremacy. He was trying to escape the modernist poetic he had renounced earlier but to which he found himself returning as he wrote poems in opposition to his beliefs. He had set out to write in a tradition that engaged the problems of choice and action, and performed a didactic function in the society around it. But when he actually wrote his political poems he used the formal and rhetorical methods of a tradition that claimed to be independent of existing society, superior to its vulgar concerns. What made the struggle between these two traditions so difficult to resolve was that the forces of one side had successfully disguised themselves in the uniform of the other. Poems like *Spain* and "September 1, 1939," which seemed unquestionably public and didactic, were in fact poetry of a very different and more equivocal kind. The conflict between two traditions produced in Auden's work a tension that served only one of them—that internal tension that twentieth-century criticism tends to value in all literature whether it is really there or not. This tension was exactly the opposite of what Auden was trying to achieve, and represented a rearguard victory for that part of himself which, out of moral and political despair, reveled in poetic mystery and power and took little thought of their consequences.

At issue in this struggle were basic and long-standing assumptions about poetic form. Despite all the claims to the contrary made by Eliot and Pound, the modernist poetic had its origins in romanticism. Modernism's theories of historical and poetic fragmentation are descended from romantic theories of organic form, however unlike each other the two generations may appear on the surface. The genealogy of English modernism is obscure because its descent from romanticism is not by direct lineal transmission through the native line, whose heirs had grown decadent by the late nineteenth century, but collaterally, through the French line that crossed the Channel and intermarried early in the twentieth century. Eliot traced his poetic ancestry to Laforgue, not Shelley, but all three were scions of the same clan.

In early romantic generations, a poem was thought to achieve its form through autonomous internal processes that were explicitly understood as analogues of individual growth. "Remember that there is a difference between form as proceeding, and shape as superinduced," Coleridge warned; "the latter is either the death or the imprisonment of the thing;—the former is its self-witnessing and self-effected sphere of agency," which characteristically manifested itself as an irregular ode, with each stanza, each poem, formally unique, never repeating an earlier form. Why should a poem aspire to imitate the formative powers of nature in this way? Schiller and Wordsworth implied the answer that would become explicit in modernism: that a poem needs a unity of its own because it comes into being as compensation for the poet's lost sense of unity with nature. The autonomy of a poem as it grew on the page corresponded to the self-awareness of the poet as he recollected childhood moments of intensity, "spots of time" that retain a "fructifying virtue"* as he writes.

* So Wordsworth wrote in the 1799 *Prelude;* "renovating" in later texts.

In the early phases of romanticism, new forms of art presaged new forms of society and the recovery of nature in a higher form. But after the disillusionments of Napoleon and the failed revolutions of 1848, the political goals of romanticism separated from its aesthetic ones. The romantic concern with perception and language increasingly became the central subject of poetry. Where the early romantics proclaimed universal renewal and transformation—*alle Menschen werden Brüder wo dein sanfter Flügel weilt*—the heirs of the romantics saw these events happening mostly in themselves or in their art. The confidence of earlier years modulated into an imperial claim for the independence of poetic language from the gross world of common speech. By the time this tradition reached its symbolist phase it had narrowed the poetic subject to an intense moment of vision detached from time and space. Other *fin-de-siècle* and early modernist movements similarly isolated the pure act of artistic performance or of aesthetic perception—and in the process, the distinction between performance and perception, which had been called into question by the early romantics, virtually disappeared.*

The great works of modernism in the 1920s—modernism on an epic scale—proclaimed an end to this narrowing tendency while in fact continuing it in a different form. Poetic language had now grown so powerfully centripetal that it could swallow up even the encyclopedic language of nineteenth-century realism. In Joyce the fictional patterns in *Ulysses* and the linguistic relations in *Finnegans Wake* take control over virtually all the data of experience, and subject them impartially to the ordered rigors of a mythographic structure. Comparably, Yeats's poems about public events—the Easter uprising, an official visit to a schoolroom—move toward a translation of external fact into inner vision: "A terrible beauty is born," "O body swayed to music, O brightening glance." The universalizing ambitions of both these methods represent the triumph of the romantic theory of autonomous form: now the form can accommodate *all* experience within itself, and can do so on its own formal and aesthetic terms. Eliot praised Joyce's discovery, and Yeats's adumbration, of the "mythical method" by which events in a book are connected not in a narrative of action but by their parallels with an earlier book—as in *Ulysses* or *The Waste Land*. Eliot, like Wordsworth

---

* Not for the first time. Socrates led the rhapsode Ion to roughly the same conclusion twenty-three centuries earlier. That this tradition has ancient roots scarcely means, however, that Socrates assigned the same value to poetic imagination that Mallarmé did.

earlier, saw this method as a compensation for loss: other ages could still use narrative because they "had not sufficiently lost all form to feel the need of something stricter." The mythical method is concerned less with imitation of action than with imitation of rhetoric. The later chapters of *Ulysses* deliberately expose the false claims of verisimilitude made by the early ones, and the spirits who dictated Yeats's system bade him translate the crude contingencies of the common world into visionary patterns of cyclic history. Content is here ruled by pattern, and the romantic heritage of autonomy is preserved by a generation that claimed to have renounced it.

The frontier between private perception and public fact therefore remained unchallenged by modernism—was even fortified by the self-consciousness of poetic vision, by systems of thought too idiosyncratic to serve as cultural myths, by the willed reflexivity of modern poetic language. Whether a poem was a masterful image which, because complete, grew in pure mind, or a personal and wholly insignificant grouse against life—the phrases are from Yeats and Eliot—it kept at bay the world of time and action. Among the methods most effective for blocking the gates were self-contradictions of the kind that made Auden's utopian poems failures in his own eyes. Stephen Dedalus despises all "kinetic" art which induces action and change; in fulfillment of his plans for "static" art, every statement in Joyce's later books is precisely balanced by its opposite. The inner conflict of styles and points of view in modernist writing holds mere reality at a respectful distance. For this reason, critical schools (psychoanalytic, formalist, structuralist, deconstructive, etc.) that thrive on the internal contradictions of the texts they examine will always treat the modernist canon and its romantic ancestry as if it were the whole of literature.

When Auden set out to write in a different tradition, his goal was a poetry that reflected the formal and linguistic lessons of modernism yet could still serve the public good. The art he wished to create was intent less on autonomy and stasis than on enlightenment and action. It was formally sophisticated but concerned more with the contradictions and order of the ethical world than with its own—a Brechtian art, conceived independently of Brecht. Yet in the 1930s Auden kept trying to adapt the techniques of modernism to contexts unsuited for them, and was not entirely willing to trust the methods most appropriate to his purposes. When he told E. R. Dodds that the poet must have direct knowledge of major political events, he was deducing his precept from Yeats. And when his utopian poems heralded the unified future that would arise from the divided present, he was adapting the method by which Yeats assigned both chaos and order to their proper stations in a determined historical cycle. Yeats was content to fit events in Ireland into his private myth. When Auden tried to fit events in Spain and China into a Marxist myth he felt he was lying. "What is the Chinese War like?" he asked in a broadcast, three days before he left England for America. "Well, at least it isn't like wars in history books. You know, those lucid tidy maps of battles . . . War isn't like that. . . . War is untidy, inefficient, obscure, and largely a matter of chance." It takes place, in fact, while someone else is eating or opening a window or just walking dully along.

In 1964, when asked by Stephen Spender for a contribution to a book of essays on Yeats, Auden gave this reply:

> I am incapable of saying a word about W. B. Yeats because, through no fault of his, he has become for me a symbol of my own devil of unauthenticity, of everything which I must try to eliminate from my own poetry, false emotions, inflated rhetoric, empty sonorities.
>
> > *No poem is ever quite true,*
> > *But a good one*
> > *Makes us desire truth.*
>
> His make me whore after lies.

The fault was no more with Yeats than it had earlier been with Shelley, but Auden made Yeats into a symbolic sacrifice. The flames fed by the discarded *Spain* and "September 1, 1939" cleansed his work of its lies and inauthenticities.

Yeats was concerned above all with visionary and personal intensity, whether in the tragic gaiety of autonomous art or in its obverse, the foul rag-and-bone shop of the heart. Auden's goal was the vast territory between these extremes, and his means of access was the literary tradition he called, somewhat defiantly, light verse. In his introduction to *The Oxford Book of Light Verse*, a work he persuaded the publishers to commission from him in 1937,* he explained that he used this term to mean: "Poetry written for performance, to be spoken or sung before an audience," as in folk-songs or the poems of Tom Moore; "Poetry in-

* It was published in 1938.

tended to be read, but having for its subject-matter the everyday social life of its period or the experiences of the poet as an ordinary human being," as in the poems of Chaucer, Pope, and Byron; and "Such nonsense poetry as, through its properties and technique, has a general appeal," as do nursery rhymes and the poems of Edward Lear. He made room in a footnote for poems like Blake's "Auguries of Innocence" that do not fall into any of these categories but whose technique is derived directly from a popular style. "Light verse can be serious," he wrote. "It has only come to mean *vers de société*, triolets, smoke-room limericks, because, under the social conditions which produced the Romantic Revival, and which have persisted, more or less, ever since, it has been only in trivial matters that poets have felt in sufficient intimacy with their audience to be able to forget themselves and their singing-robes." He concluded that serious light verse could again be written "only . . . in a society which is both integrated and free." But that did not stop him, in the unjust society of the present, from using his anthology as a pattern book for his poems.

Auden did not need Utopia to write public verse. In his poems after 1933 romantic isolation was broken, and the poetic subject released from its servitude to poetic pattern. Instead of organizing themselves according to interior or organic principles, his poems were unembarrassed to appear in conventional forms that could each be put to use for a variety of purposes. And instead of taking as their subjects the acts of imagination that called them into existence, his poems applied their familiar forms to matters common to poet and audience. The lesson he found in *The Book of Talbot* was one he repeated in a review in 1936: "The first, second and third thing in . . . any art is subject. Technique follows from and is governed by subject." Later he was less dogmatic about these priorities, and would write of subject and form searching for their appropriate partners, but now his emphasis was a therapeutic warning against his own temptation to aesthetic pride. This was why the artist had to be something of a reporting journalist—"To the journalist the first thing of importance is subject"—and one who knew what was newsworthy and what was not. "I would rather look at a painting of the Crucifixion before a painting of a still life," he wrote in his attack on Shelley—a striking choice of a newsworthy subject, a year before Spain revived his conscious thoughts about religion—and therefore he could not agree with Herbert Read's severely modernist argument that "the pattern may have some more or less remote relation to objects, but such

a relation is not necessary." Later the same year he stated his credo in
Letter to Lord Byron:

> To me Art's subject is the human clay,
> And landscape but the background to a torso;
> All Cézanne's apples I would give away
> For one small Goya or a Daumier.

Unsurprisingly, his *bête noire,* and the object of his repeated attacks in
1936, was surrealism, whose practice and theory he regarded as hypocritical and false. "The surrealist police" was a two-edged phrase.

Attitudes like these, especially his preference for Daumier over
Cézanne, called forth predictably sophisticated sneers. Even Geoffrey
Grigson's magazine *New Verse,* which tended to reserve for Auden its
few words of praise, devoted three stern editorial pages to "Remarks on
Painting and Mr. Auden." In fact Auden cared little about the visual
arts; he was arguing against a literary avant-garde whose goals and
methods he considered trivial. He had no wish to set aside the great
technical achievements of modernism or its psychological complexity,
but chose to incorporate them into a larger and more varied repertory of
subjects. He took the modernist private perspectives and subjected them
to criticism and irony, emphasizing the importance of the common
world that the private perspective imperfectly understood. He was the
first English writer to sense that modernism had exhausted its potential,
and for his emphasis on matters wider and more serious than the agonies
of the personal will, the reviewers in *Scrutiny* charged him with frivolity and diagnosed him as permanently immature.

The serious poet of the romantic kind, alone with his vision, often
seems bewildered when he appears in Auden's work. In *Spain* the poet
who prefers unpopulated nature, where he may be

> startled among the pines
> Or where the loose waterfall sings compact, or upright
> On the crag by the leaning tower,

is certainly not Auden himself, who was more likely to be startled
among the gasworks. When he was reacting most strongly against romantic conventions, he used the words *poet* and *poetry* to refer to a role
and a handiwork quite different from his own. Auden implicitly claimed
a larger and less circumscribed purpose than *poet* can signify after two

centuries of romantic coloring, and his verse suggested that *poetry* falsifies. The lover who sings poetic effusions under the arch of the railway in "As I walked out one evening" is countered by the more disturbing and truthful knowledge told by the chiming clocks.

Critics who looked to poetry for an escape into the ideal took offence at Auden's deliberately unpoetic language of description, his frequent refusal to "sing." Accustomed to the ennobling mythography of Yeats dreaming of "a Ledaean body," they found it unsettling when Auden wished for the company of a certain "squat spruce body and enormous head." But his particularizing language was his homage to the actual, his refusal of the temptation to generalize or diffuse. He had few stronger pejoratives than *vague*. His language allowed him to be didactic, and he hoped his didacticism would finally allow him to cross the barrier between poet and audience. Too often, he hectored his readers or despaired over their intransigence. But he was also learning to offer parables—didactic poems that refused to limit his readers' power of choice by telling them how to use it. Through knowledge he hoped to enlarge freedom. "There must always be two kinds of art," he wrote in 1935, "escape-art, for man needs escape as he needs food and deep sleep, and parable-art, that art which shall teach man to unlearn hatred and learn love."

Yet for all the diversity of subjects his parable-art was able to teach in the 1930s, the one subject he thought most important persistently eluded him. He reported brilliantly on history and science, literature and economics, people and places, and the many varieties of public and private hatred. What he was unable to teach, because he had yet to learn it, was love.

X

The Insufficient
Touch

When Auden sang of love he sang its privation and defeat. He had been
able to write of love in exultant tones for only a few weeks in the summer of 1933. By the following spring, his vision of agape now altogether
faded, he rejected that same personal love as a symptom of epidemic
neurosis. As a cure he recommended, of all things, indifference. Reviewing a life of T. E. Lawrence, a lonelier voyager than Talbot Clifton,
he wrote:

> Different as they appear on the surface, both he and his namesake,
> D. H. Lawrence, imply the same, that the Western-romantic concep-
> tion of personal love is a neurotic symptom only inflaming our loneli-
> ness, a bad answer to our real wish to be united to and rooted in life.
> They both say *"noli me tangere."* It is at least doubtful if in our con-
> valescence sexual relations can do anything but postpone our cure.* It
> is quite possible that the way back to real intimacy is through a kind
> of asceticism. The self must first learn to be indifferent . . .

These austere counsels are all but unrecognizable as the work of the
same author who had praised love as "the first criterion of success in any
human activity" and had praised above all the love of husband and wife.
Now relations with individuals can only feed our individuality. Instead

---

* These two sentences allude to two poems in D. H. Lawrence's *Pansies*, "Noli Me
Tangere" and "Leave Sex Alone—."

we must learn to love all of "life," through an undifferentiated rooted-
ness that will have no specific focus of desire. Behind Auden's sense of a
Western "disease" and its eventual cure is the cataclysmic vision of history, which defers personal responsibility until unity can be restored in
the future—love yesterday and love tomorrow but never love today.
Still further in the background is the frequent preference of young intellectuals to blame the times for their inability to love.

The vision of agape left other complications as well. Around 1933
Auden's sense of the value of other selves changed markedly, as did his
idea of love. Earlier, he thought love should be a matter for the senses
and powers of the body. He was happiest when he could address a poem
to a lover, "To you *simply.*" Sex was preferably an uncomplicated exchange, "The data given / The senses even." But love could be simple
only if he kept it strictly limited to the world of the flesh. The erotic objects in his earlier poems were generally from the working classes, rarely
his social or intellectual equals. They earned their living with their
bodies—some reputably, as an engineer for example ("Hands miles
away were laid on iron / That rested lately in the dark on us"), some
not. Now, from 1933 until he left England in 1939, he addressed his love
poems within his own social class.* His sexual partner might also be a
student of his intellect, whom he could imagine someday "Meeting as
equal." His erotic life developed ethical complications baffling enough
to make him contemplate a purifying abstinence. If he began a poem in
the warm pleasures of "May with its light behaving," it took him only a
stanza to find "The dangerous apple taken"; one stanza more, and "The
unjust walk the earth."

He dreamed of an equals' meeting, but it never occurred. Now that
love involved more than the anonymous unthinking flesh, he found that
his self-conscious intellect forced him into unequal relationships. Earlier
he had fantasized an erotic liberator, secure in his superiority, the "one
with power" and the Truly Strong. Now, when he actually enjoys such
erotic superiority, he discovers how large an emotional price he must

---

* These poems alluded silently to various personal names. "Underneath the abject
willow," for example, offered erotic advice to Benjamin Britten, although the intimacy of poet and composer went no further than this. Some readers have taken
Isherwood to be the subject of Auden's love poems, but this was not the case.
Auden's relation with Isherwood is best described as a sexual friendship, not sexual
love, and when Isherwood appeared in Auden's verse it was in public tributes like
the 1935 birthday poem, "August for the people."

pay in exchange. Knowing himself superior, he knows he must still look elsewhere for a meeting of equals, that his love will fade:

> Lay your sleeping head, my love,
> Human on my faithless arm . . .

He wields the power of the waking over the sleeping, the older over the younger, the thoughtful over the instinctive, but his power isolates. Nostalgic for a world of flesh his world of thought can never join, he writes of the "jealousy of the other world" which is the "besetting sin" of those who work with their minds. Hölderlin, in "*Sokrates und Alcibiades,*" provides him with a touchstone statement of the mixture of envy and desire that passes for love: "*Und es neigen die Weisen / Oft am Ende zu Schönem sich*"—and often in the end the wise incline to the beautiful. Auden would add: Yet they are not faithful to them.

There is a trace of the predator in Auden in the 1930s, and more than a trace of the perplexity that Prospero, in *The Sea and the Mirror* a few years later, would detect in seducers "sincerely puzzled at being unable to love / What they are able to possess." In his superiority Auden is still the victim of a "worm of guilt" and a "malignant doubt." In one poem only, the 1936 lyric "Dear, though the night is gone," he confesses his guilt, but by indirection, through the parable of a dream. Inverting his waking state, he dreams of erotic inferiority; the role he inflicts becomes the role he endures. It is not the poet who is faithless in this dream, but his beloved, who

>   unabashed,
> Did what I never wished,
> Confessed another love;
> And I, submissive, felt
> Unwanted and went out.

In his vision of agape Auden felt "Equal with colleagues in a ring." The power that commanded him to love gave him the means to do so: in the vision's will was his peace. When the vision faded he was left with the wish to love, which in itself could never suffice. Neither the instinctive necessity of the body nor the visionary necessity of Eros could tell him how or whom to love.

Four years before, he attributed all power of choice to evolution's impersonal powers. Now he repeated almost obsessively that nature had abdicated all authority in the world of man. We choose alone, in ignorance and guilt. Evolutionary Eros gave us the flesh we are, but left us to choose whether to use it for good or ill. Whatever our nostalgic hope for natural innocence,

> love, except at our proposal,
> Will do no trick at his disposal;
> Without opinions of his own, performs
> The programme that we think of merit,
> And through our private stuff must work
> His public spirit.

When Eros speaks it says only that it has no answers. "The life" that made all the creatures' decisions for them explicitly refuses to make ours: "I am your choice," it insists, "I am whatever you do." In the moral realm, where Eros is forever silent,

> Before the evil and the good
> How insufficient is
> The endearment and the look.

Revising this stanza in later years, Auden included the "touch" of the sexual act itself among the insufficient gestures of erotic life, and made the last line read: "Touch, endearment, look." He spelled out his meaning at the end of a rueful little Essay on Man printed as a note to *New Year Letter:* "Never will his sex belong / To his world of right and wrong, / Its libido comprehend / Who is foe and who is friend."

If the groves of Eros offered brief refuge from political chaos, they gave no relief from the difficulties of choice. The pleasures of love were always the reward of a decision made consciously. Even the most grateful and satisfied of Auden's 1930s love lyrics, "Fish in the unruffled lakes," devotes most of its attention to the painful contrast between creaturely necessity and human freedom. Fish, lion, and swan do what they must, ignorant of a future they cannot alter; man lives in inescapable anxiety. If he is to find happiness, it will not be someplace beyond time and change, not in Yeats's Byzantium or Eliot's rose-garden, but through conscious decisions made at real and specific moments:

> I must bless, I must praise
> That you, my swan, who have
> All gifts that to the swan
> Impulsive Nature gave,
> The majesty and pride,   ·
> *Last night* should add
> Your *voluntary* love.

Auden wrote the first five lines of this passage very near the edge of Yeatsian pastiche, then added two lines that Yeats could never have written. Acknowledging Yeats's preeminence among recent love poets, Auden also points to Yeats's limitations. In the previous stanza Auden had also begun by putting on Yeatsian robes—

> We till shadowed days are done,
> We must weep and sing

—but specified as our occasions for tears and song some matters that were distinctively Audenesque:

> Duty's conscious wrong
> The devil in the clock,
> The Goodness carefully worn
> For atonement or for luck.

Yeats's sense of love as custom and ceremony was suited admirably to those who live without choice—like some green laurel rooted in one dear perpetual place. But no one lives like that.

Auden made his darkest and most compressed statement of the way we really live—abandoned by Eros to our own devices—in the poem "Our hunting fathers" early in 1934, around the same time he reviewed the life of T. E. Lawrence. This poem has a reputation for obscurity, but it is an obscurity largely of the critics' making: they try to read it as an optimistic revolutionary manifesto, and object to the difficulty of fitting this purpose to a very pessimistic text. With the varnish of preconception removed, the poem's dire statements show through clearly. The first stanza is straightforward enough:

> Our hunting fathers told the story
>   Of the sadness of the creatures,
> Pitied the limits and the lack
>   Set in their finished features;
> Saw in the lion's tolerant look,
> Behind the quarry's dying glare,
> Love raging for the personal glory
>   That reason's gift would add,
> The liberal appetite and power,
>   The rightness of a god.

In the essays he wrote around this time Auden repeatedly cited the "nineteenth-century evolutionary doctrine of man moving 'upward, working out the beast, And let the ape and tiger die.' " Tennyson's lines state the confident liberal tradition of our hunting fathers, who looked back from their higher realm to the lower one of the creatures—whose evolution was "finished," and who could never share in the human dream of progress. In the world of nature the fathers saw the life force—Eros or Love—willing itself toward their own liberal condition of conscious rational love. Auden's stanza restates their liberal belief, but his first words ironically question it. It was our *hunting* fathers who imagined they saw a wish for their own glory and reason in the quarry they lovelessly and violently destroyed. Those hunters, who knew all about evolution, hunted not for the evolutionary survival of their species but for sport, and persuaded themselves that their gratuitous killing was thereby superior to the necessary violence of the lion.

"Nurtured in that fine tradition" (*fine* has the ironic sense of *fastidiously superior* as well as *noble*), they did not guess that Eros in mankind has no interest in a gloriously liberal order but works obscurely and privately, obedient to individual choice, shadowed by guilt:

> Who nurtured in that fine tradition
>   Predicted the result,

> Guessed love by nature suited to
>   The intricate ways of guilt?
> That human ligaments could so
> His southern gestures modify,
> And make it his mature ambition
>   To think no thought but ours,
>   To hunger, work illegally,
>   And be anonymous?

One of Auden's central paradoxes appears in lines 3 and 4 of this stanza. In man, Love is "*by* nature" unlike its condition *in* nature. Modified by its human ligaments, which etymologically *bind* it to mankind, Love gives up its "southern" (sunny, open, unthinking, Mediterranean) behavior for the evolutionarily "mature" human will. Now it thinks no thoughts but ours. It hungers because our conscious sense of loss cannot be satisfied; it works illegally because our acts of will violate the common law that love obeys in nature; and it is anonymous because it is concealed within each guilty personal will that gives it direction.

Auden used the words of the poem's two final lines in his review on Lawrence, but in a very different sense. There he wrote of both Lawrence and Lenin as exemplars of indifference: "The self must first learn to be indifferent; as Lenin said, 'To go hungry, work illegally and be anonymous.'" Auden's prose and verse are often at cross-purposes during the 1930s, and here they contradict each other while using the same words. Where the poem mourns Love's isolation in human ligaments, the prose welcomes that isolation as the means to a wider love. This will not be the last time Auden's verse speaks a bitter truth his prose tries to sweeten. But poem and review agree in expecting no help from social revolution—in each instance Lenin's words are appropriated from a political to an emotional context, where they preserve only faint traces of their origin. And poem and review agree in expecting no help from Eros.

⌣

Before 1933 Auden knew he had placed barriers in the way of love, but he trusted in love's power to overcome them. A free Eros, he hoped, would feel no resentment over its imprisonment, but would free him in turn to love. In Berlin in 1929 he hoped to outgrow the complexities of homosexual desire merely by letting Eros follow its natural course. Two years later he was still waiting for erotic complexity to grow into the "simplest love" that Eros could provide.

He wrote a long apostrophe to Eros, in December 1931, explaining what he had in mind. "Enter with him / These legends, Love," he began, as he sent Love on a mythical quest as companion to a youthful hero. The quest is a series of "legends," the adventures of adolescent sexuality, represented by folktale motifs of treacherous landscapes, guardians of the pass, pursuits and escapes. The point of calling these *legends* is that they are conventional: inherited, like family ghosts, from the past. Models learned from others—and this includes models of revolt—shape the erotic life of all adolescents; their choice is not between originality and convention, but between different kinds of convention. (The Airman in *The Orators* is a sexual outlaw, but he learns his outlawry from his uncle, his "real ancestor.") Although the hero of the poem does not know it when he sets out, his goal is to outgrow his own quest—to achieve, in place of conventional legend, authentic love.

The paradox the poem hopes to resolve is this: Only through legend can love begin, since lovers must learn the manner and method that will bring them together; yet if they then wish to share an authentic love they must cast off the past, since it has nothing to do with themselves and intrudes as an unwelcome third party at their private meetings. How are legends to be renounced? The poem predicts that its hero, when his romantic adventures pall, will choose to reject Love altogether. Dissatisfied with legend, unaware that any truer Love is possible, he will demand that Love "Submit your neck / To the ungrateful stroke / Of his reluctant sword." But in the very moment he destroys Love, he will be startled to find that he has summoned into being its true avatar. What apears in place of legend is "faithful . . . But disenchanted." It is "Your [Love's] simplest love."

But the poem demonstrates exactly the opposite of what Auden was trying to say. He looks forward to a moment when legend will change into truth, yet the lines describing the change are the most legendary in the poem—a folklore transformation of a beheaded phantom into something real, excellent, and whole. The poem tries to escape fiction through fiction, and this self-contradictory effort results directly from Auden's wish for a simple love, unmediated by fictions from the past. Such a love is itself a romantic fiction, created by two lovers as a standard for themselves and each other, a dream of freedom from society and their earlier lives. Although this fantasy—we two alone though the whole world oppose—has animated much of Western literature and art for seven centuries, the truth remains that all love is learned, whether it takes the form of bourgeois marriage or romantic passion. Love's conventions change over the centuries, but love never escapes them. In the 1930s Auden tried to resist this truth, first by isolating love in simple moments of satisfaction, then by hoping to grow from learned to unlearned love. But by 1940 he gave a love poem a title from the traditional marriage service, "In Sickness and In Health," and adapted much of its structure from the traditional litany; and in the final line of this poem, in a late revised version, he asked love to "hold us to the *ordinary* way."

As for the "simplest love" in the last line of "Enter with him," Auden kept changing the adjective to make it more plausible. In the 1940s he changed the line to read "Your finite love"; in the 1950s, "Your human love"; finally in the 1960s, "Love as love," each variant distinguishing a grand personified Love from the ordinary, finite, human love that occurs in any lasting relation. (The 1960s variant is incidentally the title of an unrelated poem by Laura Riding, whose other poems gave Auden the metre he used in this one.)

Auden wrote a second apostrophe to Love, in the same metre as "Enter with him," probably late in 1933 or early 1934, perhaps near the time he wrote "Our hunting fathers" and his review on T. E. Lawrence. "Love, loath to enter / The suffering winter," he begins, addressing a quester more reluctant than before. The two poems are parallel accounts of a journey to wholeness, but the trip is intentionally less exciting the second time around. Instead of the positive way of adventure, Love must embrace the negative way of suffering—which in this poem means indifference and isolation, not, as it will in later poems, the painful knowledge of one's need for forgiveness. As the poem opens, Love fears to wake from the "blithe . . . dream" of childhood, from "summer's perfect fraud" of sensual delight. Yet if it wishes to grow, it must enter the stricken grove of winter, its "heart not partial / To something special"—indifferent, that is, to any one object. The fruit of this indifference will be the spring thaw when the "frozen ghost / Begins to show / An interest"—*interest* in the sense of love, as in Auden's adaptation of James's "the interest itself." Finally, no longer dreaming and afraid but "Conscious, secure," Love will grow into an "honest summer" where lovers

> Walk in the great and general light
> In their delight and part of heaven
> Its furniture and choir.

The vague bathetic metaphors in these concluding lines are a signal that Auden is unconvinced by his own ideas. All that is lacking in his vision of mature enlightened heavenly love is the vibrato of massed violins.

Auden had read too much Freud to persuade himself that anyone, even an allegorical figure of Love, could simply grow out of childhood into serene maturity. The poetry he built on this optimistic fantasy had little merit in itself, but it was not entirely wasted. When he inverted the fantasy, in order to state a more pessimistic truth, he made one of the rare innovations in the long history of love poetry. Where earlier poets had seen the way to love blocked variously by parents, spouses, or rivals, by differences of class, nationality, or opinion, Auden saw it blocked by the psychological detritus of childhood. As in his other psychoanalytic borrowings, he altered the Freudian model in putting it to use. Freud had maintained that the barriers to adult freedom were hidden from the conscious mind in an abyss where only the analyst's probings could bring them to light. Auden, writing in the next generation, needed to expend no effort in searching for those barriers; he knew the map by heart. Psychoanalysis tended to hope that hidden barriers would dissolve when brought into the open. Auden found his visible barriers no easier to cross than Freud's hidden ones.

His wound, as he knew perfectly well, was opened by the strain of family relationships, and he made no effort to conceal this. *The Ascent of F6* (like *Paid on Both Sides*) portrays a destroying mother and her retrograde powers in parabolic style, but six months later *Letter to Lord Byron* makes the same point in direct autobiographical statement:

> We imitate our loves: well, neighbours say
> I grow more like my mother every day.

What is chilling about Auden's self-knowledge is his casual acknowledgement of its futility. With little hope that knowledge will lead to

freedom, he prefers to joke about the disaster rather than waste time
trying to change it. In an unpublished poem written in 1929 he even
played an elaborate game with the Freudian family romance in which a
child imagines that his real parents are not Mother and Dad but super-
human powers—as Oedipus himself, when the revelatory crisis was
about to break, insisted that his true mother was Nature. Auden opened
this poem by invoking "Father and mother, twin-lights of heaven"—the
sun and the moon—and continued through long apostrophes to these
deities. This sounds like the rawest possible exposure of a neurotic fantasy, but a later stanza makes clear that it is a deliberate shock effect: the
poem is a dramatic monologue spoken by the human eye.

When he considered the effects rather than the causes of his isolating
homosexuality, he was much less casually self-confident. Among friends
he tended to profess satisfaction with his emotional life; in his writings
he constantly challenged and tested it. Sometimes he blamed his homosexuality for his failure to love; sometimes he saw it as a symptom of a
deeper failure of intimacy and trust. In a review published in 1933 he
wrote of "the large number of nervous and unhappy people who are incapable of any intimate faithful relationship at all, in whom sensation
has remained at or regressed to the infantile level as an end in itself . . .
and to whom, therefore, the object is really non-existent." Auden wrote
this at a time when his descriptions of others' neuroses tended to refer
covertly to his own—as in his remarks on the attraction of communism
for the bourgeois. Although his comments here refer implicitly to his
own "backward love" and its retrograde movement toward infantile
sensation, he uses the detached impersonal tone of a clinician: "nearly all
homosexual relations are of this [regressive] kind." But he adds, perhaps defensively, "so are a large proportion of heterosexual ones and
there is nothing to choose between them."

Between the regressive past and a faithful intimate future stands another of Auden's divided frontiers. At twenty-six, in a poem he later
titled "Through the Looking-Glass," he saw himself in an unstable
middle ground in his personal history, with boyhood's narrow security
lost forever and maturity's satisfactions still invisibly distant.

It is Christmas 1933. The poem opens with an astronomical image of
passing time: "The earth turns over, our side feels the cold." There is

more to the earth's overturning than the tilt of its northern half away from the sun in winter. Six months have passed since Auden's vision of agape, and the cold he feels is both the chill of the season and the emotional chill that succeeded those warm evenings. His tone is calm, lucid, unemphatically personal: "Among the holly and the gifts I move, / The carols on the piano, the glowing hearth." But he is as detached as these objects are, at home neither in his parents' house where on holiday visits he is "loaned a room," nor in "the great bed at midnight" where he has never joined the beloved to whom he addresses his poem.

Lost between security and satisfaction, he projects on either side of him fantasies obstructing love. In his beloved's portrait he sees not the real face which might bring future happiness, but a nostalgic fantasy of his own childhood innocence, a "mirror world where logic is reversed." There, in a child's-eye transformation of his parents' world,

> move the enormous comics, drawn from life;
> My father as an Airedale and a gardener,
> My mother chasing letters with a knife . . .

All "False; but no falser than the world it matches." For the poet's fantasies transform the world outside the portrait into a setting for romantic idolatry, "Love's daytime kingdom which I say you rule." Here multitudes of emotions chastely worship the beloved's image, "All lust at once informed on and suppressed." Both these fantasies are amorous dreams, but since they reflect the poet's fear of adult love, "no one but myself is loved in these."

Stalled in self-love, he is barred from maturity and change. Where Auden had once spoken of his mental isolation in terms of the seigneur, now he uses a more accurate term, *conceit*. This is the aspect of the mind that keeps it from the shared common time of the world outside: as "time flies on above the dreamer's head," "All things he [time] takes and loses but conceit." Conceit is still aristocratic, still "The Alec who can buy the life within" and keep it from the life without; and conceit is so certain the mind is its own place that it finds reasons to be pleased with its own isolation, reasons to "Order the fireworks after the defeat." Escaping time's ravages, the mind is excluded from time's promises. Unwilling to suffer, it can never be comforted.

Two metaphors represent the poet's division. On the one hand, the looking-glass, on the other, the stormy ocean between two lost shores. He is trapped in the sea and the mirror. As he cannot move between his erotic fantasies on either side of the mirror, so, on his ocean voyage, he can find neither his home port nor his destination. Looking behind, he has "Lost in my wake" the shore of childhood and the boyish islands; looking ahead, he has "lost the way to action and to you." Conscious choice will prevent his advance: "Lost if I steer." He ends the poem in a prayerlike hope that the "Gale of desire *may*" instinctively carry him past the "illusive reef" to love's satisfactions and, instead of amorous fantasy, "the untransfigured scene." There the lovers may, in a brilliantly compressed phrase, be "Free to our favours"—freely choosing the instinctive erotic favors they share. (In a manuscript this phrase originally read "Meeting as equal.")

"Through the Looking-Glass" is a Christmas poem, written in hopes that Eros might bring a New Year of adult love. A few months later Auden admitted, in "Our hunting fathers," that Eros had done nothing of the kind. If we are divided against ourselves, Eros, whose mature ambition is to think no thought but ours, can offer no help. Then, in November 1934, Auden wrote a poem in which he looked back from the unsatisfied shore of adulthood—he reached it sooner than he hoped—to a youth now lost in the same journey.

The poem begins, "Easily, my dear, you move, easily your head." Auden added the title "A Bride in the '30's" when it was printed in *The Listener* early in 1935, and again in his volumes of collected poems in the 1940s and after, but omitted this when the poem was first published in book form in *Look, Stranger!* in 1936. The only misleadingly euphemistic title he ever used, it blurs the occasion and subject of the poem: not a marriage of two adults but a youth's emergence into adult sexuality with its dangerous variety of erotic and emotional choice.

What makes Eros so dangerous is its genuine eagerness to please. The opening lines celebrate the ease of love, and although within a few lines we hear thunder at the picnic, Eros, our obedient Ariel, makes it sound harmlessly picturesque. As easily as you, the desired one, move your head, just as easily and sensuously

I'm led
Through the night's delights and the day's impressions . . .
Though sombre the sixteen skies of Europe
And the Danube flood.

Let Europe darken, let its sky divide among hostile nations, Love's eyes see nothing but delight. "In the policed unlucky city / Lucky his bed." Intent, by our own choosing, on his "greens and lilies," Love gathers all that we see into the Yeatsian magic of the dance:

> Easy for him to find in your face
> The pool of silence and the tower of grace . . .
> Simple [for him] to excite in the air from a glance
> The horses, the fountains, the sidedrum, the trombone
>   And the dance, the dance.

Yet as it calls all these to its carnival, Love also summons, with indiscriminate attention, "Such images . . . / As vanity cannot dispel nor bless." These more disturbing images "from our time," images of "Hunger and love in their variations," now alter the poem's mood. Eros has less happy modes of expression: the chosen desires of "Grouped invalids" and "single assassins," and the more public rituals of Eros where demagogues woo their followers and the adoring masses gratefully approach:

> Ten thousand of the desperate marching by . . .
> Hitler and Mussolini in their wooing poses
> Churchill acknowledging the voters' greeting
> Roosevelt at the microphone, Van der Lubbe laughing
>   And our first meeting.

Private meeting and mass rally are equally erotic events, and it is we alone who choose which we prefer. "Love, except at our proposal / Will do no trick at his disposal"—*do a trick* has a sexual connotation—and when Love does what we decide, it does not ask what bargains we strike, what price we eventually must pay.*

---

* Auden provided a comic gloss on these matters in a 1936 lyric, "The soldier loves his rifle," published in full in *New Verse* and in part in *The Ascent of F6*, where it is sung by the promiscuously lustful David Gunn. Four stanzas provide a catalogue of Eros's satisfactions: as the soldier loves his rifle, the scholar loves his books, the trout its river, and so on. "I had an aunt who loved a plant / But you're my cup of tea." The not very flattering implication is that my personal Eros could equally be satisfied with a plant had I chosen one as my erotic object. A fifth stanza presents a variation on the theme. As Eros has many satisfactions, so also it gives various

When the poem turns to the way we came to make our choices, it expresses no more confidence in us than it does in Eros. We choose our loves not out of disinterested admiration, not even for the simple satisfaction of instinctual desire, but because our childhood development set ever more narrow limits on the polymorphous satisfactions of infancy:

> Certain it became while we were still incomplete
> There were certain prizes for which we would never compete;
> A choice was killed by each childish illness,
> The boiling tears among the hothouse plants . . .

As our choices narrowed, our "plans" for love grew "Fewer and clearer" until (here the poem shifts from *our* to *my*) "among my interesting scrawls / Appeared your portrait." It is not much of a compliment to one's lover to explain one's preference as partly a result of measles and tantrums, but it is uncommonly truthful.

With these lines the poem returns to the present, where truthfulness is needed most. The preceding half-dozen stanzas, with their history of childhood's effects, served as a didactic preparation for the choices the beloved must now make on entering adulthood. Those choices, the poem warns, are yours. "Ghosts" wish to claim you for their own, drawing you back to infantile sensation or ancestral hatred. "Are they your choices?" You possess the power of beauty; will you use it to compel others, and turn it into the "power that corrupts"? Do so, and your choice shall damn you to a hell of faithlessness "Where the engaging face is the face of the betrayer," where "you join the lost in their sneering circles, / Forfeit the beautiful interest" (and here *interest*, Auden's Jamesian metaphor for love, is corrupted by the language of bankers).

In short, will you, in exchange for hatred's "immediate pleasure" and glory's "fascinating rubbish," yield "your one treasure"? Auden takes these phrases from the shopworn romances of endangered virginity and gives them richer meaning. "Your one treasure," in a context having less to do with the physical than the moral aspects of love, is your as yet un-

---

shapes to individual bodies: "Some have sagging waistlines / And some a bulbous nose . . ." These are the results of unconscious choice, but choice nonetheless. Georg Groddeck called this private self-shaping Eros the It; in *Letter to Lord Byron* Auden wonders "what my It had on Its mind / To give me flat feet and a big behind." In *Spain*, in a more serious mood, he speaks of "the life / That shapes the individual belly and orders / The private nocturnal terror."

corrupted potential to enter a faithful intimate relation. The passage as a whole marks another of Auden's innovations in love poetry. He restates in moral terms the convention in which the poet—in the person of, say, Marlowe's Passionate Shepherd—tries to argue his lady into bed by warning her against the doom of aged virginity. Auden takes for granted that his beloved will join him in bed; what is in question is commitment and love. And where Marlowe's Shepherd knew exactly what he wanted from his Shepherdess, Auden is far less certain of his own corresponding wish for faithful intimacy. While his beloved is "standing uncertain now" on the edge of decision, for the poet himself it may already be too late. He urges the beloved to be deaf

> To what I hear and wish I did not:
> The voice of love saying lightly, brightly—
> "Be Lubbe, be Hitler, but be my good
> Daily, nightly."

The temptation to yield to that voice, to accept any satisfaction no matter how unworthy, faces the wise and the beautiful alike. Warning both poet and beloved, who would each prefer to satisfy immediate hungers than to worry about ethics, the heart still insists:

> "Yours is the choice, to whom the gods awarded
> The language of learning and the language of love,
> Crooked to move as a moneybug or a cancer
> Or straight as a dove."

The two languages and the two choices belong together, because without memory and its "language of learning" no faithful interest is possible. Of the choices these languages permit, the wrong one takes the form in the public realm of the millionaire moneybug, in the private the cancer, each with its destructive greed. The right choice flies straight as a dove—which in "A Summer Night" flew as agape's messenger.

These are straightforward moral decisions, but Auden's metaphors complicate the issue by bringing in his own sexuality. His primary meaning in calling the right choice *straight* and the wrong one *crooked* is the conventional one, but he also used *crook* and *crooked* to refer to homosexuals. "He isn't like us / He isn't a crook / The man was a heter / Who wrote this book"—thus Auden inscribed to Isherwood a volume by Robert Bridges. "Your horoscope's queer," he was told by an amateur astrologer, "and I don't like its look. / With the Moon against Virgo you might be a crook." There were moments when he tried to celebrate his opposition to Virgo: "Since our desire cannot take that route which is straightest," he wrote in "The chimneys are smoking" in 1932, "Let us choose the crooked." But now, two or three years later, in "Easily, my dear," the crooked route has become the cancerous path of hatred and greed.

His doubts about his sexuality led to a structural problem in his poetry. Soon after writing "Easily, my dear," he included it in a numbered sequence of sixteen poems which he had written mostly from the summer of 1933 to the end of 1934. Together, the poems make up a miniature psychological epic of wandering and return. The structural problem lies in the fact that the sexuality of the wanderer alters on his return.

The sequence begins in open sea with "The earth turns over." Then come a dozen sonnets and songs detailing the barriers to love—differences in age and experience, weakness of will, dreamer's conceit. In one sonnet, written in 1933, inner psychological division blocks the lover's journeys. The poet makes two metaphoric "climbs," one through the inner world of emotion, which has no means of sharing or communicating, the other through the outer world of the body, which can freely share the sex act but has no emotion to offer when it does. In the first,

> Fleeing the short-haired mad executives,
> The subtle useless faces round my home,
> Upon the mountains of our fear I climb . . .

(In a later revision Auden changed "our fear" to "my fear," clarifying the inner privacy of this ascent.) These mad executives we have met before—the personifications of what Gerald Heard called "the outer, executive, unstable side of man's nature." Fleeing them to find love within himself, the climber finds "no water" and "no col"—no pass that joins two isolated peaks. Yet when he abandons this exhausting inner climb to try the outer sexual one instead, he gets no closer to love. "Climbing *with you* was easy as a vow"—which is to say, given Auden's faithlessness in these 1930s lyrics, as meaningless as a vow. The sexual climb is simple, but we "Saw nothing but ourselves, left-handed, lost" (*left-handed* implies a variety of awkward estrangements, including homosexuality). "Love gave the power, but took the will"—Eros made possible our sensual delight, but delight sapped our wish for a deeper love.

At the close of the sequence Auden points the way out of these divisions. "Easily, my dear" is the penultimate poem, and the last is the 1933 sonnet "Love had him fast, but though he fought for breath" (later titled "Meiosis"). Now the sexuality of all the poems in the sequence—until the very end—is either ambiguous or homoerotic; many of them are addressed to an adolescent approaching the frontier of manhood. Yet the penultimate poem offers a choice between straight and crooked love, and the final poem chooses the straight—it records the fertilization by a male sperm cell of a female ovum.

In formal terms there is nothing untoward about this conclusion. The sequence as a whole is comic—it brings things together, where tragedy would take them apart—and its implied narrative movement is a conventional quest from the field of Ares to Aphrodite's bed. "Soon enough," warns one of the early poems, "you will / Enter the zone where casualties begin"; in the last poem, "he within his arms a world was holding." This is a perfectly acceptable example of modernist form: a poem shaped arbitrarily by myth, as in Eliot's account of *Ulysses*, with a deliberately fragmented narrative and discontinuous voices, as in *The Waste Land*. Yet for all Auden's sense of the virtues of conventional form, he was unwilling to let form become autonomous, to let poetic language itself act as the implied authorial presence in his work—as it does in much of modernism from Mallarmé onward—rather than the real historical author. When he tried to impose on his sequence a literary conclusion that was impossible in his life, he resisted his own poetic intention, with the result that the final sonnet not only contradicted the rest of the sequence but also contradicted itself.*

Its crossed purposes make "Meiosis" one of Auden's most obscure poems:

> Love had him fast, but though he fought for breath
> He struggled only to possess Another,

---

* In 1933 Auden used "Meiosis" as the conclusion of a sequence of five sonnets he wrote that summer (and published in *New Verse* in October); four of these sonnets were reused in the sixteen-poem sequence of 1934. The same sorts of contradiction occur in both instances.

The snare forgotten in the little death;
Till You, the seed to which he was a mother,
That never heard of Love, through Love was free,
While he within his arms a world was holding,
To take the all-night journey under sea,
Work west and northward, set up building.

Cities and years constricted to your scope,
All sorrow simplified, though almost all
Shall be as subtle when you are as tall:
Yet clearly in that "almost" all his hope
That hopeful falsehood cannot stem with love
The flood on which all move and wish to move.

As soon as one sees that the poem is an apostrophe to a sperm cell, the octave, at least, poses no real difficulty. Its wit is metaphysical. The male sexual partner was a "mother" to the sperm in the technical sense in which germ cells that give rise to gametes (either sperms or eggs) are called mother cells. The title "Meiosis" refers to the process by which the mother cell divides into two gametes, each with half the ordinary complement of genetic material in the form of chromosomes. The full complement of chromosomes is restored when a sperm unites with an egg to become a single-celled zygote, which then divides by mitosis into the differentiated cells of an embryo—as in the first three lines of Auden's sestet. Meiosis, in Audenesque terms, is the moment when a germ cell sheds half its genetic burden and therefore half its family ghosts. Depending on the specific genetic burden of the germ cell with which it later unites, it now has at least some hope of a different, perhaps easier, life in the next generation.

So, in the octave, the act of love is a struggle for mutual possession—the lover is intent on possessing another, is held fast by a love he does not resist, and forgets the snare of love in the moment of orgasm—while the sperm itself is released from his body's possession. Then the sperm proceeds on its microcosmic journey to the womb, where it fertilizes an egg and "sets up building" on the uterine wall. This is all quite straightforward, but there is an odd resonance in the line about the sperm's movement. Its "west and northward" heading is that of the futile North-West Passage, the direction of the Truly Weak. Auden lifted the octave's last two lines from a song in his unpublished 1930 play *The*

Fronny, where the implication of pointless neurotic action was clearer and more relevant. Deliberately or not, this implication carries over into the very different context of the sonnet.

The sestet's problems run deeper. Here the poem looks forward to a better future, but contradicts its own hope through its metaphoric details. The first three lines are fairly clear. The cities and years that constrict the scope of the sperm cell are the genetic memories of ancestral generations. Their accumulated "sorrow" is simplified for a moment in the new embryo's urge to grow and develop. Yet that sorrow will be almost as "subtle"—involuted, complex, guilty—in the new generation as it was in the past. These lines connect history on the public scale, the cities and years, to the private scale of the sexual act—the same connection Yeats made in "Leda and the Swan" between the fall of a city and the act of rape. Auden's sonnet revises in scientific terms the mythical history provided by Yeats's sonnet. And here the trouble begins.

Yeats printed his sonnet as the frontispiece to *A Vision*, in which he explained history as a series of two-thousand-year cycles, each inaugurated by a sexual "annunciation" joining a divinity and a mortal woman. Zeus's rape transmits to Leda the whole violent history of Greece—the burning tower and Agamemnon dead—in an annunciation made manifest by the birth of Helen and Clytemnestra from the egg. The Christ child and the rough beast slouching toward Bethlehem to be born are later products of the same historical process. Yeats's vision of history, which requires from its readers a quite extreme suspension of disbelief, is cyclically repetitive. Auden's different historical sense, which he considered rational and empirical, is linear and based on a conviction that events in history are unique. Yet this too had a mythical basis—or it did intermittently in the 1930s, whenever Auden proposed that history was meliorative, that society would inevitably grow more just in the future than it is today.

When he expresses this mythical hope in "Meiosis" he ties the poem into knots. Will the future be better than the past—"almost . . . as subtle" but not quite—or is this a vain hope? The poem gives conflicting answers. The problem is concentrated in the word *almost* in lines 10 and 12. In line 10 the word is part of a direct statement that the sorrow of earlier generations will be lessened in future ones. This statement at first seems to be the poet's, since the octave makes clear that the lover is not thinking about such matters. Yet in line 12 this changes. Now *almost* is distanced by quotation marks, part of the "hopeful falsehood" stated by the lover. The last three lines seem to say that the lover, by qualifying his hope for a better future—by hoping only that the next generation will be somewhat less sorrowful than this one, not that it will lose *all* its sorrow—hopes that his mental acts cannot stem the instinctive "flood on which all move and wish to move." This last line refers to the welcome flood of impulse, the same oceanic flood on which the poet in "Through the Looking-Glass" hopes he may be brought to port by the gale of desire. All move on this flood, because it is the flood of Eros that drives all life; all wish to move on it, because it simplifies the sorrow of consciousness and choice. The trouble is that the swelling tone of this final line does not fit the preceding lines. The meliorative hope that the poem states in line 10 it then denies in line 12; but now it reaffirms it in line 14.

Four years later, in *Spain*, Auden would trap himself in an even more difficult labyrinth through a similar effort to join private emotion to a public myth of meliorative history. But in the final line of "Meiosis" he was already pointing toward his way out. In a friend's copy he wrote the name Nietzsche next to this line, but whatever his conscious source, he used the same structure and main verb that Dante used in the final line of a greater poem about love: *"L'amor che muove il sole e l'altre stelle."* Dante's *amor* was both universal and personal at once, but Auden in 1933 was by no means prepared to accept a love so absolute and undivided, and so the love in "Meiosis" ended at cross-purposes with itself.

As for the sequence of poems that this one concluded, Auden broke it up into separate works before he had the opportunity to publish it as a whole.

The mature subject of Auden's love lyrics is the double subject of sexual success and emotional failure, and their mature tone is the double tone of celebration and regret. Thankful as he is for a lover's beauty, he has no more interest in describing it than he has in describing landscapes or still-lifes. "To me art's subject is the human clay"—but what matters is the guilty process of history and choice by which the clay takes shape.

The triumph of his double manner is the love lyric he wrote in the first week of 1937 and later titled "Lullaby." He is grateful for the pleasures of the body, but his post-coital sadness is felt as ethical self-reproach. His vocabulary is densely time-conscious and moral:

Lay your sleeping head, my love,
Human on my *faithless* arm;
Time and fevers *burn away*
Individual beauty from
Thoughtful children and the *grave*
Proves the child *ephemeral:*
But in my arms *till break of day*
Let the *living* creature lie,
Mortal, guilty, but to me
The entirely beautiful.

Beautiful indeed: but also *individual, thoughtful, ephemeral, mortal, guilty.* The cumulative effect of this vocabulary is such that *faithless* in line 2 excites faint moral reverberations in line 7's apparently innocent *lie.*

In shorter lyrics a year before Auden had apportioned the two elements of his double tone into separate stanzas. Lines praising "Beauty's conquest of your face" came first, then intimations of "unpardonable death" under whose look "my vows break." Now he devised a special rhetorical technique that allowed him to use both elements at once. The second stanza of "Lullaby" shows this technique at work:

Soul and body have no bounds:
To lovers as they lie upon
Her tolerant enchanted slope
In their ordinary swoon,
Grave the vision Venus sends
Of supernatural sympathy,
Universal love and hope;
While an abstract insight wakes
Among the glaciers and the rocks
The hermit's sensual ecstasy.

The stanza *sounds* affirmative and celebratory. It opens with a grand roll of *o*-vowels, continues with lovers swooning on Venus's enchanted slope, visions of supernatural sympathy and universal love, and ends with a phrase about sensual ecstasy. Taking his cue from the tone of these phrases, one critic has read the stanza as proposing "that on the one hand Eros can lead to Agape, and on the other that 'abstract insight' can induce Eros." As the poem celebrates a night of love, this may seem a reasonable summary of one stanza. But the rest of the poem suggests this reading may be false. This is a poem that says *my love* truthfully but says it faithlessly. The love it celebrates is unequal: the waking conscious lover, who knows all about faithlessness, speaks to a partner who is conscious of nothing. Not only is the poet faithless, but he knows that time and fevers will burn away his partner's beauty; knows that "Certainty, fidelity / On the stroke of midnight pass"; knows that midnight, like beauty and vision, dies. This night of love will exact its emotional price in a time of betrayal, when "Every farthing of the cost . . . Shall be paid." Meanwhile, in the public realm beyond the island of the bed, "fashionable madmen raise / Their pedantic boring cry."

In this dire context the line "Soul and body have no bounds" looks rather less affirmative than it does in isolation. Its tone is in fact exceptionally ambiguous. Both soul and body, the line seems to say, are unbounded or even infinite; but Auden, with his commitment to fact, was scarcely proposing that the body was unbounded by its skin. Whatever the tone may suggest, the statement of the line is that soul and body have no boundary *between* them—and, as the rest of the poem makes clear, this means that the time and fevers that burn away the body's beauty destroy the "faithless" soul as well. In the one place where a border might actually be welcome, protecting the soul from the body's decay, none is to be found. Body and soul die together, "and the grave / Proves the child ephemeral."

Auden's technique is to set affirmative-sounding phrases in a complicated syntax that, when unravelled, proves to say something very different. The vision Venus sends lovers is a grave one. What they learn from it is that there is no supernatural sympathy, no universal love and hope. The real bound is not between soul and body but between the lovers themselves, and between each of them and the possibility of love. The stanza denies what it seems to say, as its swelling praise of the unbounded soul and body modulates into a statement of the faithless soul's limits in the mortal body, and of the limits of both body and soul in time.

And as the first seven lines of the stanza take a grave view of the pleasures of the flesh, so the last three offer a chilling image of the pleasures of the mind. The hermit's sensual ecstasy is the ecstasy of thought isolated among glaciers of frozen impulse, far from the shared realm of the senses. While the body mourns its inevitable separations, the mind delights in its absolute solitude. Auden is back in the world of his 1929 journal entries about the evolutionary divergence of mind from body, but where he once saw a promise of freedom and satisfaction now he sees a future of betrayal.

So when the poem concludes by looking toward a better time, its language is resonant but hollow:

> Noons of dryness see you fed
> By the involuntary powers,
> Nights of insult let you pass
> Watched by every human love.

Loving and faithless at once, the poet hopes that the care and help he will not give his partner may come from some vaguer source instead. Yet Venus's involuntary powers have tonight offered no nourishment, and if the watchful love of this night of mutual satisfaction is already faithless, how slight must be the care to be expected in nights of insult. What the poem promises it has already denied.

"Lullaby" marks another of Auden's innovations in love poetry. It is the first English poem in which a lover proclaims, in moral terms and during a shared night of love, his own faithlessness. Hundreds of earlier poems lamented or confessed faithlessness; but the lyric tradition complained of the beloved's inconstancy, not the poet's, while the libertine tradition, in admitting inconstancy or alluding to the transience of beauty, ignored the moral consequences. Innovative as it is in the history of poetry, "Lullaby" represents a transitional stage in the history of Auden's work. He admits faithlessness, but here he blames it on the human condition. Later he will blame it on himself.

Auden sketched the innovations of "Lullaby" in a sonnet he wrote three and a half years earlier, in the summer of 1933. This appears to have been the first love poem he wrote after his vision of agape, and the first of his love poems that was not simply an erotic poem. It reads like a verse abstract of "Lullaby":

> Sleep on beside me though I wake for you:
> Stretch not your hands towards your harm and me,
> Lest, waking, you should feel the need I do
> To offer love's preposterous guarantee
> That the stars watch us, that there are no poor,

No boyish weakness justifying scorn;
To cancel off from the forgotten score
The foiled caresses from which thought was born.

Yes, sleep: how easily we may do good
To those we have no wish to see again.
Love knows he argues with himself in vain;
He means to do no mischief but he would:
Love would content us. That is untrue.
Turn not towards me lest I turn to you.

The relation of the waking lover to the sleeping partner is the same as in the later poem; love's false promise of watchful stars and a world without want corresponds to Venus's grave vision of universal love and hope; and the birth of thought from foiled caresses is the obverse of the hermit's thought-awakened ecstasy. In the sonnet's harsh admission that it is easy to do good when no obligations follow is a rough statement of the final stanza of "Lullaby," with its hope that nature and love will look after the beloved although the poet will not.

The obscure lines in the sestet about love's argument with himself are glossed in a sonnet Auden wrote at about the same time. There he said: "Love has one wish and that is, not to be"—Love desires its own satisfaction, but when satisfied it ceases to desire. Love, that is, is necessarily faithless. This was true for Auden both in the conventional sense underlying the literature of seduction and in the Freudian sense that life-instincts seek the ultimate calm of death—one of Auden's many borrowings from *Beyond the Pleasure Principle.* Love "argues with himself" that love should survive and "content us," but his argument is vain and his wish "untrue." However loving and well-meaning the poet may feel, if he were to promise truth to his partner he would lie—would offer "love's preposterous guarantee." His love makes him wish to speak lovingly, but to speak lovingly is to speak falsely, which is why he prefers his partner to remain sleeping, so that he will not feel the need to speak at all. (All this is a much clearer version of the paradoxes in "Meiosis" about "hopeful falsehood.") Language, which seeks permanence, contradicts Eros, which seeks its own ending; thought born of foiled caresses foils further ones. Warm in the arms of Titania, Bottom rightly observed that reason and love keep little company together.

"Sleep on beside me" was the first of Auden's mature love poems. It seemed for a time that "Lullaby" might be the last. A few days after writing it, in January 1937, he left for Spain, travelling from his divided private world to a divided public one. For the next two years, until after he began his career again in America, he wrote no love poems at all. Instead he wrote *faux-naïf* cabaret songs for the voice of the actress Hedli Anderson (later the wife of Louis MacNeice), parodies of popular lyrics in which he joked ventriloquistically about his own wounds. The first of these songs, in April 1937, was "Johnny," with its lonely refrain: "But he frowned like thunder and he went away." In another, in January 1938, he confessed his total ignorance of the love he had written about with such easy familiarity:

> Some say that Love's a little boy
>   And some say he's a bird . . .
>
> I've sought it since I was a child
>   But haven't found it yet;
> I'm getting on for thirty-five,
>   And still I do not know
> What kind of creature it can be
>   That bothers people so.

The song concluded: "Will it alter my life altogether? / O tell me the truth about love." Two years later Auden answered his own question and plea when he inscribed a book to a new love "who told me the truth (I was quite right; It did.)" But around 1938 he feared he would never experience love at all. In *Christopher and His Kind* Isherwood recalls Auden's anguished lonely weeping on their Chinese voyage. Auden himself, in a lighter tone, contrasted the two voyagers in a song:

> Christopher sends off letters by air,
> He longs for Someone who isn't there,
> But Wystan says: "Love is exceedingly rare."

He was echoing in his own voice words he had written for a passive loveless figure in a poem ten years earlier, who had said: "All kinds of love / Are obsolete or extremely rare." Auden had progressed no further on his quest for love than the isolation in which he began.

Yet he had learned what was required of him before he could go on. He had thought he could love only for a faithless moment, before beauty and vision died; now he knew that he might love faithfully if he accepted

imperfection and change. The time and fevers that he thought must be
the bane of love proved instead to be the soil in which it grew. In the
ballad "As I walked out one evening," written in November 1937,
the time-conscious clocks warn of the dangers facing love, but it is they
who also speak the imperatives love must obey to survive.

"Love has no ending," sings a self-deluding lover in this ballad. "I'll
love you, dear, I'll love you / Till China and Africa meet." But the poet,
with the sad weight of the traditional ballad upon him, sees the crowds
on the pavement as "fields of harvest wheat." Meanwhile the clocks
chime their warning:

> "O let not Time deceive you,
>   You cannot conquer Time.
>
> "In the burrows of the Nightmare
>   Where Justice naked is,
> Time watches from the shadow
>   And coughs when you would kiss. . . .
>
> "The glacier knocks in the cupboard,
>   The desert sighs in the bed,
> And the crack in the tea-cup opens
>   A lane to the land of the dead. . . ."

In a world of absolute necessity, a world like that of the creatures,
there would be no alternative to this prospect of emptiness and defeat.
But Auden was also coming to terms with his own insistence that Eros
leaves us free to choose our lives. There is an alternative to defeat, and
the clocks balance their warnings with commands that we are free to reject or obey. Their first command to the poet is that he see himself in
this real world of ordinary objects and recognize the failure of his pride:

> "O plunge your hands in water,
>   Plunge them in up to the wrist;
> Stare, stare in the basin
>   And wonder what you've missed."

Their second command is to recognize his failure to love as his own failure, not the fault of the world or the time:

"O look, look in the mirror,
   O look in your distress;
Life remains a blessing
   Although you cannot bless."

And the third and last command is to turn toward the world that waits beyond the enclosing walls of the self:

"O stand, stand at the window ·
   As the tears scald and start;
You shall love your crooked neighbour
   With your crooked heart."

This last command does not refute its biblical original, but explains it. We must be commanded to love because none of us has the beauty or moral perfection that would make love a matter of necessity not choice. For Auden himself the clocks' command has a hidden personal meaning. He can no longer evade the universal imperative to love by protesting that his own crooked sexuality makes love impossible. It is not only the murderer who needs to be self-forgiven in his glass, but the poet as well. Auden never approved of his sexuality, but he learned to acknowledge that it was not a uniquely isolating tribulation that barred him forever from the community of love. He came to recognize it instead as one of the infinitely varied forms of crookedness whose name, in his later work, was sin—and which was therefore open to forgiveness. What he had written in a defensive tone years earlier about the varieties of failed sexual relations, that "there is nothing to choose between them," proved true after all. It was not his sexuality that mattered but his isolation. And if the one could not be changed, the other could.

XI

Their Indifferent Redeemer

Auden's politics in the early 1930s were governed by his sense of the impending ruin of his class. In 1932, seeing no hope for the bourgeoisie, he approached a "conversion to Communism" and awaited the triumph of the workers. Then came his vision of agape in 1933. Now, all thoughts of political conversion abandoned, he knew he could not separate his fate from the fate of those he knew and loved. Within a few weeks he began to hope for deliverance. What would rescue his class would not be the oppressive power of money or arms but the liberating power of intelligence and vision. Prophets of a new life already walked the earth: Homer Lane, D. H. Lawrence, Gerald Heard, Schweitzer, Nansen, Freud. To combine their teachings into one great warning and summons, still another hero was needed. Who might be equal to the task? For a brief and secret interval, Auden glanced into the mirror as he asked himself this question.

At the same time he indulged his fantasies of heroism, late in 1933, he rebuked his own similar fantasies of erotic triumph. "Such dreams are amorous; they are indeed: / But no one but myself is loved in these." This was true of his political dreams also, but it took him a few months longer to admit it. He was seeking a role that was nothing less than redemptive—the role of the poet as messianic prophet, healer, and reconciler. While he seems to have regarded his project more as a stimulus for poems than as a plan for action—there are no traces of it in his letters or in the recollections of friends—he took it seriously enough to regret it later. The poems in which he tried out his fantasy never surfaced into print during his lifetime, and the episode was never discussed. The few signs of it that Auden did publish were incomprehensible to everyone but himself, since they were statements not of his redemptive fantasy but of his self-reproach for having harbored it.

It all began in the autumn of 1933, but it is best to approach it from a slightly later moment, in the early spring of 1934, when he wrote his review on the life of T. E. Lawrence. The review concludes:

> The self must first learn to be indifferent; as Lenin said, "To go hungry, work illegally and be anonymous." Lawrence's enlistment in the Air Force and Rimbaud's adoption of a trading career are essentially similar. "One must be absolutely modern."
>
> I mentioned Lenin. He and Lawrence seem to me the two whose lives exemplify most completely what is best and significant in our time, the most potent agents of freedom and to us, egotistical underlings, the most relevant accusation and hope.

Auden uses Lawrence as an illustration of theories of his own—theories sufficiently nonpartisan to be exemplified by Lenin as well. He says virtually nothing about Lawrence the man, only that his life is "an allegory of the transformation of the Truly Weak Man into the Truly Strong Man, an answer to the question, 'How shall the self-conscious man be saved?'" Here Auden begins to sketch in the features of his vague portrait of the Truly Strong: he is the one who escapes the paralysis of isolated thought without giving himself over to the blind impulse of undirected action. He joins within himself the two irreconcilable worlds. He is, the review insists, "indifferent"—Auden is still imagining that the union of thought and action must isolate the self-conscious man from the civil world of relations and responsibilities. In fact, all conventional forms of relationship, including the familiar rebellions of the young, must be abandoned. "One must be absolutely modern," he continues, quoting Rimbaud's "*Adieu.*" Auden now cites this poem as a summons to action. Two years earlier, in the Airman's Journal, he used it as a prelude to suicide.

"Our real wish," he writes in this review, "is to be united to and rooted in life." Yet the method he proposes requires a preliminary uprooting of all relations that have always joined us together. Nothing can be saved. The self must learn indifference (in the words of a poem written at about the same time) to "honour and sex and friendship as [we] know them." The prescription is bitter, the way negative. In passages like these Auden is writing not about politics or psychology but about a half-formed ascetic faith whose first goal is indifference to specific objects and desires and whose final goal is oneness with undifferentiated "life." All the local and individual loves of "A Summer Night" have been forgotten or abandoned.

The ultimate goal of unity proved difficult to achieve. The intermediate goal of indifference was easier—those who seek it seldom need to look very far. Auden found that the superior perspective he used in his earlier poems would now, if he adopted it again, permit an indifferent examination of the England he hoped to save. "Here on the cropped grass of the narrow ridge I stand," begins a solemn and expansive poem, written probably in the late summer or early autumn of 1933, as Auden began to think about secular redemption. After a year or more at ground level he is back at high altitudes. The poem's later title is "The Malverns"—the hills where he stands, "Aloof as an admiral on the old rocks, / England below me." When he was here last, he recalls, he was with a lover, and England seemed the "perfect setting" for their shared meditations. Now he is alone, with ideas more ambitious than amorous, and England in his eyes

> has no innocence at all;
> It is the isolation and the fear
> The mood itself . . .
> The little area we are willing to forgive
> Upon conditions.

The qualification in the last two words contrasts starkly with the universal forgiveness of "A Summer Night." England now is the locus of his solitary anxiety, his faithless refuge.

Auden takes to mountain heights not only to look down at the nation but also to understand its past ("empires stiff in their brocaded glory") and its possible future ("your last evening hastens up"). For the moment, though, his purpose is isolated and obscure: "For private reasons I must have the truth." His viewpoint private and indifferent, he takes a "closer look" down at his compatriots: the cramped clerk, the guide in shorts, "The little men and their mothers, not plain but / Dreadfully ugly." At the same time he hears from cafés, cinemas, cathedrals "The high thin rare continuous worship / Of the self-absorbed." These are people who need to be saved. Urgently emphasizing that need, the voices of the Great War dead, "the bones of the war,"* speak a warning testament from their graves, accusing their own past lives of "the will of the insane to suffer." But saner voices may be heard among the dead, the literary voices of Wilfred Owen and Katherine Mansfield, who provide watchwords for Auden's mission. Isolated in his privacy and his art, he would release England from its loveless disorder:

> "The poetry is in the pity," Wilfred said,
> And Kathy in her journal, "To be rooted in life,
>   That's what I want."

There is an inherent contradiction in the poet's wish to be rooted in a life he disdains as ugly and self-absorbed, its instincts "Deformed and imbecile, randy to shed / Real blood at last." But he cannot worry about this now: "These moods give no permission to be idle." A chiming clock reminds him he is "expected to return alive / My will effective and my nerves in order"—another phrase from Owen—"To my situation." That situation, for the moment, was just down the hill, where he was working as master at the Downs School. But in his poem he was preparing for a very large step upward.

Auden abandoned "The Malverns" in later years—to the puzzlement of critics who remarked on its vivid sweep and sharp details—but it was tainted from the start. It took over six stanzas almost without change from the most problematic poem Auden ever wrote, the unpublished poem in which he first stated his redemptive ambition. This earlier poem, probably written in the summer of 1933, opens with an apostrophe, a command to *write:*

> Friend, of the civil space by human love
> Upon the unimaginative fields imposed
> Rivalling that tie with the nearest which in nature rules . . .
>
> And of the whole human conflict you have something witnessed . . .
>
> . . . sit down and write . . .

---

* The familiar and less specific reading in *Look, Stranger!*, "the bones of war," is a typist's or printer's error. The correct reading appears in all manuscripts and early printed texts, and Auden wrote the missing *the* into friends' copies of *Look, Stranger!*

These clumsy phrases rise to a heated warning. Human love—what Auden would later call "Eros, builder of cities"—has imposed civilization on unconscious nature; but this love brought conflict also. The "Friend" must write about it for his readers' sake:

> that each upon
> This mortal star may feel himself the danger
> That under his hand is softly palpitating . . .

By recognizing their danger, both from within (under the hand) and without (this mortal star), they may change, and by changing save themselves from disaster. If they are to learn their danger, the "Friend" must warn them of it:

> So write that reading is changing in their living, these
> May save in time their generation and their race . . .

What the friend must write to save his readers is the testament they themselves would write had they not been changed by reading it here first—and so "Be saved by reading their own testament forestalled." The testament begins:

> "Know then, reader, that the simplest cause of our collapse
> Was a distortion in the human plastic by luxury produced . . ."

and continues, for six more stanzas, analyzing the collapse it will prevent from occurring. These are the stanzas Auden reused in "The Malverns," where their unrhymed triplets stand out awkwardly from the poem's eleven-line stanzas,* but where their attribution to a generation already dead, the fallen of 1914–18, avoids the circular argument of their original context.

The self-preventing mode of this testament—written in order that it may not be written—is characteristic of prophetic writing, and logical objections would be misplaced. But Auden complicates the matter even further. "Friend, of the civil space by human love" is a poem that is both

---

* In the one retrospective collection in which Auden reprinted "The Malverns" (after its first book publication in *Look, Stranger!*), the 1950 *Collected Shorter Poems*, he dropped these triplet stanzas. He omitted the whole poem from the 1945 *Collected Poetry* and the 1966 *Collected Shorter Poems*.

self-preventing and self-generating. The poet tells his prophetic friend to write the words that the poet himself immediately proceeds to write. He is the friend whom he addresses, the audience he warns. Having begun with the purpose of saving his generation, Auden ended by writing a poem concerned reflexively with its own composition, and ultimately with preventing itself from being written. This self-commanding and self-destroying mode is proper to romanticism ("Kubla Khan" is an example), but it scarcely helps rescue an endangered public. It is the opposite of the "attendant" poetry Auden would praise two years later in *Letter to Lord Byron*, where he calls "independent" poetry a literary disaster. At the same time, he would describe subject as the first thing in art—but the only subject of a self-generating poem is the poem itself.

After inserting much of this poem into "The Malverns" Auden took over some of its remaining stanzas into still another poem which he wrote a few months later, in March 1934. This third poem, again written in regular unrhymed triplets, served as his most detailed program for salvation. But now he was more wary of declaring his personal role. The responsibility that he had once placed on his imaginary friend he now assigned to real contemporaries whose names he listed and whose wisdom he conveyed.

Once again he opens with an apocalyptic warning:

> "Sweet is it," say the doomed, "to be alive though wretched";
> But here the young emerging from the closed parental circle,
> To whose uncertainty the certain years present
>
> Their syllabus of limitless anxiety and labour,
> Think: "Happy the foetus which miscarries, or the frozen idiot
> Who cannot cry mama; happy those
>
> Run over in the street to-day, or drowned at sea,
> Or sure of death to-morrow from incurable disease,
> Who cannot be made a party to the general fiasco."

The general fiasco is not the eternal human condition, but an event of our moment, the end of our familiar civilization:

> For of that growth which in maturity had seemed eternal
> 'Tis no mere tint of thought or feeling that has tarnished,
> But the great ordered flower itself is withering;

Its life-flood dwindled to an unimportant trickle
Stands under heaven now a fright and ruin,
Only to crows and larvae a happy refuge.

We have reached the point of complete isolation, "Each to his neighbour blind." Now, all of us totter "giddy on the slipping fringe of madness."

But at this last moment before disaster, the poem offers a sudden glimpse of hope:

Shuddering he [that is, "each"] waits the self-inflicted wound,
But dreading yet more the hands that hurt to heal.

Here the poem turns, for those healing hands that might avert the general fiasco do exist, "to those who choose to ask." An annotated list of healers then follows, in the form of an index to modern thought: in psychology, Freud, Homer Lane, Groddeck, and Matthias Alexander; in politics, Marx and Lenin ("that simple man who ordered / The village of Gorki to be electrified"); also "Both Lawrences," Gerald Heard, Nansen, and Schweitzer as various promoters of knowledge and justice; in physics, "Einstein of course," Planck, Rutherford, and Thompson. Auden's diction is no less naïve than this summary implies: "Yes, Freud who made a new Vienna famous" is a typical extract.

All these heroes "promise rescue" from the "disorders" that the successful, "our handsomest and best," believe can offer happiness and peace. The disorders, when Auden names them, prove for the most part to be relations between individuals, anything that might stand in the way of indifference:

From honour and sex and friendship as they know them,
These would deliver; from virtues and vices both,
And all that guilt which prisons every upright person.

So magical is the power of the healers' names that by the latter part of the poem the disaster that seemed inescapable in the beginning now seems easy and exciting to avert:

O luckiest of all the ages for a pioneer!
When the choice is simple and important, and all must choose;
When the intelligent and necessary seems also the just.

The word *seems* is a perhaps involuntary qualification to these triumphant lines, which are so oddly reticent about the pioneering choice they demand. If, as Auden's review on Lawrence suggests, the choice involves indifference, he evidently found it impossible to recommend this in the exuberant language of the poem. What he finally recommends instead is another act of writing, which is to bring about the new era. He does this in almost the same self-commanding words with which he began the first of these poems in triplets:

> So do, so speak, so write that each upon
> This mortal star may feel himself the danger
> That under his hand is softly palpitating.
>
> Quieten that hand; interpret fully the commands
> Of the four centres and the four conflicting winds;
> Those torn between the charities, O reconcile.

The "four centres" are the Lawrentian foci of impulse, but Auden has in mind an even greater reconciliation. The final lines continue the apostrophe, using phrases that would later conclude the vision of human justice in the "Commentary" to *In Time of War*:

> And to our vision lead of one great meaning
> Linking the living and the dead, within the shadow
> Of which uplifting, loving, and constraining power
> All other reasons do rejoice and operate.

By defining his redemptive program almost entirely by negatives, or by terms that cancel each other out, Auden managed to avoid giving any precise indication of what he had in mind. Certainly the choice we must make involves personal psychological healing, since Freud and Homer Lane are among the guides. Yet it is also revolutionary and collective, since Marx and Lenin play a crucial role. It includes the promise of sexual wholeness thanks to one Lawrence, and acts of lonely bravery thanks to the other. It is a choice that joins us to the universe, since we honor "the group of major physicists" who show the connectedness of all events in space and time. "Noble amateurs like Gerald Heard" do their bit, as do peacemakers like Nansen and Schweitzer "who have unlearnt our hatred ... And for our greater need, forgiveness, also work." Auden's just heroes would remit our crime of isolation, would restore us to the community of man. "Linking the living and the dead," they would pacify the ancestral ghosts. But however much these heroes recommend unity in the poem, no committee that includes Freud and Lenin, Schweitzer and D. H. Lawrence, is likely to cast a unanimous vote in the world outside.

At first Auden thought well of this poem. In the same month he wrote it, March 1934, he used it to conclude his first radio broadcast, a twenty-minute reading for the BBC. He also offered it to Eliot for publication in *The Criterion*. It never appeared there—whether because Eliot turned it down or Auden withdrew it is unclear. Finally, as he did with his earlier poem in triplets, Auden abandoned it.

The triplet form gave him almost as much difficulty as the redemptive program he used it to express. All the poems he wrote in regular unrhymed triplets in the 1930s—"O Love the interest itself," the two redemptive poems, the "Commentary" to *In Time of War*—are deeply self-contradictory or inauthentic.* The form itself became so infected that when Auden used it again in the late 1940s he deliberately applied it to fraudulent or unreal subjects: the concealed psychological horrors of "A Household" and the absence of heart, mind, and worth of "The Chimeras." Theoreticians of poetic form will note that for Auden the regular unrhymed triplet became a sign of falsity and imposture, while, at the same time, Wallace Stevens—the poet who most eagerly embraced the romantic principles Auden rejected—was adopting it as his characteristic stanza.

The contradictions in Auden's redemptive poems are signs of his buried distrust of the messianic idea. By May 1934 his doubts became explicit. Two sonnets written in this month mark the turning point. The first, "One absence closes other lives to him," he left unpublished, although it was part of the manuscript sequence of sixteen love poems he compiled at the end of the year. The occasion of the poem is the poet's irritation at a lover's absence: "his self-pity falls like rain." But there is a lesson in his irritation: he cannot bring himself to be indifferent. Sex means rather more to him than the task of saving his wretched generation:

---

* I return to the first of these in Chapter XV. See p. 334.

> Tweed pockets full of plants addressed him hours
> To him the wretched are a race apart,
> *He is not yet their indifferent redeemer*
> For only beauty still can make him kind . . .

There is a qualifying *yet* in the line I have italicized, but it is highly ironic. The pioneer's simple choice proved impossibly difficult.

The second sonnet, later titled "A Misunderstanding," is even more sceptical. Critics have good reason for finding this poem obscure: it refers to a psychological episode that is not part of ordinary experience and that Auden never mentioned anywhere else. Each element of the sonnet is clear in itself, but the whole, when read outside the context of the unpublished poems that preceded it, remains elusive. The poem is a palinode in which Auden publicly retracts a position that he had never publicly asserted:

> Just as his dream foretold, he met them all:
> The smiling grimy boy at the garage
> Ran out before he blew his horn; the tall
> Professor in the mountains with his large
> Tweed pockets full of plants addressed him hours
> Before he would have dared; the deaf girl too
> Seemed to expect him at the green chateau;
> The meal was laid, the guest room full of flowers.
>
> More, the talk always took the wished-for turn,
> Dwelt on the need for stroking and advice;
> Yet, at each meeting, he was forced to learn,
> The same misunderstanding would arise.
> Which was in need of help? Were they or he
> The physician, bridegroom and incendiary?

This precise and devastating critique of Auden's fantasy that the world needed him to save it is the first of his poems in which he writes as his own severest critic. Just as his messianic dream foretold, he was met and welcomed by those he imagined needing his aid. But the octave hints also at his sense of youthful inadequacy. The daunting professor is "tall," a word whose meaning in Auden is always relative to the "short" self-image of the observer (as in the similar child's-eye view of "the long

aunts" in "Easily, my dear"); the grimy boy does not come at the poet's
call but, disconcertingly, before it; and the girl, whose deafness suggests
her freedom from his rhetorical spells, has uncannily prepared the pleasures of nature and the flesh for his arrival.

The octave does little more than suggest these uncertainties. The first
two lines of the sestet manage to put them entirely out of mind. His talk
with those he hoped to save had turned persistently to the subject that
gratified him most, the need for the comfort and guidance that an indifferent redeemer can provide. Yet—the twist at the end is decisive—he
and they were speaking at cross-purposes. What the octave implied,
they had assumed from the start: it is the poet, not they, who needs
stroking and advice. Auden hoped to be the physician who would rescue
others from "the subjugating illness"; the tall professor is a more likely
rescuer. He hoped to be the bridegroom who could "reconcile"; the
welcoming girl at her green chateau is a better helpmeet. And he hoped
to be the incendiary who would destroy ancestral constraints; behind
the smile of the grimy boy, the real working-class incendiary may be
waiting to act.

When, during the next year or two, Auden wrote as a poetic teacher
who could "Make action urgent and its nature clear," some traces of his
redeemer fantasy still crept into his teachings. Yet he also reminded
himself of its dangers and absurdities. His song of the six beggared cripples, "O for doors to be open," written probably in the spring of 1935,
insists on the intransigence of the human will against any effort to save it
from itself. The cripples' desires—for power, sex, luck, escape, and for
"every one-legged beggar to have no legs at all"—are exaggerated versions of everyone's desires. They cry out their wishes to the "silent
statue" of a public hero who is long past promising to fulfill them. But
there were self-proclaimed heroes very much alive in Berlin and Rome
who promised all that the beggars asked and more.

Early in 1936 Auden used this implicit equation of redemptive hero
and fascist dictator in an explicit rebuke to his fantasy. He was
prompted by his experience making documentary films, when he saw
himself and his colleagues caught up in the vanity of artists trying to re-
form a society they inadequately understood. Now he was resolved to
lay the redemptive ghost forever. Soon after he left the Film Unit he

began working in collaboration with Isherwood on *The Ascent of F6*. Auden devised the central idea of the play and most of the psychological details, and arranged them in such a way that he could never again think of his fantasy without recalling its self-deluding *hubris*. The hero, Michael Ransom, wants "to save mankind"—not through poetry, but through a metaphor for poetry, his conquest of the mountain F6, and through the public adulation he will win by climbing it. Ultimately he is motivated neither by an indifferent and universal love for mankind, which he despises, nor by a pure love of his craft, but by his wish for the love his mother denied him in childhood, hoping he would compensate by growing independent and strong. As in *The Orators:* "By landscape reminded once of his mother's figure / The mountain heights he remembers get bigger and bigger." When Ransom refuses to serve the British imperialists who want him to climb the peak for the sake of a propaganda victory, his mother pressures him to agree. In making the ascent he destroys himself and his colleagues, and benefits only the government he detests. Ransom the would-be redeemer is a descendant of the Airman in *The Orators*, no longer a practical joker dangerous to himself alone, but a public figure with collaborators and an audience, and a fatal seriousness.

At his most self-important—and sometimes hysterical—moments, Ransom's speeches turn into exact transcriptions of Auden's unpublished poems in triplets. The fantasies Auden wrote in his own voice two years before he now puts into the mouth of his neurotic and self-destroying protagonist. The new dramatic context of these lines serves as Auden's most brutal criticism of their vanity. Ransom quotes the poem beginning " 'Sweet is it,' say the doomed," in his long soliloquy in the play's opening scene. He is discovered alone on a peak, looking down over England where "the stupid peasants are making their stupid children."* He begins by reading from a pocket Dante the speech Ulysses made to his crew: "ye were not formed to live like brutes, but to follow virtue and knowledge." Ransom scorns the author of these lines:

who was Dante, to speak of Virtue and Knowledge? It was not Virtue those lips, which involuntary privation had made so bitter, could pray for; it was not Knowledge; it was Power. Power to exact . . . an abso-

---

* This line is also a self-quotation, translated from a poem Auden wrote in German as an exercise some five years before.

lute revenge; with a stroke of the pen to make a neighbour's vineyard
a lake of fire and to create in his private desert the austere music of the
angels . . .

Ransom fails to recognize his own features in Dante's portrait of
Ulysses, the great explorer who destroyed himself and his crew. And he
fails to recognize his condemnation of Dante as a judgement on himself.
Ransom, not Dante, seeks power. Ransom, not Dante, sees the world as
a formless chaos awaiting a redeemer who might give it order: "Life
pants to be delivered—myself not least; all swept and driven by the possessive incompetent fury and the disbelief." Without a break, he continues in the words of the opening stanzas of Auden's poem:

> O happy the foetus that miscarries and the frozen idiot that cannot
> cry "Mama"! Happy those run over in the street today or drowned at
> sea, or sure of death tomorrow from incurable diseases! They cannot
> be made a party to the general fiasco. For of that growth which in ma-
> turity had seemed eternal it is now no tint of thought or feeling that
> has tarnished, but the great ordered flower itself is withering; its life-
> blood dwindled to an unimportant trickle, stands under heaven now a
> fright and ruin, only to crows and larvae a gracious refuge . . .

At which point one of his colleagues shouts from below: "When you've
finished saying your prayers, we should like to go down!" and the scene
closes.

   Later, on F6 itself, Ransom prays to his creator—who sounds more
like a hypothetical audience for an apostrophe than anyone Ransom
might actually believe in. The prayer repeats both the early poems in
triplets:

> Show me my path, show all of us, that each upon
> This mortal star may feel himself the danger
> That under his hand is softly palpitating.
> Quieten that hand, interpret fully the commands
> Of the four centres and the four conflicting winds.
> Those torn between the charities O reconcile.
> And to the human vision lead of one great meaning,
> Linking the living and the dead, within the shadow

Of which uplifting, loving and constraining power
All other reasons do rejoice and operate.*

The implied equation between Ransom the redemptive climber and Auden the redemptive poet would have been entirely inaccessible to the play's audience. (R. G. Collingwood, writing *The Principles of Art* in 1938, may have been alone in sensing that in the "tremendous rant at the end of *The Ascent of F6* . . . the author is expressing . . . the emotion he has towards that secret and disowned part of himself for which the character stands.") It is even possible that Ransom's meaning was inaccessible to Auden's co-author: Isherwood usually explained the story in terms of T. E. Lawrence or contemporary dictators. While the equation between Lawrence and Hitler is indeed present in the play—and it suggests how far Auden has travelled since his joint praise for Lawrence and Lenin as the most potent agents of freedom—it cannot account for most of the concluding scenes. Here the only significant parallel is between Ransom and Auden. Ransom makes soliloquies out of Auden's unpublished and therefore soliloquizing poems, and climbs mountains partly to overcome the sort of technical and emotional challenges a poet must confront on the difficult slopes of his medium. Ransom is another version of the Professor who made cat's cradles on the storm-tossed ship in "The month was April," but he adds to the Professor's harmless formalism a dangerously redemptive will.

For all his suave contemporaneity, Ransom is a figure out of the romantic age. Mountaineering itself is a romantic enterprise, which achieved its isolated early triumphs at the end of the eighteenth and the start of the nineteenth centuries, before it became institutionalized in the Alpine Club. Many of the details of Ransom's climb are lifted directly from Byron's *Manfred:* the obscure guilt, the Abbot's fruitless counsel of penitence and pity, the meeting of spirits at the close. Ransom thinks himself a Shelleyan legislator whose role will soon be acknowledged by an enormous public. As a metaphor for these poetic ambitions, the mountaineer is both historically fitting and dramatically effective. The romantic poet in his self-commanded quest for the visionary sublime cannot plausibly be represented onstage—there is nothing ob-

---

* So in the first English edition; the second, the following year, and the American edition both omit some lines and print the rest as prose.

viously dramatic about sitting at a desk with pencil and paper—but the mountaineer's ascent clothes the poet's struggle in visible action and gives it palpable suspense.

In his solitary pride, Ransom regards himself as a healer given to man. He sees his wretched patients either as pitiable beasts with "rodent faces, those ragged denizens of the waterfronts," or as helpless isolates like "the sad artist on the crowded beaches," all longing for salvation. He says of a moment of vision: "I thought I saw the raddled sick cheeks of the world light up at my approach as at the home-coming of an only son." But he could no more share this vision with his friends and colleagues—"How could I tell them that?"—than Auden could finally bring himself to publish his redemptive poems.

On his way up F6, Ransom stops at a monastery and conducts a long dialogue with its Abbot. Auden did his best to keep the meaning of their exchange hidden within its baroque complexity. (When Isherwood re-read the scene some years later, he told interviewers, he was baffled by it.) The Abbot begins by explaining what Ransom already knows: that behind the native legend of an avenging Demon at the summit is a psychological truth. The Demon is the projection of the will, the image of human isolation or "sorrow," the guardian of the unity lost in the birth of consciousness—a unity the will tries constantly and confusedly to regain. The Abbot recognizes Ransom's temptation: "You wish to conquer the Demon and then to save mankind. Am I right?" Ransom does not dispute him. The Abbot sees that Ransom has yielded to the "temptation of pity: the temptation to overcome the demon by will." Ransom is interested not in forgiveness, but in conquering his isolation by force—a futile and self-contradictory effort. Pity is not charity: it looks down on those it saves, so no real union is possible. (The poetry, that is, is not in the pity; and Auden in effect withdraws the quotation he made two years earlier from Wilfred Owen.*) "You could ask the world to follow you," the Abbot observes, "and it would serve you with blind

---

* He also retracts the "pity" he felt—in his 1929 verse letter to Isherwood—for man's "opposite strivings for entropic peace." In 1949, echoing Nietzsche but with a very different purpose, Auden would write of "the vice of pity, that corrupt parody of love and compassion," through which one regards oneself as superior to those one pities—"and from that eminence the step to the torture chamber and the corrective labor camp is shorter than one thinks" (*Renascence*, Spring 1949). His vehemence is partly self-reproach.

obedience." Ransom's gifts have made him a governor, and by his effort to save those he pities, he himself is "lost," for "government requires the exercise of the human will: and the human will is from the Demon." Ransom's wish to destroy the Demon is itself the Demon's curse.

The Abbot offers Ransom an alternative to his ambition: a penitent's journey to "the complete abnegation of the will." In the first-edition text, Auden makes it clear that the Abbot has sufficient moral authority to make this kind of challenge. In his monastery the contemplative life has not destroyed the Demon of the will, but has effectively controlled and confined it. In revising the play in the autumn of 1936 Auden added a passage that denied the Abbot even this limited redemptive power. Ransom asks the Abbot in the new version: "You rule this monastery?" The Abbot accepts Ransom's implication: he too is a governor, tempted by power, vanquished by the Demon, "already among the lost." It is too late for him to change. A few lines later, it becomes too late for Ransom also, as he accedes to the enthusiasm of his men and leads them to the fatal last ascent.

All this amounts to a psychological critique of the redemptive fantasy, but with theological overtones. No secular hero can be adequate to the task of redemption. The Abbot's speeches to Ransom have a whiff of parody about them—behind his robes one detects the improbable figure of A. E. Housman—but they add a religious note that will resound again in the play's final moment. In the intervening scenes, the concluding scenes of Ransom's story, the religious argument is buried beneath the crashing sounds of psychological revelations. But their confusion and disorder suggest that Auden found a psychological conclusion inadequate to the problems the play had raised earlier.

The details of the ending are impossibly muddled, and remained so through its revisons and rewritings, but the basic outline is reasonably clear. The scene presents Ransom's dream as he dies on the summit. In his dream he wills the death of the brother whom his mother had always seemed to favor. This murder is then mysteriously accomplished by the veiled figure of the Demon who sits on the highest peak. As the brother dies he repeats to Ransom his own charge against Dante: it was not virtue and knowledge he sought, but power. Ransom then accuses the Demon of his brother's death. There is a trial. Ransom now evidently loves the Demon he had charged with murder, and he withdraws the accusation in the midst of the proceedings. But "the case is being

brought by the Crown." The Abbot, acting as judge, declares the
Demon to be real—the *external* cause of Ransom's temptation, not, as he
had said earlier, only the projected symbol of an inner disorder. The
chorus, an aspect of Ransom himself, shouts its guilty verdict against the
Demon; Ransom rushes to protect it. Its veils fall, and it is revealed to be
his mother when young. His quest was a North-West Passage to regain
the love she denied him, to regain it by winning the adulation of multitudes. The redemptive ambition proves to be the adult distortion of a
childhood desire, and when Ransom finally recognizes this, he gives up
his ambition and dies. His mother sings a consoling lullaby as she
strokes his hair. Darkness falls. Then, as the sun rises over Ransom's
body alone on the peak, a hidden chorus sings in four-part harmony.
The music is a Bach chorale from the *St. Matthew Passion*. In the original text, "*Wer hat dich so geschlagen*," the chorus acknowledges the
sinlessness of the tormented Christ; now Auden's chorus also tells of one
who was despised and rejected of men:

> By all his virtues flouted,
> From every refuge routed
> And driven far from home;
> At last his journey ended,
> Forgiven and befriended,
> See him to his salvation come.

On the printed page the effect is mild, but in the theatre this can be a
profoundly unsettling moment. The music identifies Ransom as precisely the suffering innocent redeemer that the play has relentlessly
demonstrated he is not. How this rich and disturbing ambiguity follows
from the fuss and bluster of the dying hero's dream vision is unclear.
The dream scene, with its jazz elegy and comic horseplay, said nothing
about religion. Instead it blamed the destructive acts of a self-obsessed
leader on his wish for the love denied him in childhood. The religious
ending suggests that the elaborate business of Ransom's dream served to
compensate for its meagre explanatory content. The authors tried to sort
it all out in three different revisions within a few years after they first
wrote the play, but, as Auden told an interviewer in the 1950s, "we
never did get that ending right." The problem that persists through
every version lies in the attempt to resolve the play's political and ethical

issues through a psychoanalytic case study capped with a hymn.* The conclusion was not, in fact, designed to resolve these public issues at all, but to exorcise the private disorders that gave rise to the redemptive ambition in the first place. The play inverts the psychological causes— Auden was the son his mother favored most, not least—but the effects were the same. More concerned with private catharsis than public benefit, Auden used Ransom's death to discredit his own ambitious fantasies. He achieved his therapeutic purposes, but at the cost of a successfully resolved play.

As for the psychological cost, he meditated on this in a short lyric he composed in Iceland a few months later. It asks, "O who can ever praise enough / The world of his belief?" The dreamer finds a warm welcome in "the vivid tree / And grass of phantasy," but no one else is welcome to join him there. His "whole reward" is "to create it and to guard," no other benefit. "The Price"—Auden's later title for this poem—is much greater. "He shall watch and he shall weep," and after loneliness and adventure told in folktale terms, "in the pit of terror thrown / Shall bear the wrath alone." The pit of terror is the mirror image of Ransom's fatal summit.†

* In the first edition, following the dream vision and chorale, there was a brief epilogue in which the survivors irrelevantly praise Ransom's courage while the anonymous public claims possession of his memory. This makes no effort to resolve the public issues in the play, but at least it acknowledges their existence. As a conclusion it may have seemed too sardonic and hopeless to survive the urgent political mood of the Spanish Civil War, which began a few months after the first edition appeared, and it was dropped from later texts, along with the chorale stanza about Ransom's salvation. The chorale stanza that replaced it belongs to another phase of Auden's career entirely; see Chapter XIV, p. 315.

† There was a more tangible price to be paid some thirty years later. After the death of Dag Hammarskjöld Auden was asked to translate his private diaries, *Markings*. In his introduction, which was full of praise for the book and its author, whom he knew as a friend, Auden alluded to Hammarskjöld's messianic temptations and discussed their source, dangers, and eventual resolution. Auden did not say so, but he knew these temptations at first hand, and this allowed him to write about Hammarskjöld's experience with insight and force. When certain Swedish dignitaries read the introduction in typescript, early in 1964, they saw it as a desecration of a national martyr. Auden had been Hammarskjöld's candidate for the Nobel Prize, and his chances were known to be excellent for receiving it that year. But now it was discreetly made clear that his chances would vanish if the introduction appeared without change. Auden believed Hammarskjöld would have approved of everything he had written, and refused to alter it. The Prize went elsewhere.

After *F6* there remained only one detail of the episode still to be resolved. Auden had buried the notion that he himself could save his readers; but what of his notion that other secular heroes could do the same?
In 1934 he could compile a catalogue of healers, because he then believed that "such, to those who choose to ask, exist." Two years later
they existed no longer. The "Epilogue" to *Look, Stranger!*—the poem
beginning "Certainly our city"—asks rhetorically

> where now are They
>
> Who without reproaches shewed us what our vanity has chosen,
> Who pursued understanding with patience like a sex, had unlearnt
> > Our hatred, and towards the really better
> > World had turned their face?

These were the healers' triumphs in the earlier poem, and now Auden
provides a variation on the catalogue he had given then: "There was
Nansen," and Schweitzer, Lenin, Freud, Groddeck, D. H. Lawrence,
Kafka, and Proust. To the question "where now are They?" the
straightforward answer in 1936 would have been: Two out of eight are
alive and at work. But the poem's question is concerned not with the real
existence of these men in the world of fact, but with the possibility of
heroic healing in the world as Auden understands it. "Are They dead
here?" the last stanza asks. "Yes," comes the answer, because for Auden
in 1936 redemptive heroism is dead as a possibility, for himself and for
everyone else; and, in the words of a poem written at almost the same
moment, the only way to be "godlike in this generation / Was never to
be born."

XII

Parables of Action: 1

By 1934 Auden had thoroughly absorbed his own lesson that a poet has better hopes of teaching his audience than of saving it. He could not liberate his readers into the future he chose for them, but he might be able to help them learn to choose a future of their own. A tyrant or a secular redeemer held his followers in contempt, did their thinking for them; a teacher worked to increase the freedom he cherished in his students. "You cannot tell people what to do," he wrote in his 1935 essay on "Psychology and Art To-Day"; "you can only tell them parables; and that is what art really is, particular stories of particular people and experiences, from which each according to his immediate and peculiar needs may draw his own conclusions." In the same year, in his introduction to *The Poet's Tongue*, an anthology compiled in collaboration with a schoolmaster friend, John Garrett, he explained that "Poetry is not concerned with telling people what to do, but with extending our knowledge of good and evil, perhaps making the necessity of action more urgent and its nature more clear, but only leading us to the point where it is possible for us to make a rational and moral choice." In editing this anthology he was so intent on denying any personal authority to the poets he included that he banished their names to an appendix and arranged their poems by alphabetical order of first lines. What mattered most about a poem was not who wrote it, but its capacity to delight and to instruct.*

* Auden used the same alphabetical arrangement in his 1945 *Collected Poems* and 1950 *Collected Shorter Poems*, hoping that the poems might be read for their individual merits rather than as events in his personal history.

That Auden should think it possible to teach anything at all is a sign of how deeply and rapidly he had changed. In 1932 he was willing to postpone education until after a change in society: "Education succeeds social revolution, not precedes," he had argued; "You cannot train children to be good citizens of a state which you despise." But by March 1934 he was taking almost the opposite position. In a review printed in *Scrutiny* he wrote: "The progress of the realization of values is like that of scientific inventions; it renders obsolete its predecessors. A state has to train its youth not only to be good citizens, but to change it, *i.e.* to destroy its present existence. Educationalists must always be revolutionaries."

While the vocabulary of this passage is as revolutionary as that of his earlier remarks, the argument is very different, and the phrase that follows "*i.e.*" means something less violent than it would have meant a year before. Now, instead of a single decisive revolution, society is to be altered by a continuing Hegelian realization of values, which corresponds to the continuing process of "scientific inventions." In neither the political process nor the scientific one is there a single realization of ultimate truth. Auden's position has become reformist, for all the bluster of its vocabulary, and expresses a homeostatic view of history. Educationalists must *always* be revolutionaries; there will be no revolution to free them from their role.

He chose poetic drama as his didactic vehicle. The first work he wrote for public performance was the ambiguously revolutionary playlet *The Dance of Death* (1933). Then came the three longer plays, each somewhat less revolutionary than the last, all written in collaboration with Isherwood: *The Dog Beneath the Skin* (1935), *The Ascent of F6* (1936), and *On the Frontier* (1938). By the time the last of them had been produced, he was praising drama for its "supremely conservative" portrayal of "the relation between man's free will and the forces which limit and frustrate that will." This conservatism of vision had nothing to do with reactionary politics; in fact it made drama the proper medium for a just society. Lecturing in Paris on "The Outlook for 'Poetic Drama'" in December 1938, he described the theatre as the best of all didactic media, with clear advantages over its great competitors, the novel and cinema. Unlike the novel, it was a public medium that required the cooperation of a large number of people; unlike the cinema, it was inexpensive enough not to need the large financial support that could only come from "people who have very good reasons not to wish the truth to be known." Furthermore, the drama lacks the freedom of movement enjoyed by both novel and cinema, and so (in the words of a poem written at about the same time) cannot "betray us / To belief in our infinite powers." Instead, the drama "holds temperately to the belief in the free will of man; it also is humble and is aware of all those forces which limit it. It is therefore . . . not a form for a completely laissez-faire community, nor is it a form for totalitarian states, which much prefer the cinema. It is a form for social democracy."*

The prose drama of the nineteenth century, he said, gave the illusion that human action takes place only on the local private scale of the family. "It was possible for a character to confront her father and say: 'I will leave the house!' and for one to feel that an immense moral victory had been gained." But now we are learning "how enormously the social structure and the cultural power of an age contribute to dictate individual characters and the kind of liberty which is permitted." Both psychology and economics have taught us to think of ourselves collectively—in the double contexts of the unconscious which is shared by all mankind, and of the social roles we share with others of our class and community. The drama must now combine personal uniqueness—inherited from nineteenth-century conceptions—"with the realization of collectivity as well." One of the ways this can be achieved "is by the use of poetry, because poetry is a medium which expresses the collective and universal feeling."

This lecture, which amounts to a retrospective program for Auden and Isherwood's collaborative work in 1934–38, also refers obliquely to an important difference between the collaborators. Isherwood had observed earlier that "When we collaborate, I have to keep a sharp eye on him—or down flop the characters on their knees." Now Auden's lecture acknowledges that "poetry unalloyed tends, if one is not very careful, to introduce a rather holy note. You cannot have poetry unless you have a certain amount of faith in something, but faith is never unalloyed with doubts, and requires prose to act as an ironic antidote." Agnostic Auden wrote the verse in the plays, ironic Isherwood most of the prose.

Auden's lecture refers to the drama's just portrayal of the balance between freedom and necessity, but he and Isherwood never quite achieved that balance in their plays. They always concluded by empha-

---

* When he wrote this in 1938 Auden was no longer attacking social democracy as inadequate, as he had done in 1935; see Chapter XIII, p. 301.

sizing one side or the other, either ascending on hymns of poetic vision,
or collapsing in the flat necessity of prose. Then, recognizing the imbal-
ance, they would rewrite the endings to reverse the emphasis, and leave
the plays just as imbalanced as before. Isherwood explained the
genuflecting tendencies of Auden's characters as a recollection of his
childhood Anglicanism, but Auden had a more urgent and immediate
purpose. He was trying to find in practice the supremely conservative
view of free will and necessity that he praised in theory in 1938, but he
was still unwilling to find it in religious belief. So he kept trying to resolve his plays by using the language of religiosity instead.

Like Yeats and Eliot before him, Auden went to the stage to recover
for poetry an audience and a social function. For all three, poetic drama
promised to reunite the private world of the poet with the public world
of the theatre. They expected wholesale reconciliations. Barriers would
dissolve between artist and audience, ivory tower and marketplace, vision and action, art and society. Motivating all their hopes was an intense and unexamined nostalgia. Yeats in the theatre tried to recover the
archaic Irish legends that would reconstitute the Irish nation and its ancient social order of nobles and peasants, free from the modern intrusion
of the half-educated bourgeois paudeen. Eliot also found "the half-
educated and ill-educated" a barrier to his poetic vocation; he would
have preferred "an audience which could neither read nor write," to
whom he might address socially useful poetry that "could cut across all
the present stratifications of public taste." The ideal medium for such
poetry, he thought, would be the theatre. And Auden, at least when he
first had access to a stage, wanted to recover the original condition of
drama in a lost world, a world so unified that drama was "the act of a
whole community."

Nostalgia is not the soundest basis for action, and all these efforts
fell short of their impossible goals. But each effort served as a warning
lesson for the next. Yeats's Abbey Theatre audience loudly refused to
accept the myths he told them were their own. So he turned away in
disgust, and worked in his later plays to "create for myself an unpopular
theatre and an audience like a secret society where admission is by fa-
vour and never to many." Where Yeats contemptuously admitted defeat
in his attempt to make high art entertaining to a large public, Eliot
hoped to succeed by taking the opposite course. The audiences of the
past may have tolerated the high style, but the modern audience in these
fallen days would not. "The Elizabethan drama," Eliot wrote in 1920,

with more snobbery than accuracy, "was aimed at a public which wanted *entertainment* of a crude sort, but would *stand* a good deal of poetry; our problem should be to take a form of entertainment, and subject it to the process which would leave it a form of art. Perhaps the music-hall comedian is the best material. I am aware that this is a dangerous suggestion to make," he modestly continued, and he found it too dangerous to follow even to the end of *Sweeney Agonistes,* which he left unfinished. But he found in the music hall, as in no other theatre, a complete sympathy between performer and audience—a community that came together to sing the refrains. He wrote in his tribute to Marie Lloyd that only the lower classes could achieve this sympathy, not the middle classes. "The middle classes are morally corrupt." So Eliot, like Yeats, found himself holding his only potential audience in contempt. When he wrote *Sweeney Agonistes* he did not try to achieve sympathy with his audience—the music-hall echoes told his listeners what they lacked, not what they shared—but hoped to transmit his secret knowledge exclusively to the audience's "most sensitive and intelligent members." The rest, their responses "material, literal-minded and visionless," were deliberately to be left in the dark; Eliot seems not to have doubted that they would buy tickets for this purpose. Eventually, as Yeats had withdrawn to the symbolic intensities of the drawing-room, Eliot took the opposite road to Broadway and the West End, bringing drama with him but leaving behind much of the poetry.

Auden, despite all the imperfections of his plays, came closer than anyone writing in English to solving the problems of modern poetic drama—although he never managed to solve them all in the same work. Only Brecht solved more of them, and the techniques Brecht developed in depth and detail closely resembled the sketchier ones devised independently by Auden. Brecht's commitment to the stage was far stronger and more consistent, but he and Auden shared a similar didactic purpose. Each rejected a theatre that, however "advanced" its technique, made the audience a passive spectator of the inexorable movement of character or fate. Each tried to alert his audience to the urgency of choice and change. Like Brecht, but unlike Eliot, Auden wanted to educate all his audience, and not share secrets with selected members of it; like Brecht, but unlike Yeats, he preferred to use symbols his audience already knew rather than insist they accept symbols he felt they ought to know but didn't. He took up Eliot's suggestion that the music hall could be a source of dramatic technique, but did so without Eliot's finical shiver. He proposed instead to adapt the techniques of music hall and Christmas pantomime to the dramatic conventions familiar to the middle classes where he knew he could find his only real audience. Auden's disdain for the solemn high art of the bourgeoisie never extended to its amusements.

Reviewing a book on modern poetic drama in *The Listener* for 9 May 1934, he wrote (anonymously, as in the case of all brief reviews there) that Yeats and other poetic dramatists had failed, because "The truth is that those who would write poetic drama, refuse to start from the only place where they can start, from the dramatic forms actually in use. These are the variety-show, the pantomime, the musical comedy and revue . . . , the thriller, the drama of ideas, the comedy of manners, and, standing somewhat eccentrically to these, the ballet." Eliot had dismissed the revue as corrupt: it "expresses almost nothing," he said. Auden was now ready to use the revue and anything else that might be at hand. "Poetic drama," he continued, "should start with the stock musical comedy characters—the rich uncle, the vamp, the mother-in-law, the sheik, and so forth—and make them, as only poetry can, memorable." He concluded with a young man's rebuke to the middle-aged fastidiousness of Eliot's 1920 essay: "If the would-be poetic dramatist . . . is willing to be humble and sympathetic, to accept what he finds to his hand and develop its latent possibilities, he may be agreeably surprised to find that after all the public will *stand, nay even enjoy, a good deal of poetry*" (italics added).

Replying to some letters published in response to this review, Auden claimed even more for the stock characters of musical comedy. Not only does "their popularity and familiarity [give] the public a handle to hold on to," but this "would seem to imply that they have some psychological and perhaps poetic symbolic value." His review and reply are the credo of a civil poet, receptive to the full range of literary tradition that lies between the extremes known to the aristocrat and the peasant, and ready to educate an audience from a position among them, not somewhere up above.

When Auden wrote this review he had not yet attached a political motive to his dramatic theory. As early as 1928, when he had no interest in politics at all, he had similarly thought of the drama in terms of communal symbols, and had rejected the naturalistic drama of individual characters with unique personal psychologies. *Paid on Both Sides* quotes long fragments from the ritualized mummers' play performed in English villages at Christmas. In his 1929 journal he noted his approval of a tenth-century Latin dramatist whose plays had recently been published in translation, and he equated her literary technique with the stylized acts and deeds of schoolboys: "A play is poetry of action. The dialogue should be correspondingly a simplification. (E.g. Hrotswitha.) The Prep School atmosphere. That is what I want."

This was his intention for the play he was then starting, with *The Reformatory* as its working title (he finished it with Isherwood's help as *The Enemies of a Bishop*). When the play was complete he appended a "Preliminary Statement" that defined his simplified style in terms of its effects:

> Dramatic action is ritual. "Real" action is directed towards the satisfaction of an instinctive need of the actor [i.e. *not* a stage actor, but anyone who performs a deed] who passes thereby from a state of excitement to a state of rest. Ritual is directed towards the stimulation of the spectator who passes thereby from a state of indifference to a state of acute awareness.

This last point has become familiar as an aspect of Brecht's dramatic theory, but Auden came to the idea on his own. His attendance at an early performance of *Die Dreigroschenoper* in Berlin in 1928 may have had some effect on his thinking, but he was working primarily out of the traditions of pantomime and medieval drama, which he had used in *Paid on Both Sides* before he arrived in Berlin. Brecht's more elaborate version of the theory, as set out in the notes to his opera *Mahagonny*, did not appear until two years afterward, in 1930.

Auden was still emphasizing the ritual aspect of drama as late as 1935, when he wrote a brief manifesto for the program of the first public production of *The Dance of Death*. This was one of a series of statements by different writers, all headed "I Want the Theatre to Be . . ." Among the characters in *The Dance of Death* was a "Mr. Karl Marx," but Auden's statement, while entirely consistent with Marx's philosophy, omits Marx's practical purposes:

> Drama began as the act of a whole community. Ideally there would be no spectators. In practice every member of the audience should feel like an understudy. . . .

The development of the film has deprived drama of any excuse for being documentary [Auden had just begun his film work when he wrote this]. It is not in its nature to provide an ignorant and passive spectator with exciting news.

The subject of the drama . . . is the commonly known, the universally familiar stories of the society or generation in which it is written. The audience, like the child listening to the fairy tale, ought to know what is going to happen next.

Similarly the drama is not suited to the analysis of character, which is the province of the novel. Dramatic characters are simplified, easily recognisable and over life-size. . . .

Drama in fact deals with the general and universal, not with the particular and local.

And a year later he wrote to a reviewer, Dilys Powell, to confirm her observations on his plays' use of "symbols of *action*" rather than symbols of states of mind or being—Auden as Aristotle, one might say, against Yeats as Plato:

as you said, I want to objectify the images, into symbols of action. I do want the drama I write to become more and not less like a boy's adventure story. The significance on the external plane must be as childishly simple as possible. . . . at present my trouble is not that the behaviour of my characters is too schoolboyish, but that their schoolboyishness is sometimes only that, i.e. the real significance has failed to get itself projected into terms of their behaviour . . .*

Auden's first opportunity to turn theory into practice came in 1932 when Rupert Doone, who had recently founded the Group Theatre, commissioned him to write a play. Doone had begun his career as a dancer, worked extensively in classical ballet, and spent some years in

* Dilys Powell had also noted that Auden's poems, in contrast to the plays, were strikingly *non*dramatic. Auden agreed: "I want lyric verse to be really lyrical, because at least in my own work when I get onto the dramatic lyric I hear far too often the shrill tones of the hockey-mistress."

Paris absorbing the tenets of modernism from Jean Cocteau (with whom he once collaborated) and Serge Diaghilev. In 1929 he joined Diaghilev's Ballets Russes as a soloist for a London tour; two months later Diaghilev died and the company disbanded. Back in England, Doone turned to the study of acting and directing, and soon conceived the idea of a dramatic counterpart to the Ballets Russes—a permanent repertory company whose productions would use speech, mime, and dance, and bring together the most advanced techniques in all the arts. In London, in February 1932, he formally organized the Group Theatre. Nothing like it existed in England, and Doone quickly found many artists and writers who were eager for his projects to succeed. Eliot and Yeats took an active interest; Auden, Spender, and MacNeice wrote plays; Henry Moore and John Piper provided designs; Benjamin Britten wrote music. Doone's co-intendant was Tyrone Guthrie, with whom he had discussed his plans at a very early stage. Within a few months of its founding, the Group had taken rooms in London and begun regular series of lectures, classes, and play-readings. By 1935 it listed more than 250 paying members.

Auden came to the Group through Robert Medley, his friend at school who in 1922 had first prompted him to write poetry. Medley was now living with Doone, and in the spring of 1932 he arranged for Auden to visit and talk over the possibility of working together. Auden found the idea of a Group sympathetic—he had been writing about groups for the past few months—and welcomed the chance to write plays that might actually be produced. But he did not much care for Doone personally, and was sceptical of Doone's ideas about theatre. He made it clear from the start that he detested ballet—"an art fit only for adolescents"—and in his *Listener* review grudgingly allowed it only an eccentric position among theatrical forms. He advised Doone on plays that might be produced, and helped with productions of his own, but on the whole he tended to keep his distance from the Group's everyday activities.

For the first three years Doone thought of the Group in collective terms but not yet political ones. The Group's early manifestoes, hammered into shape by Auden but not necessarily reflecting his ideas, emphasized that it was to be an aesthetic community, with a paying audience for an economic base. A 1933 appeal for membership began:

the GROUP THEATRE is a co-operative. It is a community, not a building.

the GROUP THEATRE is a troupe, not of actors only but of

                              Actors
                              Producers
                              Writers
                              Musicians
                              Painters
                              Technicians
                              etc, etc and
                              AUDIENCE

Because you are not moving or speaking, you are not therefore [merely] a
passenger. If you are seeing and hearing you are co-operating.

A 1934 prospectus explains that the Group's audience and artists "do
everything, and do it together, and are thus creating a theatre representative of the spirit of to-day." These pronouncements were somewhat
optimistic. The Group was perennially short of funds, and instead of
becoming a permanent repertory company, depended largely on intermittent volunteer work by inexperienced young performers. Its productions during its first three years were given in suburban theatres during
the summer, or were club performances given on Sundays when the
commercial theatres were closed.

Then, in 1935–36, a London theatre-owner offered financial backing
for a full season, and the Group's activities began in earnest. Carrying
out the pluralist intentions of Auden's 1934 *Listener* review, it staged
Timon of Athens, a comedy by Goldoni, and a prewar comedy of manners, in the same series with *The Dog Beneath the Skin* and a double bill
of *Sweeney Agonistes* and Auden's *The Dance of Death*. During this
season Doone first began to talk, in a rather woolly fashion, of making
the theatre "a social force, where the painter and author and choreogra-
pher . . . combine with the audience to make realism fantasy and fantasy
real." By the time Doone came round to this social view of drama, possibly through Auden's influence, Auden himself was beginning to have
doubts. Having left his teaching job in the summer of 1935, he was now
living in London, growing disillusioned with his film work, and losing
patience with Doone's erratic methods and dictatorial manner.* The

* Benjamin Britten came home from one of Doone's rehearsals in 1936 and wrote in
his diary: "Rupert is really beyond all endurance sometimes—his appalling vague-
ness & quasi-surrealist directions—& completely impractical for all his talents."

Group could not manage without Doone, but Auden began to feel it could not manage with him. When, evidently at Doone's request, he wrote a statement for the first number of the *Group Theatre Paper* in the spring of 1936, he readily acknowledged the effect society had on art, but he was much more circumspect about any influence in the reverse direction. He suggested that the Group could serve as an "experimental laboratory" whose work might prove useful to society, although—perhaps recalling Doone's productions—he admitted that many of the experiments would fail. His statement, a masterpiece of tact, praises art for its general didactic value but omits any specific praise for the Group Theatre itself:

> Art is of secondary importance compared with the basic needs of Hunger and Love, but it is not therefore a dispensable luxury. Its power to deepen understanding, to enlarge sympathy, to strengthen the will to action and last but not least, to entertain, give it an honourable function in any community.
>
> The content and structure of social life affect the content and structure of art, and art only becomes decadent and a luxury article when there is no living relation between the two. But because of natural laziness and the friction of opposing and vested interests, development in art as in society, is not a purely unconscious process that happens automatically. It has to be willed; it has to be fought for. Experiments have to be made, and truth and error discovered in their making. An experimental theatre ought to be regarded [as] as normal and useful a feature of modern life as an experimental laboratory. In both cases not every experiment will be a success . . . but, in its successes important avenues of development may be opened out, which would not otherwise have been noticed.

He neglects to say who might explore those avenues when they open.

The plays Auden had written for the Group up to this time were similarly uncertain about their public effect. *The Dance of Death* presents itself as propaganda, but of an elusive, almost frivolous kind, ending with Karl Marx's entrance to the tune of Mendelssohn's wedding march. *The Dog Beneath the Skin* combines some musical-comedy froth about a missing heir disguised as a dog with hortatory choruses about repentance, unity, and action. Each of these plays moves only erratically toward its moral and political warnings. *The Ascent of F6* moves erratically away, and forgets its opening satire as it follows its solitary hero to his final psychological redemption.

But with the outbreak of civil war in Spain in the summer of 1936 Auden's attitude changed. Political action was now urgent, and if the Group Theatre was a flawed instrument, it was better than nothing. In November he wrote a fund-raising program note (entitled "Are You Dissatisfied With This Performance?" and opening with the answer, "Quite possibly") in which he said the Group had "the possibilities . . . for a vital theatre, neither drawing-room drama, nor something private and arty, but a social force. We have a lot to learn," he continued, chastened but hopeful, "but are willing, we think, to do so if we get the right support."

Four months later he returned from his disillusioning visit to Spain with very different attitudes to both politics and the theatre. He made less effort to hide his contempt for Doone, and during a summer meeting of the Group in 1937 he and Isherwood at last precipitated a bitter policy dispute, which was only partly and warily resolved. They conceived their next play, *On the Frontier,* more for commercial production than for the Group (although in fact Doone produced it with backing from J. M. Keynes), and the play itself, their weakest, begins by striding forth among the simplicities of propaganda and ends by sitting down to weep.

Auden found it difficult from the start to write for the Group. At his first professional meeting with Doone in the spring of 1932 he brought along a late medieval *danse macabre* poem and suggested it as the possible basis for a play. Doone was inclined instead toward a ballet libretto on the theme of Orpheus in the underworld, in which he could star as lead dancer. In the end they agreed that Auden would try to write a single work combining both ideas. Although in later years Auden found commissions, formal or informal, to be unfailing stimuli to his imagination, now he made little progress. He told Doone in the summer of 1932 that he was "getting on with the Orpheus stuff," but in October he reported that he had "written a thing but frankly it's no use. I'm afraid you'll think I've let you down but I know it's no good. Perhaps one day I shall be able to manage it but not yet." At the end of the year he talked

over some of his ideas with Isherwood, but he does not seem to have re-
sumed work until the summer of 1933. By August he finished *The
Dance of Death*, a one-act play in about eight hundred lines of doggerel
verse and slapstick prose.

The Orpheus theme survives sketchily in the play's traversal of the
hell of bourgeois society in its late decline, but the *danse macabre* motif
predominates. To keep himself alive through the course of the play,
Death the dancer makes use of the favorite stimulants and distractions of
the dying middle class: sunbathing, religious patriotism, anti-Semitism,
Lawrentian blood-consciousness, drugs, mysticism, and the sexual nostalgia that is satisfied in a night club called Alma Mater. When all these
have been exhausted the dancer makes his will, leaving "the power and
glory of his kingdom" to the working class. Then he dies.

This brief playlet seemed unspecific enough in its sentiments to earn
the praises of both the *Daily Worker* and the *Catholic Herald*. Its portrayal of "the decline of a class" is divided into two separate accounts—
one economic and public, the other psychological and private—which
never quite coincide. Auden quarantines the political interpretation in a
choral commentary that has little to do with the main action. A throw-
away Marxist history of Western thought, sung to the tune of "Casey
Jones" while the dancer writes his will, includes, for example, this
stanza on the Reformation:

> Luther and Calvin put in a word
> The god of your priests, they said, is absurd.
> His laws are inscrutable and depend upon grace
> So laissez-faire please for the chosen race.

The play is more deeply concerned with the psychological allegory of
the dancer. He is—the announcer's opening lines explain—the "death
inside" the declining middle class, the death the class wishes for itself.
This is a wish no economic history can explain. The dancer is an epileptic who suffers a fit; he is a practical joker who steals the sunbathers'
clothes; and he is "the Pilot" who attempts a mystic flight to "the very
heart of Reality." We have met him before. He is the Airman of *The
Orators*, the epileptic-trickster-pilot who wills his own destruction, and
a portrait of that secret part of Auden himself whose anarchic fevers he
half hoped to exorcise and half hoped to enjoy. The Airman and the
dancer would appear to be opposites—one is something of a revolu-

tionary hero, the other embodies the death wish of the ruling class—but they are in fact two different expressions of the same idea. The death wish of the ruling class—the dancer—manifests itself as the revolutionary hero—the Airman—who arises from that class and wishes to destroy it, but is infected by its suicidal passions. The play gives its final words to Marx, but these words are deliberately inadequate to the events they purport to explain. After the dancer collapses there is a brief silence, then noises off, and finally:

> Quick under the table, it's the 'tecs and their narks,
> O no, salute—it's Mr. Karl Marx.
> Chorus. (*Singing to Mendelssohn's "Wedding March."*)
> O Mr. Marx, you've gathered
> All the material facts
> You know the economic
> Reasons for our acts.
> [*Enter* Karl Marx *with two young communists.*]
> K.M.   The instruments of production have been too much for him.
> He is liquidated.
> [*Exeunt to a Dead March.*]

Any Marxist who found this satisfying was deaf to irony, and to the calculated tactlessness with which the last word in the dialogue calls attention to a newly minted euphemism. Auden wrote in a copy of the play, in the early 1940s: "The communists never spotted that this was a nihilistic leg-pull."

The play makes some efforts to be an "act of the whole community," but these are little more than perfunctory gestures—comic cockneys, for example, planted embarrassingly in the auditorium. At one point the audience as a whole takes a speaking part, playing a storm dialectically opposed to the "ship of England" played by the actors. (Audience: "We are the lightning. Crash. Fizz.") Near the end, according to a rather impractical stage direction, the audience joins the actors on the stage. All this has a propagandistic air, but—as Brecht was now arguing in his theoretical writings—an audience that is implicated in the stage action, and made to feel like a participant in it, is not educated at all. Instead it loses its capacity for independent action and becomes the playwright's passive instrument.

When Auden wrote *The Dance of Death* he had begun to think England might need a redeeming leader if it were ever to change, and he had too little confidence in his audience to expect it to change on its own. A year later he thought differently. Now he was ready to be didactic in a thoroughly Brechtian sense by keeping his audience at a deliberate distance from the stage action, so that it might decide for itself what action it might take in the days ahead. The concluding chorus of *The Dog Beneath the Skin* explains that the play has shown a prospect of moral and political disaster, and now the chorus offers the choice of a different future:

Mourn not for these; these are ghosts who chose their pain,
Mourn rather for yourselves; and your inability to make up your minds . . .
Choose therefore that you may recover;* both your charity and your place
Determining not this we have lately witnessed: but another country
Where grace may grow outward . . .

Then, after lines (lifted from the poem "Love, loath to enter / The suffering winter") that evoke lovers walking "in the great and general light / In their delight a part of heaven," the final line proclaims a famous slogan: "To each his need: from each his power." The chorus challenges its audience to choose between lonely indecisive pain and shared responsible delight—a condition it defines in both social and religious terms.

   The Dog Beneath the Skin arrives at this challenge by a number of circuitous routes. The final chorus, and much else, comes from *The Dog*'s immediate ancestor, *The Chase*, a propaganda play Auden wrote in the summer of 1934, which in turn contains elements from two earlier plays, *The Enemies of a Bishop*, written by Auden and Isherwood in 1929, and *The Fronny*, a 1930 work by Auden alone.† Faber accepted *The Chase* for publication, but Auden withdrew it for rewriting only a few weeks later. Isherwood's advice on the revisions led to a collaboration, and the published text of *The Dog Beneath the Skin* was complete by January 1935. For the Group Theatre production one year later the

---

* The medial punctuation in these long lines often indicates a breathing pause rather than a grammatical break.
† *The Enemies of a Bishop* seems never to have been submitted to a publisher; *The Fronny* was briefly considered at Faber & Faber, and at one point was supposed to appear in the same volume with *The Orators*, but publisher and author both lost interest in it.

authors devised a new ending—a practice they repeated in their later plays.

The evolution of *Dogskin* (the authors' informal title) is most easily traced in reverse chronological order, working backward through the ancestral generations. *The Chase*, although its details are muddled and Auden's attention keeps wandering from the point, has a political moral and a Brechtian didactic method. Of its three plots, one—about Alan Norman, a young man from the village of Pressan Ambo who is chosen by lot to search for the missing heir to the manor—survived into *Dogskin*, where it grew much more elaborate. In *The Chase* it involves little more than Alan's distraction from the search when he becomes infatuated with a film star who exploits him—until he realizes he is acting against his true desires. The second plot is about two boys who escape from a nearby reformatory, one disguised as a dog, while the other, dressed as a young woman, attracts the newly awakened desires of the reformatory principal. The third plot concerns a nearby lead mine that is shut down by a strike, which the escaped boys join just before it is violently broken by the police. One of the boys is killed, as is the missing heir, who, it is revealed, had earlier joined the workers' movement. Auden did little to portray this local battle of the class war in dramatic action. Its events are reported in vague terms by a chorus, and no one directly involved in the strike ever appears on stage. The reformatory subplot, which gets a lot more attention, treats class conflict as a sexual matter, with much being made of the attraction felt by the repressed middle classes for the impulsive poor. Thematically, these plots are connected in this tenuous way: the class struggle in the strike plot modulates into the conjunction of class and sex in the reformatory plot, which modulates into the sexual crises of the search plot—these last two being designed to expose the falsity of "honour and sex and friendship" as the middle classes know them. Formally, the play is held together by the omniscient consciousness of two "Witnesses"—variants of Auden's earlier Lords of Limit—and by the convergence of most of the characters in the bloody conclusion to the strike. This in turn prompts a final choral challenge to choose otherwise—the challenge that survived almost unchanged in *Dogskin*.*

* *The Chase*, unlike *The Dance of Death*, has only one brief exchange between the audience and the actors on stage. The escaped boy in the dogskin steps before the curtain and asks the audience to guess who he is. Among the incorrect answers is an undergraduate's: "You're a s-s-symbol of M-m-marx and Lenin." The correct an-

The full text of the 1930 play *The Fronny* is lost, and the few surviving fragments permit only the sketchiest reconstruction, but it is clear that the search plot in *The Chase* had its origin here. The title pays friendly homage to Francis Turville-Petre, a dissolute young English archaeologist who bar-crawled with Auden in Berlin. There he acquired the German diminutive *der Franni* which Auden and Isherwood anglicized as The Fronny. By the time he found his way into *The Chase* and *Dogskin*, and was fitted out with a baronetcy and revolutionary principles, any resemblance to his living original had disappeared. In the play that bears his name, he is sought by Alan Norman through scenes of modern civilization (this provides the first context for the poem Auden later titled "The Wanderer"), including the Nineveh Hotel where, as in *The Chase* and *Dogskin*, Alan becomes infatuated with a film star. At the end, the Fronny makes his will and dies. Auden reused this idea at the end of *The Dance of Death*, where the dancer is wheeled into the Alma Mater bar and bequeaths the power and glory of the bourgeoisie to the working class. In *The Fronny* the dying hero bequeaths various items (his flat, his binoculars) to Auden's friends, in stanzas that, had the play ever been performed, were libellous enough to bring lawyers in. The air of theatrical impracticality is heightened by a note Auden wrote in one draft fragment to the effect that different stanzas of the will could be substituted when different people were in the audience.

The Chase's reformatory plot, and the lead mine in the background, first appeared in the even earlier play *The Enemies of a Bishop, or, Die When I Say When: A Morality in Four Acts*, which Auden and Isherwood cobbled together in 1929. After the title the play goes rapidly downhill. As in *The Chase*, a reformatory principal becomes infatuated with an escapee in drag, but here the escapee is also the target of a white-slave ring whose agents are unwittingly abetted by a female detective-psychologist. The principal's sex-obsessed brother, the manager of the lead mine, seduces his under-manager's wife. The mine is shut down not by political action but by the pandemic economic doom that afflicts the landscape of Auden's work at the time (before the start of the Great Depression). At the end the faults of the characters are all exposed by Bishop Law, a stern healer whom the authors seem to have intended as an ideal portrait of Homer Lane. The play is entirely in

---

swer is given by a Dreadfully Clever Little Girl: "You're the dog." The shared symbolic meanings of the earlier play are neatly and casually refuted.

prose, except when the demonic spectre who haunts the mine manager stops the action at inconvenient moments and recites most of the poems Auden wrote during 1929. The play contains no further technical novelties, although Auden added a few lines for a drunk in the audience when he made some revisions in 1932. This summary suggests a comic extravaganza, but what the authors actually wrote was a meagre outline of one, using few more details than were needed to establish the neurotic limits of the characters.

Auden made some changes in all these plots when he forced them into *The Chase*, but it was impossible to make them fit his new interest in freedom and choice. After reading the typescript in November 1934, Isherwood suggested a revised scenario—omitting the mine and the reformatory altogether, while retaining and elaborating the search for the missing heir as the thread on which to hang the political message. At first Isherwood did not think of himself as a collaborator—Auden insisted on sharing title-page credit later—but his ideas gave the play its final shape. Auden persuaded Faber to pay the plane fare for a three-day visit he made to Isherwood in Copenhagen in January 1935 in order to work on the play, and after Auden's return to England Isherwood prepared a final version by the end of the month. The title had now become *Where is Francis?* Robert Medley (or possibly Rupert Doone) reduced this to a subtitle and provided the final title, a spoof on Eliot's "skull beneath the skin."

Isherwood's scenario gave *Dogskin* its efficient plot—efficient when compared with *The Chase*—and provided Auden with an outline to be filled in with a latter-day Candide's tour of Europe. (Some details, like the refreshments at an execution, are in fact lifted directly from *Candide*.) Isherwood wrote most of the transition scenes, where Alan, accompanied by the disguised Francis, travels by boat or train and, in a discarded scene, confronts some customs officers. Auden avoided these border-crossing passages, keeping to the scenes that took place in each country along the way.

If Auden did not portray crossings in space, he did take the opportunity to portray movement in time. The pattern he introduced beneath the wanderings of the hero amounts to a parabolic lesson in history. This takes the form of a progress from innocence, in both the hero and his native village, to experience, of two opposed kinds: the revolutionary awareness awakened in the hero and the reactionary hysteria that emerges in the village. The play begins and ends in the vicarage garden at Pressan Ambo. In the opening scene, according to the stage direction, this "suggests the setting of a pre-war musical comedy." Here Alan Norman is chosen by lot to search for the missing heir. The dramatic method, the blissful illogic of the action, the style of verse all derive from Gilbert and Sullivan:

> *Vicar.* Here come I, the Vicar good
> Of Pressan Ambo, it's understood;
>   Within this parish border
> I labour to expound the truth
> To train the tender plant of Youth
>   And guard the moral order.
> *Chorus.* With troops of scouts for village louts
> And preaching zest he does his best
>   To guard the moral order.

By the final scene, the Vicar's scout troops—and his sense of the moral order—have grown less jolly. When Alan returns with Francis—who had of course been in the village all along, disguised as the dog—Pressan has become a proto-Fascist camp, with a Lads' Brigade led by the Vicar pledging to "succour England in times of national crisis." The Vicar's language has changed from Gilbertian stanzas and end-stopped couplets to the hysterical prose of a manichaean sermon in which freedom of action is equated with treachery to God and obedience equated with purity.* Only a few weeks have passed in the time of the action, yet the village has grown, at least in the eyes of the hero, from an Edwardian childhood to an anxious militant adulthood *entre deux guerres.* This sinister rapidity echoes a device in *Women in Love,* where Lawrence brings his characters forward from a languorous Edwardian

---

* Auden wrote this travesty of spiritual pride as a separate piece in 1933 and published it under the title "Sermon by an Armament Manufacturer" the following year. After inserting it in *The Chase* and *Dogskin,* he detached it again for the 1945 *Collected Poetry,* titling it "Depravity: A Sermon" and adding a prefatory note explaining that it is "concerned with two temptations," the treatment of spiritual life as an aesthetic performance and the confusion of one's Super-Ego with God. The point of course is that the sermon blatantly manifests these temptations (it says nothing *directly* about them), but some critics solemnly reported that Auden, having renovated his past, was now presenting the satire as straight unironic admonition. This dizzyingly imbecile misreading is encountered less frequently than before, but it has by no means died out.

idyll to an expressionist nightmare. It is a habit of modernism to imagine that time passes more rapidly in the present age.

The play includes still more history lessons. Alan's European travels take him from the old tired monarchy of Ostnia (trumpets and tramlines) to the new lunatic fascism of Westland (wireless and airplanes). In Westland, Alan finds Chimp Eagle—the names are among the play's minor splendors—who was one of those sent out earlier to find Francis, but gave it up to join the workers' movement; now he has been shot by the police at a strike. With Chimp Eagle the possibility of revolutionary social change first enters the play, although the only visible revolutionaries are not workers but bourgeois (Chimp to Alan: "I say, you aren't in with our lot, too, are you?"). The new revolutionary glimmer is accompanied by a shift in content in the choruses that are spoken between the scenes. Having emphasized the nostalgic past—"Wherever you were a child or had your first affair"—now the chorus tells of man's knowledge of his own future—"when death shall cut him short"—and from this point forward speaks insistently of what is to be done. Meanwhile, Alan Norman, having had his first brush with the revolution, spends much of the rest of the play getting distracted from it, mainly by sex. In the Nineveh Hotel he is transfixed by the sight of a film star represented on stage by a shop-window dummy. When he speaks to it he also gives its answers by running behind it and speaking in falsetto. The point of the scene is the narcissism of romantic love—Auden had recently described sexual relations as a way of postponing our cure—but its tone is misogynist. Social revolution in this play is a male preserve, the work of a band of brothers, and Alan's eye must be stopped from roving away from it.

While the hero's mind is elsewhere, the chorus continues to give lessons to the audience. Just before the final scene, it speaks of the failure of nostalgia. Seeking to recover the arcadian waters of childhood, we inadvertently summon up from the depths our hidden neurotic terrors:

So, under the local images your blood has conjured,
We show you man caught in the trap of his terror, destroying himself.
From his favourite pool between the yew-hedge and the roses, it is no
    fairy-tale his line catches
But grey-white and horrid, the monster of his childhood raises its
    huge domed forehead
And death moves in to take his inner luck . . .

An audience might object that it has been shown no such thing. But Auden is representing in psychological terms the political horror Alan will find when he seeks the comforts of his native village. In the final scene he must make the choice of yielding to this horror or resisting it, as the moment of decision threatened by the chorus finally arrives. Alan and Francis return to Pressan, where Francis—still wearing the dogskin "but with the head thrown back, like a monk's cowl"—denounces the villagers as "obscene, cruel, hypocritical, mean, vulgar creatures," who, however, no longer matter very much:

> I don't hate you any more. I see how you fit into the whole scheme. You are significant, but not in the way I used to imagine. You are units in an immense army: most of you will die without ever knowing what your leaders are really fighting for or even that you are fighting at all. Well, I am going to be a unit in the army of the other side . . .

With this he leaves, taking Alan and a few recruits. The play ends with the chorus's final exhortation to choose.

This final scene, except for the Vicar's sermon and a few other lines, was the work of Isherwood, who left the scene inconsistent with the offstage choruses Auden had provided before and after it.* The preceding chorus speaks of impending destruction; the following chorus asks the audience to choose "not this we have lately witnessed." But the scene we witnessed showed a choice being made that, in the authors' eyes, was unquestionably the right one. There is nothing to regret; so when the final chorus tells us to "Mourn not for these," one wonders whom it has in mind. Francis and Alan exit at the height of their powers. The confusion results from the authors' decision simply to reuse choruses from *The Chase*, choruses that urged the audience not to mourn the deaths of Alan and Francis in the workers' struggle, but to take action outside the theatre in order that such deaths might not occur in reality.

* I base this attribution on a letter Auden wrote to Spender after the play was published, and on an earlier letter from Isherwood to Auden following their joint labors in Copenhagen. Isherwood wrote: "I have made Francis' speech quite simple and comparatively short." Auden quickly reused a line from the speech in a review in *The New Statesman*, 23 March 1935: "The difficulty about the class war is that few on either side know what they are fighting for or even that they are fighting at all." Auden may have been borrowing from his collaborator; or Isherwood in writing the speech may have used a remark Auden made at the time.

The conclusion of *The Chase* was didactic in a Brechtian way. The conclusion Isherwood wrote for *Dogskin*, using his characteristic rhetoric of *we* against *they*, works far more crudely, and gives explicit instructions of the kind Auden said art could never provide. Although Auden agreed to this scene, it includes a small Audenesque demur in the person of a curate, who speaks in rhyme and stands proleptically for Auden's later Christianity. The curate cannot choose between the two sides, and so gives no counsel to the audience. Instead he goes off "to pray / To One who is greater." (General: "Greater than who?" Curate: "Greater than you.")

This was the ending that appeared in the published text in 1935. When the play was finally produced in January 1936, the authors decided to rewrite it. Isherwood sketched out the revision in a letter to Auden, but it was Auden who actually wrote the text, and who decided on the new version of Francis's address to the villagers. He threw out Francis's abandonment of Pressan and threw out the reference to "the army of the other side." Instead he made Francis into an Audenesque instructor in history and choice. The opening of Francis's speech corresponds to Isherwood's earlier version, but the conclusion is entirely different. The transition between the old and new strata occurs in a passage that corresponds to the excerpt from the 1935 version quoted above. In 1936 this reads:

> I don't hate you any more. You are significant but not in the way I used to imagine. You are not the extraordinary monsters I thought. You are not individually important. You are just units in an immense army; and most of you would probably die without knowing either what your leaders are really fighting for or even what you are fighting for at all . . . That ignorance at least I can do something to remove. I can't dictate to you what to do and I don't want to either. I can only try to show you what you are doing and so force you to choose. For choice is what you are all afraid of.

He continues in this vein, reiterating the words *choose* and *choice* every few sentences, offering lessons in history, challenging each villager in turn to elect a different life.

It is all too much for Pressan. Finally Francis comes to Mildred Luce. Earlier in the play, in both versions, she had spoken hysterically of her hatred for the Germans who, she said, had killed her two sons in the war. Francis now explains that this was all a neurotic fantasy. She never even married, because she could not bring herself to abandon her mother to poverty. But Francis's exposition is somewhat deficient in tact:

> A doctor [he explains] would say you hate the Germans because you dare not hate your mother and he would be mistaken. It is foolish and neurotic to hate anybody. What you really hate is a social system in which love is controlled by money. Won't you help us to destroy it?

Mildred, not entirely without good cause, takes hold of a gun and kills him. Only Alan mourns, while the two journalists in attendance arrange to suppress all public knowledge of the incident. Life goes on unchanged in Pressan Ambo, but the audience knows better.

In this 1936 version Francis's death is the disaster the chorus urges us not to repeat in our lives, and the conclusion of the action is now consistent with the hortatory interludes. But Francis's crude didactic methods do not inspire much confidence in their powers beyond the stage. He has about him an air of Auden's redemptive fantasy: he admits no faults of his own and asks others to follow him to a truth he never quite defines. In this final version, Francis does at the end what the chorus has been doing all along—explaining everything, never giving the audience much chance to make the decisions that the play demands. Whenever he got into his redeemer mood Auden found himself separating the things he was otherwise trying to unite: the knowing artist from the ignorant audience, the didactic from the amusing aspects of art.

At the time he was working on *Dogskin* Auden explained these disunities as the fault of circumstances he could not alter. When Spender noted some of the problems in the play, Auden replied, in a letter of around June 1935:

> Certain of the faults, though not excused, are partially explained by the circumstances of writing for dramatic performance, e.g.,
>
> The audience. The theatre-going audience is a bourgeois one. I must not let them yawn, I must not keep their minds too long at a stretch (i.e. scenes like the financier and the poet* must intersperse more serious stuff). The average level of appeal must not be much

---

* Both of these were Isherwood's work, except for the songs.

higher than the average level of response. There must even be something to keep the young man who has come with his girl by mistake,
thinking it was a detective story.

This is not the tone of the "humble and sympathetic" poetic dramatist
of his *Listener* review a year before. Auden's letter adds that he segre-
gated the play's moral lessons in the choruses because the actors could
not handle "heavy parts, or complicated characters." The choruses
address only the thinkers, "the part of the audience which will listen to
poetry at all," while the prose action is there for the sake of those who
prefer spectacle. "Actually," he wrote in an afterthought, "the moral I
tried to draw is always: 'You have the choice. You can make the world
or mar it.' Free-will means you can choose either to fear or to love." Yet
he was teaching this moral only to that part of his audience that would
think, and so he was back in Eliot's dilemma of the divided audience,
and was still unwilling to see that he could make the didactic elements of
his work entertaining in themselves, and accessible to anyone who
might listen.

   At about the same time, he was offering a veiled excuse, on similar
grounds, for the divisions that still afflicted his lyric poems. In his introduction to *The Poet's Tongue* he wrote that "a universal art can only be
the product of a community united in sympathy, sense of worth, and as-
piration; and it is improbable that the artist can do his best except in
such a society." The limits of an artist's powers to educate and unite his
audience were the limits imposed by social division. Although undivided societies in the past had fostered universal art, and future societies
might do so again, the society of the present day made any wholeness or
fulfillment impossible to achieve. Ultimately it was nobody's fault and
nobody's responsibility.

XIII

Parables of Action: 2

The early years of documentary film brought hopes of revolutionary progress in the arts. All across Europe, artists and technicians came together to build a new *Gesamtkunstwerk* as an instrument of social change. With the introduction of sound, documentary began to reach a large and receptive audience. In the late 1920s, John Grierson, a pioneer of the movement, set up a Film Unit in a British government department that promoted Commonwealth trade, and persuaded his superiors to give him a virtually free hand in his choice of subject matter. The Unit moved in 1933 to the General Post Office, where it kept its artistic autonomy and obtained technical equipment equal to its ambitions. Grierson hired experienced technicians and artists who had never worked in film. Eventually he hired Auden.

Auden approached the Unit through Basil Wright, a friend from undergraduate days who had been Grierson's first recruit. Early in 1935 Auden, then twenty-eight, sent Wright a letter asking if there might be any film work for him. Grierson looked at the letter and told Wright, "Don't be a fool, fetch him." Auden's first commission from the Unit, during the spring, while he was still teaching at the Downs School, was to provide a text for the last moments of *Coal Face*, a short film about mining. He wrote the luminous madrigal "O lurcher-loving collier, black as night,"* which was set to music by Benjamin Britten, whom

---

* Luminous, and also a seven-line triumph of craft and wit. E.g., "For *Monday comes when none may kiss*"—a line that manages to include double internal rhymes

Grierson had signed up shortly before. His next commission was a verse commentary for the last reel of *Night Mail*, a more elaborate documentary about the postal express train from London to Glasgow. In September, while this film was still being made, he moved to London to work four days a week as an "apprentice" at the Unit's offices in Soho Square.

To Auden the Film Unit may have seemed everything the Group Theatre promised to be but wasn't. Grierson headed an active permanent company of artists and craftsmen working full-time, and he had a genius for finding new talent and encouraging its independent growth. Disdaining the commercial theatre, Grierson arranged to show his films in stores, railway stations, trade shows—anywhere they might be seen by audiences unlikely to seek out art films. He was the first British filmmaker who discarded comic stereotypes of the working classes and instead portrayed fishermen and miners in a dignified and realistic light. He had a clearheaded socialist purpose, and by creating an aura of prestige around the documentary movement he was able to win government funding without direct government control. Films like *Night Mail* were nominally made to publicize Post Office activities, but Grierson and his co-workers managed to escape the taint of propaganda and create permanently satisfying works of art.

At first Auden enjoyed his apprenticeship with its varied practical tasks. He sat at a desk in a noisy corridor, imperturbably writing verse commentaries; he carried cans of film and dragged heavy cables; he learned how to edit film; he directed a brief sequence or two. But he also grew irritated by the Unit's bureaucratic inefficiency, its days of complete idleness followed by frantic bursts of all-night labor. He also grew disturbed by what he sensed as a contradiction between the means and ends of the documentary movement. How could bourgeois artists— which most of Grierson's recruits were—serve revolutionary purposes in a medium that required funding from government or big business? This contradiction was less malign than was the filmmakers' refusal to acknowledge it. No one could survive as an artist in an atmosphere of self-deception. Where a few months earlier Auden had blamed external circumstances—society, the audience, unskilled actors—for the difficulties of socially didactic art, now he placed the blame on the vanity and

---

and rich consonance while it cheerfully alters St. John's warning that "The night cometh, when no man can work."

impatience of artists who convinced themselves there were no such difficulties at all.

He kept silent about his disillusionment until it erupted in a long bitter argument with Basil Wright in late 1935 or early 1936. This began as a minor blowup over production details but quickly grew into a wider dispute over the whole documentary movement. Soon Auden's other colleagues began to sense his disaffection. As he recalled a few months later, in a verse letter to his closest friend in the Unit, the painter William Coldstream, the two of them "sneaked out for coffee . . . And were suspected, quite rightly, of being disloyal." Early in February 1936 he took what he expected to be a two-month leave to work on his own writings. He also wrote a politely devastating review of the movement—using the publication of Paul Rotha's *Documentary Film* as a pretext—in *The Listener*, 19 February 1936. The review opens with some dilute praise for the movement's rejection of the star system and shallow themes in the commercial cinema, and for documentary's commitment to fact—even if the results "to the ordinary film-goer were finally and fatally dull."* Then, after noting Rotha's willingness to "criticize so acutely his own movement," Auden proceeds to list the obstacles—each in the form of a contradiction—that Rotha does "not point out quite clearly enough." One involves class. "It is doubtful whether an artist can ever deal more than superficially . . . with characters outside his own class, and most British documentary directors are upper middle." Another is time. Documentary requires knowledge of complex social issues, knowledge that takes time to gain, yet films are too expensive to be made at anything less than breakneck speed. This leads to the obstacle of financial support. The documentary filmmaker hopes to tell the truth about society, but "truth rarely has advertisement value" to the governments or industries who pay the bills.

The implication is clear. However truthful and independent Grierson and his colleagues thought themselves—and they repeatedly praised the officials who let them do as they chose—anyone in their position would inevitably hesitate before offending the paymaster. Problems of censorship and self-censorship, although seldom discussed, did in fact arise. Auden recalled later that when he set up a scene in a telephone exchange on a busy New Year's Eve, a supervisor objected to the realistic details:

---

* Auden was probably writing before the first showing of *Night Mail*, whose popular success surprised everyone who worked on it.

"We can't show government officials in their shirt sleeves."* This was scarcely the Big Lie, but it was a step in the wrong direction.

Grierson published a condescending note on Auden's review in the April number of *World Film News*. He pointed out that the "human element" whose absence Auden had deplored in the Unit's work "increases as the apprentices learn their job. As Auden's own apprenticeship matures he may feel less despondent." But by the time Auden saw this he had already sent in his resignation from the Unit.

He was in Portugal when he resigned, on a month-long visit to Isherwood in March–April 1936. There they wrote *The Ascent of F6*. While this play's central concern is Auden's redeemer fantasy, it also casts a baleful light on some less exalted temptations to which artists are susceptible.

The summit of F6 stands on the border between two colonies, British and Ostnian Sudoland. When the play opens, the British government—in the person of Michael Ransom's brother James who heads the Colonial Office—needs a climber who can conquer the peak almost immediately. Ostnia has secretly sent out an expedition, and its agents are spreading a legend among the natives that the first white man who climbs the mountain will rule over both the Sudolands for a thousand years. James persuades a newspaper peer to put up funds for a British expedition and proposes his brother as its leader. Michael Ransom feels no sympathy with James's politics, or with any politics at all. It is only his mother who can induce him to make the ascent, as a symbolic quest for the love she withheld. None the less, Ransom knowingly commits his energy and talent to a cause he does not share.

Ransom's mountain ordeal is more spectacular than anything that happened to the G.P.O. Film Unit, but the issues of government sponsorship that Auden raised in his review are among the issues raised in the play. Ransom's colleagues, caught up in their rivalry with the Ostnian climbers, forget the imperialist motives behind the race to the peak. Ransom, after an inner struggle, submits to their enthusiasm: he prefers to retain his leadership rather than teach them an unflattering truth. He reaches the summit, but like a filmmaker who must finish at breakneck

---

* Auden told this story in his 1938 lecture on poetic drama to illustrate the relative disadvantage of the cinema. The incident occurred during the filming of *Calendar of the Year*, in which Auden appears briefly as an Oxford-accented Father Christmas, and may have primed his argument with Basil Wright. The argument was triggered by a minor disagreement over the production costs of this film.

speed, he makes the final ascent without adequate preparation, scrambles to the top in a blizzard, and dies. The official support that gave him his opportunity finally destroys him.

But more seductive than the influence of cabinet ministers and bureaucrats is the vague indiscriminate praise of a mass audience. Ransom compromises his gifts in return for the brief adulation of a public he cannot respect, to whose community he can never belong. And he seeks this unsatisfying public goal partly in the hope—which he knows perfectly well is futile—of easing his private psychological terrors. The route he takes up F6 goes by the "north face" to the "West Buttress"—the North-West Passage made visible. The story's origin in its author's own temptations is obscured by the fact that Ransom is perceived by his onstage public, the representatively suburban Mr. and Mrs. A., to be serving England's imperial glory—scarcely a beneficiary of Auden's recent writings. But if one reads "the socialist revolution" in place of "England's imperial glory" the parable becomes clear. In Ransom Auden was delineating a double contradiction that he knew threatened himself: the contradiction between an artist's work and his beliefs, and the contradiction between the public pursuit of fame and the private neurosis that makes it so fatally attractive. These contradictions are especially harrowing to an artist, for even when he most wants to write about his personal psychology, he is constrained to keep it secret from his public if he hopes to maintain their approval.* A mountaineer's triumph seems rather less impressive if he announces that he conquered his peak neither for England nor because it was there, but because it symbolized his mother's inaccessible breast.

When Auden became famous as the leading writer of his generation, the poetic prophet of the English Left, he was little more than twenty-three years old. Now, at twenty-nine, he was praying to be made chaste but not yet, warning himself against the compromises of fame while still enjoying its pleasures. He told an interviewer later it was while writing *The Ascent of F6* that he realized he must someday leave England.

While he gladly explained *The Orators* or *Dogskin* to anyone who asked, Auden seems to have kept quiet about *F6*. He left the explanations to Isherwood, who thought the play was all about T. E. Lawrence

---

* There is of course a large audience for artists whose only subject is their personal psychology. This audience provides, rather than critical judgement and approval, a superior form of public charity.

and contemporary dictators. Later Isherwood added that while the play did have a central theme, "mixed up in it are definite obscurantist elements which seem designed simply to confuse critics, professors, members of the audience"—and, he might have added, the authors' friends. E. M. Forster said in a review that the play was "not easy to focus," that he needed "at least four pairs of spectacles" to read it—the heroic, the politico-economic, the character-test, the psychoanalytic. Yet all these perspectives resolve into one when the play is read as a parable of the fate Auden had avoided, the fate of the indifferent redeemer destroyed by a public role his private terrors tempted him to accept.

None of this, of course, would have been of much didactic use to an audience. The play presents no challenge to awareness or action, other than through some conventional satire on colonial officials and newspaper peers, and on jazz music as a public opiate. If there is a warning for the audience in the parable of Michael Ransom, it is to be wary of artists out to save them from themselves—artists like those two didactic playwrights so highly praised last season, the authors of *The Dog Beneath the Skin.* *

If in *F6* this lesson got lost in the obscurities and horseplay, Auden carefully made it plain in a long poem he wrote a few months later, during the summer of 1936. *Letter to Lord Byron* is a discursive poem in five parts, urbane, conversational, *au courant*, tolerantly amused by the literary scene, savagely amused by the political one. The poem is often splendidly funny, but it has none of the uncontrolled slapstick of *The Orators*. Auden adds a note of comic self-mocking irony whenever the poem gets didactic, but he is more didactic than in anything he wrote before. He claims at the end to have reached only "the rather tame conclusion / That no man by himself has life's solution"—lines which demonstrate the art of sinking in poetry—but along the way he offers three

* Auden finally reworked *F6* as an explicitly personal parable in 1945 when he wrote a new ending for a production at Swarthmore College. Now the final scene was the climax of a Jungian quest for self-realization. Ransom's mother, revealed at last on the summit, makes her son "repeat after me" that he had been dreaming all his life, and must now wake "And see the real world and find a true reason for being"—as he dies. This ending is hardly an improvement on its predecessors, and effectively trivializes the play by ignoring the issue of the artist's public responsibility that the revision left standing in earlier scenes.

sharply parabolic lessons in history. In presenting these, Auden repeatedly insists on distinguishing between the subjects he writes about and his own authority to write. It is the subjects that matter. His poetic gift provides him with no special privileges, but with a perspective not much better or worse than anyone else's. The unacknowledged model here is not so much Byron as Dante, who claimed to have equal honor with the great poetic masters he visited in the upper circle of Hell, but needed grace and love, not poetry, to raise him to Paradise. Auden had spoken *ex cathedra* in his plays and redemptive poems; now he is a citizen among citizens. At one point he makes explicit what *F6* had implied—that what fascinates an artist most is really "The Trap" set by the "Complex or Poverty" that started him writing in the first place. Auden immediately qualifies this psychoanalytic dismissal of art, but not to the benefit of the artist:

> Freud's not quite O.K.
> No artist works a twenty-four-hour day.
> In bed, asleep or dead, it's hard to tell
> The highbrow from l'homme moyen sensuel.

The didactic prophet who wrote the choruses of *Dogskin,* and implied like any indifferent redeemer that he worked only for the benefit of his audience, now cheerfully admits that teaching has its rewards. Not only is the pay good and the hours reasonable; also

> It's pleasant as it's easy to secure
> The hero worship of the immature.

After this, neither poet nor audience has any excuse for fantasies about the artist as prophet to his age.

All these disclaimers of authority conceal a sting, and a serious purpose as well. Auden keeps denying he is equal to the many tasks—metrical, intellectual, didactic—that he then proceeds to accomplish. His stanza form is his first problem. He can't possibly manage Byron's Ottava Rima, he says, and his own "Rhyme-royal's difficult enough to play." He is reduced to woeful expedients for filling out the form, lines like "There is no other rhyme except anoint." But he counts on his readers to recognize these fumbles as deliberate imitations of *Don Juan*—and, in any event, Auden showed himself capable of writing perfectly adequate rhyme-royal in "A Happy New Year" in 1932. Having made his self-mocking point in the first part of the *Letter*, he dispenses with his deliberate awkwardness in the remaining four parts. But he also has a problem, he says, with the range of subjects he wants to deal with. A novelist could do it better. "The average poet by comparison / Is unobservant, immature, and lazy." He had thought of writing to Jane Austen, but he scarcely dares address someone so superior; safer to intrude on a mere poet like Byron. After all this self-deprecation he still feels compelled to ask forgiveness all round,

> humbly begging everybody's pardon.
> From Faber first in case the book's a flop,
>> Then from the critics lest they should be hard on
>> The author when he leads them up the garden,
> Last from the general public he must beg
> Permission now and then to pull their leg.

But his tone is not especially repentant, since he is still trying to achieve a cure. "I make no claim to certain diagnosis," he admits. He can only "offer thought in homoeopathic doses / (But someone may get better in the process.)" He makes his therapeutic claims in an unassuming parenthesis, implicitly acknowledging that the massive doses he administered in his plays did little good for the patient. Furthermore, the medicine is different now. In his plays, the serious choruses for thinkers were separated from the groundlings' farce. In the *Letter*, where the whole audience is addressed at the same time, the serious parts *are* the comic ones.

In the poem's three history lessons the focus grows progressively sharper. Auden starts with a quick survey of the changes in English society since Byron's day ("Crying went out and the cold bath came in"), then presents a capsule history of romantic and modernist isolation in the arts, and finally offers the "plain, perhaps . . . cautionary tale" of his own personal history as a representative of artists and of his class. The underlying concern throughout is the proper relation of an artist to his audience and subject. Why is it, the poem asks, that culture and litera-ture should in recent years have turned their attention from the local realm of human society to the outer realm of natural objects? Our modern interests are a tea party to which "We can't, of course, invite a Jew or Red / But birds and nebulae will do instead." How did art follow science into these inhuman regions? The answer, not surprisingly, may be found with the help of "a little dose of history."

Auden's brief history of art goes like this. In the English eighteenth century there were two arts, one "Relying on his lordship's patronage," the other "Appealing mainly to the poor and lowly"—the arts of Pope and Isaac Watts. A poet in either class "knew for whom he had to write, / Because their life was still the same as his." Then came the Industrial Revolution, represented by "Savoury* and Newcomen and Watt / And all those names that I was told to get up / In history preparation and forgot." These established a new class of *rentier* artists who, like Shelley, lived on dividends but "lost responsibilities and friends." The finest of these new artists, and those most affected by the change, "started what I'll call the Poet's Party."† It all began brilliantly. The poets—like Auden himself in his earliest poems—looked disdainfully out on the rest of the world from their "upper window." But the night wore on and the perfumed air turned rancid. In the party's final stages, surrealism and other lesser modernisms set the tone:

> many are in tears:
> Some have retired to bed and locked the door;
> And some swing madly from the chandeliers;
> Some have passed out entirely in the rears;
> Some have been sick in corners.

At least "the sobering few / Are trying hard to think of something new."

Like everyone else, Auden has no answers, but he can suggest where to begin the search. What is most important for an artist, if he is to be reintegrated with his lost responsibilities, is that he be something of a reporting journalist, that his subject be "the human clay." Just as he must avoid the "disaster" of isolated autonomy, so he must avoid the desire to be a legislator, acknowledged or not. Art should be "attendant"—not on agreeable abstractions like Mankind but on an actual and finite "class of persons."

---

* He means Thomas Savery, who made the first commercially successful steam engine, followed by Thomas Newcomen and James Watt.
† Auden neatly joins the political and the festive senses of *party* by following this line with a parenthesis: "(Most of the guests were painters, never mind)."

Auden's own finite category includes everyone who can call himself "An intellectual of the middle classes."* His third history lesson is his own life story, told not as a unique Rousseauistic confession, but as an exemplary tale set within the common contexts of political history, school, university, work, and sex. "The part can stand as symbol for the whole." Auden's portrait of the artist as a young man says nothing about a lonely superior vocation, and a great deal about the relativism of individual perspectives: "what we see depends on who's observing, / And what we think on our activities." So he offers his own story as a parable that others, with perspectives of their own, might find instructive in contrast. In the distant future, a child may ask "During a history lesson" about the nature of a middle-class intellectual—" 'Is he a maker of ceramic pots / Or does he choose his king by drawing lots?' " Auden's self-portrait is designed as an answer.

The *Letter* shows traces of the tripartite vision of history Auden had adopted the year before, but now only as a fantasy. The resolved future will never arrive:

> The Great Utopia, free of all complexes,
>   The Withered State is, at the moment, such
> A dream as that of being both the sexes.

The future union of the divided world seems so improbable that Auden can only imagine it as a form of hermaphroditism. Still, he adds the qualifying phrase "at the moment." It may be relevant that when he wrote these lines he was half-seriously theorizing to his friends that the sexes ought to dress alike, perhaps in a modified nurse's uniform.

Hermaphroditism was an unlikely road to Utopia, but Auden knew better than to rush down any alternative routes that might seem more plausible. He doubted the world-historical claims of Marxism and doubted even more the romantic claims of visionary or aesthetic revolution. When he wrote

---

* From 1933 to 1935 Auden tended to use *middle class* as the form of the noun; his use of *middle classes* after 1936 represents a shift from a Marxist vocabulary to a politically more neutral one.

> I like Wolf's *Goethe-Lieder* very much
> But doubt if *Ganymede*'s appeal will touch
> —That marvellous cry with its ascending phrases—
> Capitalism in its later phases

he was making a complex irony. The surface sense of the lines is that art cannot affect society, but the tone—which opposes personal enthusiasm about art against the dry impersonal rhetoric of politics—adds the converse argument that utopian politics ignore the marvels of the aesthetic imagination.

He finished *Letter to Lord Byron* in the autumn of 1936. Around this time, under the pressure of the Spanish Civil War, he imagined—or tried to imagine—that the determined forces of History might after all bring about a universal harmony of person and *polis*, although no individual or collective acts seemed able to do anything of the kind. No one could be educated into Utopia. The grave vision he saw on the slopes of Venus he saw in the political arena as well. His 1937 visit to Spain confirmed that no single faction could claim the future's blessings. In Spain all the available choices seemed wrong, and if some were less wrong than others, these still offered little hope of justice and freedom should they lead to political victory. The summer after he returned from Spain he joined Isherwood in the last of their plays, *On the Frontier*, where history is a chaos of random irrational causes leading impartially to disaster—although some unconvincing choruses try to argue otherwise.

Not very much needs to be said about *On the Frontier*. It consists of two unrelated plots and a series of choral interludes each spoken by an entirely different group. One plot, entirely conventional in dramatic technique, concerns the mad childlike Leader of Fascist Westland and his manipulation by Valerian the steel magnate. The latter, a fount of cynical wisdom on the futility of progressive politics, is also far too wise for his own good. Events continually escape his control. He prefers to keep the arms race going "for another five years at least," but when he soothes the Leader into renouncing war with neighboring Ostnia, he miscalculates his timing. Ostnia has already invaded; war has begun. Soon both sides are ravaged by plague, rebellion, and civil war. The Leader, who came to power on a pledge to smash the Valerian Trust but then became its pawn, is murdered by one of his disillusioned troopers. This trooper, named Grimm, had once been fired unjustly by Valerian's company, and now arrives at the magnate's office to commit a second murder. Valerian, cool as ever, suspects that Grimm can't go through with it and tries to wear him down psychologically. But he makes one last miscalculation:

> *Valerian.* . . . Tell me about your mother, though. That's always interesting. I expect you were an only child. Her pet. . . . The son who was to achieve wonders. What did she teach you, at nights, beside the cot? What did she whisper?
>
> *Grimm* [*screams and shoots*]. Leave my mother alone, you bastard!

Valerian does not die by a conscious act of vengeance from an aroused proletariat, but in an explosion of maternally induced hatred of a kind Auden has portrayed before.

The second plot, and the play's watery dramatic poetry, is set in "The Ostnia-Westland Room" an image of the impassable border. As the stage direction puts it,

> It is not to be supposed that the Frontier between the two countries does actually pass through this room: the scene is only intended to convey the *idea* of the Frontier—the L. half of the stage being in Westland: the R. half in Ostnia.

On the Westland side lives the academic Thorvald family, on the Ostnian side the bourgeois Vrodny-Husseks. The plot, such as it is, traces their reactions to the war, as the children, Eric Thorvald and Anna Vrodny, fall mystically in love. Their bodies never meet, but they find each other in a dream world represented on stage by a circle of light in the surrounding darkness. There the frontier dissolves. Outside space and time, far from hatred and change, they find an unshakable "tower," an "unsuspected island," an "everlasting garden." But they find it only in dreams:

> O if we take one step
> Towards our love, the grace will vanish,
> Our peace smash like a vase. O we shall see
> The threatening faces sudden at the window . . .

In the early draft of the play this contrast between mortal reality and the inaccessible ideal was even more clearly underlined: Valerian and his

aide were homosexual lovers, crooked counterparts to the young heterosexual lovers who are so pure they never set eyes on each other.

At the end of the play Eric and Anna lie on their separate deathbeds,
he succumbing to a wound received while fighting among the workers in
the Westland civil war, she to the plague she caught nursing the sick.
But their images meet in the circle of light at center stage. They sing of a
future "guarded" from the world of today, that "lucky" time when

> Others like us shall meet, the frontier gone,
> And find the real world happy.
> The place of love, the good place.

"Thousands have worked and work" to build that place—

> the city where
> The will of love is done
> And brought to its full flower
> The dignity of man.

When *On the Frontier* was published it was noted that the leading
left-wing poet of his generation had concluded this highly topical play
with something very like a Christian hymn to a better world. But only
like a Christian hymn: it foresees no union with a divine authority and
source, only an ultimate flowering of human dignity. As in the "Commentary" to *In Time of War*, written shortly afterward, Auden concludes the play with an attempt to join two irreconcilables: a Utopia
defined in vaguely religious terms, where in love's will is our peace, and
the present "work" of the will that may somehow bring about the rule of
love. Once again the familiar contradiction: in man, Eros has no will of
its own, and so no acts of will can lead to the loving harmony Auden
wants to predict. The play in fact dramatizes precisely this dilemma. All
the willed actions portrayed on stage lead to failure and death; the rule
of love must be deferred indefinitely; and in their final lines the doomed
lovers ask "Pardon" for those who "die to make man just / And worthy
of the earth." But as Auden cannot portray their struggle, neither can he
say who is to forgive their trespasses. He can only hope the indifferent
earth he invokes in the play's last words can somehow stand as a measure of justice and virtue.

In the unpublished first version of the play, written in the late summer of 1937 and now mostly lost, there seems to have been a choral report of the workers' victory in the long civil war. But a delay in production and publication, until after Auden and Isherwood returned from their 1938 trip to China, gave them time to revise their political forecast. They lost hope in the workers' triumph and let the civil war drag on indefinitely while Soviet and Fascist intervention threatens a world conflict. Although the finished play makes a perfunctory tribute to the workers' struggle in the choruses for activists and prisoners, the verse is far too tired to take seriously. As with *F6*, there are no demands for action and no Brechtian challenges to alter history. The forces described are too large and uncontrollable for the audience to find any hope of changing them. Auden rose to verbal and prosodic invention only in two songs for a chorus of soldiers disaffected with all factions and authorities—a feeling he was beginning to share. The sole public purpose of the play was to serve as a stimulus for weeping over the coming disaster. Its public effect proved rather different. MacNeice, reviewing the production, said the mystical love scenes "made one long for a sack to put one's head in." After a few performances the play, in Isherwood's words, "passed away painlessly."

Auden's disaffection extended to all his old hopes and projects for a better future. When he returned from Spain, having discarded any serious wish to affect the political future, he agreed to resume his schoolmaster's post at the Downs for a single term. In the schoolroom as in Europe, education proved more difficult than he had thought. Soon after his arrival, he wrote "Schoolchildren," a poem that sees no glorious future in the eyes of the young, and knows of no way to excite any passionate hopes there. The children "dissent so little" against the rule of the schoolroom; "the bars of love" that hold them in captivity are as strong as the cells in prison. "The tyranny is so easy." The poem punctures the nostalgic "professor's dream" of innocent children simply by pointing out that "the sex is there." Auden among schoolchildren rises to no Yeatsian dream of visionary compensation. He sees only a doomed futile revolt against the reality of this world:

> The improper word
> Scribbled upon the fountain, is that all the rebellion?
> The storm of tears shed in the corner, are these
> The seeds of the new life?

As at school, so at university. A few months later Auden wrote about "Oxford," where the intellectual "Eros Paidagogos / Weeps on his virginal bed"—bound, like all Eros's human incarnations, to the limited will of those it occupies. Here as elsewhere, it is not universal harmony but "the knowledge of death" that for everyone "Is a consuming love." Even at Oxford "the natural heart refuses / The low unflattering voice / That rests not till it find a hearing"—Freud's "voice of the intellect," which "is soft and low but . . . persistent and continues until it has secured a hearing." A year and a half earlier, in a verse letter from Iceland, Auden had been able to write about "dons of good will." They existed no longer. The young poet-healer who made England his schoolroom, whom Wyndham Lewis called "Auden . . . with playground whistle," had retired to give some new thought to the curriculum.

By the time he got back from six months in China in 1938, where he and Isherwood gathered material for a book about the Sino-Japanese War, he was ready to throw out the curriculum altogether. Education, he said, had become peripheral. Lecturing to a teachers' conference in October 1938, he told his audience "that their first job now is to take part in political action, for as long as society is unequal as it is, the whole idea of democratic education is a sham. Unless all the members of a community are educated to the point where they can make a rational choice, democracy is a sham." This statement may have been something of a sham as well, because although Auden had indeed convinced himself that education was impossible, he was not at all convinced that political action held any better hope for the future of England.

Around the same time he wrote this lecture he was also preparing two other prose works, an essay and a parable, designed to undeceive his readers about the political effectiveness of art. After all his didactic efforts, poetry seemed as socially useless as education itself, and the obscure warning hidden in the story of Michael Ransom became fully explicit.

The essay had been commissioned for a Left Book Club anthology, *Poems of Freedom*, by its editor John Mulgan—who got to know Auden while working at the Oxford University Press on Auden's *Oxford Book of Light Verse* the year before. Mulgan probably expected an essay considerably more partisan than the one Auden provided. In his introduction to the Oxford volume, Auden had foreseen a planned democracy in which all poetry would enjoy a social role. Now, for the Left Book Club, he began by dismissing as "bosh" the "Great claims . . . made for poets as a social force" and the charge that they are "introverted neurotics." Poets are in fact "fairly ordinary men and women . . . some intelligent, others stupid," who happen to have "a particular interest and skill in handling words in a particular kind of way." They do for society only what they do for themselves: "crystallize and define with greater precision thoughts and feelings which are generally present in their class and age." Auden still insists, as he did in *The Poet's Tongue* in 1935, that the aim of poetry is knowledge, "to make us more aware of ourselves and the world around us," but he no longer imagines that poetry makes action urgent or its nature clear. It promotes awareness, but "I do not know if such increased awareness makes us more moral or more efficient: I hope not." To readers who saw Auden as the didactic bard of the socialist revolution, the last phrase would have come as a shock. But he was recalling the Group Theatre, his broadcasts in Spain, his fantasies of cure—and the political futility of all of them. Poetry serves freedom in ways neither a party official nor a cabinet minister is likely to appreciate: "I think it makes us more human, and I am quite certain it makes us more difficult to deceive, which is why, perhaps, all totalitarian theories of the State, from Plato's downwards, have deeply mistrusted the arts. They notice and say too much, and the neighbours start talking." But even as he evoked an image of the vigilant, undeceiving artist, he knew from his own example and from many others that the portrait was idealized. Not all artists were committed to undeception, and it was always possible to find a compelling motive for deceiving oneself and one's readers.

At about the same time he was avoiding this problem in his preface, he confronted it elsewhere. The Autumn 1938 issue of *New Verse* was given over to prose essays commissioned by the editor on the subject of "Commitments." All the other contributors provided straightforward exposition; Auden sent in an elusive parable entitled "The Sportsmen." The sportsmen are the poets; their quarry are their poems; and the history of their technique and social role is a summary history of poetry. The parable coincides almost point for point with the more explicit history Auden wrote late in 1937 in the introduction to *The Oxford Book of Light Verse*, except that the utopian predictions with which he ended that essay are now conspicuously absent.

The story begins in a village long ago, when poets were integrated in society and lived the same kind of life as everyone else. The only thing that distinguished the sportsmen-poets was their interest in shooting duck, which they hunted for food "in the slack season between harvest and ploughing." A few hundred years pass, and the parable arrives at the English eighteenth century of Isaac Watts and Pope, when although most of the sportsmen "still shot duck to sell in the open market, the best shots had been hired by the village squire who preferred partridge, a taste with which they were inclined to agree." This was an age when poets became professionals and achieved a high "standard of marksmanship"—prosody and rhetoric—because most did nothing else, and, unlike their fellow villagers, "wouldn't have known what to do with a sickle if they saw one." Then, in the isolating industrial age when the "country had become so densely wooded that . . . it was only possible to see a tiny circle of sky immediately overhead," the sportsmen no longer worked for the village squire but for their own artistic and emotional satisfaction: "boys from rich homes who had run away . . . an occasional eccentric who, even when he was in the nursery, had a passion for playing with toy firearms." Village and squire "had almost forgotten what birds tasted like . . . and were living on tinned food sent down in vans from the city." Since no one wanted birds anyway, the sportsmen began "to feel that the only excitement in shooting lay in the skill required"—a theory of *l'art pour l'art* that led to terrible aesthetic squabbles in the *Sporting Quarterly*.

Now the parable comes to the present day. "Rumours" began to reach the village of a far country "where the inhabitants had cleared the land of timber, so that duck had once more become plentiful and shooting parties were again in fashion." (Auden makes it clear that he is referring to the reports that reached England of renewed popular art in the Soviet Union; he says nothing about the accuracy of these reports.) Among the few sportsmen remaining in the village the response to this news was mixed. The aesthetes were too proud to shoot a bird as ugly as a duck; others hesitated to offend the squire, from whom they expected a legacy. These went away, ignoring those villagers whose social purpose was to clear the forest. When the sportsmen who remained offered to do something to help, they were told not to bother shooting duck but to join in the more useful tasks of felling trees and clearing the undergrowth. A few agreed, but most "were alarmed and offended, saying: 'Me, turn woodcutter? I am a sportsman.'" And indeed they were right: to look at them was to see without a doubt that they were incapable of working at anything but art.

But when these withdrew and reconsidered, some felt they could impress the villagers, not by joining them in their labors, but by strolling in one evening with "a couple of fine duck." Yet when they tried to write straightforward popular poetry, "they were so accustomed to trick targets that they missed." Humiliated and angry, they set out to counterfeit popular art instead:

> "Bah!" they said, "those villagers are a stupid lot: if they want duck, they shall have them"; and ... they sat down to model duck out of clay and old newspapers, using to guide them some coloured plates which they had torn out of ornithological textbooks in their fathers' libraries.
>
> When the models were finished and dry, they returned with them to the village, and said: "Look what we have shot." Some of the younger villagers who had never seen a duck except in a museum were impressed, and praised the sportsmen highly for their skill; but the older and wiser among them fingered the models, and smelt them, and said: "These are not duck; they are only clay and old newspapers."

With this critique of recent efforts, his own included, to make a new popular poetry the parable ends.

As described in this summary, the parable leaves an artist with only two choices—public action at the cost of poetic silence, or self-serving poetic fraudulence. But another passage offers a third possibility. When the villagers propose to clear the land, an older man, "perhaps, the finest marksman of them all," stands in long silence, then wishes the villagers every success, but adds:

> "I must ask you to forgive me if I do not help you. For many years now I have been spending all my waking hours in the study of eagles. I do not know if there are any others who share my passion; I do not suppose that there will ever be many who feel as I do about those rare and beautiful birds; but for me, it is my vocation and my life. So I must ask you to excuse me." And having said this, he went his way.

This sounds like the indecisive curate of *Dogskin* who, caught between two sides, withdraws into prayer, but the allusion is specifically to Eliot, who had asked himself in *Ash-Wednesday*, "Why should the agèd eagle spread its wings?" (He was forty-two at the time.) After five years of bending his art to political pressure, of joining poetry to politics through the visionary rhetoric of Yeats, Auden honors Eliot's persistent refusal to corrupt his vocation.

Auden was acknowledging once again the lessons of his early master, but was not quite ready to accept them. While writing a parable he could honor the idea of vocation, but when writing essayistic prose he twisted it almost beyond recognition. Late in 1938 the publishers of a projected volume entitled *I Believe* asked Auden for an essay of "personal philosophy." What he provided was a chillingly impersonal philosophy that described vocation strictly in terms of social function and made no reference at all to his work as a poet. His essay prescribes an ideal society, a Republic from which he does not even bother to banish the poets because he does not acknowledge they exist. There is no hint of a psychological interior in this essay, and no place for anyone like the Eliot of the parable. All the division and sorrow Auden recorded in his love poems now seem to belong to some other species.

Writing in brisk classroom style, Auden begins by defining personal goodness in social terms:

> For me, the least unsatisfactory description [of goodness] is to say that any thing or creature is good which is discharging its proper function, using its powers to the fullest extent permitted by its environment and its own nature ... Thus, people are happy and good who have found their vocation: what vocations there are will depend upon the society within which they are practised.

Then, after a dozen numbered paragraphs describing man's external relations to nature and society, Auden offers his definition of social good, which proves to be the corollary of his idea of personal good. A society, he writes, is good to the extent that "it allows the widest possible range of choices to its members to follow those vocations to which they are suited," and also constantly develops new and more demanding vocations for them. He then lists the forces that hinder vocational development—all of them external, since any that might seem internal and psychological are really the product of social forces outside the individual.

This personal philosophy has no room for persons—no one has any inner life that is not simply a response to a stimulus outside. The terms *good* and *evil* recur throughout the essay, usually in a functional or mechanical sense, but Auden says nothing about personal good and evil as expressed in love and hate. He had recently written—in a poem—about man's crooked heart, but in prose he declares himself "fairly optimistic" about human nature because "bad environment is the chief cause of badness in individuals."

Perhaps at moments Auden convinced himself he believed this wretched stuff. But he was to write in very different terms a few years later. In a 1945 lecture on "Vocation and Society," vocation was no longer a functional discharge but a form of love, a personal commitment unalterable in time. Now,

> to acknowledge vocation is, like marriage, to take a vow, to live henceforth by grace of the Absurd, to love for better or for worse, for richer or for poorer, in sickness and in health, until death do us part. No one can hope to have a vocation, in fact, if he makes a private reservation that, should circumstances alter, he can get divorced.

In the same lecture he spoke of the "impossibility" of any society built on "such stimuli as happiness, success, utility, avoidance of pain," or anything else that leads to a society "without passion." Such a society "must inevitably dissolve into an amorphous abstraction called the General Public." In 1938, although he denied there was any "such thing as a general will of society," he had found no place in his social diagram for passion or individuality in any form. Yet without individuality, the whole idea of a coherent differentiated society—one that unlike those of ants or bees is voluntary—collapses into nonsense.

He drew the practical lessons of his social theory in the lecture he gave at a teachers' conference in October 1938—the lecture in which he said teachers should make political action their first task, not education. The educational system of liberal democracy had failed because liberalism as a whole had failed. Its articles of faith were that social coercion is always evil and that man is innately rational; it believed that one only had to teach the good for all men to choose it freely. But as liberalism spoke of freedom it ignored injustice, and "made people feel that freedom is not worth while." Now fascism was succeeding through its appeal to the avenging sense of justice that liberalism ignored and through its promise of a secure unified society that will last for ever.* If fascism were to be defeated, it would not be by liberalism but by "something which I shall call Social Democracy."

Three years earlier Auden slighted Social Democracy in favor of communism. Now he prefers it, although his hopes for it are moderate: "I am not very optimistic about the future of Social Democracy in this country during the next twenty years at least." Social Democracy, he says, holds that no society can ever be perfect, because man is born neither free nor good. This tends to dispute his "fairly optimistic" assessment of man in the *I Believe* essay, written at about the same time, but he comes to the same conclusion in each instance. In the lecture, Social Democracy must reject liberal doctrine and use coercion to "control the interests of groups which threaten to upset the justice of society"; and in the essay, at a time of crisis it is necessary to "accept the responsibility of our convictions" and use the "intolerance" and "coercion" that are also practiced by large collective groups: "Thus I cannot see how a Socialist country could tolerate the existence of a Fascist party any more than a Fascist country could tolerate the existence of a Socialist party. I judge them differently because I think that the Socialists are right and the Fascists are wrong in their view of society." That is: we must, in all good conscience, call out the guard for the sake of a good society—*good* in the functional sense the essay has already specified, the condition in which everyone knows his proper task and does it.

Auden is ignoring in his prose everything he learned in his poems: that it is persons, not theories, who wield power; that the inequality of force corrupts; that the governors of a society nominally dedicated to social justice will, if given repressive powers, wield them no more wisely than any other governors have ever done. In later years Auden would again write that civilization needs force to maintain itself, but he would also emphasize its brutalizing cost and the inevitable suffering of

* In the "Commentary" to *In Time of War*, written in the same month, the humble dead say all this in leaden verse:

You talked of Liberty, but were not just; and now
Your enemies have called your bluff; for in your city,
Only the man behind the rifle had free-will.

One wish is common to you both [you and your enemies], the wish to build
A world united as that Europe was in which
The flint-faced exile wrote his three-act comedy.

the innocent. In 1938, when he tries to ignore these matters, he traps himself in an unacknowledged contradiction. Convinced as he is that liberal education has failed to bring about social cohesion and social conscience, he still expects the society of the future—twenty years from now, perhaps—somehow to have educated itself to use coercion only for the sake of justice. He would know better in 1942 when he wrote Herod's monologue in *For the Time Being*.

Having chosen to write his prose in absolute terms of political right and wrong, terms he found intolerable in his poems, he found himself doing precisely what he said he must never do—tell his readers how to act. His essay concludes:

> we do have to choose, every one of us. We have the misfortune or the good luck to be living in one of the great critical historical periods, when the whole structure of our society and its cultural and meta-physical values are undergoing a radical change. . . .
>
> In periods of steady evolution, it is possible for the common man to pursue his private life without bothering his head very much over the principles and assumptions by which he lives, and to leave politics in the hands of professionals. But ours is not such an age. It is idle to la-ment that the world is becoming divided into hostile ideological camps; the division is a fact. No policy of isolation is possible. . . .

This is stirring rhetoric, but confused. Precisely because the world is divided into hostile ideological camps, the choice Auden demands of the ordinary citizen has already been made for him. The essay's tone takes little account of political reality: in time of war, with universal conscrip-tion and total mobilization, few citizens are free to choose between so-cialism and fascism. The choice available is far more likely to involve different degrees of complicity in causes, just or unjust, already adopted by the state. The choice Auden explicitly reserves for times of crisis must in fact be made at all times if it is to have any effect. In rejecting a "policy of isolation" Auden uses the same phrase to cover both personal isolation and the national isolation then under debate in America—where the essay was published—but the connection is more metaphoric than real.

Three years later in *For the Time Being* Auden let his Narrator recite a comparably stirring and comparably false celebration of public action at a time of crisis: "These are stirring times for the editors of newspapers: /

History is in the making; Mankind is on the march," and so forth. The tone is that used by the collective ideologies, with traces of Auden's own manner from 1938. But in the Narrator's lines the voice of the inescapable personal will and personal consciousness soon breaks through the collective mask. We might almost believe all this grand rhetoric, he says, "If we were never alone or always too busy . . . / But no one is taken in, at least not all of the time." The dream of public unity is a charm against our private terrors, not simply a response to an "unlucky" moment of European crisis. "We know very well we are not unlucky but evil, / That the dream of a Perfect State or No State at all, / To which we fly for refuge, is a part of our punishment."

In 1938 Auden came close to endorsing the dream of a perfect state, which he disguised as an admittedly imperfect state somehow infallibly equipped to detect and suppress its own imperfections. The times seemed too urgent to ask whether the solution might not be as fatal as the problem. As Auden prepared to depart from the English setting of his didactic efforts, he made this last attempt to devise a curriculum for Western society. It took everything into account except the real nature of his pupils. And when he turned to write it on the blackboard, the schoolroom erupted in chaos.

XIV
History to the
Defeated

In Auden's vocabulary, history and love were words with double senses. There was *love* and *Love*, the first a voluntary relation between individuals, the second the involuntary evolutionary Eros that rules all of nature but in mankind has abdicated to the personal will. Corresponding to these in the social realm were *history*, the set of personal and collective acts done in the past that shape the present, and—for three years of Auden's career only—*History*, the determined and purposive force that will bring mankind to its ultimate fulfillment.* This latter History, which dictators are forever claiming will absolve them, gave Auden hope that he might salvage the utopian dreams which he also knew he must abandon. Evolutionary Love has long since shrugged and left us free to choose our errors, but however chaotic the world we make with our freedom, we can perhaps trust in History, Love's purposive sister, to sort it out in the end.

History, seen in this light, takes sides. It favors the progressive movements of socialism and opposes the dying struggles of capitalism. It never compels any individual to choose one side or the other, but the only real choice it allows is between joining the winning side or the losing: either you attend History's progress and share the spoils of its victory, or you fight a vain resistance against its preordained triumph. As

---

* Auden intermittently used capital and lower-case initials to make these distinctions; in this chapter I do so consistently, although without tampering with Auden's usage in passages quoted.

Auden kept insisting, in the idiom of the times, "we do have to choose, every one of us." Finally this choice was practical not moral, but Auden nonetheless wished to see History's movement in moral terms, as progress toward the fulfillment of Love. This had less to do with the class struggle than with visionary hopes to build Jerusalem in England's green and pleasant land. In Auden's rather vague prognosis, the bourgeois individualist tendencies of five hundred years were either to be reversed or somehow to be channeled into a society where individualism would harmonize with collectivity. The people's army in *Spain* blossoms from "Our moments of tenderness"; the future city for which the workers and the young are fighting (offstage) in *On the Frontier* is the place where "The will of love is done." But when Auden tried to find the will of love at work in the political present, what he found, especially in Spain, were expedient lies and necessary murders.

In writing the didactic historical parables of *The Dog Beneath the Skin* Auden had in mind not a determined History but a history whose direction could be altered by human choice. The purpose of education was to enlarge the freedom in which such choices were made. Then, from late 1936, near the start of the Spanish Civil War, until late 1939, at the end of the European peace, he tried to hold a rather different attitude. The choices being made all through Europe were leading to catastrophe; education had done no good. Perhaps the only hope of ultimate salvation lay in Historical processes that moved inevitably toward a just society. A long and honorable tradition in religion and philosophy spoke in more or less these terms; perhaps it was right. Perhaps, after all, the crises of the present day would finally be seen as minor deviations in History's progress to Utopia. If this were so, then education of sorts might still be possible, but not to increase the freedom of its pupils to choose their lives. Education would teach the inexorable aims of History, and save its pupils from wasting their lives making choices History opposed.

Auden's interest in History, however troubled its outcome, began as a wish for certitude. He hoped to find a secure foundation for his belief that fascism was absolutely wrong and that opposition to fascism was obligatory. He knew enough about recent political history to sense that the doctrines of liberalism were not enough. As he recalled later,

> The novelty and shock of the Nazis was that they made no pretense of believing in justice and liberty for all . . . Moreover, this utter denial

of everything liberalism had ever stood for was arousing wild enthusiasm, not in some remote barbaric land outside the pale, but in one of
the most highly educated countries of Europe ... Confronted by
such a phenomenon, it was impossible any longer to believe that the
values of liberal humanism were self-evident. Unless one was prepared to take a relativist view that all values are a matter of personal
taste, one could hardly avoid asking the question: "If, as I am convinced, the Nazis are wrong and we are right, what is it that validates
our values and invalidates theirs?"

He was prepared at least to experiment with the idea that purposive
History might suffice. If History were opposed to fascism, then its necessary direction would justify one's moral feelings. One's faith in History could serve as a natural religion in the realm of politics.

Auden was convinced that Marxist interpretations of economic factors in society exposed the lies used in defending the status quo; yet because Marxism ignored psychology, or treated it as a manifestation of
deeper economic factors, he could give little credence to its prophetic
powers or moral authority. So long as he took both sides of this divided
attitude into account in his writings, he gave himself no cause for later
regret. But whenever expedience or urgency led him to suppress his
reservations, he produced what he later called, referring to himself in
the third person, "trash which he is ashamed to have written." Even
at the time he could never entirely repress his doubts. They took their
revenge, and returned as self-contradictions.

When Auden eventually rejected all his poems that had given credence to partisan History, critics rebuked him for judging his younger
self by the standards of his older one, or for trying to rewrite his poetic
biography. It tends to be accepted without question that when Auden
wrote these poems he thoroughly believed in them, and discarded them
only when he changed his mind. Eliot's retention of "The Hippopota-
mus" in volumes that also included *Four Quartets* is cited as an instructive counter-example. The poems Auden rejected, however, were not
the ones to whose ideology he had once been committed, but poems
whose ideology seemed socially expedient enough to make him hope it
might someday prove true. The real trouble was the gulf between his
hope and his convictions. He knew, even in the 1930s, that any claim for
the existence of purposive History was a dangerous lie. However much
he tried to drown out his knowledge with high-sounding sentiments, he

understood that to celebrate the necessary course of History was passively to accept the decisions made by political leaders who were not at all passive in the face of events. To believe in a deliberate world-spirit meant finally to believe, like Hegel at Jena, in the world-spirit on horseback.

Auden was too sceptical ever to accept the willed naïveté enjoyed by Stalin's apologists. His Marxism was more a matter of attitude than of action, more a hope for a better future than an excuse for current policy. The tone of all his political writings in the 1930s is consistent with this recollection made twenty years later:

> Looking back, it seems to me that the interest in Marx taken by myself and my friends ... was more psychological than political; we were interested in Marx in the same way that we were interested in Freud, as a technique of unmasking middle-class ideologies; ... our great error was not a false admiration for Russia but a snobbish feeling that nothing which happened in a semi-barbarous country which had experienced neither the Renaissance nor the Enlightenment could be of any importance ... Nobody I know who went to Spain during the Civil War who was not a dyed-in-the-wool stalinist came back with his illusions intact.

When Auden wrote about psychology in the 1930s he cited cases and authorities, but when he wrote about communism he never indicated which Marxist writers, if any, he was reading. He almost always coupled the names of Marx and Freud, but his portrait of Freud was vastly more detailed. Even in his exposition of Communist theory in his essay in *Christianity and the Social Revolution* in 1935, he devoted more space to objections to the theory, and the appropriate refutations, than to the theory itself. He certainly read deeply in Marx, and he seems to have set informal reading courses for some of his friends, but he undoubtedly absorbed his Marxism from other sources as well—Communist Party publications and the intellectual climate. When he wrote about politics in Marxist terms, he tended to replace Marx's materialist base with an idealist one, as in his accounts of History moving toward the reign of Love. When he wrote about poetry, a subject in which he was more secure of his knowledge, he was steady, even exuberant, in his materialist approach.

The broad outline of his idea of History corresponds to the crude "classical" Marxism of Plekhanov, who held that while individuals can affect particular events and their consequences, the trend of History is inexorably determined by larger forces. The Third International, taking its cue from some paragraphs in Marx, identified the Communist Party as History's chosen agent; those who opposed the Party, those who made the wrong choices, were doomed to defeat by History itself. Auden was willing to try out the general theory, but he persistently refused to accept that the Communist Party, or anyone else, was the advance guard of Utopia. Hidden in the final lines of *Spain* is the even more sceptical implication that those who fight for the Communist cause may themselves be among those who have made the wrong choices— may be among the defeated whom History will abandon. If History had agents, they were not easy to find. Yet if there were no one to carry out its predestined purposes, in what sense could History be said to exist?

Auden first encountered the name and idea of purposive History in a short story by Edward Upward. "Sunday," one of the political writings Upward showed Auden in 1932,* is a thinly disguised autobiographical record of a well-educated young man's conversion to Marxism. It begins in the first person but shifts near the end to the second person, as the narrative is taken up by a voice which is partly the narrator's own and partly a disembodied intelligence. The voice accuses him of denying realities like History by thinking of them as mere abstractions:

> it's well known that comfortably-paid university experts have warned us again and again against mistaking abstract generalisations for concrete things. Don't you suspect that after all they may have been right, that history is nothing more than a convenient figment, an abstraction . . . Isn't that what you have been trying to convince yourself of all along? . . .—and every day you have failed completely. . . . You have failed to deny history . . .
>
> History is here in the park, in the town . . . It was once in the castle on the cliff, in the sooty churches, in your mind; but it is abandoning them, leaving them with only the failing energy of desperation, going to live elsewhere. It is already living elsewhere. It is living in the op-

* See p. 143.

pression and hustle of your work, in the sordid isolation of your lodgings. . . .

But history will not always be living here. . . . History abandoned the brutal fatherliness of the castle and it will abandon Sunday and the oppression of the office too. It will go to live elsewhere. It is going already to live with the enemies of suffering . . . And the man who doesn't prefer suicide or madness to fighting . . . will join with those people . . .

Here History is a tangible force, a *mana* that infuses certain persons and objects with power, while it abandons others to subsist on a debased form of energy instead. As in Fascist or imperialist claims of historical national destiny, History provides a metaphysical excuse to make obeisance to force. Upward adds an ethical reason for following History as it moves from the bourgeoisie to the working classes: it is going to live with the enemies of suffering. Why it should turn altruistic after so many centuries is unclear, but it hardly matters. The main reason for following history is that if you don't, you will be left behind to suicide or madness. This has nothing to do with altruism. A few centuries earlier, a young man who wished to be closeted with History would have applied at the castle on the cliff.

Upward's story added new meanings to an idea Auden had used already in a different form. Evolution, in the 1929 poem "Since you are going to begin to-day," granted power to various nations and classes in turn, but did so in an apolitical way, and sooner or later it abandoned everyone. Since no one could choose to follow Evolution, as the young man in "Sunday" follows History, neither practical nor moral choices had any meaning. As Auden recalled in a birthday poem to Isherwood in 1935, "The close-set eyes of mother's boy / Saw nothing to be done." Before he began using the word in Upward's sense, Auden saw history as the carrier of defeat. The schoolchild's "lunar beauty" as yet "Has no history," meaning that sorrow has not yet intruded with the anxieties of choice and loss. In a chorus of *Paid on Both Sides*, others' wisdom is "the following wind of history" which fails to sustain our flight when we come upon air pockets where, falling, we must choose our own acts. The July 1932 doggerel poem, "The sun shines down on the ships at sea," glances toward Upward's sense of the word in suggesting that in this generation "History seems to have struck a bad patch." But the

poem goes on to suggest that if times are indeed changing for the worse
they can perhaps be turned again—not by political action but by love.

Only a year later Auden had abandoned his dream that Love could be
sufficient before the evil and the good. Eros, Love, would make no
choices for us, but Auden made some fitful efforts to find some equivalent force that would. He said in a letter to Spender in 1934 that "I believe the Unconscious to be collective, creative and purposive," but he
knew better than to suppose that its purposes were anything other than
inscrutable. The flood of Eros he wrote about in 1933, "The flood
on which all move and wish to move," was little more than a self-
contradictory hope. Yet two years later he used the same fluent metaphor, no longer for Eros but for History. The final lines of his birthday
poem to Isherwood, "August for the people and their favourite islands,"
evoke this hour of crisis and dismay when

> all sway forward on the dangerous flood
> Of history, which never sleeps or dies,
> And, held one moment, burns the hand.

In this poem Auden makes explicit his renunciation of faith in Eros as
reconciler, but a few stanzas later he begins to use Upward's History
as a vehicle for maintaining that faith under another name. Early in the
poem he looks back over his nine-year friendship with Isherwood. As
adolescents they saw the world in terms of spy-fiction and aesthetic performance ("Prizing the glasses and the old felt hat . . . The enemy were
sighted from the Norman tower"); in their early twenties they believed
the world's million fevers could be cured by love ("Was there a dragon
who had closed the works . . . Then love would tame it with his trainer's
look"). Delusions, all. Now Auden asks forgiveness: "Pardon for these
and every flabby fancy," pardon for his romantic faith in the "solitary
vitality of tramps and madmen" and in the curative "whisper in the
double bed." Today, as "the wireless roars / Its warnings and its lies,"
where once he saw nothing to be done, "we look again," and see a
masque of crisis:

> See Scandal praying with her sharp knees up,
> And Virtue stood at Weeping Cross,
> The green thumb to the ledger knuckled down,
> And Courage to his leaking ship appointed,

Slim Truth dismissed without a character,
And gaga Falsehood highly recommended.

Greed showing shamelessly her naked money . . .
And Reason stoned by Mediocrity,
Freedom by Power shockingly maltreated,
And Justice exiled till Saint Geoffrey's Day

—a day so distant it is not found in the calendar. The time demands action, but the poem takes so much pleasure in its witty images of crisis that it manages to avoid saying what is to be done. Perhaps Isherwood will know: "What better than your strict and adult pen," Auden asks rhetorically, borrowing a phrase from *The Poet's Tongue*, can "Make action urgent and its nature clear?" What indeed? Waiting in the poem's final lines is the answer Auden would try to accept when the war in Spain, the following year, made action even more urgent than it was now. Those final lines suggest that the way to keep one's balance on History's flood is to make certain one is facing in the right direction. History is as yet neither purpose nor partisan, but for all the poem's insistence on the urgency of decision, the best way to ride the flood is not to make one's own choices but to move forward in the direction History is taking anyway. Those who try, even for a moment, to hold it back or alter its course, burn their hands.

This, in essence, was Auden's philosophy of History in the late 1930s. But before he made it explicit he went through an interval in which he renounced the whole idea. This occurred in the summer of 1936, during his months of truthtelling and self-reproach that began when he left the Film Unit, continued through the catharsis of *F6*, and culminated in *Letter to Lord Byron*. In June he began his holiday journey to Iceland, leaving behind the European madness he could not cure. There, on 8 July, he wrote a verse letter to his Oxford contemporary Richard Crossman, now an Oxford don; he published it in *Letters From Iceland*. The letter is not a very good poem, but Auden used it to give himself very good advice about the dangers of words like History.

The poem contrasts two realms: the real world of unique particulars and the imaginary world of abstract historical forces. The real world is an orthodoxy, "the common faith from which we've all dissented" in our individual perspectives.* Dissent is universal, but "Only the mad will never never come back," while doctors, lovers, and artists return most often, thriving on the actual world which is the material of their passion. "Let me find pure all that can happen," prays the artist, asking freedom from consuming generalities. "Only uniqueness is success!" All this is part of Auden's campaign for subject as the first, second, and third thing in art, and in this as in his other letters from Iceland he reports on a unique locality—its politics, vanities, landscape, literature. "Justice or not," he writes to Crossman, "it is a world."† What he must see in Iceland's particulars are "Not symbols of an end, not cold extremities / Of a tradition sick at heart"—not, that is, the death wish of the English bourgeoisie that he saw in his plays. Instead "I must see all," must especially "see there if I can the growth, the wonder."

Auden draws out the moral reasoning behind this argument in an extended religious metaphor. To recognize uniqueness, his argument runs, is to recognize one's personal responsibility for the world's disorder; to escape into abstractions like History is to blame the world for one's own sufferings. In his metaphor this evasion is

> our vulgar error, isn't it,
> When we see nothing but the law and order.
> The formal interdiction from the garden,
> A legend of a sword, and quite forget
> The rusting apple core we're clutching still.

Refusing to accept responsibility for eating the apple, we blame our expulsion from Eden on the flaming sword. This fantasy of "law and order," and of our lack of freedom, emerges whenever we blame our sorrow on society, capitalism, fate—anything but the human will. A year earlier, Auden had placed the blame in precisely this fashion in his birthday poem to Isherwood, where the masque of disorder represented the world's doing, not ours. Now, he acknowledges, "It's that that makes us really selfish: / When the whole fault's mechanical, / A maladjustment in the circling stars."

In these lines Auden renounces the frame of mind that gives rise to a

---

* These lines strikingly anticipate Auden's thinking in the 1940s and after.
† He is echoing a line he wrote a few months earlier, "It's a world. It's a way," at the end of the "Epilogue" to *Look, Stranger!*, the poem in which he turned away from a generalizing redemptive fantasy to a more difficult reality.

cataclysmic vision of history—the notion that it is the fault of some impersonal breakdown, like a dissociation of sensibility, if the times are out of joint; and the corollary notion that an ethical civil life must be deferred until the fault is corrected. If we accept these notions, then the only moral acts we can imagine being performed now are the acts of heroes who might restore the proper order for us. "Goodness" seems "just an abstract principle / Which by hypothesis some men must have." Evading our own concrete obligations to goodness, "we spend our idle lives in looking" for these Truly Strong leaders—"And are so lazy that we quickly find them." Two years before Auden had found one in T. E. Lawrence.

Now this temptation takes a special form, blurring the particular scene into purposive abstraction:

> Until indeed the Markafljöt I see
> Wasting these fields, is no glacial flood
> But history, hostile . . .

The generalizing force of History stands opposed to all individuality and choice. If we believe such a power exists, it becomes "Time the destroyer / Everywhere washing our will" and eroding our powers. It flows through Oxford—the address to which Auden sent this verse letter—"past dons of good will, / Stroking their truths away." To those it baptises in its illusory faith, the only voice that sounds "distinctly human" is not the voice of conscious responsibility, but the "anarchist's loony refusing cry"—a cry no less unreasoning and suicidal for the grandeur of its rhetoric:

> "Harden the heart as the might lessens.
> Fame shall be ours of a noble defence
> In a narrow place. No choices are good.
> And the word of fate can never be altered
> Though it be spoken to our own destruction."*

---

* The first line of this stanza is the same line from *The Battle of Maldon* Auden already quoted in his Ode to his pupils in *The Orators*. The rest of the stanza sounds as if it might also be quotations. The second sentence seems to allude to Thermopylae or Roncevaux, although it can be found in neither Herodotus nor *Le Chanson de Roland.* If the final sentence is not from an Icelandic saga, that is the result of an oversight by the saga-writers.

Under the rule of History, the only possible action is mad resistance to inevitable defeat.

The artistic price a poet pays for a resonant abstraction like History is the forfeiture of truth. Auden's poem suggests political costs as well. In celebrating History, an artist implicitly defends those public figures who claim to be History's avenging agents, and permits the haze of his rhetoric to conceal the human reality of their victims. This was one of Auden's central subjects in later years, and he made an oblique, obscure approach to it in "Detective Story," a poem apparently written soon after the verse letter, in July 1936. The poem makes an expressionistic dash through various whodunit conventions in search for the murderer of "our happiness." There is a chase, capture, and kill. Legal justice and our wish for vengeance are both satisfied. "Yet on the last page" of the story there remains "just a lingering doubt" about the verdict: "That clue, that protestation from the gallows, / And our own smile . . . why yes . . ." (the ellipses are in the poem). The truth is that we, not the victim we condemn, killed our happiness. But we require always that "Someone must pay," in this case the time we squander in evading our obligations: "time is always killed." Auden would acknowledge more palpable victims later.

On 21 July 1936, the day when Auden heard the first news of the Spanish Civil War, he finished the poem "Journey to Iceland." In its final lines "again the writer / Runs howling to his art." He stayed in Iceland six more weeks, but his mood had altered. The same abstractions he had renounced he now began to embrace, as in lines where he saw reactionaries "defend / Each dying force of history to the end." When he returned to England at the end of the summer he wrote a new final stanza for *The Ascent of F6*, predicting the dissolution of those "Whom history has deserted." At the end of the year he looked forward to "the intolerable tightening of the mesh / Of history" round the dictators' necks. And in *Spain*, the following spring, he came close to ascribing to History the power to require the murder of its enemies.

The new final stanza of *The Ascent of F6* is the crudest and clearest example of Auden's Historical doublethink. The graveyard of so many of his earlier illusions, *F6* now became the seedbed of a newer, more pernicious one. Having rejected the fantasy that he could alter history

with his poems, he now accepts the fantasy that no one can alter History
at all. Revising the first-edition text, he and Isherwood threw out the
sardonic and pessimistic prose epilogue, in which the surviving characters claimed the dead Ransom as a spokesman for honor, duty, sacrifice,
and England, and put in its place a new stanza for the hidden chorus of
the preceding scene, where Ransom dies on the mountain. This new
stanza, now the final words of the play, imposes on Ransom's story a
meaning never suggested in the original version:

> Whom history has deserted
> These have their power exerted,
> In one convulsive throe;
> With sudden drowning suction
> Drew him to his destruction.
> [*Cresc.*] But they to dissolution go.

This is an unlikely text for the Bach chorale to which it is supposed to
be sung. And when Auden writes verse as awkwardly as he does here it
is generally a sign that he cannot make himself believe what he is making himself say. The crescendo in the final line is a way of drowning out
the circularity of the argument. The ruling class, whom History has deserted, sent Ransom for their own purposes on his fatal expedition. Now
he is dead, but the ruling class has done very well by him. He reached
the summit before his Ostnian rivals. England won. If History has deserted the imperialists, if they are defending a dying force, the play has
given no hint of it. The only evidence it offers in support of this stanza's
statement that History has deserted the ruling class is the statement in
the same stanza that they go to dissolution. The first version of the play
held out little hope for a better future. Now the Spanish War made this
attitude defeatist, even dangerous.

By the following spring this circular account of History had blos-
somed into something far more elaborate. In January 1937 Auden left
for Valencia and Barcelona. In March he was back in England, and
within a few weeks had written *Spain*. This extraordinarily complex
poem is the record of a disillusionment half accepted, half denied. In it
Auden asserts that a certain form of partisan political action can express
the will of love and foster ultimate justice; but he also knows that the
political action today claiming to express these things in fact does nothing of the kind. *Spain* is by far the best of the hundreds of English

poems written in support of the beleaguered Spanish Republic; it is also, in part because of its allegiance to generalizing History, the one that expresses the least sympathy for the Republic and its defenders.

History waits until the final lines of *Spain* to make its personified appearance:

> The stars are dead. The animals will not look.
> We are left alone with our day, and the time is short, and
> > History to the defeated
> May say Alas but cannot help nor pardon.

The critical literature on this stanza is divided between two factions. One of them includes Auden and perhaps no one else. In his preface to the 1966 *Collected Shorter Poems* he wrote of the two final lines: "To say this is to equate goodness with success." He added, "It would have been bad enough if I had ever held this wicked doctrine, but that I should have stated it simply because it sounded to me rhetorically effective is quite inexcusable." The other, larger faction insists that the lines say something entirely different, that the final stanza merely extends a quite innocuous argument made earlier in the poem to the effect that history is the product of human choices, and affirms that once these choices are made they cannot be altered, that if we fail to act now, we shall get no second chance. The trouble with *Spain* is that both factions are right.

The large structure of the poem is essentially the same one Auden used in his 1935 chart of European history in "Psychology and Art To-day." The poem presents a cataclysmic account of human time, organized according to Auden's characteristic pattern of two integrated periods separated from each other by a third, divided one. "Yesterday all the past," the poem begins, initiating six stanzas of grand synechdochal panorama that embrace all of time from the aboriginal taming of horses to the romantic adoration of madmen. "To-morrow, perhaps the future," it tentatively predicts in four of its later stanzas, looking toward a time of "perfect communion" and "the rediscovery of romantic love." Between these two periods is "to-day the struggle": the divided present with its irresolute balance of love and hate, private desire and public violence—as in the soldier's "fumbled and unsatisfactory embrace before hurting."

In *Spain* Auden makes his first real effort to describe the transition from division to unity, from the struggling present to the fulfilled future. He introduces the issue by affirming, as he had often done before, the irreducible privacy in which all choices are made. When the poet asks for "the luck of the sailor," the scientist for the answer to his experimental inquiries, and the poor for a purposive "History the operator, the / Organiser," all are asking a divine power to "descend" and "intervene." (Similarly, in "The Creatures," Auden saw indecisive mankind awaiting "the extraordinary compulsion of the deluge and the earthquake.") They address their pleas to evolutionary Eros, to "the life / That shapes the individual belly and orders / The private nocturnal terror." But "the life, if it answers at all, replies" that it is "not the mover; / Not to-day," not in the human realm. Among the creatures "the life" did indeed provide civil order, did "found once the city-state of the sponge" and "establish the robin's plucky canton." But in human ligaments it thinks no thoughts but ours. "What's your proposal," it asks,

> To build the Just City? I will.
> I agree. Or is it the suicide pact, the romantic
> Death? Very well, I accept, for
> I am your choice, your decision. Yes, I am Spain.

These lines heed all the warnings Auden gave himself in his verse letter to Crossman. They insist on unique personal responsibility, on man's equal freedom to build the Just City, if he chooses, or to rush into romantic death.

But when "the life" concludes with the politically charged words, "Yes, I am Spain," then the poem begins to contradict itself. From this point onward it diverges into two mutually exclusive arguments, two entirely distinct ideas of history and responsibility. One argument may be called the expository or *manifest* argument, as it occurs in the poem's direct statements, including those made by "the life" when it insists that man makes his own choices. The other is the figurative or *metaphoric* argument, which is found in the poem's various rhetorical figures. After "the life" ends its speech, the poem gives an account of the volunteers who came to fight in Spain. In the manifest argument, these hear "the life" tell them their choice is their own, and consciously choose to serve the Republican cause. But the poem uses metaphors of unconscious nature to describe their coming: they "migrated like gulls or the seeds of a flower"; they "clung like burrs" to the sides of trains; they "floated over the oceans" like clouds or flotsam. The effect of these rhetorical figures is to suggest that the volunteers are exempt from the doubt and division that the poem has insisted are the universal condition of conscious mankind; there are no such natural metaphors in the stanzas where the poet and the scientist and the poor ask "the life" to assist them. The volunteers, having been told by "the life" that they are forever separated from the unthinking processes of nature, immediately become part of those processes by going to Spain.* The poem moves from private choice to collective action through a subtle sleight-of-hand: it slips unthinking nature back into the deck after setting it ostentatiously off to the side.

Now the poem arrives at Spain itself, and describes both the country and the civil war as physical expressions of a divided condition. The Iberian peninsula is yet another of Auden's divided middle realms, a "tableland scored by rivers" that is a "fragment nipped off from" Africa and "soldered so crudely" to Europe. On this divided geography the war projects our mental division. Here "Our thoughts have bodies," which have separated into two opposing armies. On one side, our fearful wish to escape our lives through quack cures or a holiday's brief respite has embodied itself in the great fascist denial of conscious responsibility—

> the fears which made us respond
> To the medicine ad. and the brochure of winter cruises
> Have become invading battalions

—while, in the same way, "our faces, the institute-face, the chain-store, the ruin," behind which façades we plot our private wish to withdraw or control, "are projecting their greed as the firing squad and the bomb." But this psychopathology applies to one side only—as if firing squads were the exclusive property of Franco's invading forces. The poem covers its transition to the other side with a brief metaphoric sentence: "Madrid is the heart"—both the inner heart for which our thoughts contend and the outer one for which armies fight in battle. Now the

* The one phrase that attributes choice to the volunteers—"All presented their lives"—also takes it away from them. They present their lives to be used by others who will now make their choices for them.

poem leaves behind our fears and fever for the very different psychology of the Republican side:

> Our moments of tenderness blossom
> As the ambulance and the sandbag;
> Our hours of friendship into a people's army.

Our friendship *blossoms* into an army, as the volunteers *migrated* to Spain. These natural metaphors apply only to one side in the war, while the human metaphors of hatred and division apply to the other. Yet the war as a whole is a projection of our inner struggle between hatred and love, a struggle that occurs in everyone. The poem maintains simultaneously that the war projects "our" division and that those of us who fight on the correct side are undivided. Auden manages to have it both ways by suggesting that those who fight on the correct side are exempt from the human condition, that for them the undivided future has already arrived as the charity of warriors. So while the poem's manifest argument asserts that all human actions are chosen by the will, the metaphoric argument maintains that some special actions in the political realm, actions directed at certain social goals, are the product not of will but of something very much like unconscious instinctive nature.

The final stanza proves to be divided evenly between these two positions. In the first two lines the manifest argument applies. The stars are dead and the animals will not look. "The life" has withdrawn to its evolutionary and astronomical fastness and has left us alone with the brief moment of our day. Yet the two final lines extend the metaphoric argument. "The life" that in the manifest argument refuses to act as "History the operator" now appears under that same name and has opinions of its own. It feels regret; it chooses sides. There are those whose defeat it will mourn, and the poem shows unmistakably that the only side worth mourning is the people's army, which in the metaphoric argument is the manifest form of love.

In Auden's prose statement on the Civil War he said he supported the Republic because its defeat would encourage European fascism. Elsewhere he wrote that History was moving toward a utopian fulfillment which Fascist victories could delay but not prevent. Auden's disillusioning visit to Spain showed him that while the Valencia government was infinitely preferable to Franco, it was not the force of justice and love that would promote History's final triumph. He could no longer see the movement of History as a simple struggle between rising and dying forces. Matters were now complicated by the obvious fact that some of the supposedly rising forces were infected by the same murderous disorders that Auden had preferred to attribute only to dying ones. If, as seemed likely, the Valencia government were defeated, this would be because it failed to conform to the ultimate democratic course of History. And so History would regretfully abandon it as it had abandoned other societies. The Republic had begun with good intentions, but not good enough, and now it would fail. It would not be saved by History, which is concerned with larger matters.

Yet in *Spain*'s final words Auden indicates how deeply he abhors the idea of History in his own poem. What purposive History cannot give is *pardon*, a word that carries special force in Auden's vocabulary. Pardon has nothing to do with vague notions of courteous tolerance; it is the means by which one who is isolated by guilt or circumstance may be restored to wholeness and community. Other needs are vital—hunger and love—but as Auden implied in 1934, it is "our greater need, forgiveness," that matters most. With all its powers, History cannot help and cannot pardon; and the sense of the two final lines of *Spain* is that History cannot help or pardon the defeated, those whose need for pardon is greatest of all. This is not to say that the converse is true, that History necessarily helps or pardons the victors. The Fascist victors in today's struggle will not deserve pardon; and the ultimate victors who will eventually establish Utopia will have done nothing, in History's eyes, that needs pardon. This implies, as the metaphoric argument of the poem has already implied, that the right political actions are acts of love, even when performed by men at arms, and that these acts are exempt from the universal guilt and isolation that make pardon an urgent need. Furthermore, these guiltless actions, because they conform to History's purposes, will finally succeed. Precisely as Auden insisted, "To say this is to equate goodness with success."

The two contradictory arguments in *Spain* gave Auden the insoluble problem of reconciling his image of the hours of love that blossom into a people's army with the violent acts that armies actually commit. "Today the struggle," even among the people's army, is not a time for the good and the beautiful. Quite the reverse:

To-day the deliberate increase in the chances of death,
The conscious acceptance of guilt in the necessary murder;
To-day the expending of powers
On the flat ephemeral pamphlet and the boring meeting.

George Orwell, in a celebrated paragraph from *Inside the Whale*, commented that this stanza provides

> a sort of thumb-nail sketch of a day in the life of a "good party man."
> In the morning a couple of political murders, a ten-minutes' interlude
> to stifle "bourgeois" remorse, and then a hurried luncheon and a busy
> afternoon and evening chalking walls and distributing leaflets. All
> very edifying. But notice the phrase "necessary murder." It could
> only be written by a person to whom murder is at most a *word*.
> Personally I would not speak so lightly of murder.... The Hitlers
> and Stalins find murder necessary, but they don't advertise their cal-
> lousness, and they don't speak of it as murder; it is "liquidation,"
> "elimination," or some other soothing phrase. Mr. Auden's brand of
> amoralism is only possible if you are the kind of person who is always
> somewhere else when the trigger is pulled. So much of left-wing
> thought is a kind of playing with fire by people who don't even know
> that fire is hot....*

There is something very wrong with Auden's stanza, but not what
Orwell saw there. These lines do not present a day in the life of a Party
apparatchik; they allude to Auden's brief and nugatory work broadcasting propaganda for Valencia. By speaking for the Republic, he accepted
a degree of complicity in the actions done in its name, actions that included political and judicial murders. Other poets of the Spanish war
had no trouble ignoring this uncomfortable truth; Auden insisted on
facing it. Divided between his moral revulsion and what he felt to be his
public obligations, he chose, almost despairingly, the "conscious acceptance of guilt." To the extent that his stanza reflects this deliberate

---

* This is an expanded version of a milder complaint Orwell made in passing in his
"Political Reflections on the Crisis," in *The Adelphi*, December 1938: "Mr. Auden
can write about 'the acceptance of guilt for the necessary murder' because he has
never committed a murder, perhaps never had one of his friends murdered, possibly
never even seen a murdered man's corpse."

choice, it does exactly what Orwell said it didn't do—illuminate the moral difficulties of war.

Yet the stanza also calls murder "necessary." This word can have two different meanings: either required by circumstance, as in the common phrase "a necessary evil," or inevitably fixed and determined, as in the necessary obedience of matter to the laws of physics. Orwell assumed that *Spain* used the word in the first of these senses, as a casual justification of murder on the grounds of expedience.* But context indicates that the word must be read in the second sense. "The *conscious* acceptance of guilt in the *necessary* murder" is a paradox, the one line in the poem in which the manifest argument about choice directly confronts the metaphoric argument about necessity. The necessary murder is the harshest of the unchosen unconscious processes associated, in the metaphoric argument, with the people's army. The poet chooses to accept guilt in this murder, but the act itself is a necessary step taken by others toward History's inevitable fulfillment. This contemptible idea, brought into the poem for the sake of a paradox, is precisely what Auden had hoped to exorcise from his work when he wrote his verse letter to Crossman less than a year before.

Spain first appeared as a pamphlet—price one shilling, royalties to Medical Aid for Spain—in May 1937, a few weeks after Auden wrote it. Late in 1939 he revised it for book publication in *Another Time*. His revisions changed the poem in such a way as to remove virtually all the passages that associated natural processes with acts of war. Out went the statement that Franco's invaders incarnate our greeds and hatreds; out went the hours of tenderness blossoming into a people's army. Out went the "necessary murder," replaced by the unextenuated "fact of murder"—a change that eliminated the paradox and detached this line from the metaphoric argument. (Reversing the pattern in the original text, the only death the poem now deemed necessary was not someone else's but our own: the consciously heroic "deliberate increase in the

* Auden read the word in the same way when he defended the poem more than twenty-five years after writing it. He told Monroe K. Spears: "I was *not* excusing totalitarian crimes but only trying to say what, surely, every decent person thinks if he finds himself unable to adopt the absolute pacifist position. (1) To kill another human being is always murder and should never be called anything else. (2) In a war, the members of two rival groups try to murder their opponents. (3) *If* there is such a thing as a just war, then murder can be necessary for the sake of justice." (Letter quoted in Spears's *The Poetry of W. H. Auden*, 1963, p. 157.)

chances of death" became the "inevitable increase.") Also discarded was an unlikely stanza about an enthusiastically united future, with "The eager election of chairmen / By the sudden forest of hands"—another metaphor from nature. None of these changes has anything to do with Orwell's objections; their purpose is to rid the poem of all traces of determined History. But the poem's infection was still too severe for Auden to retain it in the volumes of collected poems that he published after the 1950s.

Even in 1937 Auden grew more reticent about History after finishing *Spain*. In May, adopting an almost entirely apolitical tone, he wrote a brief Essay on Man, the poem beginning "Wrapped in a yielding air" (later entitled "As He Is"). Here again he foresaw an inevitable resolution to sorrow and division, but he did not call it History. All but the last lines of the poem catalogue the discontents Auden had already identified in the human condition: isolation from natural objects, entrapment by the past, faithlessness in love. Only in the poem's final phrase does he quietly predict something different:

> Fresh loves betray him, every day
> Over his green horizon
> A fresh deserter rides away,
> And miles away birds mutter
> Of ambush and of treason;
> To fresh defeats he must move,
> To further griefs and greater,
> And the defeat of grief.

There is a faint political undertone to these lines, and a less faint religious one. Man must move to fresh defeats, must be deserted by those who join the great totalitarian surrender, but he must also move inevitably to the defeat of grief. As in *Spain*, Auden uses the word *defeat* in his lines about this final goal, but here he uses it in the opposite sense, as a sign not of our abandonment but of our triumph.*

"As He Is" has by far the most elaborate and arbitrary stanza form of

---

* Auden was to continue this series of transformations in a June 1939 poem, "The Riddle," which uses the same large pattern and some of the same metaphors in "As He Is," but with this crucial difference: where the earlier poem looks to the end of history for its resolution, the later one finds the end of sorrow in the present, in a personal love that at last is not faithless.

all Auden's poems in the late 1930s. In addition to its *abacbdcd* rhyme
scheme, which deviates subtly from the related pattern of line lengths, it
uses a network of internal repetitions: a word or syllable in line 3 repeated in line 4, another in line 7 repeated in line 8, with further repetitions *ad libitum* in other lines. These are the signature of a metrical vir-
tuoso experimenting in his workshop. Nothing could be less like *Spain*,
which borrows its technique from public orators at mass rallies. *Spain* is
of course just as artificial as "As He Is," but it conceals its artifice, and
pretends that its division into three historical periods is less a trick of
rhetoric than a serious interpretation of events. "As He Is" retains the
idea of purposive History, but distances it from the realm of politics by
framing it in a playfully ornate poetic form.

   History now disappeared from Auden's work for the rest of the summer of 1937, its hidden presence indicated only by certain corollary
ideas. At the end of the summer History's name—in the sense of purposive, necessary History—appeared in his verse for the last time. In a
chorus of *On the Frontier* he allows a doomed prisoner some defiant last
words against his Fascist captors. The verse is the kind Auden could
have written in his sleep, and perhaps did:

> They boast: "We shall last for a thousand long years,"
> But History, it happens, has other ideas.
> "We shall live on for ever!" they cry, but instead
> They shall die soon defending the cause of the dead!

At the end of this chorus all the prisoners—who clearly never read *Letters From Iceland*—sing about purposive abstractions like Time with its
patience and Truth with its ultimate flowering. This is not Auden's
voice but, as he suggested in his letter to Crossman, the voice of the defeated who accept the will of fate. Real events offer no hope, so the
defeated look forward to the illusory triumph of abstract ideas.

Although this was the last time Auden said anything in print about
purposive History, he alluded to it again two years later, during his first
summer in America, in an essay he never published and in a stanza he
deleted from "September 1, 1939" before the poem appeared in print.
   In this poem, as in some earlier ones, Auden keeps History hidden

until the end, when he lowers it on stage to impose an order that seems unattainable without it. The first seven stanzas speak in the voice of the orthodox Auden of the 1930s transplanted to Fifty-second Street. They recapitulate in American terms all his earlier accounts of public and private sorrow. Here again are the rapid historical etiologies, tracing fascism's public madness back to Luther, Hitler's private madness back to his childhood at Linz; and, even more telling, the stark moral logic of unforgiveness: "Those to whom evil is done / Do evil in return." Here too is Auden's characteristic shift in tone between inclusive sympathy and superior isolation, as he first shares, then disdains, the unhappiness of the "Faces along the bar," the "dense commuters," the "sensual man-in-the-street." All, whether the exceptional Diaghilev or "the normal heart," share the same isolating wish—"Not universal love / But to be loved alone."

These stanzas end in a despairing cry over helpless mankind: "Who can release them now, / Who can reach the deaf, / Who can speak for the dumb?" These are questions that associate the power of speech with the power of redemption, and are in effect the same questions Auden asked himself six years earlier, when he answered that a redemptive poet could release mankind. Now, again, his next line replies: "All I have is a voice . . ."

What the poet's voice can achieve is revelation. To expose a hidden truth, it can "undo the folded lie." The truth it reveals proves to be a summary version of what Auden had already written in the first seven stanzas. There he described the egoistic fantasies in the private realm. Now, he says, his voice can expose the "romantic lie in the brain / Of the sensual man-in-the-street." In earlier stanzas he described the "vain / Competitive excuse" and the "elderly rubbish" spoken in the public realm. Now his voice can reveal "the lie of Authority / Whose buildings grope the sky."* His earlier stanzas exposed both the lie of "Collective Man" and the private "error bred in the bone," the error of selfish love. Now he can assert again: "There is no such thing as the State / And no one exists alone." The poem turns back on itself, shifting its attention from the moral agonies of war to the poet who is writing about them.

After exposing the lies told by others, the stanza ends with a resonant

---

* The verb *grope*, used transitively, may have a deliberately indecorous undertone; Auden used the word in this sense in limericks and other trifles. This line of the poem may also allude to a couplet in Rochester's "A Ramble in St. James's Park": "Whence rows of mandrakes tall did rise / Whose lewd tops fucked the very skies."

affirmation: "We must love one another or die." But a few years later
Auden decided this too was a lie. He recalled in 1964 that when he
reread the poem after it was published, he came to this line

> and said to myself: "That's a damned lie! We must die anyway." So,
> in the next edition, I altered it to
>
> We must love one another and die.
>
> This didn't seem to do either; so I cut the stanza. Still no good. The
> whole poem, I realised, was infected with an incurable dishonesty and
> must be scrapped.*

Auden's rejection of his best-known line has always struck readers as
pedantic or misguided. E. M. Forster saw the line as a great moral affirmation: "Because he once wrote 'We must love one another or die,' he
can command me to follow him." Others observed that the Christian
Auden should have found nothing objectionable in his own echo of the
First Epistle of John iii.14: "He that loveth not his brother abideth in
death." Yet all such readings treat the line simply as a touchstone or
apothegm and ignore the poem around it. The line is in fact inseparable
from the two lines that precede it:

> Hunger allows no choice
> To the citizen or the police;
> We must love one another or die.

The connection between the two clauses is obscured by Auden's misleading punctuation. Unless corrected by editors, he invariably used a
semicolon where conventional usage requires a colon: to introduce further matter. His lines say we must love one another because hunger
allows us no choice. This is a statement of necessity: love is a biological
need which must be satisfied lest we die. Auden had said as much repeatedly during the past five years. He cited the authority of both Freud

---

* For the record, the textual history was in fact more complicated than this. Auden
may have intended to use "and die" in a new edition, but by the time he had an opportunity to revise the text, for the 1945 *Collected Poetry*, he dropped the whole
stanza. The reading "and die" appeared ten years later, in *The New Pocket Anthology of American Verse*, edited by Oscar Williams; Williams asked to restore the
omitted stanza, and Auden agreed on condition that he make this change.

and Marx for regarding "human behaviour [as] determined, not consciously, but by instinctive needs, hunger and love"; he wrote that art was of secondary importance "compared with the basic needs of Hunger and Love"; and in *Letter to Lord Byron* he bracketed "The drives of love and hunger." But he did not need his later Christian beliefs to see in "September 1, 1939" the "damned lie" that love *is* a hunger, an instinctive determined need rather than a gift voluntarily offered to another as a form of forgiveness. As early as 1936 he knew that what he valued most in love was not the satisfaction of a hunger but the gift of "Your *voluntary* love"; he knew later that not even an international crisis was an adequate excuse for forgetting this. It was in answer to "September 1, 1939" that many years later he concluded the poem "First Things First" with the line: "Thousands have lived without love, not one without water."

By writing of love under the aspect of necessity—"Hunger allows no choice"—Auden entangled himself yet again with necessary History. The typescript of the poem as he submitted it for publication in *The New Republic* (where it appeared on 18 October 1939) included two stanzas that he had already crossed out, one preceding the stanza just described, the other following it.* The latter makes explicit the suggestion in *Spain* that nothing can prevent History's ultimate fulfillment. Its syntax is governed by the earlier line, "All I have is a voice"—

* In the typescript the first seven stanzas correspond to all printed texts. Then comes this deleted stanza:

> No promises can stay
> The ruling of the court
> In session on an act
> Nor magic wish away
> Its summary effect;
> What can I do but recall
> What everyone knows in his heart,
> One Law applies to us all;
> In spite of terror and death
> The continuum of truth
> May not be torn apart.

This introduces the subject of Auden's own powers ("What can I do but recall"), a matter then elaborated in the stanza beginning "All I have is a voice" and ending "We must love one another or die" (the stanza dropped *after* publication). This is followed in the typescript by the deleted stanza beginning "To testify my faith," and then by the stanza that concludes all versions, "Defenceless under the night."

> To testify my faith
> That reason's roman path
> And the trek of punishment
> Lead both to a single goal;
> Individual death,
> Each pert philosopher's
> Concupiscence or, worse,
> Practical wisdom, all
> Our public impatience can
> Delay but may not prevent
> The education of man.

This inept stanza says that what the poet's voice can do, beside exposing lies, is proclaim that individual acts and lies finally make no difference. History—unnamed here, but something identical in all but name is at work—will settle everything in the end. Whatever happens, History never loses sight of its single goal. Individual death, the pride of philosophers, the practical wisdom that places ends before means, the public impatience that does the same—all these only delay man's education into Utopia. To say this is morally comparable to calling love a hunger. It implies that our chosen acts, including the individual death that results from denying our hunger for love, only get in the way of History's inexorable movement. It implies also that our chosen acts issue from the mad delusions catalogued earlier in the poem. This passive attitude is another of those that Auden warned himself against in his verse letter to Crossman.

A few weeks before writing these verses Auden had said much the same thing in prose. During the summer of 1939 he wrote a book of *pensées* and recollections titled (after Blake) *The Prolific and the Devourer*. After an opening autobiographical section, he proceeds through reflections on religion, society, and politics, all written in functional terms like those he used in his 1938 essay for *I Believe*—although now he ends not in a call to choose sides but in a defence of pacifism. Along the way he offers a determinist prediction of the future:

> Socialism is correct in saying that the world will inevitably become socialist, and that the actions of an individual can only either accelerate or retard that development, but in accepting the use of violence and hatred now, in believing that the laws which govern history to-

day differ from those that will govern it to-morrow, they are doing the opposite of what they imagine: they are ranging themselves on the side of the retarders. . . .

I certainly don't think that the world will be saved only by a change of heart. I believe that the world will be saved though, that historical development through every channel, wars, technology, psychology etc. etc. will compel a change of heart, that both our mistakes and our successes increase our understanding, the latter directly, the former indirectly by inducing another kind of mistake. . . .*

The concluding stanza of "September 1, 1939" prays that the poet might bear witness to these ultimate truths. But one's confidence in his foresight is lessened by a curious parallel between this final stanza and the final stanza of "Lullaby." Like the sleeping lover in the earlier poem, "Defenceless under the night / Our world in stupor lies." As Auden had hoped, implausibly, that his beloved would be watched by every human love, so now, over the earth's darkness, another watch is kept:

> Ironic points of light
> Flash out wherever the Just
> Exchange their messages.

The night may be dark and long, but the dawn of man's education will come eventually, and the Just maintain their lesser lights until the rise of the greater one. What rings especially false about this conclusion is that the Just, like the History to which they bear witness, appear out of nowhere. The earlier stanzas described universal pride, envy, fear, greed, but somehow the Just are exempt from all this, like the invisible revolutionary workers in the Auden-Isherwood plays. Auden tried at the last minute to rescue the Just from total implausibility by making their lights "Ironic." Originally in the typescript they were "The little points of light" instead.†

---

* But a few weeks after the war began, Auden decided against publishing this book, and by the end of 1939, when he acknowledged the intensity and ineradicability of wartime hatred, he regarded both the pacifism and the determinism in the book as pernicious nonsense.

† As they were in his source, a passage in E. M. Forster's essay "What I Believe" about the "aristocracy of the sensitive, the considerate and the plucky." Even in the dreadful modern world, Forster found hope in these, because "the greater the darkness, the brighter shine the little lights, reassuring one another, signalling, 'Well, at

All Auden tells us about the Just is that they exchange messages, which is, in this poem, precisely what he has been doing with his readers. So while disaster worsens around us, you and I may be confident that we too belong to that fortunate company, no matter what the poem may have said in earlier stanzas about our heart and our wish. We are not the defeated who lie beyond pardon. Like the Just, we are "composed . . . Of Eros and of dust." And so Love finds its way back into the poem to do the work of its unnamed partner History, and we, "Beleaguered by the same / Negation and despair" that even the Just must endure, may, like them, "Show an affirming flame."

Implausible as it is, this stanza makes a resonant conclusion to a poem filled with rhetorical splendors. The combination of grandeur and hollowness in "September 1, 1939" results in large part from Auden's explicit echoes of the metre and form of Yeats's "Easter 1916." Auden tried to use Yeats in the way the English Augustans used Horace—as the stable anchor for a tradition of public poetry—but a tradition of twenty years carries less weight than one of twenty centuries. Nor did Yeats's poem provide the most secure base for a poetry of war. His sense of "terrible beauty," like Auden's ironic points of light, has more to do with private vision than with the public order that is the ostensible subject. Auden's last word on "September 1, 1939" came in a letter he wrote, but apparently did not send, to Naomi Mitchison in 1967: "The reason (artistic) I left England and went to the U.S. was precisely to *stop* me writing poems like '*Sept. 1st, 1939*' the most dishonest poem I have ever written. A hang-over from the U.K. It takes time to cure oneself."

Auden had warned himself in his verse letter to Crossman of some of the secondary effects of a belief in History. These also appeared in his work, following in the train of History itself, during the first year of the Spanish Civil War.

---

all events I'm still here. I don't like it very much, but how are you?' Unquenchable lights of my aristocracy!" Auden presumably saw this essay first when it appeared along with one of his own in the volume *I Believe*, published in August 1939, a few days before he wrote his poem. When an interviewer asked about "September 1, 1939" in the early 1960s, Auden said he felt the points-of-light image was "frivolous."

One effect was a sense that only "The anarchist's loony refusing cry," longing for death and sure that no choice is good, was distinctly human. A few days before he left for Spain in January 1937 Auden transcribed that loony cry in a poem he later titled "Danse Macabre." It is in the voice of a mad dictator, saying "farewell to the drawing-room's civilised cry" and summoning his followers to their death with a lover's endearments. He has a modest proposal for defeating the devil with whom he is obsessed: since the devil's existence is the diseased will of man, he will destroy the devil by destroying mankind.

> For I, after all, am the Fortunate One,
> The Happy-Go-Lucky, the spoilt Third Son;
> For me it is written the Devil to chase
> And to rid the earth of the human race.

What joins History to the mad dictator is that both act involuntarily. He is as trapped by his madness as mankind is trapped by the teleological compulsions of History. But where History moves to one great goal, the dictator, by equal necessity, moves to destruction. Auden wrote this poem as a piece of psychological grotesquerie, but it implies a political critique that in fact has little to do with actual events. What Eliot said about the helpless Leader in *On the Frontier*—"I am afraid that Hitler is not the simpleton that the authors made him out to be"—applies equally to the jolly genocide of "Danse Macabre." The poem parabolically assigns responsibility for the European disaster not to real conscious choices by Hitler and his allies but to irrational forces as impersonal as History itself. In "September 1, 1939" the same idea recurs in the lines about "helpless governors" at their "compulsory games."

In 1937 Auden was denying any hope of conscious responsibility in anyone, dictator or citizen. While the mad rulers spread their gospel of death, each of their subjects (in "Dover" for example) "prays in the dusk for himself," and none "Controls the years." A year earlier, in *Letter to Lord Byron*, Auden saw fascist despair as the result whenever man "endorses Hobbes' report / 'The life of man is nasty, brutish, short.' " Now, during the spring and summer of 1937, he endorsed that report by portraying helpless citizens in a series of macabre ballads, with disdainfully jingling metres set to familiar tunes. His *galère* of self-defeat and self-destruction included the ingrown virgin Miss Gee (to the tune of "St. James' Infirmary"), the religious maniac Victor

("Frankie and Johnny"), the brilliant but blind-to-consequences James Honeyman ("Stagolee"), and the emptily leisured self-absorbed Sue.* Auden had no snobbish intention of looking only outside his own circle for examples of helplessness and defeat. He planned a similar ballad about Isherwood's recent separation from a lover whom the Germans had arrested. Isherwood, however, objected to being pinned to the page in the manner of Miss Gee.

In these ballads Auden was obeying his own warning in the Crossman letter to observe individuals instead of abstractions, but he was doing so with a vengeance, scarcely finding "the growth, the wonder" he had hoped to reveal. None of his helpless citizens can grow, none can see beyond himself to the tasks of an urgent time. Among "Schoolchildren," around the same moment, Auden could find no "seeds" that might blossom into a "new life." It is not surprising that so many of the figures in the poems he wrote around this time—farmer and fishermen, lover and traveller, drunkard and dreamer—hear in their inevitable defeat the voice of Death, offering Sophoclean wisdom in the frantic rhythms of the dance:

> *The desires of the heart are as crooked as corkscrews*
> *Not to be born is best for man . . .*

Auden could find no hope, either for himself or for Europe. It did not matter in the end whether History was determined by its own necessary forces, or by universal instinctive needs and their individual distortions, or by the diseased will of a mad dictator. If any of these forces ruled events, then conscious moral choice was futile or impossible. No one was free, neither dictator, citizen, nor poet. It was not a limited class of the politically erring who could be called "the defeated," because everyone was defeated—barred from choice, denied both help and pardon. Better, perhaps, not to be born. After all his warnings and precautions, Auden needed no one's help to argue himself into this hopeless position. But he would need both help and pardon to find his way out of it.

---

* Her tune was lost with the final draft of her ballad. Auden showed the manuscript to a friend who thought it so offensive she tore it up. This was the only fair copy, and Auden never bothered to rewrite it. A partly conjectural reconstruction from an early draft was published by the Sycamore Press, Oxford, in 1977.

XV
From This Island

In the early 1930s Auden dreamed of innocent islands. He woke on a
guilty one. From the end of 1935 to the end of 1938, whenever he
needed an emblem for his separation from responsibility, audience, love,
history, all that is real outside the mind's inner chambers, he invoked the
solitary island. This was both the image of isolation and its etymological
source, the *isola*. The island supplanted the border as Auden's geo-
graphical sign of entrapment and enclosure. It was not that he was held
captive like Odysseus by Calypso—he found his own Calypsos all too
easy to abandon—but that every place he went became another lonely
island, far from everything that mattered. He carried his isolation
everywhere, and in this period his poems travelled all over the map: Iceland, Spain, Egypt, Hong Kong, Macao, China, Brussels. The only
poems he explicitly set in England at this time were a bitter valedictory
to Oxford, an enclosed place isolated from "the shops, the works, the
whole green county," and a poem about Dover, the city where the decisive exit is seen as a futile repetitive routine. His constant subject became the journey; and his constant frustration, the journey's failure to
take him someplace different from his starting point. He knew that what
he needed was engagement with the real, with "All that I push away
with doubt and travel," and that his journeys altered nothing. The traveller, he wrote, "seeks the hostile unfamiliar place . . . the strangeness"—yet when he arrives "he and his are always the Expected." There
are no discoveries; and neither Dover nor Hong Kong can ever be as-

tonished. The "crowds make room for him without a murmur, / As the earth has patience with the life of man."

Before he set out on his international wanderings Auden had tried to make all England his arena and audience, the place he could alter with his poems. This was an ambitious change from his early work where he kept to a narrow declining landscape in the north. As late as 1931, England as a whole was still a place he observed clinically when he observed it at all, as in the "English Study" of *The Orators*. His change from clinical distance to didactic exhortation, in regard to England, can be dated precisely: May 1932, in "O Love, the interest itself in thoughtless Heaven," when he wrote in praise of "This fortress perched on the edge of the Atlantic scarp, / The mole [breakwater] between all Europe and the exile-crowded sea." He prayed to Love to make him

> as Newton was, who in his garden watching
> The apple falling towards England, became aware
> Between himself and her of an eternal tie.

The analogy is imperfect, as Newton's eternal tie was less nationalistic than geocentric, but Auden moves rapidly on to a stanza that ranges across Britain, naming industrial sites on "Lancashire moss" and in "Glamorgan valleys." A few stanzas later he writes of those "inland" in Europe who are "watching these islands" to see prefigured here their own future. As England, in Auden's border-metaphor, is the fortress on the edge dividing Europe from the Atlantic, so also it is the leading edge between the European past and "Some possible dream, long coiled in the ammonite's slumber," now emerging as the future. England bears the world's promise, and Europe watches her to learn what will happen—

> As children in Chester look to Moel Fammau to decide
> On picnics by the clearness or withdrawal of her treeless crown.

Metaphors like this one, scenes where we look toward some English prominence, grew frequent in Auden's poems. A year later, in "A Summer Night," he recalled "The Oxford colleges, Big Ben, / And all the birds in Wicken Fen." Soon afterward, in "The Malverns," he looked to Wales, where from their mansions the retired and rich

See the Sugarloaf standing, an upright sentinel
   Over Abergavenny.

As in his lines about Chester and Moel Fammau, Auden is claiming a
large perspective. Not only does he see what is visible from his own
standpoint, but he knows what others see from theirs. He is a poet for
the nation, he contains multitudes.

All this culminates in the opening chorus he wrote for *The Dog Beneath the Skin* around the end of 1934 or early 1935. To begin the one
play in which he hoped to educate the nation, he evoked the full range of
England's landscape, with examples of every kind of place an audience
might recognize as its focus of nostalgia. Everyone who watches the
play is urged to think of the village of Pressan Ambo as the place he
loves best, "Wherever you were a child or had your first affair." Auden
knows all these places, and like Hardy in *The Dynasts* can sweep from
the wide panorama of Europe down to the local details of any setting he
prefers:

The Summer holds: upon its glittering lake
Lie Europe and the islands . . .
Calm at this moment the Dutch sea so shallow
That sunk St. Paul's would ever show its golden cross
And still the deep water that divides us still from Norway.

We would show you at first an English village: You shall choose its
   location
Wherever your heart directs you most longingly to look; you are lov-
   ing towards it:
Whether north to Scots Gap and Bellingham where the black rams
   defy the panting engine:
Or west to the Welsh Marches; to the lilting speech and the magicians'
   faces:
Wherever you were a child or had your first affair
There it stands amidst your darling scenery:
A parish bounded by the wreckers' cliff; or meadows where browse
   the Shorthorn and maplike Frisian
As at Trent Junction where the Soar comes gliding; out of green
   Leicestershire to swell the ampler current.

Critics for whom the young Auden is the One True Auden like to cite
this passage as, in one recent instance, "the most beautiful of all . . .

revelations of the deep structure of Auden's imaginative world." Certainly the lines are memorable, the work of a writer with tireless curiosity, wide sympathy, and a deep love for the English realm. The trouble is that the curiosity, sympathy, and love are not Auden's at all and have little to do with the "deep structure" of his imagination. He copied it all out of a book. Every geographic image quoted above derives from Anthony Collett's *The Changing Face of England*, first published in 1926 and reissued in a cheap edition in May 1932. Auden must have snapped up the reissue as soon as it appeared, because almost immediately, in the poem where he hoped to feel Newton's eternal tie to England, he adopted a topographic image from a sentence by Collett: "Chester knows Moel Fammau ... and divines the coming weather by the clearness or withdrawal of her bare crown" (1932 edition, p. 91). From Collett also came the "Lancashire ... mosses" and the "valleys of the Glamorganshire coal-field" (pp. 197–98). The line about a possible dream coiled in the ammonite's slumber adapts Collett's phrases "a likely dream" (p. 121) and "coiled ammonites in eternal snakelike slumber" (p. 115). A year or so later Auden recalled Collett's list of all the birds in Wicken Fen (p. 67). Then he borrowed "the peaked Sugarloaf standing sentinel over Abergavenny" (p. 94). When he needed material for *Dogskin*'s opening chorus he lifted passages from Collett in almost the same sequence he found them in the book:

> Not only is the North Sea so shallow that if St. Paul's was planted anywhere between the Dutch and English coasts the golden cross would shine above water ... [p. 9]

> the deep water that divided us from Norway, and divides us still. [p. 9]

> that wildest and most leisurely of railway journeys from Scot's Gap on to Reedsmouth and Bellingham, and the rams that gaze defiantly at the panting engine are horned black-faces. [pp. 112–13]

> the lilting speech of the Welsh border ... a still stranger face ... it is the magician out of the fairy-book. [pp. 213–14]

> the mild-eyed shorthorn or the maplike Friesian. [p. 235]

> the Trent, or where Soar comes gliding at leisure out of green Leicestershire to swell the ampler river. [p. 148]

The settings of Auden's earliest poems were places he knew and loved, whose names he learned to treasure before it ever occurred to him to write poems about them. When he decided to write verse that could move an audience to action, he discarded the settings he loved for ones he felt would be poetically and politically useful. In the summer of 1934, even before the *Dogskin* chorus was written, Spender smelled something fishy in Auden's appeals to national symbols and suggested in a letter that he had a tendency to "National Socialism." (In 1934 it was still possible to use this term without referring exclusively to Nazism; Spender meant any socialism with a national appeal rather than international goals.) Auden defended himself by claiming first that personal necessity forced him to write this way, then that political expedience was justification also:

> I entirely agree with you about my tendency to National Socialism and its dangers. It is difficult to be otherwise when one's surroundings and emotional symbols are of necessity national emblems.
>
> I'm no more of a communist than you are but to achieve the kind of society I think we both wish for, it is fatal to ignore the national psychological factor. The number of the completely disinterested is never quite large enough.
>
> The success of fascism seems to show that if people have any share, even only a cultural one (e.g. the secondary school clerk), he [*sic*] responds to the national call and if the right appeal is not made, the wrong one will be.

This suggests fighting fire with fire, using the psychological methods of fascism to serve fascism's enemies. Auden is ignoring, for the moment, the possibility that fascism is its methods, but at least he is writing in the *faute de mieux* manner that always indicates he doubts what he is trying to say.

By 1935 Auden knew he could no longer justify or excuse his national symbols. His real setting was "this island now," not England at all, but the holiday island of his art. Far away were the "urgent voluntary errands" his isolated art could not perform. After he realized this, he used national symbols only to expose their falsity, as in the case of Ransom in *F6*, or to reduce them by ironic realism, as in *Letter to Lord Byron:* "Where is the John Bull of the good old days, / The swaggering bully with the clumsy jest?" Dead at Ypres is the answer, replaced by "The bowler hat who straphangs in the tube." So much for England's masculine symbol. Britannia, its feminine symbol, is strangely altered also: "Mother looks odd to-day dressed up in peers, / Slums, aspidistras, shooting-sticks, and queers." Soon afterward Auden and Isherwood deleted the final return to England from the second edition of *F6;* then, when they wrote *On the Frontier,* the only scene they set in England was a prose chorus of newspaper readers worrying over Europe—a scene replaced in the production text by a chorus of journalists in Europe itself. As for Anthony Collett, Auden plundered another phrase or two from him in 1935, and again in the late 1940s, but never in search of a place-name and never to claim Collett's love of England as his own.* When he wrote "Dover" in 1937 he looked up at aeroplanes flying "in the new European air, / On the edge of that air that makes England of minor importance."

"August for the people and their favourite islands": the first line of the birthday poem Auden sent Isherwood in 1935 gives the date and return address. As the summer visitors arrive here to enjoy the "complicated apparatus of amusement," Auden looks back over his life and sees an archipelago of irresponsible islands. Nine years before, he and Isherwood played at espionage on the Isle of Wight, "that southern island / Where the wild Tennyson became a fossil." Five years passed, and "we watch / The Baltic from a balcony"; he does not say so, but they were on Reugen Island, where Auden and Spender made a holiday visit to Isherwood. Now he is on another island where, "in this hour of crisis and dismay," again "I smoke into the night, and watch reflections / Stretch in the harbour." The poem's geography suggests the Isle of Man, but its location matters less than its insularity.

When he wrote his next poem, three months later, he was in London,

---

* In his birthday poem to Isherwood in 1935 he took Collett's "The face is a narrow oval . . . the skin is a little sallow and brownish, the eyes are rather close together" (pp. 245–46) for "The sallow oval faces of the city" and "The close-set eyes of mother's boy." The same year he took "the tide's pluck" (p. 9) for "the pluck / And knock of the tide" in "Look, stranger." Evidently he reread the book in 1948, when he took Collett's "network of caves and conduits" (p. 138) for "A secret system of caves and conduits" in "In Praise of Limestone," and "those deep, slow hovers" (p. 87) for "the slow, deep hover" in "Deftly, admiral."

working at the G.P.O. Film Unit. But he was still writing about islands. Marion Grierson, John Grierson's sister, commissioned him to write some verses for a documentary film to be titled *Beside the Seaside*, which she was making for a travel association. Auden provided the memorable descriptive lyric, "Look, stranger, at this island now." Marion Grierson found the poem unsuitable; only a few phrases found their way into her film. Auden found it a decisive self-reproach.

There is far more in "Look, stranger" than its warm slow language of description. It also illustrates a theory of perception and its ethical consequences. In the first stanza "The swaying sound of the sea" can "wander like a river" through the ear's "channels." Here perception is imitative: the mind acts as a microcosm of what it observes. The sound of the large body of water moves in the ear like a small body of water, and both sounds move aimlessly. In the third stanza, visual images move in a similar way. The "full view / Indeed may enter / And move in memory," just as "these clouds" appear to "pass the harbour mirror," moving from reality in air to reflection in water, where they "saunter" all summer.

No urgency intrudes on this holiday island, where sound and image move in memory but have no other effect. The visiting "stranger"—as in "The Watershed" apparently a double for the poet himself—should simply enjoy his passivity, "Stand stable here / and silent be," and "pause" where the cliff forever opposes the foam. Here all motion is part of an unchanging natural balance, and no deliberate human acts require action in response.

It is different elsewhere:

> Far off like floating seeds the ships
> Diverge on urgent voluntary errands . . .

Everything else in the poem is a matter of passive sensory impressions of unconscious natural objects; here Auden adds a deliberate interpretive understanding of conscious artifice and actions. These two varieties of perception oppose each other even in these two lines. To the perceiving eye the ships seem purposeless, part of nature. The truth is different and less poetic. The phrase *urgent voluntary errands* abjures all sensory metaphors. The sympathy with nature sought and mourned by the romantics, the wisdom of the senses, is not enough. The senses discover facts but evade meanings. Implicit in the poem are challenges to its author to find his own urgent errand, to leave his poetic isolation behind him, and to learn that he and his audience can be more active than the unmoving stranger the poem addresses.

In the film *Beside the Seaside* the island was no more than the Isle of Wight and its pleasures. In Auden's lyric it took on a more immediate and personal significance. A few months later he used it in the title he chose for his second book of poems, as a reference both to England and to the isolation of the poems themselves from any purpose outside their own existence. When he compiled this second book, in the spring of 1936, he began with the working title *Thirty-One Poems*, then changed it to *Poems 1936*. Faber & Faber used this latter title in the proofs, but the directors of the firm decided it sounded too much like the title of a full collected edition and asked Auden for something more specific. Writing from Iceland, he suggested either *It's a Way*, from the book's final line, or *The Island* (or, he added, "On the analogy of *Burnt Norton* I might call it *Piddle-in-the-hole*"). But the mails were slow, and by the time Auden's reply reached England, the printing schedule had obliged Faber's directors to come up with a title of their own. They chose *Look, Stranger!*, complete with exclamation mark. With his redemptive fantasies behind him, Auden was in no mood to buttonhole passing strangers with a title like this one. "It sounds," he wrote to his American publisher, "like the work of a vegetarian lady novelist. Will you please call the American edition *On this island.*"

Auden's more urgent problem was to find his way off this island, and he had begun trying as soon as he turned in the book of poems in the spring. The first journey he wrote about at length was his summer visit to Iceland. There, perhaps, the past might simply be left behind— "North means to all: 'Reject!'" As a miniature quest epic, the poem "Journey to Iceland" begins syntactically *in medias res:*

> And the traveller hopes: "Let me be far from any
> Physician"; and the ports have names for the sea;
>   The citiless, the corroding, the sorrow . . .

The traveller's hope to be far from physicians sounds like a circuitous way of wishing not to get ill, but it is also a sign of Auden's rejection of his redeemer fantasies. He wants to keep his distance from meddlers with ideas of their own about how to cure others. He wants only to be left alone, and Iceland seems the perfect setting:

> For Europe is absent. This is an island and therefore
> Unreal. . . .

But the traveller has another hope. He has bought his passage to a place rich in history, where he hopes to find a version of faithful love— not love among the living, but between faithless mortals and the unchanging spirit of their ancestors. On this island, the traveller imagines, "the steadfast affections of its dead may be bought / By those whose dreams accuse them of being / Spitefully alive"—an assertion qualified immediately by the doubting question, "Can they?" Can steadfast affection ever be bought? The truth is that here too "the world is, and the present, and the lie." Here, too, love is faithless: "the weak vow of fidelity is formed by the cairn." In human ligaments, here as everywhere, "The blood moves also by crooked and furtive inches." The island proves all too real. The unreal refuge withdraws beyond every horizon:

> For our time has no favourite suburb; no local features
> Are those of the young for whom all wish to care;
> > The promise is only a promise, the fabulous
> > Country impartially far.

Auden's dilemma is not that he is compelled to return—although he does so, loudly, in the final line where "again the writer runs howling to his art"—but that he has not really gone anywhere. *"Caelum non animum mutant qui trans mare currunt,"* wrote Horace; "they change their sky, not their soul, who rush across the sea." Auden, writing in Horatian stanzas, concurred.

On his poetic voyages Auden never reaches the goal for which he sets out. Either his goal is illusory; or it refuses to offer the challenge a traveller needs if he is to change; or, simply, "he does not want to arrive." Auden is constantly setting forth in one direction, only to turn back or away somewhere else. These deviating voyages became so habitual in his verse that by 1938 he had invented a rhetorical device that corresponded to them. He would open a poem by pursuing one subject, and then, after two or four lines, would swerve on the word *But* to a differ-

ent or opposite subject. He used the device repeatedly in the sonnets of
In Time of War:

> The life of man is never quite completed;
> The daring and the chatter will go on:
> But, as an artist feels his power gone,
> These walk the earth and know themselves defeated.

The first two lines indicate that the poem will have something to do
with man's insuperable vigor, but then the subject abruptly changes to
"these" who, not insuperable at all, know themselves defeated. Normally a pronoun like *these*, in the middle of a sentence, refers to an antecedent noun, whether stated or implied; here there is no such noun.
Only later in the poem does it become clear that *these* are political exiles
whose daring and chatter have long since ended.

In the 1930s Auden's voyages are like his loves, beginning splendidly
and turning false. In "The Voyage," written on the boat to China early
in 1938, the traveller on board thinks of himself as the real center of his
world. From his perspective, "the mountains swim away with slow calm
strokes" and the gulls that had accompanied the ship "abandon their
vow"—precisely what both traveller and lover do. Left behind on the
quay, a watcher envies the chance that the voyage might reach, somewhere else, "the Juster Life." Yet the poem casts doubt on the traveller's
hope from the start. "Where does the journey look," asks the opening
phrase. The traveller does not know. Does he find, the poem asks, any
proof of "the Good Place" through his senses, through "the vaguer
touch of the wind and the fickle flash of the sea"? The question implies
its answer. The Juster Life and the Good Place can never be found in a
vague touch or a *fickle* flash. In short,

> he discovers nothing: he does not want to arrive.
> The journey is false; the false journey really an illness
> On the false island where the heart cannot act and will not suffer . . .

False sounds out three times in two lines. The journey is false because
the traveller refuses to change; the ship is a false island both because it is
only *like* an island and, in a moral sense, because it is a place of faithless
isolation.

In "Journey to Iceland," eighteen months before, the false island was everywhere, but much has happened since then. Now, although the traveller cannot end his entrapment, perhaps it can be broken for him. "At moments"—no more than moments—he can hope for a "true journey" ending in faithful love. This hope rises whenever something real outside him summons his attention. So,

> when the real dolphins with leap and abandon
> Cajole for recognition, or, far away, a real island
> Gets up to catch his eye, the trance is broken: he remembers
> The hours, the places where he was well; he believes in joy.

And if he was well once, then perhaps again

> the fever shall have a cure, the true journey an end
> Where hearts meet and are really true.

However, this will remain only a hope until Auden stops disclaiming moral responsibility for his isolation by equating it with disease as he does here; the therapeutic metaphor by which he tries to explain his problem is part of the problem itself. The poem's final lines show him still unsure of what he means by a "true journey" and caught in self-contradiction when he tries to describe it. When the true journey ends, he writes, then "away" will be

> this sea that parts
> The hearts that alter, but is the same, always; and goes
> Everywhere, joining the false and the true, but cannot suffer.

First the sea *parts* altering hearts, then it *joins* them. Auden has not decided if the sea is a medium or a barrier—whether a voyage can ever really take him anywhere by movement through space, or whether the sea's unfeeling sameness represents the barrier in time that he creates by his own refusal to suffer, act, and change. If the second of these alternatives is true, if his own inner refusal blocks him from love, then no journey in the world outside can ever bring him anywhere that matters.*

* When he revised the poem in the 1960s Auden resolved the contradiction in the metaphors of these final lines by replacing "joining the false and the true" with "as truth and falsehood go."

The fortunes of Auden's private life were always analogous to the fortunes of his poetry. He saw his emotional isolation in the midst of sexual success as parallel to his ethical dissatisfaction with his literary fame. He felt too little conviction in his political writings to share the passions they helped arouse or justify in his audience, while his darker personal writings seemed to him too private and obscure to communicate their meaning. *Where does the journey look?* asks the first line of "The Voyage." This was the wrong question to ask, for the real goal of faithful love was distant not in space but in time. *What does the song hope for?* asks the first line of "Orpheus." This, too, was the wrong question.

"Orpheus," the most gnomic and compressed of Auden's poems in the 1930s, was the one poem that he later acknowledged to have been deliberately obscure. Writing in April 1937, immediately after finishing the resounding polemic of *Spain*, he posed no challenges and offered no answers. Instead he withdrew briefly from the public realm to ask what he had meant by being there. "Orpheus" is almost all questions, as in the first of its two stanzas:

> What does the song hope for? And the moved hands
> A little way from the birds, the shy, the delightful?
>   To be bewildered and happy,
>   Or most of all the knowledge of life?

The poet, Auden told John Pudney in 1932, must be "a little outside of the group." Now the poet's hands, moved by inspiration across the strings of his lyre, are "A little way" from his audience of shy delightful birds.* Does his song—does the art of poetry—seek to share the happy bewilderment of the listening birds, the unwilled enchantment a song can induce in those who hear it? Or is the end of poetry the cold deliberate knowledge that observes and controls? Orpheus induced ecstasy in others, but no one suggests he experienced it himself. Does he long to share it, or does he prefer after all to watch its effect from his distant and lonely perspective?

Auden is restating a theme from the start of his career, the division

* The detail is from Ovid.

between the communistic body with its sensual delights and the aristocratic mind with its conscious authority. On which side of this division does he wish to belong? The second stanza leaves the question unanswered:

> But the beautiful are content with the sharp notes of the air;
> The warmth is enough. O if winter really
> > Oppose, if the weak snowflake,
> > What will the wish, what will the dance do?

These two sentences parallel the two possible hopes expressed in the first stanza. The beautiful, those instinctive beings *denen sich die Weisen neigen,* have no need for poems; nature's artless sounds and restful warmth suffice. And as summer warmth is enough for the beautiful, so the winter chill is unaffected by the poet's wish, by his willful knowledge. In Ovid, all the powers of Orpheus come to nothing. He summons Hymen to his wedding, but the god brings no good luck, and Eurydice dies; he charms the gods of the underworld into releasing her from death, but as he leads her to the upper world he looks back at her despite their command, and she dies again; at last, his voice, which can protect him from all hostile missiles, is drowned out by the cries of maenads who destroy him. Neither the poet's inner "wish" nor his outer "dance" can avert his ruin.

"Orpheus" is Auden's rebuke to his art. Neither of the alternative wishes he explores in the poem has any hope of being accomplished. What does his song hope for? If he writes to share the bewildered delight felt by the beautiful—felt by the sleeping objects of his faithless love, felt by the awed incomprehending audience—he is trapped in the conscious isolation of his artistry. But if he writes to gain knowledge and control, he is still trapped in his mental isolation, opposed by the weak snowflake no knowledge can defeat. Whatever the song hopes for, it cannot have. This is a compressed statement of the romantic convention of the poet's disillusionment: starting in gladness, confident in the powers of his art until he finds them ineffectual, then ending in despondency and madness. Auden dreamed of overcoming his isolation by using his power to enchant, whether poetically, erotically, or politically; but the inequality of those who use power and those on whom it is used—like the inequality of the waking and sleeping lover in "Lullaby"—can only deepen isolation, never end it. Orpheus is barred forever from the community of the enchanted and enthralled.

It was a counterfeit poetry that dictated to an audience the choices the poet secretly refused, just as seduction was a counterfeit love. To say "Repent . . . Unite . . . Act" was to leave the difficult tasks to someone else. To find a large audience by modelling plaster birds out of clay and old newspapers—the metaphor Auden used in "The Sportsmen"—was to ensure isolation from those who gathered to admire. Between his final decision to leave England, in July 1938, and his departure for America, in January 1939, Auden took it upon himself to learn acceptance rather than authority. He sought poetic subjects in knowledge that he could share, rather than in knowledge that set him apart. Where he had mourned the illusive powers of poetry, now he learned to accept the real possibilities of his poetic gift. If he could not accomplish "the defeat of grief," he could at least "Sing of human unsuccess / In a rapture of distress."

The chronology of these last months before his departure for America is simple in its public outline, complex in its private details. Auden and Isherwood, having been commissioned by their publishers to write a travel book about Asia, decided, when Japan invaded China, to write about the Sino-Japanese War. They sailed for the Far East in January 1938. On the voyage out they revised *On the Frontier* and began a joint travel diary, and Auden wrote his poems about the ship and its ports of call.* During their four months in China they wrote little outside their diary. They left China in June, made a brief stopover in Japan, sailed across the Pacific to Vancouver, and took the train to New York. There, during a ten-day visit, they agreed to come back to America to live. Isherwood seems at first to have thought in terms of an indefinite stay, not an emigration. Auden, without saying much about it to Isherwood or to anyone else, had resolved on a categoric break. He had known for more than two years, since finishing *The Ascent of F6*, that he would eventually leave England. Now he knew when he would depart, and where he was going.

* This sequence consisted of "The Voyage," "The Sphinx," "The Ship," and "The Traveller," all written during the journey, and "Macao" and "Hongkong," tacked on in Brussels about ten months later.

After making his decision, he spent as little time as possible in England. He and Isherwood returned from their China trip in the middle of July, but by the first week in August, after giving a lecture or two, Auden slipped away to Brussels to work on his poems. He stayed to the end of September, then spent two months in England rushing about giving lectures on China and speeches against fascism. He also assisted in the long-delayed production of *On the Frontier*, a play that began to seem somewhat irrelevant after the dismemberment of Czechoslovakia upset its political prophecies. Early in December he left for Brussels again, this time with Isherwood. They came back to England in January 1939, allowed themselves a week for farewells, and sailed for New York on 19 January, the anniversary of their departure for China the previous year.

This was all that was visible to Auden's audience and friends, but privately he was hard at work uprooting his earlier ways of thinking and cultivating new ones. His disenchantment with partisan politics proceeded quickly, but when he spoke in public he maintained the tones of the committed left-wing writer that the newspapers took him to be. His close friends had no better sense of his real feelings than the journalists did. As the public figure diverged from the private man, his reticence grew more constraining. It had already become one of his more urgent reasons for leaving England. He was reticent not because he liked to keep his feelings secret from those around him, but because he felt the political struggle was far more important than his doubts about it— doubts that, had he expressed them, could only serve his enemies and hurt his friends. As Isherwood recalls, Auden not only was convinced of his undiminished obligation to speak against fascism, but also "wanted to show his solidarity with left-wing friends he admired and loved." Even if his public activity served virtually no useful purpose, he still kept at it. He did this partly because English life was for him a larger form of family life. He wanted to escape his family, but he had no wish to give them pain. While he lived among them he maintained their conventions. "The bars of love are so strong."*

---

* It was of course impossible to live this way for long without falling victim to the emotional strain. Auden's family feeling, in both the personal sense and the more general one, led to some moments of bitterness in the letters and verses he wrote in the last weeks before his departure. He ended a poem written to entertain friends in Brussels on New Year's Eve 1938 with an unpleasant stanza (which later embarrassed him) listing "Fascists, policemen and women" among "the haters of

During his last months in Europe he wrote far better poems when he
was in Brussels than he did at home. In Brussels in August and September he worked on the sonnets of *In Time of War*, devising a method of
writing about history that focused on the moral links between past and
present and accepted responsibility for the future. Again in Brussels in
December he wrote a group of poems about art and artists in which he
explored the assumptions that would govern his later work. In England,
in October and November, he did little more than gather up scraps and
fragments of a half-dozen earlier poems and piece them together with
some new material to make up the "Commentary" to *In Time of War*.
He was clearing out his workshop before moving on.

In Time of War—the sonnet sequence, not the verse commentary—is
Auden's most profound and audacious poem of the 1930s, perhaps the
greatest English poem of the decade. Writing in a form that could easily
have turned into a garland of miniatures, he achieved monumental dignity and strength. The harsh crude textures of its verse, its emotional
clarity in the face of disaster, the rigor and inclusiveness of its moral
logic, all contribute to the poem's extraordinary weight and force.
Auden accomplished all this partly by abandoning the large loose forms
he had earlier preferred in writing about history—the forms of his unfinished cantos, his redemptive choruses, and *Spain*—and would adopt
again in the "Commentary." Instead he used the sonnet form he had reserved mostly for love poems, and brought to his writing on public
themes the same conviction he had brought to his writing on Eros. The
brevity of the sonnet encouraged precise local details while forestalling
shapeless lists and bloated generalities. And by arranging sonnets in sequence Auden accumulated their intense particulars into a dense im-

---

Man." When he was told by John Mulgan at the Oxford Press that a Dunbar poem
would have to be dropped from the reprint of *The Oxford Book of Light Verse* because its sexual language made the book impossible to sell to schools, he agreed, but
added that the poem was "better than the English deserve." Both his misogyny and
his distaste for the English proved to be short-lived responses to family strains at a
moment when he was preparing to walk out and slam the door. About eight years
later, his feelings changed to the point where he planned to write a guidebook to
England and, at the same time, enjoyed a gratifying sexual relationship with a
woman. As for his reticence: this ended, during his first years in America, when he
lived among friends and readers who could respond to his new opinions without
constantly measuring them against his old ones. For a few months in 1939–40 his
book reviews in the liberal weeklies amounted to bulletins on his emotional state and
his rediscovery of religion.

plicit pattern, one sufficiently confident of its own order to allow the reader to reconstruct its logic and confront its moral issues.

All Auden's historical surveys extend over vast ranges of time, but *In Time of War* (like *Horae Canonicae* later) goes as far back as the Creation. The opening sonnet makes Auden's characteristic contrast between man and the creatures, but in a new way, defining for the first time in his work both man and creature in terms of their actions. The creatures acted only once, at the moment their separate species emerged into time, and took their "gifts" from "the years" rather than from any guiding evolutionary force. "Bee took the politics that made a hive." "Successful at their first endeavour," they never tried anything else. Natural objects, in this metaphor, are no more free than they were when Auden attributed their forms to Eros or "the life," but now his rhetorical emphasis is on choice and act rather than a plastic passivity in the hands of larger powers. Man himself, in the first sonnet, is the one creature who cannot decide what he is finally to be, the creature who changes, inquires, errs, envies, "and chose his love." (The same human creature is found, at the end of the sequence, "Wandering lost upon the mountains of our choice.")

The creatures chose once; man must choose always. His choices are his history, a word that refers not to an abstract force but to the weight of human events, not to a utopian future but to a sorrowful past. "History opposes its grief to our buoyant song." The first half* of the sequence is historical (the second half focuses on the present) in a manner that Auden had not attempted before. *Spain* summarized the past in a series of disconnected tableaux with no relation to the present struggle. Now the sonnets trace the chain of consequences that connects ancient choices with present-day effects. Each sonnet presents the history of a human type—farmer, poet, scientist—as if it were compressed into a single individual who experiences centuries of change in one lifetime. Auden achieves this metaphoric connection between the general case and the particular example by portraying figures who are not quite allegorical, since their relations with others are not allegorical relations, and not quite exemplary, since their experience is more extensive than any exemplar's could be. English poetry has nothing else quite like them. They are shaped partly by the habit of German romanticism to modu-

---

* The architecture is different in the 1965 revision, which is retitled *Sonnets From China*.

late between abstractions and particulars, as Schiller did in the essay
Auden used for "The Creatures," and by the cruder tendency of Socialist Realism to make a single larger-than-life figure stand for the vil-
lainies or heroics of a class. But Auden's figures are neither villains
nor heroes nor larger than life. They are representative men, fallible
and complex, as bewildered as everyone is by the outcome of their
choices.

Auden's earlier notations of personality relied on catalogues of symptoms like the liar's quinsy. While writing *In Time of War* he finally
discarded such physical metaphors of health and disease in favor of ethical metaphors of knowledge and authority. The builder of cities, in
Sonnet VIII, long ago "turned his field into a meeting-place"; after centuries of sophisticated urbanization, he can no longer "find the earth
which he had paid for, / Nor feel the love which he knew all about."
The martial hero of Sonnet V, whose once "generous bearing was a new
invention," grew into sedentary age, "sat in offices and stole, / And
spoke approvingly of Law and Order." Besides using ethical action, not
physical symptoms, as his measure for man, Auden makes his first gesture toward finding the ground of ethics in religion, rather than in Earth
or History or Eros. Events in Christian time, the Fall and the Incarna-
tion, have a status equal in his historical survey to events like the rise of
modern science and the Industrial Revolution.

Yet even as he deepened the moral range of his speculations on history, Auden was also drawing back from his ambitions to preach. The
sonnets (again the "Commentary" is another matter) offer nothing that
can be taken as a guide to action but are, rather, parables showing the
effect of actions done already. *Journey to a War*, the volume of prose
and verse by Auden and Isherwood in which the sequence first appeared, includes a dedicatory sonnet to E. M. Forster, who in the eyes of
both authors was the paragon of undeceivers. When "we are closeted
with Madness" it is Forster's clearsighted sense of motives that breaks
the comforting illusion: "You interrupt us like the telephone." Forster's
telephone, prosaic as it is, communicates more than his flashing points of
light that signal their messages in "September 1, 1939." Art "makes us
more difficult to deceive": so Auden wrote in his preface to *Poems of
Freedom* at about the same time he wrote these sonnets. The point of his
earlier political writings had been to make it harder for the dictators to
deceive us— but any audience likely to read Auden's poems did not

need to be warned against believing Hitler. The less comfortable but more valuable didactic point of *In Time of War* was to make it harder for us to deceive ourselves.

Auden was writing against his own self-deceptions as well as his readers'. His emphasis on responsibility and freedom in these sonnets rebukes two of his lingering fantasies: the self-deception that nothing anyone can do will alter determined History; and the obverse delusion that resistance to fascist evil makes us participate in the unconscious goodness of nature. The first of these leads to a tyranny practiced by others, the second to a tyranny practiced by ourselves. Near the end of the historical half of the sequence, Auden inserted (as Sonnet XII) a poem he had written in the spring of 1936 as a rebuke to his redemptive fantasies. Its subject is the Renaissance conquest of superstition and the rise of "The Economic Man"—its original title. This conquest, the work of the indifferent redeemers of an earlier time, was flawed from the start. "And the age ended, and the last deliverer died / In bed." The land seemed safe; dragon and kobold were seen no more. Yet the "vanquished powers," those human sorrows that formerly took visible shape, simply transformed themselves into the inner sorrows of neurosis and madness, "glad / To be invisible and free." Those who promise deliverance in our own era, we are left to infer, may leave us exposed to dangers equally fatal.

After this warning the sequence leaves history and arrives at the present moment and the field of war. Here, in Sonnet XIII, Auden attains the double tone of celebration and reproach that will be the characteristic note of his later work. At the end of *Letters From Iceland* he prayed for "The wish and power to act, forgive and bless"; in "As I walked out" he heard the clocks insist that life remained a blessing "Although you cannot bless." Now he finds the power to do so. He borrows from Rilke's tone of *dennoch preisen* a way of praising that is not specifically religious—not yet. He begins Sonnet XIII with a self-command, but one that has nothing to do with his earlier self-commands to his redemptive powers:

> Certainly praise: let the song mount again and again
> For life as it blossoms out in a jar or a face,
> For the vegetable patience, the animal grace;
> Some people have been happy; there have been great men.

Certainly praise: the emphasis of the opening intimates the qualifying *But* that will soon follow. The poet's task is both to speak and to hear, to celebrate and to understand:

> But hear the morning's injured weeping, and know why:
> Cities and men have fallen; the will of the Unjust
> Has never lost its power . . .

And this double obligation has brought him to China's "Eighteen Provinces," to *this* war and *this* morning's injured.

Now, in Sonnet XIV, Auden begins to treat the actors and events of the war itself. He begins with an air raid—a method of warfare unique to the present day. The moral infamy of strategic bombing, its resistance to heroicizing myth, its indiscriminate destruction of combatant and civilian alike, its intimate connection with the violent triumph of fascism in Spain—all this made it the proper focus of a poem written in time of war in 1938. With the arrival of the bomber pilots Auden discards all the theorizing and horseplay of his earlier Airman in *The Orators*, and knows that "Yes, we are going to suffer, now."

Auden evidently found this central sonnet the most difficult to get right of any in the sequence. During the latter months of 1938, before the sequence was published, he wrote three separate versions of Sonnet XIV, the third after all the other sonnets had reached their finished state. His insistence that *we* are going to suffer, *now*, did not appear until the third version. When he started the poem, his attention was focused mostly on the Japanese bombers, and his metaphors for their condition and ours were his old physiological ones. By the time he finished revising, he had replaced them with metaphors of conscious responsibility and choice.

The first version retains Auden's earlier perspectives, his distance and detachment. He is still denying the reality of suffering, as he had refused it on the false island of the ship. All that the bombing can do is "make us cry" as if from a childhood illness. In this first text the octave reads less like a meditation on war than a dispatch by a partisan journalist on the evils of the other side:

> Our rays investigate the throbbing sky
> Till, suddenly, within that brilliant field,
> Alone and bad, their bombers are revealed,

> The dread bacillus all identify,
> The little natures that can make us cry:
> Some sad request has sent them to do ill
> Who are not sad, but execute the will
> Of the intelligent and evil till they die.

The bombers are unconscious bacilli, sent to us in a form of germ warfare by the intelligent and evil. The pilots are merely carriers of the disease, obedient to a "sad request" whose isolating sorrow they do not share. As the disease and sorrow of their side is the subject of the octave, the subject of the sestet is ours:

> Yet not in us the clear unerring blood:
> Our fit breed germs, our greatest are not free.
> Defective and remote in history
> Our average, our talent and our good.
> The cured years and the well are yet to be;
> Happy their wish and mild to flower and flood.

This says that no matter how wrong they are, we are not therefore in the right—but says it in a way that subtly qualifies the self-rebuke. The metaphors, as in the octave, denote physical illness: our fault is not in our will but in our blood, and so even our greatest are not to be blamed for their unfreedom.

All this changes in the second version. Now the bacillus is reduced from a metaphor to a visual simile; the line about the mild happy wish of the possible future moves to another sonnet (XXIV) where it refers instead to the wish of the modest and humble in the past; and the cured years and the well vanish entirely. It is not disease that afflicts us now but deliberate acts of will, acts no longer indirect but immediate:

> It exists, identified like a bacillus;
> The searchlights focus on it in the sky;
> Those little natures can make cities cry;
> There is a power that has the will to kill us.

> Resist then; be destructive and as strong:
> All killing hurts, but it will always matter
> Whose dust the twelve winds lift and scatter;
> All people are not equal; some are wrong.

The Japanese pilots and their commanders have also virtually disappeared (into another sonnet, XV), and in their place Auden adds a perhaps superfluous exhortation to resist and kill. This has the warlike tone of his essay in *I Believe*, but the sestet qualifies it. The difference between us and them is not that they are wrong and we are right, but that they act on their evil wish while we repress ours in private fantasies and hatreds. But both we and they see our real or intended victims as plural and impersonal:

> Behind each sociable home-loving eye
> The private massacres are taking place;
> All Women, Jews, the Rich, the Human Race.
>
> The mountains cannot judge us when we lie;
> We dwell upon the earth; the earth obeys
> The intelligent and evil till they die.

We dwell upon the earth. Hölderlin had written: "*dichterisch, wohnet der Mensch auf dieser Erde*"—man dwells *poetically* upon this earth. But Auden's final sentence discards the romantic wish that the life we lead might be understood poetically not morally, the wish that in a world without moral absolutes our sense of nature might serve as a criterion for action.* This wish Auden had indulged as early as 1930 when he wrote of the earth as "the virtuous thing," and as late as 1938, a few months before the China sonnets, when he concluded *On the Frontier*

---

* Martin Heidegger used the same phrase from Hölderlin to conclude an argument that Being itself is founded by poetic language, with the implication that there can be no absolutes beyond the fiats of verbal imagination—we dwell *poetically* upon this earth that poetry has made (*Hölderlin und das Wesen der Dichtung*, 1936; the essay has become a touchstone for certain schools of modern literary theory). It is possible but unlikely that Auden read this essay and responded to it in his poem. Probably he and Heidegger independently recognized the power of Hölderlin's phrase to illuminate the ethical crisis brought about by fascism. But Heidegger regarded the phrase as a truth given to Hölderlin in his madness, and used it to deny any reality to ethical judgement, to support a philosophy that celebrated the manifestation of Being in the German national will—as in his praises, three years before, of the heroic rigors of the new Reich. Auden was less willing to justify political madness by poetic madness, and, writing in the same moment of crisis, used Hölderlin's phrase to expose the corruption of any system of thought that regards the ethically neutral powers of language or nature as the measure of all things. *The mountains cannot judge us when we lie.*

by evoking those who die to make man "worthy of the earth." Now he knew better. Earlier that year Louis MacNeice published a book of poems titled *The Earth Compels*. Auden's poem answered: *the earth obeys*.

This is the form the sonnet had reached when Auden prepared a typescript of the sequence for *Journey to a War*. The other sonnets appeared in the book in this typescript version, but Auden revised Sonnet XIV yet once more. He left the sestet unchanged while substituting an entirely new text for the octave. He no longer tells the guns to resist, and he discards all justification for killing. The guns' resistance is now a fact, and the battle is no longer between the actively evil and the evil by intent, but between the warring halves of the human psyche, which share equally in the pain of their guilt. The bombers still will "make us cry," but even before their physical pain assaults us, we feel the psychological hurt that comes when our illusion of safety is broken. Disease, still present in this version, is now as ordinary as a headache, induced not by external enmity but by our own inner struggle between memory and conscience:

> Yes, we are going to suffer, now; the sky
> Throbs like a feverish forehead; pain is real;
> The groping searchlights suddenly reveal
> The little natures that will make us cry,
>
> Who never quite believed they could exist,
> Not where we were. They take us by surprise
> Like ugly long-forgotten memories,
> And like a conscience all the guns resist.

In this final text the poem further justifies its central position by connecting—as does none of the other sonnets—the subject of the sequence's first half, the individual choices made in the past, with that of the second half, today's collective acts of war. The sequence turns on this pivot from various types of action in history to various types of actors in the present: pilots, soldiers, diplomats, the wounded and the exiled, and the dancers who in their natural beauty ignore war entirely. All are defeated or ineffectual, and Auden describes them not as unique responsible figures with singular pronouns, as he did in the first half, but in each instance as a generalized plural *they*. (Only a dead Chinese sol-

dier earns a singular pronoun, too late for it to matter.*) One evil of war
is that it reduces its actors to their anonymous functions.

Not until Sonnet XXIII, "When all the apparatus of report / Con-
firms the triumph of our enemies," can Auden hope to "think of *one*"
who might serve as an example. This is Rilke, emerging in person from
Auden's echoes of his voice, standing now as a model for the independence of poetry from the demands of party or expedience. Rilke's lonely
patience was rewarded by *Die Sonnette an Orpheus*, when after con-
centration and silence, unexpectedly "all his powers spoke, / And
everything was given once for all." But this verbal triumph is not
enough. In the next sonnet Auden balances Rilke's unique poetic iden-
tity with the countless anonymous humble "they" who equally deserve
praise, having had no greater ambition than to love. "They grew ripe
and seeded," and left as their only monument "our better faces," which
are in fact all the memorials they want. It was "the others" who, lacking
love, built monuments of stone. In these two sonnets Auden maintains
his old distinction between individual will and collective flesh, but
begins to sense that where there was isolating antagonism between
them, there might be mutual gratitude instead.

In the penultimate sonnet the thankfulness of Rilke and the mild wish
of the humble combine in Auden's amazed discovery of love's consis-
tency and strength. He finds neither an instinctual Eros separate from
the will nor a faithless desire bound to it, but a new love, one that persists and rewards. The sonnet speaks of these issues in economic metaphors of business cycles, profits, and expansion planning—metaphors
that mischievously violate the decorum of love poetry, but make the serious ethical point that pride defeats itself while love increases and ex-
pands. In the large industrial landscape of our personalities, love is a
"little workshop," at the outskirts of our ambitious projects, "Always far
from the centre of our names." Nonetheless, we chose to build it, even if
we imagine as Auden once did that it came into being instinctively, as
one of the natural functions of the flesh:

---

* There is one sonnet about a dead soldier and another about living ones. The former seems to be the only poem in the sequence actually written in China, in the
spring of 1938, and its first version took a propagandistic buttonholing tone: "Professors of Europe, hostess, citizen, / Respect this boy." Revising this later in the
year Auden lowered his voice: "He neither knew nor chose the Good, but taught us,
/ And added meaning like a comma . . ."

> We can't believe that we ourselves designed it,
> A minor item of our daring plan
> That caused no trouble; we took no notice of it.

Only when "Disaster comes" and our clever hopes expire do we notice its faithful productivity and service:

> we're amazed to find it
> The single project that since work began
> Through all the cycle showed a steady profit.

Without pomp or melodrama Auden has made the one discovery that can release him from his private island. All his daring splendid projects for changes of heart and history led to contradiction and defeat. But his small private hopes, which he had scarcely noticed, brought lasting rewards. For a young poet, praised by the crowd and conscious of his genius, this realization was both unsettling and exhilarating: if he was not so special as he hoped, then he need not be so isolated as he feared. Knowing this did not make the future any easier, but it ended his self-deception about the past. There were errors he need no longer repeat, truths he was at liberty to discover.

Still, the charity of love's workshop was easier to praise than practice. The sequence ends without a conclusion, "Wandering lost upon the mountains of our choice." Once again, in this final sonnet, Auden evokes our fantasies of escape: the dream of a free arcadian past, "the warm nude ages of instinctive poise," and the dream of a planned utopian future where "the disciplined movements of the heart / Can follow for ever and ever its harmless ways." But—and the entire sequence depends on the dialectic implied by this recurring word—"*But* we are articled to error," bound immutably to change. We "were never nude and calm . . . And never will be perfect." We retain our arduous birthright of freedom, "A mountain people dwelling among mountains." A few years before, Auden ended another sonnet sequence on the flood of Eros, a setting as dangerous and uncertain as these mountains. Two years later, in the final poem of his third and last sonnet sequence, he will find solid level ground in the resolved peace of "The Garden."

In 1938 he had taken only the first steps; and in England, after finishing his sonnets, he took the backward step of the verse "Commentary." During September and October, while fulfilling what he took to be his public duties of lectures and speeches, he wrote three hundred lines in the unrhymed triplet form that had given so much trouble in his redemptive poems of 1933–34. Hortatory in Auden's least convincing style, the "Commentary" praises the "civil reconciliation" in China (and tactfully ignores the enmity between Communists and Nationalists that made reconciliation necessary, and also made it limited and pragmatic) and concludes in a triumphant vision of utopian justice. The poem includes a tired version of Auden's tripartite historical schema, using Rome, the Middle Ages, and "the epoch of the Third Great Disappointment"—the modern era of capitalist individualism. In the "Commentary," even at its finest moments, Auden was marking time.

Most of the "Commentary" performs the service promised by its title. It elucidates at great length the historical sonnets in the first half of the sequence, using many schoolmasterly epithets and proper names ("generalising *Hegel* and quiet *Bosanquet*") and none of the irony of comparable passages in *Letter to Lord Byron*. Then it enlarges wordily on the second half of the sequence, while at the same time drastically simplifying the sonnets' moral complexity. The modest anonymous dead of Sonnet XXIV, identified there only by their actions, "not their names," are here elevated into "the Invisible College of the Humble," whence they offer high-sounding admonitions: "Only the free have disposition to be truthful, / Only the truthful have the interest to be just, / Only the just possess the will-power to be free." There is nothing so wooden or circular as these lame formulae anywhere in the sonnets. The "Commentary" ends with the self-contradictory stanza* that sees the forces of the will released to create at last a human justice. This conclusion pretends that the final sonnet in the sequence itself had never been written. After sending the typescript to a friend with a note saying he was "very uncertain whether this kind of thing is possible without becoming a prosy pompous old bore," Auden returned to Brussels for a second visit, and once again wrote what he believed rather than what he felt was expected of him.

---

* Discussed in Chapter IX, p. 199–200.

Auden's ethical imagination had always been divided between the two extremes of solitary authority and passive acceptance, aristocratic mind and obedient flesh. The Airman had begun as a leader and then, accepting the rule of the enemy, crossed over into silent resignation. Michael Ransom, in the same way, first inspired his followers to action, but at last rested silently in his mother's lap. A third alternative, which might resolve these extremes, was implicit in much of Auden's writings, but he did not acknowledge it until now. Trying to overcome division, he had succeeded only in moving from one side to the other; he had not guessed that by *accepting division itself,* he could start a dialectic between its opposing aspects. If a divided self or a divided society could not be made whole, at least each part might consent to learn from each other, and might yet make a vineyard of the curse. If there could be no final concord in the dialogue of mind and flesh, authority and submission, there could be mutual responsibility and aid. The enduring "Social Democracy" that Auden had imagined, where everyone perfectly fulfilled his function, was a lethal fantasy; a responsible dialectical democracy, never resolved, always changing, was the best and only hope for justice. "We live in freedom by necessity." Throughout the 1930s he had hoped for some political or visionary or predestined end to division. It could not happen. In America, when he had given up his last hopes for Utopia, he learned instead to "honour the fate you are," with all its incorrigible divisions, "Travelling and tormented, / Dialectic and bizarre." The endings endured by Ransom and the Airman were misshapen symbols of a new beginning. Instead of wishing vainly for unity, Auden could achieve a dialectic relation. The two worlds, divided less by evolutionary fate than by ignorance and pride, could not merge into one. Yet they could marry.

Shortly after his second arrival in Brussels Auden set out a brief program for his dialectic future. In a note on Byron, written in December 1938 for the anthology *Fifteen Poets* (and not published until 1941), Auden chose to learn from the example of a poet to whom, two years before, he had offered lessons in history. Isolated by his pride in his gift, as Byron had been, Auden now saw that others had isolating burdens of their own and that these might be shared. He was referring implicitly to himself when he wrote that "Byron was an egoist and, like all egoists, capable of falling in love with a succession of dream-figures, but incapable of genuine love or fidelity which accepts a personality completely." Yet Byron, again like Auden, "was not only an egoist; he was also acutely conscious of guilt and sin." In Byron the conjunction of egoism and guilt issued in a defiant irony; in Auden it developed further, into a need for forgiveness. Like all great secular teachers, Byron was an example that could be followed only in part. But Auden's concluding comments somewhat stretch the facts in order to emphasize the lessons he himself must follow now:

> No egoist can become a mature writer until he has learnt to recognize and to accept, a little ruefully perhaps, his egoism. When Byron had ceased to identify his moral sense with himself and had discovered how to extract the Byronic Satanism from his lonely hero and to turn it into the Byronic Irony which illuminated the whole setting, when he realized that he was a little ridiculous, but also not as odd as he had imagined, he became a great poet. For Byron was not really odd like Wordsworth; his experiences were those of the ordinary man. . . .
>
> . . . he fashioned a style of poetry which for speed, wit, and moral seriousness combined with lack of pulpit pomposity is unique, and a lesson to all young would-be writers who are conscious of similar temptations and defects.

"Young would-be writers" was a phrase that referred implicitly to Auden at thirty-two, as he looked to a new start in America.

He devoted five of the sonnets he wrote during this second stay in Brussels to artists and writers, each chosen for his personal relevance as an object lesson. Two poems served as warnings of entrapment in one or the other of the two worlds: "Rimbaud" renouncing poetry for action, "A. E. Housman" withdrawing into pedantry and nostalgia. Two further poems suggested ways of countering these temptations. To avoid Rimbaud's silence Auden looked to the example of "The Novelist," who grows out of the egoistic "boyish gift" of the romantic poet into an adult sense of common humanity. And the counter-example to Housman's "savage footnotes" was the "absolute gift" of "The Composer," whose art is "unable to say an existence is wrong." Auden took details for these two sonnets from the lives of Isherwood and Britten, but in the poems the novelist and composer are types, not individuals, and their actions have a religious resonance. In the novelist's willingness to "suffer dully all the wrongs of Man" is a muted hint of Christian atonement;* while the composer's music officiates at a metaphoric Communion, pouring out its "presence" and "forgiveness like a wine."

Both novelist and composer reconcile, one by suffering, the other by praise. For an example of reconciliation in the realm of poetry, Auden chose none of the great masters, but the modest figure of Edward Lear. Whenever he wrote that he hoped to be ranked on Parnassus with "Firbank, Potter, Carroll, Lear," Auden deliberately—and disdainfully—gave weapons to critics innocent of irony, but he was also making a serious point about his poetic ambitions. These were all writers who had absolutely no wish to write anything more grandiose than their gifts allowed. By the time Auden began his career, the romantic parabola of youthful ambition and self-praise leading to middle-aged disillusionment and self-pity had long been a matter of routine. Auden preferred to follow poets like Shakespeare who had better things to worry about than their aspirations, and who were able to achieve what they attempted because their reach was exactly equal to their grasp. So, in his sonnet on Edward Lear (written a few days after his return from Brussels in January 1939), Auden portrays a poet who, like Byron, fulfilled his gift when he accepted its real nature. Lear began in fear and self-hatred, "But guided by tears he successfully reached his Regret." Acknowledging and accepting his fears, he transformed them into comic art. Starting out as a lonely voyager, like Auden in search of islands, he grew to be the goal of other voyagers: "Children swarmed to him like settlers. He became a land."

An artist's conciliation with his gift corresponded to a citizen's concern for his city. In earlier years Auden justified his civic detachment by a series of romantic and utopian arguments—an artist's mind was too complex and abstract to be soiled with politics; poets belong a little outside the group; there could be no obligations to society until society made itself worthy of love; public life was ruled by self-destroying madmen; and so on. In Brussels he began to renounce all these evasions.

"The Capital," probably the first poem he wrote there, is a throwback to his earlier styles, a detached survey of the city's temptations and de-

---

* Auden's seriously unserious style allows this resonance to coincide with an allusion to Isherwood's recent case of the clap.

lusions. But "Brussels in Winter," although also a threnody of urban desolation, has traces of a different attitude. "The homeless and the really humbled" in this poem, if they have nothing else, at least "Seem to be sure exactly where they are, / And in their misery are all assembled." And in the poem's concluding lines, "fifty francs will earn the stranger right / To warm the heartless city in his arms." This bitterly unequal bargain—the stranger pays to give his own warmth to the city—scarcely marries the private and public worlds, but it prefigures their union in a distorted and inverse form. The sexual metaphor in this poem is Auden's first intimation of his later sense of responsibility to the imperfect city.

As for Auden's simplifying fantasy that no one was consciously responsible for political catastrophe, that Hitler and Franco were trapped in involuntary manias, that totalitarianism was a problem in medicine not ethics—the six lines of "Epitaph on a Tyrant" repudiate all this. The tyrant of this poem (written, like "Edward Lear," just after Auden's return from Brussels) is neither the apocalyptic madman of "Danse Macabre" nor the compliant simpleton of *On the Frontier*, but a sharp-witted perfectionist, even something of a polymath:

> the poetry he invented was easy to understand;
> He knew human folly like the back of his hand,
> And was greatly interested in armies and fleets.

His death will bring no peace; terror will find other agents. A dictator exits in "Epitaph on a Tyrant," but in "Gare du Midi" an anonymous figure enters the scene, "to infect a city / Whose terrible future may have just arrived."

However it might arrive, the future was certain to bring pain. Auden had already begun to accept in himself the dull ordinariness of suffering, but responsibility for others' suffering was a different matter. Writing of the wounded in *In Time of War*, he could only "stand elsewhere" and observe. Now, in Brussels, standing before the Brueghels in the Musées Royaux des Beaux-Arts, he began to sense a more immediate relation.

"Musée des Beaux Arts" is a poem that pointedly rejects the grand manner of *Spain* and of the Auden-Isherwood plays—where the crucial agon happened at the "heart" or the summit, at the highest point of a rhetorical flight. The truth was considerably less dramatic. As Auden said in a broadcast a few weeks later, "War is untidy, inefficient, obscure." In one of his China sonnets he concluded gratefully that love's obscure workshop mattered more than the grandiose projects of the will. "Musée des Beaux Arts" reaches a similar but more disturbing conclusion about pain. Brueghel's *The Fall of Icarus*—like the other paintings alluded to in the poem, *The Numbering at Bethlehem* and *The Massacre of the Innocents*—quietly points out that events of the greatest pathos and importance occur in settings that seem to be out at the edge of history, ordinary places where we pursue our normal unobservant lives. The poetic imagination that seeks out grandeur and sublimity could scarcely be bothered with those insignificant figures lost in the background or in the crowd. But Auden sees in them an example of Christianity's great and enduring transformation of classical rhetoric: its inversion of the principle that the most important subjects require the highest style. If the sufferings of a carpenter turned preacher mattered more to the world than the doom of princes, then the high style, for all its splendor, was a limited instrument, more suitable to the narrow intensities of personal isolation than to the infinite complexities of responsibility and relationship.

Auden's later work would follow Brueghel's example, to the bafflement of critics who preferred bright colors and loud noises. The Old Masters he accepted as his teachers in "Musée des Beaux Arts" were never awed by the grand rhetoric of History or by appeals to the autonomy of art. Their subject was the human clay; their sympathy extended to the silent and the obscure; and about suffering they were never wrong. They understood how readily we ignore its true nature,

> how it takes place
> While someone else is eating or opening a window or just walking
> dully along . . .

In Brueghel's *Icarus*, for instance: how everything turns away
Quite leisurely from the disaster . . .

These casually irregular lines make none of the demands for action and attention that marked Auden's earlier harangues on the urgency of the times, yet beneath the apparent surface disorder a deeper pattern of connectedness gradually makes itself felt. The unassertive rhymes, easily overlooked on a first reading, hold the poem together: they affirm, with Brueghel, that suffering is no less crucial because it happens somewhere else, or when we are too busy to notice.

Whether or not we are aware of it, our connection with others' suffering is inescapably real. "Musée des Beaux Arts" comes close to spelling out that connection in its final lines, but does not quite do so. In Brueghel's *Icarus*, these last lines report,

> the expensive delicate ship that must have seen
> Something amazing, a boy falling out of the sky,
> Had somewhere to get to and sailed calmly on.

This is another view of one of the ships that diverged on urgent voluntary errands in "Look, stranger." But now that ship has a different aspect: it leaves behind not merely a holiday island but isolated suffering and death. What is implicit in this, and will soon become manifest in Auden's writings, is his recognition that a "voluntary errand" does not merely ignore suffering but causes it. All acts of will, all errands that have "somewhere to get to," exert force over a person or object outside the self. There is always someone who gets in the way, deliberately or by chance, someone who must be dealt with, because hunger allows no choice. The animal victim who died at the origin of language—as Auden had imagined in his essay on "Writing"—proved to have a human shape and a human face. What in the words of a later poem is "revealed to a child in some chance rhyme / Like *will* and *kill*, comes to pass / Before we realize it." In the public realm as in the private one the will demands its victim.

And this most of all is why it needs forgiveness. The only answer to the isolating will is the absolute gift of pardon. Until Auden learned to distinguish between hunger and love, between will and responsibility, he could not accept the forgiveness he required, and could not give faithful love.

At the start of 1939 he was still on his island. But he was ready to begin his personal and public life anew, and was ready to begin alone. After years of resistance, he knew he had chosen his isolation and could accept another future.

Epilogue

Mutual forgiveness of each vice:
Such are the Gates of Paradise.
—BLAKE

Auden's early poetry is the record of his passage from indifference to forgiveness. When the latter word first appeared in his work, in the second of the "1929" poems, it was still trapped in *unforgiveness*. Man could not find wholeness; "unforgiving is in his living." A few lines later, the poem celebrates a moment of isolation in nature and memory, a moment when the poet stands "Without wishing and with forgiving." But, as the final "1929" poem acknowledges by making death a condition of love, this forgiveness is hollow. To be without wishing is to do nothing that needs others' forgiveness in return. As Auden wrote in *Horae Canonicae* twenty years later, "It is only our victim who is without a wish." In his vision of agape in 1933 Auden had imagined for the first time a love that could "Forgive the murderer in his glass" but whose reign he could only hope to see in an apocalyptic future. Not until *New Year Letter* in 1940 could he thank his friend Elizabeth Mayer for showing by her own example that "*always* there are such as you, / Forgiving, helping what we do."

Both *forgiveness* and *pardon* have their root in the verb *to give*, or *donare*. As Auden had guessed in 1938, it was the gift of charity that reconciled where all else failed. It could reconcile even the past and the present. In the elegy he wrote for Yeats in his first weeks in America, Yeats's "gift survived it all," and now spoke to the living. In another elegy later that year, Auden praised Freud's charity, his wish to share the gifts of mercy that restore and recover:

> he would *unite*
> *The unequal moieties* fractured
> By our own well-meaning sense of justice,

> Would *restore* to the larger the wit and will
> The smaller possesses but can only use
> For arid disputes, would *give back* to
> The son the mother's richness of feeling.

These elegies are unlike any others. Instead of a conventional mourning for a lost perfection that we must distantly observe and then leave behind, they use the example of the dead in order to teach the living. When Yeats elegizes Major Robert Gregory, in life an admirable man but of no extraordinary distinction, as "Soldier, scholar, horseman, he, / And all he did done perfectly," it is an inspiring vision, but you and I must give up hope of doing likewise. When Auden elegizes Yeats and Freud, men of whose greatness we need not be persuaded, he emphasizes that they performed extraordinary deeds despite their ordinary imperfections. Yeats "was silly like us," Freud "wasn't clever at all," yet they learned to use the gifts they had, and so might we.

In "Orpheus" Auden wrote of the poet whose charm is so powerful he *makes* the trees move; he does not give them any choice in the matter. But as Auden would write in his elegy for Yeats, poetry *makes* nothing happen. "Orpheus who moved stones," he wrote some years later, "is the archetype, not of the poet, but of Goebbels." The poet who fulfills his gift does not enchant his readers but teaches them their capabilities. And what he can teach best is the capability of their language to respond to the real world in which they live. It was no loss to a poet that he could not charm his readers out of the difficult world of time into the intensity of the image or an eternity of pure form. It was poetry's triumph that it could, even "In the prison of his days / Teach the free man how to praise."

NOTES
AND
INDEX

Reference Notes

For Auden's writings before 1939 I refer wherever possible to the text in *The English Auden* and to the new (1979) edition of *Selected Poems;* both these volumes print the early texts of poems Auden revised in his collected and selected editions published between 1945 and 1976. For work written after 1939 I give a page reference to the 1976 *Collected Poetry,* whenever its reading is substantially the same as the original version quoted in my text, and refer also to the 1979 *Selected Poems.* For work not found in these volumes I cite readily available clothbound reprints if these preserve the original readings. Otherwise, references are to the first editions. Works by other authors that have been published in various reset editions are normally cited by chapter or section number rather than by a page reference to one specific edition. I cite texts or translations that were available to Auden in the 1930s; more recent versions (as in the case of Freud) may differ very slightly. I hope learned readers will accept the customary apology for overannotation; at least there are no flyspeck numbers in the text to cause needless distraction.

These abbreviations are used for books by Auden:

AF6   *The Ascent of F6,* by Auden and Christopher Isherwood (second Faber edition, 1937, and its clothbound reprints; where I cite the 1936 first edition, this is indicated in parentheses)

CP   *Collected Poems* (Faber or Random House editions, 1976)

DBS   *The Dog Beneath the Skin,* by Auden and Isherwood (Faber edition, 1935, and all Faber reprints)

DD   *The Dance of Death* (Faber edition, 1933)

EA   *The English Auden* (Faber or Random House editions, 1978)

FAA   *Forewords and Afterwords* (Faber or Random House editions, 1973, and all reprints)

LFI   *Letters From Iceland*, by Auden and Louis MacNeice (second Faber edition, 1967, and second Random House edition, 1969)

OTF   *On the Frontier*, by Auden and Isherwood (Faber edition, 1938)

SP   *Selected Poems: New Edition* (Faber or Vintage editions, 1979)

Full bibliographical details of Auden's writings through 1969 may be found in *W. H. Auden: A Bibliography*, by B. C. Bloomfield and Edward Mendelson, second edition (University Press of Virginia, 1972).

Locations of manuscripts and typescripts, and the present owners of letters no longer in the hands of their recipients, are given in parentheses. These abbreviations are used:

Berg   The Henry W. and Albert A. Berg Collection of English and American Literature, The New York Public Library, Astor, Lenox, and Tilden Foundations

BL   British Library Manuscript Room

HRC   The Humanities Research Center, The University of Texas at Austin

I am grateful to the curators of these and other libraries for their help and for permission to quote from manuscripts in their care.

All previously unpublished writings of W. H. Auden quoted in this book are copyright © 1981 by the Executors of The Estate of W. H. Auden, and may not be reproduced without written permission. The quotation from Benjamin Britten's diary in Chapter XII is © 1981 by the Executors of The Britten Estate, and may not be reproduced without written permission.

INTRODUCTION

xiii   "the construction and": *FAA* 502

"I decided, or": *A Certain World* (1970), p. 424

xiv   "Plain cooking made": *CP* 470

"Riddles and all": *The Dyer's Hand* (1962), p. 47

"It is no doubt": *A Certain World*, p. 423

xv   "forbid automatic responses": *CP* 642

xvi   "have won their own discipline": Eliot, "*Ulysses*, Order, and Myth," rptd. in *Selected Prose* (1975)

"A man who does": Yeats, "The Fisherman"

"lords over fact": Pound, "Vorticism," rptd. in *Gaudier-Brzeska* (1916)

xvii   "dissociation of sensibility": Eliot, "The Metaphysical Poets"
        "break the pentameter": Pound, "Canto LXXXI"
        "a formless age": Eliot, "The Possibility of a Poetic Drama," in *The Sacred Wood* (1920)
xviii   "force, . . . dislocate": Eliot, "The Metaphysical Poets"
        "*JE est un*": Rimbaud, letter to Paul Demeny, 15 May 1871
        "The pure work": Mallarmé, "*Crise de Vers,*" in "*Variations sur un sujet*"
xix   "by a singular": Balzac, *Illusions Perdues,* part 2, ch. 8
xx   "a sort of gutless": Orwell, *The Road to Wigan Pier* (1937), ch. 11; Orwell retracts the phrase in *Inside the Whale* (1940)
        "Fighters for no": *EA* 28
        "who were doing": *SP* 91; revised text, *CP* 215
        "rather the": Eliot, "Last Words," *Criterion,* January 1939
        "great labour": Eliot, "Tradition and the Individual Talent"
xxi   "probably / were among": *CP* 521; *SP* 256
xxii   when Jungian terminology: "A Literary Transference," *Southern Review,* Summer 1940, p. 80; rptd. in *Hardy: A Collection of Critical Essays,* ed. Albert J. Guerard (1963), p. 137
xxiii   "a game of": Nabokov, *Conclusive Evidence* (1951), ch. 6; rptd. in *Speak, Memory* (1966), ch. 6
        "In so far": *The Dyer's Hand,* p. 27

I: THE EXILED WORD

3   "the divided face": *EA* 53
        "Sentries against inner": *EA* 33
        "frontier-conscious": *EA* 106; *SP* 20
        "One sold all": *EA* 26
        "Consider this and": *EA* 46; *SP* 14
        "The Airman's Alphabet": *EA* 79
4   "They ignored his": *EA* 25; *SP* 3
        "Did not believe": *EA* 28
        "he dreams of": *EA* 7
        "winter for earth": *EA* 40; *SP* 11
        "snow down to": *EA* 109; *SP* 24
        "this . . . the Age": *EA* 32
        "sound behind our": *EA* 56
5   "the peace-time stories": *EA* 106; *SP* 20
        "sheer off from": *EA* 29
        "Our old right": *EA* 26
6   "They forget": *EA* 15

"Before this loved": *EA* 31

7   "The sexual act": MS Journal (Berg); similarly all quotations identi-
     fied as appearing in the journal Auden kept in 1929
     "cheek to cheek": *EA* 30
     Edouard Roditi: His draft translation with Auden's MS comments
       [November 1931] (UCLA)
     "the problem of": *Criterion,* January 1932, p. 318

8   "Is first baby": *EA* 38; *SP* 9
     "For love recover": *EA* 55; *SP* 18
     "Needs more than": *EA* 40; *SP* 12
     "new conditions": *EA* 40; *SP* 11
     "Prolonged drowning shall": *EA* 12

9   "Winter for earth": *EA* 40; *SP* 11
     "complete" beauty of a child: *EA* 52; *SP* 16
     "Completeness of gesture": *EA* 38; *SP* 10
     "tall unwounded leader": *EA* 28
     "truly strong man": *EA* 37; *SP* 8
     "Neither in the": *EA* 96
     "on the arm": *EA* 37; *SP* 7
     Yeats uses *labour:* "Among School Children"
     "absolute unity": *EA* 38; *SP* 10

11   "Only remembering": *EA* 54; *SP* 17

12   "Have things gone": *EA* 49
     "It is later": *EA* 47; *SP* 15

13   "Can speak of": *EA* 2
     "Often the man": *EA* 5
     "I used to try": Letter to unidentified recipient, 8 November 1937
       (HRC)

14   Stephen Spender implied: "Five Notes on W. H. Auden's Writing,"
       Twentieth Century, July 1932
     "But there waited": Charles Madge, "Letter to the Intelligentsia," *New
       Country,* ed. Michael Roberts (1933), p. 231

15   "the dreadful literary": MS Journal (Berg)
     "Writing": *EA* 303

16   "Wystan Auden (born 1907)": *An Outline for Boys and Girls and
       Their Parents,* ed. Naomi Mitchison (1932), p. 851; cf. letter to
       Mitchison, 4 March 1932 (Berg)

17   "They're looking for you": *EA* 110; *SP* 20
     "The game is up": *EA* 47; *SP* 15
     "Do not imagine": *EA* 45; *SP* 14
     "Among the foes": *EA* 122
     "It is time": *EA* 40; *SP* 11

"Get there if": *EA* 48

"Brothers, who when": *EA* 120

18 "It's no use": *EA* 42

"increasing attraction for": *EA* 314

19 "No. I am": Letter to Rupert Doone, 19 October 1932 (Berg)

"sounded note is": *CP* 340; *SP* 174

"The Garrison": *CP* 633

20 "The failure of": *EA* 315

"You cannot train": *Criterion*, January 1933, p. 289

"without a cement": *CP* 484; *SP* 229

22 "Much more research": *EA* 91

23 "the smaller group": *EA* 105

"Re groups and": Letter to John Pudney, 28 July 1932 (Berg)

24 "Create the group": "To a Young Man on His Twenty-First Birthday," *New Oxford Outlook*, May 1933, p. 73; "when" emended to "where" as in MS Notebook (Harvard) and MS (Isherwood)

"Permit our town": *EA* 421

"Everyone knows": *EA* 325

"these movements use": "The Group Movement and the Middle Classes," *Oxford and the Groups*, ed. R. H. S. Crossman (1934), p. 98

26 "essential first step": Heard (as described in text), p. 307

II: THE WATERSHED

27 "At nineteen": *FAA* 513

"Crazes had come": *EA* 194

"de la Mare": "A Literary Transference," *Southern Review*, Summer 1940, p. 78; rptd. in *Hardy: A Collection of Critical Essays*, ed. Albert J. Guerard (1963), p. 135; spelling corrected

28 Politicians, he told his friends: Cf. Stephen Spender, "W. H. Auden and His Poetry," *Atlantic Monthly*, July 1953; rptd. in *Auden: A Collection of Critical Essays*, ed. Monroe K. Spears (1964)

"the formation of": "Preface" by Auden and C. Day-Lewis, *Oxford Poetry 1927*, p. v (this passage by Auden)

"through the quads": *EA* 195

"read it, at": Tom Driberg, *Ruling Passions* (1977), p. 58

29 "In Spring we": "In Due Season," *Oxford Outlook*, December 1926, p. 298

"Under such pines": "Consequences," *Oxford University Review*, 18 November 1926, p. 177

"This peace can": *EA* 437

"Can change me": This early reading is from MS (Isherwood), printed in Isherwood's *Lions and Shadows* (1938), p. 187; the revised reading quoted in my footnote is from Auden's *Poems* (1928), reprinted in *EA* 437

30   "Taller to-day": *EA* 26; *SP* 3

"The Letter" ("He reads and"): *Oxford Poetry 1926*, p. 4

"Your letter comes": *EA* 25; *SP* 2

31   "Consider if you": *EA* 438

"On the frontier": *EA* 440

32   "Who stands, the": *EA* 22; *SP* 1

33   "hawk's vision": *Southern Review* (as above), p. 83

35   "Utterly lost": *CP* 271

"Control of the": *EA* 25; *SP* 3

36   "The crowing of": *EA* 23

"Am I really": Letter to Naomi Mitchison, 28 October 1930 (Berg)

37   "When life fails": *EA* 43

"real meeting": *EA* 31

"pairing off in": *EA* 27

"Upon this line": *EA* 32

38   "Renewal of traditional": MS (Isherwood); published posthumously in *Pearl* (Odense), Autumn 1976, p. 1

"Although your medium": MS (Isherwood)

39   "made a slum": *EA* 11

"Watch any day": *EA* 31; *SP* 24

"The silly fool": *EA* 34

40   "The question is": Another entry from the 1929 MS Journal (Berg)

41   "Freud's not quite": *EA* 198

43   "raw provincial": *EA* 195

44   "Doom is dark": *EA* 55; *SP* 18

III: FAMILY GHOSTS

47   "ancestral curse": *EA* 29

Paid on Both Sides: EA 1

"A parable of": MS note [1942] in copy of *Poems* (1934) (Albert and Angelyn Stevens)

48   "His mother and": *EA* 17

50   "makes us well": *EA* 12

52   "All pasts": *EA* 12

"These I remember": *EA* 14

53   "They refuse to": Letter to Isherwood, n.d. [August 1928]

54   "staying with a": Letter to David Ayerst, n.d. [August 1928]

"To throw away": *EA* 12

55 "It may examine": These lines are from MS Notebook (Berg)
56 "I met a": *EA* 195
57 "There is the": *EA* 11
59 "I am having": Letter to W. L. McElwee, 31 December 1928 (BL)
    "This is a": Letter to W. L. McElwee, n.d. [Summer 1929] (BL)
    "certain occult": *CP* 535; *SP* 274
    "The only duality": *EA* 302
    "cancel the inertia": *EA* 31; *SP* 4
60 "On Sunday walks": *EA* 33
61 "The strings' excitement": *EA* 32
    "scamper after darlings": *EA* 7
62 "backward love": *EA* 31
    "this despair with": The MS reading "better" is from MS Notebook
        (W. S. Johnson)
    "My family ghosts": *CP* 638
64 "simply for mental": Hardy, *The Dynasts*, preface

IV: THE EVOLUTIONARY DEFILE

67 "I want something": Roditi's TS with Auden's MS comments [No-
        vember 1931] (UCLA)
69 "Coming out of": *EA* 37; *SP* 8
70 "Seen clearly, man's": Burrow, p. 131
73 "non-communistic self": MS Journal (Berg)
    "Out of the common": MS (Isherwood)
74 "sheer off from": *EA* 29
75 "Startled by the": MS (Isherwood)
76 "Body and mind": MS Notebook (BL Add. MS. 52430)
    "The reason is": *EA* 302
77 "The account of": *EA* 418
78 "the recognition of": Burrow (as above), p. 133
    "In sanitoriums they": This quotes the published text as in *EA* 40; *SP*
        12 gives an MS revision from around 1931–32 which Auden ne-
        glected in later editions, changing "The intricate play of the mind"
        to "To censor the play of the mind"—from MS note in copy of
        Poems (1930) (Bodleian)
79 "Which of you": *EA* 41
80 "All organic life": Lane, p. 177
    "pompous trash": Letter to Naomi Mitchison, 28 October 1930
        (Berg)
    "It's no use": *EA* 42
81 "Since you are": *EA* 44; *SP* 12

"For you amusements": These lines from MS Notebook (W. S. Johnson)

82   "Consider if you": *EA* 438
"This lunar beauty": *EA* 52; *SP* 16

83   "refuse the tasks": *CP* 407
"Schoolchildren": *EA* 216

V: TRICKSTER AND TRIBE

84   "From scars where": *EA* 28
85   a drunken purposeless drive: Cf. Isherwood, *Lions and Shadows*
(1938), p. 269
"Will you turn": *EA* 35; *SP* 5
86   title from Blake: From "Auguries of Innocence"
87   "Sir, no man's": *EA* 36; *SP* 7
88   "To have found": *EA* 43
searchlights: *EA* 36; *SP* 7 ("Cover in time with beams those in retreat")
"sidecar" and "C.P.S.": *EA* 4
89   "Consider this and": *EA* 46; *SP* 14
"Get there if": *EA* 48
90   "a text book of": Postcard to Naomi Mitchison, n.d. [April 1930]
(Berg)
"The friends of": MS (Isherwood)
91   "I saw them": MS (Isherwood)
92   "Bring joy, bring": *EA* 56; *SP* 19
"To ask the": *EA* 54; *SP* 17
"Is beginning history": MS (Isherwood)
93   *The Orators*: *EA* 59
94   "a case of": *CP* 15
95   "On the whole": Letter to Pudney, n.d. [April 1931] (Berg)
96   "As a rule": *The Orators*, 3rd edn. (1966), p. 7
"I feel this": Letter to T. S. Eliot, n.d. [?March 1932] (Valerie Eliot)
97   "dance of males": *EA* 65
"In a sense": Letter to Mitchison, 12 August 1931 (Berg)
102   "Mourning and Melancholia": Quoted from translation in Freud's *Collected Papers*, vol. 4 (1925), p. 163
103   "the crucial problem": *EA* 91
"Self-care is": *EA* 73
"One must draw": *EA* 84
"awareness of interdependence": *EA* 75
"real ancestor": *EA* 85

"avenge": *EA* 84

"absorption," "self-destruction": *EA* 93

"I am now": Letter to Mitchison, 12 August 1931 (Berg)

104   "*Orators* / I am": Letter to Mrs. Kuratt, 16 August 1932 (Lockwood Memorial Library, SUNY at Buffalo)

105   "well-known epileptic": Layard, p. 521

"The new batch": *EA* 88

"The aeroplane has": *EA* 76

"ancestor worship": *EA* 82

"ghost stories": *EA* 76

106   "likeness," "awareness of difference," "the Airman is": *EA* 75 (the last of these is in capitals in the original)

"whatever you do": *EA* 77

"Though there appears": Layard, p. 504

107   "such as is": Layard, p. 549

"A system organises": *EA* 73

108   "catchwords": *EA* 82

"The effect of": *EA* 73

"theft, that attempt": *Criterion*, July 1932, p. 752

"My whole life": *EA* 93

109   "I have crossed": *EA* 85

"nerves are in": *The Poems of Wilfred Owen* (1931), pp. 36 and 38

"O understand darling": *EA* 94

110   "the suppression of": Layard, p. 524

"nearly all homosexual": *Criterion*, January 1933, p. 289

111   "the Stigmata of": Letter to John Layard, n.d. [February 1930] (Richard Layard)

112   "Religion is the": Marx, "A Contribution to the Critique of Hegel's *Philosophy of Right:* Introduction"

114   "Can't bear this": MS note [1942] in copy of *Poems* (1934) (Albert and Angelyn Stevens)

"Enemy Gambits": *EA* 86

116   "a place / I may": *CP* 521; *SP* 255

VI: PRIVATE PLACES

117   "I think that": *Échanges*, December 1931, p. 170

118   "In criticizing a": *Criterion*, January 1932, p. 319

119   "Private faces": *EA* 59

"Get there if": *EA* 48

"Bishops and headmasters": MS (Isherwood)

120   "Bob and Miss Belmairs": All edns. of *The Orators* prior to *EA*
       "Middleton Murry's": MS Notebook (Harvard); *EA* 105
121   "Beethameer, Beethameer": *EA* 86
       "possible bases": *EA* 76, but with Auden's original misspellings of
           place names left uncorrected (save for a probable typographical
           error)
122   "The couples are": *EA* 106
       "Between attention and": *EA* 52
123   "Who will endure": *EA* 53
       "We have brought": *EA* 77
       "There are some": *EA* 89
124   "That night when": *EA* 113
       "For what as": *EA* 113
125   "A Happy New Year": *EA* 444
       "Now from my": *EA* 115; MS reading from MS Notebook (Har-
           vard)
127   "put a limit": Lawrence, ch. 14
128   "O Love, the": *EA* 118; *SP* 25
129   "Son of a": *EA* 145
       "Problems of Education": *EA* 314
       "an unsatisfactory educational": *Criterion*, April 1933, p. 537
       "Education, whatever it": *EA* 315
       "In the meantime": *EA* 314
130   "It is going": *EA* 312
       "isolated, feel themselves": *EA* 315
       "dual conceptions": *EA* 302
131   "Whoever possesses the": *Criterion*, January 1933, p. 289
       "masterful images because": Yeats, "The Circus Animals' Desertion"
132   "all the gyres": Yeats, "There"
133   "part of the environment": *EA* 318
       "Who to their": *EA* 116
       "The Witnesses": *EA* 126
       a dream vision in cantos: MS Notebook (Swarthmore College); pub-
           lished posthumously in *Review of English Studies*, August 1978,
           pp. 281–309
134   "mind is the": Lawrence, *Psychoanalysis and the Unconscious* (1921),
           ch. 6
       "What's in your": *EA* 56
135   "blind action without": *EA* 321
       "Pick a quarrel": MS Journal (Berg); *EA* 50
       "Gerhart Meyer": *EA* 37; *SP* 8
       "the transformation of": *EA* 320

VII: LOOKING FOR LAND

137   "you must first": *EA* 317
138   "some kind of revolution": *EA* 317
      "If we want": *Criterion*, January 1933, p. 289
      "Education succeeds social": *ibid.*
      "unconsciously the liberal": *EA* 313
      "The chimneys are": *EA* 116
139   "communist orator": *EA* 421
140   "What we do": *EA* 421
141   "super-consciousness": Heard, *The Ascent of Humanity* (1929), p. 6
      "O Love, the": *EA* 118; *SP* 25
142   "called out of": *New Country*, ed. Michael Roberts (1933), p. 194
143   "unhappy poet": *EA* 422
144   "driven not by": Heard, *Social Substance of Religion* (1931), p. 311
      "I have a": *EA* 123
145   "O what is": *EA* 125; *SP* 26
146   "What is the": *Criterion*, January 1933, p. 289
148   "my epic": Letter to Naomi Mitchison, 18 October 1932 (Berg); the
      poem was published posthumously in *Review of English Studies*,
      August 1978, pp. 281–309, with a commentary by Lucy McDiarmid
      to which I am deeply indebted
149   "limen . . . rises between": Heard, p. 89
150   "outer, executive, unstable": Heard, p. 30
151   "as I didn't": letter to Henry Bamford Parkes, 6 December 1932
      (Colby College)
      "the army of": *DBS* 174
      "a society defeated": Spender, "The Poetic Dramas of W. H. Auden
      and Christopher Isherwood," *New Writing*, Autumn 1938; rptd. in
      his *The Thirties and After* (1978)
152   "The month was": MS Notebook (Swarthmore College); punctuation
      supplied as in *EA* 130
154   "far from the": *EA* 26; *SP* 3
      "deep in clear": *EA* 40; *SP* 12
      "Hearing of harvests": *EA* 135; *SP* 28

VIII: LUCKY THIS POINT

159   "a new chapter": *CP* 16
160   "Since I cannot": *FAA* 69
161   "intensity of attention": *EA* 319
163   "To return to": *EA* 87

"I have a handsome": *EA* 123
"O Love, the": *EA* 118; *SP* 25
164   "Out on the lawn": *EA* 136; *SP* 29
168   "So, to remember": *CP* 325; *SP* 148
"this round O": *CP* 249; *SP* 114
172   "ghosts must do": *EA* 55; *SP* 17
174   "For it is not meters": Emerson, "The Poet"
"this filthy modern": Yeats, "The Statues"
175   "Reflections on *Vers Libre*": rptd. in Eliot's *To Criticize the Critic* (1965) and *Selected Prose* (1975)
"martyr to corns": "Foreword," B. C. Bloomfield, *W. H. Auden: A Bibliography* (1st edn., 1964), p. viii
176   "We are left": *CP* 480; *SP* 224
"large the hate": *AF6* 122
"stand where luck": *EA* 146

IX: THE GREAT DIVIDE

177   "Unable to choose": This is from the *c.* 1942 revised text in *CP* 107; the original 1933 reading in *EA* 145 is "Son of a nurse and doctor, loaned a room"
"The liberal appetite": *EA* 151; *SP* 33
"Heaven and Hell": *EA* 361
178   "for our greater": MS (Valerie Eliot), MS (BBC Written Archives Centre); published posthumously in *TLS*, 16 January 1976, p. 53
179   "From natural scenery": *EA* 172
"Easily, my dear": *EA* 152; *SP* 33
"the phases of": *LFI* 234
"To think like": Yeats, *Dramatis Personae* (1936), §4; rptd. in *Autobiography* (1938) and *Autobiographies* (1955)
180   "Personally the kind": *EA* 360
"Time the destroyer": *LFI* 91
181   "These moods give": *EA* 144
"Language of moderation": *EA* 145
"unmasking hidden conflicts": *EA* 351
"Make action urgent": *EA* 157; cf. *EA* 329
"Let us honour": *EA* 19 (dedicatory poem to *Poems* [1930 and 1933])
"exemplify most completely": *EA* 321
"A shilling life": *EA* 150
182   "Mountains": *CP* 428; *SP* 206
"Others like us": *OTF* 122

"without . . . the immense": *EA* 222

183   "There must be": "The Group Movement and the Middle Classes," *Oxford and the Groups*, ed. R. H. S. Crossman (1934), p. 94

184   "The problem of": *ibid.*, p. 100

"Modern Liberalism": *ibid.*, p. 96

185   "international democracy": *EA* 338

"There is a rough": "Honest Doubt," *New Verse*, June–July 1936, p. 16 (this piece is signed J. B. but is unquestionably by Auden; cf. MS at HRC)

186   "for whom it": "Poet and Politician," *Common Sense*, January 1940, p. 23

"the clever hopes": *EA* 245; *SP* 86

"You must of": Letter to John Johnson, n.d. [early 1935]

187   "Do not speak": *EA* 280; *DBS* 155

"People and civilizations": "Lowes Dickinson," *Scrutiny*, December 1934, p. 306

"the period of": "John Skelton," *The Great Tudors*, ed. Katharine Garvin (1935), p. 57

188   "just beginning": *EA* 337; the chart appears on *EA* 338

190   "a quack religion": *EA* 352

191   "The Creatures": *EA* 158

193   "The young *Rimbaud*": *CP* 164

194   "The match of": *EA* 199

"reflect on one's": *LFI* 139

"One goes North": Louis MacNeice, *I Crossed the Minch* (1938), p. 18

195   "Obsessing our private": *EA* 245; *SP* 86

"If you have": *LFI* 28

"I so dislike": Letter to E. R. Dodds, n.d. [December 1936] (Bodleian)

"I am not": Letter to E. R. Dodds, 8 December 1936 (Bodleian)

196   "Any disillusionment": Unpublished interview with Timothy Foote, 1963

197   "To my astonishment": *Modern Canterbury Pilgrims*, ed. James A. Pike (1956), p. 41

"everywhere there are": *EA* 361

198   "only offer two": *EA* 361

"Our hours of": *EA* 425; *SP* 54

"Here danger works": *EA* 263

199   "among the just": *EA* 269

"O happy the": MS (Isherwood); *EA* 288

200   "We are articled": *EA* 262

political exigence: Reported by Spender, *World Within World* (1951), p. 247

201   "the bulk of": *EA* 358

"never hesitate to": "In Defence of Gossip," *Listener*, 22 December 1937, p. 1372 (Auden's italics)

"infected with an": "Foreword," B. C. Bloomfield, *W. H. Auden: A Bibliography* (1st edn., 1964), p. viii

"vain fornications": *CP* 485; *SP* 230

202   Anxiety found itself: These similes may be found at *EA* 260, 236, 238, 265, 238

"preacher's loose immodest": *CP* 165

203   "Remember that there": Coleridge, "On Poesy or Art"

204   "mythical method": Eliot, "*Ulysses*, Order, and Myth," rptd. in *Selected Prose* (1975)

206   "What is the": "What the Chinese War is Like," *Listener*, 2 February 1939, p. 247

"I am incapable": Letter to Spender, 20 May 1964

"Poetry written for": *EA* 364

207   "The first, second": *EA* 355

"To the journalist": *EA* 357

"I would rather": *ibid.*

208   "To me Art's": *EA* 185

"The surrealist police": *EA* 111

"Remarks on Painting": *New Verse*, January 1939

"startled among the": Text from 1937 version, *SP* 52; slightly revised 1940 text, *EA* 211

209   "Ledaean body": Yeats, "Among School Children"

"squat spruce body": *EA* 156

"There must always": *EA* 341

X: THE INSUFFICIENT TOUCH

210   "Different as they": *EA* 321

211   "To you *simply*": *EA* 113 (italics added)

"Hands miles away": *EA* 444

"Meeting as equal": This reading is found in MS Notebook (Swarthmore), and was revised as "Free to our favours," as in *EA* 146

"May with its": *EA* 152

212   "Lay your sleeping": *EA* 207; *SP* 50

"jealousy of the": "Lowes Dickinson," *Scrutiny*, December 1934, p. 305

"*Und es neigen*": Auden quotes this poem at *EA* 199 and 362 "sincerely puzzled": *CP* 312; *SP* 129

"worm of guilt": *EA* 161; *SP* 45

213   "love, except at": *EA* 153; *SP* 34

"I am your": *EA* 211; *SP* 53

"Before the evil": *EA* 152

"Touch, endearment": *CP* 110

"Never will his": *The Double Man* (1941), p. 99; *New Year Letter* (1941), p. 103; revised text at *CP* 232

"Fish in the": *EA* 162

214   "Our hunting fathers": *EA* 151; *SP* 33

215   "nineteenth-century evolutionary": *EA* 346; cf. *EA* 340

216   "The self must": *EA* 321; cf. Auden writing about a schoolmaster, the same year: "He was in the best sense of the word indifferent"—*EA* 324

217   "Enter with him": *EA* 114 ("Love" is capitalized in various MSS and earlier printed texts)

218   "In Sickness and": *CP* 247; original text at *SP* 111

"Your finite love": *Collected Poetry* (1945), p. 41; *Collected Shorter Poems 1930-1944* (1950), p. 56

"Your human love": *W. H. Auden: A Selection by the Author* (1958), p. 26; *Selected Poetry* (1959), p. 19

"Love as love": *CP* 71 (First published in 1966)

"Love, loath to": *New Oxford Outlook*, May 1934, p. 82; cf. fragment of this poem rptd. in *DBS* 179 and *EA* 277

219   "We imitate our": *EA* 191

220   "Father and mother": MS (Isherwood), MS Notebook (W. S. Johnson); published posthumously in *TLS*, 16 January 1976, p. 52

"the large number": *Criterion*, January 1933, p. 288

"The earth turns": *EA* 144

222   "Gale of desire": italics added

"Easily, my dear": *EA* 152; *SP* 33

225   "He isn't like": Quoted in *W. H. Auden: A Tribute*, ed. Stephen Spender (1975), p. 79

226   "Your horoscope's queer": MS Notebook (Isherwood), *EA* 233

"Since our desire": *EA* 118

"Fleeing the short-haired": *EA* 149

"my fear": *CP* 108

"Climbing *with you*": italics added

227   "Love had him": *EA* 150

"Soon enough": *EA* 146

231   "Lay your sleeping": *EA* 207; *SP* 50 (italics added)

"Beauty's conquest": *EA* 158

233   "Sleep on beside": *New Verse*, October 1933, p. 14; revised text from
           1934 MS (Isherwood), with different first line, *EA* 146
234   "Love has one": *EA* 147
235   "Johnny": *EA* 213
           "Some say that": *EA* 230
           "who told me": MS inscription to Chester Kallman [1939] in copy of
           On This Island (HRC)
           "Christopher sends off": MS Notebook (Isherwood); *EA* 234
           "All kinds of": *EA* 412
236   "As I walked": *EA* 227; *SP* 60

XI: THEIR INDIFFERENT REDEEMER

238   "Such dreams are": *EA* 145
239   "The self must": *EA* 320
           "honour and sex": MS (Valerie Eliot), MS (BBC Written Archives
           Centre); published posthumously in *TLS*, 16 January 1976, p. 53
240   "Here on the": *EA* 141
241   "Deformed and imbecile": *EA* 423
           "Friend, of the": MS Notebook (Swarthmore College)
243   "attendant" and "independent": *EA* 186
           " 'Sweet is it' ": MS (Valerie Eliot) (as above)
246   "One absence closes": MS (Isherwood); *EA* 147
247   "Just as his": *EA* 148
           "the long aunts": *EA* 153; *SP* 35; cf. the small birds' view of "the tall
           bird-catcher" in the Auden-Kallman translation of *The Magic Flute*
           (1956), Act I, scene 1, and the translators' explanation in *Tempo*,
           Spring 1958, p. 23
248   "Make action urgent": *EA* 157
           "O for doors": *EA* 154; *SP* 42
249   "to save mankind": *AF6* 73
           "By landscape reminded": *EA* 61
           "the stupid peasants": *AF6* 15
250   "Show me my": *AF6* (1st edn.) 73; cf. 2nd edn. text at *AF6* 76
251   "tremendous rant": Collingwood, p. 123
252   "rodent faces": *AF6* 70 (the second edition text quoted here portrays
           Ransom's contempt for his fellow-man in somewhat sharper focus
           than does the 1st edn. text prepared six months earlier, but does not
           otherwise alter the point of this exchange; the 1st edn. text refers to
           "the swooning faces of the crowd"—p. 68)
           "You wish to conquer": *Af6* 73 (1st edn. reads: "You would like to be
           great among men, to have power. Am I right?"—p. 71)

"temptation of pity": *AF6* 73 (the temptation is left unspecific in the
    1st edn.)

"You could ask": *AF6* 73 (same in 1st edn.)

253   "government requires": *AF6* 73 (1st edn. has the Abbot cite Lord
    Acton to the effect that absolute power corrupts absolutely)

"the complete abnegation": *AF6* 74 (1st edn. refers more generally to
    "knowledge and contemplation" which can confine the Demon al-
    though not entirely destroy him—p. 72)

"the case is": *AF6* 120

254   "By all his": *AF6* (1st edn.) 119

"we never did": Interview with B. C. Bloomfield quoted in his *W. H.
    Auden: A Bibliography* (2nd edn., 1972), p. 21

255   "O who can": *EA* 205

256   "Certainly our city": *EA* 165

"godlike in this": *EA* 165; *SP* 46

XII: PARABLES OF ACTION: 1

257   "You cannot tell": *EA* 341

"Poetry is not": *EA* 329

258   "Education succeeds social": *Criterion*, January 1933, p. 289 (probably
    written late in 1932)

"The progress of": "Life's Old Boy," *Scrutiny*, March 1934, p. 408

"supremely conservative": "The Outlook for 'Poetic Drama,'"
    France-Grande Bretagne, July–August 1939, p. 230

259   "betray us": *EA* 236

"When we collaborate": Isherwood, "Some Notes on Auden's Early
    Poetry" (1937); rptd. in his *Exhumations* (1966) and in *W. H.
    Auden: A Tribute*, ed. Stephen Spender (1975)

260   "the half-educated": Eliot, *The Use of Poetry and the Use of Criticism*
    (1933), "Conclusion"

"the act of a whole": *EA* 273

"create for myself": Yeats, "A People's Theatre," §6, rptd. in *Plays and
    Controversies* (1923), and *Explorations* (1962)

"The Elizabethan drama": Eliot, "The Possibility of Poetic Drama," in
    The Sacred Wood (1920)

261   "The middle classes": Eliot, "Marie Lloyd"; rptd. in *Selected Essays*
    (1932) and *Selected Prose* (1975)

"most sensitive and": Eliot, *The Use of Poetry* . . . (as above)

262   "The truth is": *Listener*, 9 May 1934, p. 808

"expresses almost nothing": Eliot, "Marie Lloyd"

"their popularity and": *Listener*, 27 June 1934, p. 1102

263   "A play is": MS Journal (Berg)

"Preliminary Statement": MS (Fowke Mangeot)

"Drama began as": *EA* 273

264   "symbols of *action*": Dilys Powell, *London Mercury*, October 1936,
p. 561 (italics in original)

"as you said": Letter to Dilys Powell, n.d. [November 1936] (HRC);
this letter also refers to a second review by Powell in *London Mercury*, November 1936, p. 76

265   "an art fit": Information from Robert Medley

266   "the GROUP THEATRE": *The Group Theatre* [prospectus], April 1933
(Berg)

"do everything": *The Group Theatre* [prospectus], January 1934
(Berg)

"a social force": Doone, "I Want the Theatre to Be . . . ," Westminster
Theatre program, 29 October 1935; cf. similar statement by Doone
in *New Verse*, December 1935, p. 10

267   "Art is of": "Selling the Group Theatre," *Group Theatre Paper*, June
1936, p. 3; emended according to MS (John Johnson)

268   "Are You Dissatisfied": Westminster Theatre program, 1 & 8 November 1936

"getting on with": Letter to Doone, 20 July 1932 (Berg)

"written a thing": Letter to Doone, 19 October 1932 (Berg)

269   "the power and": *DD* 33

"the decline of": *DD* 7

"Luther and Calvin": *DD* 34

"death inside": *DD* 7

"the Pilot": *DD* 28

270   "Quick under the": *DD* 37

"The communists never": MS note [1942] in copy of *Poems* (1934)
(Albert and Angelyn Stevens)

"ship of England": *DD* 19

271   "Mourn not for": *DBS* 179

The Chase: TS and carbon copies (Lockwood Memorial Library,
SUNY at Buffalo; Exeter College, Oxford; Berg; Isherwood)

The Enemies of a Bishop: TS and carbon copy (Berg; Isherwood)

The Fronny: MSS of songs and fragments (Isherwood)

275   "suggests the setting": *DBS* 17

"succour England in": *DBS* 160

276   "I say, you": *DBS* 100

"Wherever you were": *DBS* 11; *EA* 282; *SP* 37

"when death shall": *DBS* 91; *EA* 283

"So, under the": *DBS* 155; *EA* 280

277 "but with the": *DBS* 158

"obscene, cruel, hypocritical": *DBS* 173

"I don't hate": *DBS* 174

"not this we": *DBS* 180

278 "to pray / To": *DBS* 175

"I don't hate" (revised version): TS (BL Lord Chamberlain's Collection); cf. MS drafts (Berg)

279 "Certain of the": Letter to Spender, n.d.

280 "a universal art": *EA* 329

XIII: PARABLES OF ACTION: 2

281 "Don't be a": Elizabeth Sussex, *The Rise and Fall of British Documentary* (1975), p. 65

"O lurcher-loving": *EA* 290

283 "sneaked out for": *LFI* 218

"to the ordinary": *EA* 355

284 "We can't show": *France-Grande Bretagne*, July–August 1939, p. 229

"human element": Grierson, *World Film News*, April 1936, p. 13 (because of the conventions of this magazine and *The Listener* both the review and reply were unsigned, but there was no secret about the authorship of either, and Grierson refers to Auden as the reviewer just as he would have done had the review been signed)

285 "north face": *AF6* 90

"West Buttress": *AF6* 83

He told an interviewer: Unpublished interview with Timothy Foote, 1963

286 "mixed up in": Isherwood, interview with Shirley K. Hood, 1966, TS (UCLA)

"not easy to": Forster, *Listener*, 14 October 1936; rptd. in *Two Cheers for Democracy* (1951)

"the rather tame": *EA* 196

287 "Rhyme-royal's": *EA* 172

288 "I make no": *EA* 182

"Crying went out": *EA* 174

"plain, perhaps": *EA* 189

"We can't, of": *EA* 184

289 "many are in": *EA* 187

"the human clay": *EA* 185

290 "An intellectual of": *EA* 189

"The Great Utopia": *EA* 199

291   "I like Wolf's": *ibid.*

"for another five": *OTF* 78

292   "Tell me about": *OTF* 115

"tower": *OTF* 69

293   "Others like us": *OTF* 122

294   "made one long": MacNeice, *Spectator*, 18 November 1938, p. 858

"passed away painlessly": Isherwood, *Christopher and His Kind* (1976), ch. 16

"Schoolchildren": *EA* 216

295   "Oxford": *EA* 229; *SP* 63 (italics added)

"voice of the": Freud, *The Future of an Illusion* (1928), ch. 10

"Auden . . . with": Wyndham Lewis, *One-Way Song* (1933), p. 74

"that their first": "Democracy's Reply to the Challenge of the Dictators," *New Era in Home and School*, January 1939, p. 7

296   "Great claims": *EA* 370

"The Sportsmen": *EA* 368

299   "For me, the": *EA* 372

300   "Vocation and Society": TS (Swarthmore College)

"made people feel": "Democracy's Reply . . ." (as above), p. 6

302   "These are stirring"; *CP* 288

XIV: HISTORY TO THE DEFEATED

305   "we do have": *EA* 379

"The novelty and": *Modern Canterbury Pilgrims*, ed. James A. Pike (1956), p. 40

306   "trash which he": *Poetry of the Thirties*, ed. Robin Skelton (1964), p. 41

307   "Looking back": "Authority in America," *The Griffin*, March 1955, p. 8

308   "Sunday": *New Country*, ed. Michael Roberts (1933); the passage quoted is from p. 187

309   "The close-set": *EA* 157

"lunar beauty": *EA* 52; *SP* 16

"the following wind": *EA* 7

"History seems to": *EA* 120

310   "I believe the": Letter to Spender, n.d. [Autumn 1934]

"August for the": *EA* 155

311   verse letter to Richard Crossman: *LFI* 89

312   "It's a world": *EA* 166

314 "Detective Story": *EA* 204
"Journey to Iceland": *EA* 203; *SP* 46
"defend / Each dying": *EA* 180
"the intolerable tightening": *LFI* 249

315 "Whom history has": *AF6* 123
Spain: SP 51 gives the original text based on the two pamphlet editions of 1937; *EA* 210 has the 1940 revision, with major variants from 1937 described at *EA* 424

316 "To say this": *CP* 15

321 "a sort of thumb-nail": Orwell, *Inside the Whale* (1940), §2

323 "Wrapped in a": *EA* 217; *SP* 59

324 "They boast": *OTF* 41
"September 1, 1939": *EA* 245

326 "and said to": "Foreword," B. C. Bloomfield, *W. H. Auden: A Bibliography* (1st edn., 1964), p. viii
"Because he once": Forster, "The Enchafèd Flood," rptd. in *Two Cheers for Democracy* (1951)

327 "human behaviour": *EA* 341
"compared with the": *Group Theatre Paper* June 1936, p. 3
"The drives of": *EA* 177

328 "To testify my": TS (Berg) (the semicolon in line 3 is an emendation for the colon in the TS, since Auden's perennial confusion of these points would lead to a nonsensical reading if left uncorrected: i.e. the "single goal" is in fact the "education of man" in the final line, while the "individual death" mentioned in line 4 is only one of a number of things that can delay that goal)
The Prolific and the Devourer: TS (HRC)

329 "What I Believe": Rptd. in Forster's *Two Cheers for Democracy* (1951)

330 "The reason (artistic)": Draft letter to Naomi Mitchison, 1 April 1967 (Berg)

331 "Danse Macabre": *EA* 208
"I am afraid": Eliot, letter to J. M. Keynes, 15 November 1938 (King's College, Cambridge)
"prays in the": *EA* 223
"endorses Hobbes' report": *EA* 181
"Miss Gee": The music for these poems is specified in their periodical appearances, "Miss Gee" and "Victor" in *New Writing*, Autumn 1937, and "James Honeyman" in *Ploughshare*, November–December 1937

332 "Schoolchildren": *EA* 216
"The desires of ": EA 206; *SP* 50

XV: FROM THIS ISLAND

333   "the shops, the": *EA* 229; *SP* 64

"All that I": *LFI* 90

"seeks the hostile": *EA* 234

334   "O Love, the": *EA* 118; *SP* 25

"Some possible dream": This is the reading in *Look, Stranger!* (1936); *New Country* (1933) reads: "Some dream, say yes, long coiled . . ."

"The Oxford colleges": *EA* 138; *SP* 31

335   "See the Sugarloaf": *EA* 141

"The Summer holds": *DBS* 11; *EA* 281; *SP* 36

337   "I entirely agree": Letter to Spender, n.d. [Summer 1934]

"Where is the": *EA* 178

338   "Mother looks odd": *EA* 198

"in the new": *EA* 223

"August for the": *EA* 155

339   "Look, stranger": *EA* 157; *SP* 43

340   "On the analogy": Postcard to T. S. Eliot, n.d. [postmarked in England 7 July 1936 but evidently sent there earlier from Iceland to be forwarded] (Valerie Eliot)

"It sounds": Letter to Bennett Cerf, n.d. [October 1936] (Columbia University)

"Journey to Iceland": *EA* 203; *SP* 46

341   "*Caelum non animum*": Horace, *Epistles*, I, xi

"he does not want": *EA* 231

342   "The life of man": *EA* 259; *SP* 75

"The Voyage": *EA* 231

344   "Orpheus": *EA* 212; *SP* 55

346   "Repent . . . Unite": *DBS* 157; *EA* 281

"the defeat of": *EA* 218; *SP* 60

"Sing of human": *EA* 243; *SP* 83

347   "wanted to show": Isherwood, *Christopher and His Kind* (1976), ch. 16

"The bars of": *EA* 216

349   "Bee took the": *EA* 251; *SP* 64

"History opposes its": *EA* 256; *SP* 71

350   "we are closeted": *EA* 249

"makes us more": *EA* 371

351   "And the age": *EA* 255; *SP* 70 (the title "The Economic Man" is from *New Verse*, June–July 1936, p. 8)

"The wish and power": *LFI* 250
"Although you cannot": *EA* 228; *SP* 62
352 "Our rays investigate": *EA* 426
353 "It exists, identified": TS (Berg); *EA* 427
354 "*dichterisch, wohnet*": Hölderlin, "*In lieblicher Bläue*"
"The virtuous thing": *EA* 53
355 "worthy of the": *OTF* 123
"Yes, we are": *EA* 256; *SP* 71
357 "The Garden": *CP* 230 (sonnet XX); *SP* 110
358 "civil reconciliation": *EA* 263
"the epoch of": *EA* 265
"generalising *Hegel*": *EA* 267 (Auden's italics)
"very uncertain whether": Letter to Mrs. A. E. Dodds, n.d. [?November 1938] (Bodleian)
359 "We live in freedom": *EA* 262; *SP* 78
"honour the fate": *CP* 246; *SP* 118
360 "Byron was an": *Fifteen Poets* [editor not named] (1941), p. 295
"Rimbaud": *EA* 237
"A. E. Housman": *EA* 238
"The Novelist": *EA* 238
"The Composer": *EA* 239
361 "Firbank, Potter": *EA* 190
"Edward Lear": *EA* 239
"The Capital": *EA* 235; *SP* 78
362 "Brussels in Winter": *EA* 236
"Epitaph on a Tyrant": *EA* 239; *SP* 80
"Gare du Midi": *EA* 236
"stand elsewhere": *EA* 258; *SP* 73
"Musée des Beaux Arts": *EA* 237; *SP* 79
"War is untidy": "What the Chinese War is Like," *Listener*, 2 February 1939, p. 248
364 "revealed to a": *CP* 480; *SP* 223

EPILOGUE

365 "Mutual forgiveness": Blake, "For the Sexes"
"unforgiving is in": *EA* 38; *SP* 9
"It is only": *CP* 476; *SP* 219
"Forgive the murderer": *EA* 138; *SP* 32
"*always* there are": *CP* 193 (italics added)

"gift survived it": *EA* 242; *SP* 81

"he would *unite*": *SP* 94; *CP* 217 has revised text (italics added)

366   "Orpheus who moved": "Squares and Oblongs," *Poets at Work*, ed.
       Charles D. Abbott (1948), p. 180

"In the prison": *EA* 243; *SP* 83

Index

Dates of birth and death are supplied for Auden's family and acquaintances.